STUDIES IN

RATIONALISM

JUDAISM & UNIVERSALISM

1896–1963

Studies in
Rationalism
Judaism & Universalism

IN MEMORY OF LEON ROTH

EDITED BY RAPHAEL LOEWE

LONDON

ROUTLEDGE AND KEGAN PAUL

NEW YORK : THE HUMANITIES PRESS

First published 1966
by Routledge & Kegan Paul Limited
Broadway House, 68–74 Carter Lane
London, E.C.4

Printed in Great Britain
by William Clowes & Sons, Limited
London and Beccles

M. S.

HYAM LEON ROTH

CARTESII SPINOZÆQVE INTERPRETIS

SPECTATI

ACADEMICIS HIEROSOLYMITANIS

RECTORIS ATQVE LVMINIS

IVDÆORVM GENERATIONI

PERPLEXISSIMÆ

DVCTORIS PERIPATETICI EXEMPLI

PRÆSTANTIS

PROVT

MAGISTRI SVI MAIMONIDIS FIDELIS

DISCIPVLI

זכרנו לחיים · אל מלך חפץ בחיים · כתבנו בספר חיים

CONTENTS

CONTENTS

PREFACE

A memorial volume ought, as far as is possible, to speak for itself. All that is called for here by way of introduction is a note as to the scope of the following essays as they are intended to reflect various aspects of Leon Roth's character, work, and interests. A short biographical sketch has been appended below (pp. 1 f.), together with a bibliography (pp. 323 f.), as complete as it has been possible to assemble, of his writings.

The title — *Rationalism Judaism Universalism* — has been chosen with deliberation: and it corresponds to a triangle which — although he never discussed it with me — must, I feel, have been consciously present in Roth's own mind. Professor D. D. Raphael begins his contribution (p. 197) by explaining the possible meanings of the term rationalist and the sense in which Roth may properly be described as one. That Roth was himself a person of deep faith was unmistakable to all who knew him. He was also fully awake to the problems of communication[1] that are typified by the whole question of the feasibility of translation to which Professor Ullendorff adverts (p. 273), and conscious that Jewish tradition, too, is fully aware of the existence of such problems and looks (as the late Dr Wilhelm points out, pp. 298 f.) to the messianic age to resolve them. For artificially contrived harmonisations, on the other hand, he had no use. The original act wherein faith is conceived is personal, possibly not communicable, and one in which reason can have no role. But the act of faith is not without corollaries, and Roth (one must think) would have regarded it as an act of little significance in those of intellectual capacities unless its consequences were in themselves capable of surviving a rational examination. He could himself find no basis for discussion with a religious emphasis that would implicitly inhibit, or constructively stultify the human intelligence vouchsafed (in traditional Jewish terminology) by a God who, of His grace, affords man knowledge and teaches mortals understanding. His training as a philosopher, and his quality as an expositor of Descartes and Spinoza, thus fashioned the faith within his breast into an intellectually disciplined Judaism. But Judaism itself, if it

were to be regarded as co-extensive with Jewish self-interest –
material, political or even spiritual – would have seemed to him
incomplete and misconceived. Its universalistic implications and
presuppositions have to be recognised and, wherever they are of
practical relevance, to be implemented unreservedly. One of his
favourite quotations[2] was the letter in which Maimonides assured
Obadiah the proselyte that it was not only his right, but his
positive obligation to use in his prayers the liturgical formula
'Our God and the God of our Fathers'; and in the last piece of his
writing to appear in print in his lifetime[3] he studied the universalist implications of the interconnection, in rabbinic thought, of the
commandment to love one's neighbour and the notion that each
several man is made in the image of God.[4] *Rationalism Judaism
Universalism* were not, then, for Roth (as I believe) ideas
patient of serial arrangement in any order of importance, but
rather a triangle, each apex equidistant from the act of faith
enclosed within, as irresistible on the spiritual field as was once,
on the field of battle, the Macedonian *phalanx*.

Contributors to this volume are drawn from England, the
United States of America, France and Israel, in all but one of
which countries Roth had at some time taught. Some of them
deal with one or other of the aforementioned three components;
others endeavour to correlate two or more of them. It is apposite
to say something here about two of the essays in particular.

Roth had been one of the early recruits to the staff of Jerusalem
University as its first Ahad Ha'am Professor of philosophy, and
later served the University well as Rector. He was regarded – correctly – as standing aloof from Zionism in the sense in which that
term has for some time now been conventionally understood.
This is not the place to dilate upon his alienation; but the following ought to be said by way of corrective to possible misunderstandings. Jewish peoplehood was, for Leon Roth (I venture
confidently to surmise), a value of enduring significance. I doubt
whether he was ever able to look at Jewish statehood in the same
light, notwithstanding its importance as a contemporary political
phenomenon. Nationalism and statehood were not, indeed, for
him a challenge that Jewry has any moral right to avoid: but the

very circumstance that claims are sometimes advanced for these concepts, as being valid means for implanting the fundamental teachings of Judaism, imposes certain ethical responsibilities, which must always control and sometimes, by prohibiting, transcend merely political considerations. Mr H. D. Schmidt refers below (p. 268) to the acute distress in this respect that was occasioned to Roth by certain happenings during the closing years of the British Mandate in Palestine. Those sentiments were shared by Rabbi Dr K. Wilhelm, whose congregation in Jerusalem Roth then joined. It required some moral courage at that time to carry through, as Wilhelm did from his own pulpit, a demonstrative disavowal of what was going on with the condonation or approval of most of the Jewish public in Palestine; and Wilhelm's courage was shared by Roth in his own unswerving pursuit of the course of idealism that he had set himself. Dr Wilhelm's contribution on the Jewish concept of humanity (pp. 289 f.) is therefore a particularly appropriate one for the occasion, for the theme is one, as Roth made clear, that requires constant reassertion. To my regret, Kurt Wilhelm − whose friendship I, too, had the privilege and good fortune to enjoy − died suddenly in Sweden (of which country he was latterly the Chief Rabbi) early in 1965, while this volume was being assembled, and he never saw proofs of the English version of his article, which may now stand as a memorial not only to Leon Roth, but to the spiritual fellowship which Wilhelm shared with him.

Leon Roth's uprightness and intellectual honesty commanded respect − never grudging, though sometimes tinged with a condescending commiseration − from some of those who were aware of his lack of sympathy for their own causes or programmes. An eloquent example of this is afforded by his having been considered (although not a politician himself) as a possibility for the portfolio of education in a coalition government of Israel, which suggestion carried the endorsement of the Mizrachi (i.e. religiously orientated) Party. The Mizrachists knew well enough that Roth had scant regard for either their political philosophy or its practical aspects, but they also knew that from him they could expect a fair deal in a matter of cardinal importance to them and of close interest also to Roth, who devoted a number of publications to the question of education.[5] This makes particularly apposite the contribution of Roth's successor in the Jerusalem Chair of philosophy, Professor N. Rotenstreich (pp. 231f.), which deals with educational philosophy and not at all with the specifically Jewish educational situation. Professor Rotenstreich concludes that ethics are inevitably an integral component of education despite the claims of some educationists that it is possible, and perhaps even desirable, to deny so close an association of education and ethics. Roth would, we may be sure, have endorsed that conclusion; and he had a big enough mind to presuppose its endorsement even by some of those from whom he felt himself widely separated.

Throughout his life Roth was the conscious disciple, though never the adulator, of Maimonides. Time deals hardly with those who in their lifetime did not seek office or limelight, and it may soon consign Roth's name to a popular oblivion with which he would have been content. But for those who are concerned with straightforwardness, substance and sincerity rather than with slogans, symbols and self-importance Leon Roth's stature will, it may be predicted, grow each time that it is rediscovered. It is, I trust I may say, the hope of all contributors to this volume that its contents may stimulate a few readers to tread the same path of honest enquiry and, after they have allowed the original sources to speak to them through no intermediate veil of tendentious glossation, to formulate conclusions that will be their own.

In addition to those who so readily agreed to contribute articles to this volume, I wish to record my gratitude to Mr Stanley Burton, and the Israel Zangwill and the Arthur Davis Memorial Funds, whose generous financial subventions have rendered the publication feasible; also to Professor Norman Bentwich and the Secretariat of the Friends of the Hebrew University, for lending their good offices at certain stages; and to Mr Colin Franklin of the publishers, Messrs Routledge & Kegan Paul. Leon Roth (as I was informed by Dr Wilhelm) himself frowned on *Festschriften* as being but 'academic morgues', and he would certainly have disapproved of my having organised the present volume in his memory. But perhaps we may venture to hope that even if the book is caught *in flagrante delicto*, its themes – and perhaps even some of its contents – are not unworthy of its occasion. The Editor has, indeed, but one regret only, which concerns the sixth essay in the volume; for he feels certain that its subject could have been dealt with more effectively, and more economically, by Leon Roth himself.

London, September 1966   RAPHAEL LOEWE

NOTES

1 See for example his review of S. Belkin's *In His Image*, *Jewish Chronicle*, 17th March, 1961, p. 29.

2 He printed a translation of it on several occasions, e.g. in his *Judaism, A Portrait*, pp. 96 f.

3 See *Bibliography*, no. lxxi, *infra*, p. 328, and K. Wilhelm's article, *infra*, p. 305, note 49.

4 In a private letter, Dr S. Radhakrishnan writes, 'I had known Professor Roth for a number of years. . . . His work on Judaism showed accurate learning and profound insight. He used Judaism as a universal religion. I hope some people are carrying out investigations in the themes set forth by him.'

5 See *Bibliography*, nos. xxvii, xxxv, 7, 26, 29, 36, 51, 57, 61, 68, 72, 73, *infra*, pp. 325f.

MEMOIR[1]

Leon Roth was born in London, on Tuesday 31st March, 1896, corresponding to the third day of Passover (17th Nisan) 5656 according to the Jewish calendar, 'at 10.15 a.m.' (as his father noted in a family Bible) at 32 Victoria Park Road, Hackney. 'Leon' was in point of fact his second English name, the first (the use of which he dropped early in life) being Hyam – corresponding to the first of his two Hebrew names, Hayyim Yehudah: these being the names under which his Hebrew publications in due course appeared, their initial letters together with his surname happily forming the Hebrew word *heruth, liberty*. Leon was the third of four sons, his youngest brother, Cecil Roth, being destined as his contemporary at Oxford and, like him, to rise to a position of academic distinction and world recognition in the sphere of Jewish studies. Their father, Joseph Roth, had been born in Poland, settled in England, and married a Sheffield-born Jewish girl named Etty Jacobs. He was himself a merchant, whose business lay in north London: and the family moved, shortly after Leon's birth, first over the shop at 91 Kingsland Road, and later to Queen Elizabeth's Walk. The Dalston, Stoke Newington, Stamford Hill area is one which, in the late nineteenth century, was popular amongst middle-class English Jewry characterised by a strong Jewish allegiance and sturdy degree of Jewish practical observance, not infrequently combined with an awareness and concern for English and western European values – its vernacular, until the waves of refugees from Russian pogroms began to filter northwards from the East End of London, was English rather than Judaeo-German.

The home environment typified this. Joseph Roth would, whenever opportunity offered, lead his sons off to inspect the latest arrivals on the booksellers' shelves, and he himself gave them a first-class Jewish education, employing for the purpose the '*Ivrith be'ivrith* method – i.e., Hebrew taught as a spoken language – an approach which David Yellin was endeavouring to popularise from Palestine but which, in spite of its having a sponsor of recognised English academic standing in Israel

1

Abrahams, was then still a somewhat quizzically regarded novelty in Anglo-Jewish educational circles. As a Hebrew teacher for his sons he engaged Mr Moses Vilensky, a gentleman of deep Hebrew learning (at the time of writing happily still alive), who has since become well known as an educationist and freelance adviser on Jewish literary topics; and for the secular component of their education he sent them to the City of London School, into the strong classical traditions of which Leon Roth was swept – in due course to win thence a scholarship in Classics to Exeter College, Oxford. Throughout his life he remained conscious of his debt to his early training in Latin and Greek, first and foremost for the mental discipline that its rigorousness taught him to apply to self-expression in English, but also for the literary and historical content of the old-style classical syllabus; but (as he wrote in his last letter to me, just before leaving England within a few weeks of his death) he was 'saved by World War I from becoming a philologist'. Of other interests at school no record is known to me; but a hint of things to come is given by the report of his having opened a debate on the relations between the individual and the state on 26th January, 1915 (*City of London School Magazine*, 39, 1915, p. 34; cf. Bibliography, Hebrew section, nos. 64, 81, *infra*, pp. 334 f.).

Roth went up to Oxford briefly in 1915, and was on active service in the Army from 1916 to 1918, first in France and then with the Jewish Regiment (in which he held a commission), but to his disappointment he was not sent to Palestine. On his return to an Oxford overcrowded both with ex-service undergraduates and the memories of that golden generation which had not returned, he applied himself to academic studies and played his part in the reestablishment of Jewish undergraduate activities – his Jewish contemporaries and friends including Mordecai Eliash, later the first minister accredited by the State of Israel to the Court of St James's. He was awarded, in 1920, the John Locke Scholarship in Mental Philosophy – one of Oxford's most coveted distinctions in Humanities, tenure of which in a sense opens the door to an academic career in philosophy—and also, in the following year, the James Mew Scholarship in Rabbinic Hebrew. The

2

latter is a hurdle for which an academic and disciplined handling of the post-biblical language is requisite, and a mere familiarity with texts inadequate. This gave him the means to prosecute research for a while, and he spent a year in Zurich. The Regius Professor of Hebrew, G. A. Cooke, was a scholar of broad enough horizons to approve his devoting himself during his tenure of the scholarship to studying the relationship of Spinoza to Descartes and Maimonides: and in his preface to what was the fruit of that work (*Spinoza Descartes and Maimonides*, Oxford, 1924) Roth acknowledged the encouragement that he had received from Cooke.

There was, however, no academic niche immediately open to him, and he had resigned himself to making a living in the legal profession. He had, in fact, actually arranged to meet Herbert Bentwich with a view to entering into articles when, on the very day of their appointment, he received a telegram from Samuel Alexander, an unforeseeable vacancy having occurred in Manchester University, offering him a lectureship in philosophy. To Manchester he accordingly went in 1923 to join a department that included also J. L. Stocks among its staff, and he represented Manchester University at the opening of the Hebrew University, Jerusalem, in 1925. This visit to Palestine – something which he had long hoped to achieve – was also his honeymoon; for on 11th March of that year he had been married to Winifred, daughter of Alderman Abraham Davis, J.P. (by whom he had three sons and a daughter). The publication of his book (Bibliography, no. ii, *infra*, p. 323) on Descartes' correspondence with Huygens (1926) was hailed as an event of scholarly importance; and it was signalised in France by Roth's being appointed, in the year of its appearance, *Officier d'Academie*.

Roth's whole Jewish background and upbringing was such as would almost inevitably imbue him with a keen interest in what post-biblical Hebrew styles *Eretz Israel*, the Land of Israel. As a philosopher he was conscious, too, of the reality (and importance) of the political dimension of life: but it is more than doubtful if he could at any period of his life have been correctly described as a political Zionist. The infant University of Jerusalem, however, was an obvious focus for his Palestinian interests. When, in 1927, the philosophical essayist in Hebrew Ahad Ha'am (i.e. Asher Ginzberg, born 1856) died, the University established a Chair of philosophy named after him; and (within the English-speaking world) Roth was a clear choice as its first occupant. He had, incidentally, once met Ahad Ha'am during his latter years. He held the professorship for 25 years, until 1953, serving the University as Rector in 1940–43 and as Dean of the Faculty of Humanities from 1949 to 1951.

On taking up his appointment he set himself, later with two colleagues from Europe – Julius Guttmann and S. H. Bergman – to lay the foundations of a school of philosophy. Roth's own contribution was twofold. While maintaining his own interest in Spinoza and in ethics (his *Science of Morals*, prepared in Manchester, appeared in 1928) and continually increasing his interest in Maimonides (on whom he published a masterly summary in English, see Bibliography, no. vii, *infra*, p. 324), he also undertook a wider enterprise, *viz.* that of making available in Hebrew some of the classical texts of philosophy. The establishment of a technical Hebrew vocabulary for the discussion of modern western philosophy (as opposed to the mediaeval Hebrew vocabulary evolved for translation from Arabic) also formed a major part of this purpose. Roth himself rendered certain portions of Aristotle, and he supervised and assisted the translation of Plato, Descartes, Leibniz, Locke, Hume, Rousseau, Berkeley, John Stuart Mill, Muirhead, Bosanquet and Bertrand Russell (see Bibliography, Hebrew section, nos. 9–30, pp. 330 f.). He sought also to interpret British democracy and English values and institutions (see nos. 37, 38, 52, pp. 332 f.) to a Jewish public in Palestine that was largely born in, or but half a generation distant from eastern and central Europe and Russia, and whose political patience with Britain as the Mandatory Power for Palestine was fast running out.

For almost from the moment of Roth's taking up his professorship until the outbreak of the second World War, extremist elements within together with foreign Arab intransigence fomented discontent amongst the Arabs of Palestine, while also

4

(within a few years) the flood of Jewish refugees from Germany and German-occupied countries increased. The political climate was continuously in decline. It is not easy to express the sorrow that this state of affairs caused to those who, like Roth himself, had looked to a future in which Palestine should be an enterprise of Jewish and Arab partnership and an object-lesson to the world in mutual understanding, appreciation, and forbearance (he was himself a founder-member, and later president, of the Jerusalem Rotary Club, intended as a focus for the meeting of Arab and Jew); and the few Jews who were prepared, as tempers deteriorated and political atrocities increased, to disavow violence and to make a stand on their own principles of political ethics, found themselves isolated. Roth stood here in close sympathy with J. L. Magnes (see Bibliography, xxxiva, xliii, 71, *infra*, pp. 326 f.), the President of the Hebrew University, whose death in 1948 left him even more on his own. When eventually, on the British withdrawal, Jewish Jerusalem came under siege conditions, Roth took his own share of guard duties uncomplainingly and with dignity. The pre-natal experiences of the State of Israel which emerged in 1948 endowed it (hardly surprisingly) with certain characteristics with which Roth felt himself out of sympathy ethically as well as ideologically (and to this we shall perforce have to revert below); and after a few years he resigned his Chair. The University was at first more than reluctant to accept his resignation: and the Government of Israel, for all his disapproval of much of what it was doing and more of its methods, appreciated what an asset to the country he was. Strenuous efforts were accordingly made to persuade him to remain in Israel. He was offered the presidency of the University, and, as related elsewhere (*supra*, p. xi), his appointment as minister of education was mooted. But he was not to be dissuaded of his purpose, and, in July 1951, he returned to England, where, in 1948, he had been elected a Fellow of the British Academy. In 1952 he made his home in Cambridge, whence he moved to Brighton in 1959.

During the last phase of his life (approximately ten years), Roth devoted himself more particularly to the interpretation of Judaism, and especially the specifically Jewish integration of theology

5

into both bible-exposition and ethical behaviour. He had travelled quite widely (including in America) during his earlier years, and after his retirement he did so more extensively, accepting several invitations as a visiting professor and undertaking lecturing tours. He went on one lecturing visit to India, and found in Indian thought a congenial stimulus (albeit in some respects at least a negative one, as the following postcard which I received from him gently implies: '13.1.56 Still going strong, with our puzzlement growing daily. A fortune waiting here for Buber! yours LR'). He taught for a session in the College of Jewish Studies in Chicago, and also (his last assignment) in the Department of Philosophy at Brown University, Providence, Rhode Island, where he also gave some public lectures on Judaism. His last public appearance in England was (I suppose) in December 1962, at Church House, Westminster, on the occasion of the Archbishop of Canterbury's Robert Waley Cohen Lecture; and I recall a picture of him engaged in animated conversation with the Archbishop over tea preceding the lecture. He left England with his wife on 30th December, 1962, on board the *Canberra*, to fulfil a long-cherished project of seeing Australia and New Zealand. Owing to a fire on board they were delayed, and put in at Malta where they were transferred to another ship. He died in Wellington, New Zealand (where he was buried), as a result of a sudden heart attack, just after his 67th birthday, on 2nd April, 1963; and I have it on Mrs Roth's testimony that the last weeks – and especially the last five days – were among some of the best of his whole life.

Roth would never allow himself to be used as the vehicle for propagating any cause or appeal, but he was always ready to find time to speak to an audience, whether Jewish or general, if he felt that he had anything to say to them; and his limpidity and economy of expression gave him remarkable powers of communication at different levels, without any group's feeling that he was talking down. He had always read widely, and kept his reading enviably up-to-date: frequently taking as his starting-point for an address or article some quotation from a recent literary production (always a significant one, though not always one that had entered into the evanescent currency of literary journalism), or from an important new publication within the field of Jewish scholarship. He gave generously of his time, especially during these last years, to various organisations whose purpose is to promote inter-group understanding – notably the Spalding Trust, which is concerned with the interpretation of the East to the West and *vice versa*, to the Council of Christians and Jews and some of its associated organisations, and to the World Congress of Faiths. He would sometimes join in a week-end meeting of some of these groups, his participation bringing a touch, as individual as it was clearly spiritual, which those who experienced it will not soon forget.

It would be quite a pointless endeavour to attempt an analysis of precisely what Roth owed to his Jewish and his general European cultural heritages respectively. The two were so welded and wedded within him as to produce that interpenetration of personalities which informs the atmosphere of a home in which married love reigns supreme. As far as concerns his achievements as a scholar and a thinker, it lies beyond my competence to say anything regarding his work as a student of western philosophy, and for an estimate of it I must refer to Professor T. E. Jessop's *Memoir* written at the request of the British Academy.[2] On his work in Jewish studies a word may, however, be in order. I have written below (pp. 115 f.) of his capacity for divining and elucidating points of cardinal significance in ethics or philosophy, which had been expressed by the Rabbis or symbolised by them in an idiom that is not philosophical, frequently quaint, and sometimes (to the modern mind) grotesque. Perhaps it was his early training in the Classics that gave him such remarkable powers of translation from this sort of language into something meaningful to the plain man today, without ever forcing the language into some straitjacket of inappropriate symbolism or half-accurate modern counterpart. There is here no new contribution; but merely the successful performance of the ever-indispensable function of making palpable the contemporary relevance of what is timeless. The same holds good of his own construction of Judaism, so impressively portrayed in his last

7

book (Bibliography, no. ix, *infra*, p. 324). Composed of comparatively short pieces, some of them delivered as papers on various occasions, it is no picture in the style of Holman Hunt, fascinating the eye with a mass of accurately reproduced detail, nor yet a kind of catechetical identikit designed to enable the reader to affix or withold a Jewish label when considering professions of faith, programmes, or persons: but rather, as Roth himself styled it, a portrait, classical in its restraint from all exuberance (the technical scholarship in it being restricted to the minimum), which succeeds by a few master-strokes in suggesting what it leaves unsaid. If – as in so much of Roth's later writing – Maimonides is here the key-piece, it is not merely on account of his eminence as a thinker or his clarity of expression; but because Maimonides had appreciated the importance and inter-relationship of three things, and had drawn the relevant conclusions in terms which, though not always tenable in the light of twentieth-century scientific knowledge and patterns of thought, yet did justice to the science and categories of the twelfth. These are (i) the uniqueness of God and, as a corollary thereto, the universal implications (and, to a limited extent, the universal relevance) of Judaism, as instituted and sanctioned by God: (ii) the progressive potentiality of the human intellect, the capacities of which, although God may arbitrarily and unaccountably inhibit them, man has not himself the moral right to abdicate, or to allow to atrophy: and (iii) the Hebrew Bible as constituting a field of spiritual energy flowing between God and man, with the corollary that the interpretation of the Bible, for all its practical conservatism, is of possibly cumulative relevance and is not a static affair, but a process in which both poles must always be dynamically involved.

Leon Roth was essentially practical – perhaps pragmatic – in his outlook: ideas had to be relevant to modern everyday problems if their value was to be reckoned an abiding value, and, if their import was practical, they must be applied in fact. In no sphere was he more conscious of this requirement than in that of ethics. This was the principal reason for his disappointment with Jewish statehood when it was ultimately realised. He had gone

out to Palestine in the hope that it was to constitute a truly
Jewish contribution to the polity of man. It being his experience
that Jewish ethics and notions of justice were not given any
marked enunciation in the national life of Israel (notwithstanding full many a domestic example of their continuing liveliness),
he saw no reason to remain in the country any longer. As he saw
it, lip service was being offered to the ethical teachings of the
Bible which were at the same time being ignored in political
concerns when they were inconvenient, material advantage often
(as he considered) being secured through means which political
leadership was constrained to condemn whilst in fact condoning.
He expressed his viewpoint in impressive accents in a letter
published in *The Jewish Chronicle* (4th December, 1953, p. 21)
in the weeks following the Qibya raid. In it he trounced (as always,
urbanely) a prominent Anglo-Jewish apologist who, whilst
conceding that the Israeli action was deserving of censure, went
on to declare that such Jewish protests as it had evoked were
mainly insincere and inspired by sensitivity to gentile recrimina-
tion. The whole letter deserves study: but the following sentences
at least must be reproduced here:

> It is surely a truism that the very meaning of morality is the
> correction of feeling by judgment. Judgment to be judgment
> must be external to the facts judged . . . even assuming his
> suspicion to be true, is it so wrong to take into account, and
> even to be guided by, other people's judgments? Is not that the
> way in which moral ideas are in fact inculcated and spread? . . .
> Is it not perhaps a compliment to Jews and Judaism that our
> friends say to us: 'We expected better of *you*'.

It was not until the 1950s brought us together in Cambridge
that I really got to know Leon Roth; and the stimulus of his
conversation, the help of his criticism, the joy of his company, and
the encouragement of his unspoken support are for me an abiding
memory that I prefer not to attempt to express in words. I recall
talking with him about the Hebrew language – a subject in which
his approach, though differing from my own, overlapped – and
in retrospect I regret not having endeavoured to lure him into

9

some collaborative discussion of the question on paper. But above all I treasure – as, I suppose, do all his friends – the memory of faith and of idealism, proof against disillusionment; a faith in Judaism, not dissipated by Jewish indifference, and in the Jewish people, not shattered by Jewish materialistic opportunism; a faith in England and in British values (and their American counterparts) not soured by an educational revolution that has dethroned the Classics or by a changed political climate that has all but despatched the Liberal Party from the House of Commons and has exorcised the ghost of Palmerston from the Foreign Office; and a faith in man, not withered by cynicism even in the face of the twentieth century.

The whole of life is, in some sense, a battle fought (simultaneously) on several fronts; and Jewish tradition, recognising that such tensions are not merely inevitable but also potentially positive and productive, makes quite frequent use of military metaphors for the enunciation of its own truths. It is in the language of war that it can sometimes describe the struggle against the Evil Inclination that it bids each several Jew prosecute continuously within his own heart; and it speaks in the same strain when treating of those technical procedures of scholarship, debate, and the application of reason, by which the specific apparatus of Judaism ought to be applied to speculative and theoretical elaboration of a view of life and a pattern for it, as well as to the practical implementation of the logical consequences of these. All of this is embraced within the scope of what Hebrew calls *milḥamtahh shel torah*, 'the warfare of Torah'. And in a play which Aristophanes makes Aeschylus regard as his foremost dramatic achievement, *the Seven against Thebes* – a play 'brimful of War' – there occurs a description of Amphiareus the Prophet, the sixth of the heroes who stand in readiness to lead the attack on the City's seven gates. His shield, unlike those of his comrades in arms, bore no device – he preferred the substance of bravery to its repute. Plutarch records a tradition that when the play was first performed in Athens, the following lines turned the heads of the audience instinctively towards Aristides;

10

and with them we may fittingly here conclude:

οὐ γὰρ δοκεῖν ἄριστος, ἀλλ᾽ εἶναι θέλει,
βαθεῖαν ἄλοκα διὰ φρενὸς καρπούμενος,
ἐξ ἧς τὰ κεδνὰ βλαστάνει βουλεύματα.
τούτῳ σοφούς τε κἀγαθοὺς ἀντηρέτας
πέμπειν ἐπαινῶ. δεινὸς ὅς θεοὺς σεβεῖ.³

R. L.

NOTES

1 At the time of Leon Roth's death obituary notices appeared in *The Times* (5th April, 1963, supplemented by E. Ullendorff, 8th April, p. 12) and in *The Jewish Chronicle* (5th April). A tribute by the present writer was printed in *Common Ground* (Council of Christians and Jews), xvii, 2, Summer, 1963. The Israeli press published obituaries, the *Jerusalem Post* (English) on 4th April, 1963, by Norman Bentwich; *Haaretz* (Hebrew), by S. H. Bergman; *Molad* (Tel Aviv), xxi, 181–2, Sept.–Oct. 1963, p. 448, by Ruth Kleinberger. *The New York Times*, 5th April, p. 47. The Magnes Press of the Hebrew University, Jerusalem, also produced a memorial brochure containing a portrait, addresses delivered by S. H. Bergman, M. Sternberg, N. Rotenstreich, and a bibliography of Roth's writings. See also note 2.

2 In the Academy's *Proceedings*, vol. L, 1965, pp. 317–29.

3 Aeschylus, *Septem contra Thebas*, ll. 592–6; cf. Aristophanes, *Frogs*, l. 1021, and Plutarch, *Aristides*, 3, 253z, ed. I. D. Limentani, 1964, p. 16. Gilbert Murray's translation of these lines of Aeschylus (p. 54) is as follows:

Not to seem great he seeketh, but to be.
The fruit of a deep furrow reapeth he
In a rich heart, whence his good counsels rise.
Oh, find a valiant champion and a wise
To meet him. Great is he who feareth God.

1

Moses Mendelssohn
on Leibniz and Spinoza

ALEXANDER ALTMANN

Moses Mendelssohn's first literary effort, the *Philosophische Gespräche* of 1755,[1] was motivated by a desire to rehabilitate the merits of the Leibniz–Wolffian philosophy, then under attack by the Berlin Academy members who were admirers of Voltaire. It was akin in spirit to the essay *Pope ein Metaphysiker!* written jointly by Lessing and Mendelssohn and published in the late autumn of the same year.[2] How deeply Mendelssohn was committed to Leibniz' thought may be gauged from a passage in his *Über die Empfindungen* (which also appeared in 1755) extolling, beside Locke and Wolff, the 'immortal Leibniz', who had rescued the writer (Palemon) from his tormenting doubts about the existence and providence of God and had proved his guide to 'true knowledge and virtue'.[3] The moving tribute put into the mouth of Palemon has all the marks of an autobiographical confession. In the *Gespräche* 'our' Leibniz is hailed as 'the greatest philosopher' and the Germans are chided for copying the French, who, since Malbranche, had failed to produce a single metaphysician, and for lacking pride in their own Leibniz and Wolff, who had brought philosophy to perfection.[4]

13

Thus it is Leibniz who claims Mendelssohn's unquestionable allegiance, yet the foreground of the first two dialogues in the *Gespräche* (out of the four) is occupied by another figure whose identity emerges in almost dramatic fashion and whose rehabilitation, rather than Leibniz', seems to be the author's real concern in the first half of the book. This figure is Spinoza. Not that Mendelssohn wishes to divide his loyalty between the two. Spinoza's system is 'absurd' and his principles are 'mistaken and distasteful'. One who has read Wolff's painstaking critique of Spinoza 'will, surely, never be tempted to agree with Spinoza'.[5] Mendelssohn rejects Spinoza, yet he pleads on his behalf. Having reminded the Germans of their neglected pride in Leibniz and Wolff, Neophil tells his interlocutor Philopon that, in justice, one ought to admit that 'also someone other than a German, and, I would add, someone other than a Christian, i.e. Spinoza, has a great share in the improvement of philosophy.'[6] It almost seems as if the theme of the Germans' pride in Leibniz and Wolff was introduced merely as a curtain-raiser to the assertion of Mendelssohn's pride in his fellow-Jew Spinoza. He mingles this sentiment with that of pity for the 'misfortune' of this man who 'lived moderately, withdrawn and blamelessly'; who 'gave up all human delights, dedicating as he was his entire life to contemplation, and behold, in the maze of his reflections he went astray and, misled into error, asserted what the most abject knave would desire in order to be free to indulge his evil inclinations.'[7] Mendelssohn's sense of pity for Spinoza is not that of Leibniz' deploring Spinoza's *infelix ingenium* which carried the overtone of *esprit malin*.[8] He 'went astray from error, not from a wickedness of heart.'[9] Nor was he far from the truth. 'The step from him to truth was but a small one.'[10] The 'truth' is, of course, the Leibnizian philosophy, and Mendelssohn is anxious to show the proximity between Leibniz and Spinoza. Putting it differently, the development of modern philosophy from Descartes to Leibniz leads *via* Spinoza. The tragedy of Spinoza consists in the role of a mediator in which fate had cast him. 'Before the transition from Cartesian to Leibnizian philosophy could take place, someone had to fall into the tremendous abyss lying between them. This was Spinoza's hapless fate. How much one has to regret his destiny! He became a sacrifice for the sake of the human mind; a sacrifice, however, that deserves to be adorned with flowers. Without him, philosophy could never have extended its borders thus far.' Hence, 'how unjust is the implacable hatred of the learned towards such a hapless one!'[11] The melodramatic manner in which Mendelssohn describes Spinoza's fate reflects the categories of the Greek tragedy. Spinoza is clearly viewed as the hero of a *Trauerspiel*.[12] Moreover, he is portrayed in almost Christ-like fashion as a mediator who is sacrificed, or rather who sacrifices himself. He 'falls' into the 'tremendous abyss' between Cartesian and Leibnizian philosophy, yet there is only a 'small step' from him to the truth.

How does Mendelssohn attempt to substantiate his rather sweeping thesis? He does it in two stages. In the first dialogue he sets out to prove that Leibniz' doctrine of the pre-established harmony was essentially taken over from Spinoza. Leibniz, who was 'not only the greatest but also the most cautious philosopher', took care not to reveal his source in order not to incur the odium attached to Spinoza's name.[13] In the second dialogue he offers the ingenuous suggestion that Spinoza's system is identical with the archetypal world which, according to Leibniz, pre-existed in God's mind before it became real (*antecedenter ad decretum*). Thus understood, he argues, Spinoza's pantheism (or acosmism, as we might say) can be reconciled with religion. We propose to deal with this second proposition first.

The second proposition is advanced with the clearly expressed intention of showing that 'Spinoza's system is compatible with reason and religion'.[14] The Leibnizians attribute to the world a twofold existence as it were. It existed first, prior to God's choice, as one of a number of possible worlds in the divine mind. It was then made real and external to God because, being the best, God gave it preference before all other possible worlds. Now Spinoza stopped short at its first existence. He believed that no world ever became real outside God, and that all visible things were to be found in the divine mind alone. In other words, Spinoza characterises the visible world in the terms applied by

15

the Leibnizians to the plan of the world as it existed in the divine mind *antecedenter ad decretum.* According to the Leibnizians God conceived the possibility of accidental things by thinking His own perfections as limited to some degree.[15] Spinoza says the same: 'All individual things express the divine attributes in a certain limited way.'[16] In the Leibnizians' view the nature of accidental things in the mind of God consists in this, that they cannot be conceived without attributing to them an infinite series of causes.[17] Spinoza says in almost identical words: 'The idea of an individual thing actually existing has God for a cause, not in so far as He is infinite, but in so far as there is found in Him the idea of another thing which also actually exists. God is, likewise, the cause of this latter one in so far there is found in Him the idea of a third, and so on *ad infinitum.*'[18] Mendelssohn asks: 'What objection can a sound philosopher raise against this doctrine as applied to the world which existed in the divine mind?' In such a world there was no room for the Leibnizian soul as a 'special force'[19] since there existed in it only the idea by which God conceived the human soul. In this noumenal (*verständlichen*) world the distinction between necessary and accidental things does, however, have its place according to Spinoza. The common assumption to the contrary is refuted by Spinoza's statement that the necessary derives from the divine attributes in so far as He is infinite, while the accidental is explained by reference to God in so far as there exists in Him an infinite series of other accidentals. Hence there was but a 'small step' from Spinoza to Leibniz.

Having shown how close Spinoza came to Leibniz, Mendelssohn raises the question: 'Yet what may have motivated him to deny freedom to God?'[20] Obviously, no reconciliation is possible between Spinoza's and Leibniz' respective positions on the question of God's freedom. All Mendelssohn can hope to do is explain how Spinoza was misled on this issue. His answer is entirely in the spirit of his *apologia pro Spinoza.* 'If ever he committed an error innocently, it was this particular one.' He considered as genuine freedom the *aequilibrium indifferentiae* only, *viz.* the freedom to act from indifference and by a certain absolute will.[21]

16

He shared this concept of freedom with many orthodox philosophers. He was, on the other hand, sagacious enough to understand that the choice made by an intelligent being is invariably
determined by motives. Hence he regarded this equilibrium as
impossible and denied freedom to all intelligent beings. Leibniz
has happily dispelled this error and demonstrated that genuine
freedom consists in the choice of the best; moreover, that motives
do determine the choice and, while they abolish chance, never
bring about necessity.

How firmly Mendelssohn was convinced of the correctness and
relevance of the two lines of argument which we have traced is
evident from the fact that they re-appear toward the end of his
life in his Morgenstunden (1785). The occasion is the famous
controversy with Friedrich Heinrich Jacobi about Lessing's
alleged Spinozism. Mendelssohn is deeply disturbed by Jacobi's
disclosures, and in an effort to clear his friend's memory of the
charge of rank pantheism he offers the concept of a 'purified
pantheism' which is innocuous and reconcilable with religion
and morality in so far as they are practical.[22] This purified pantheism is identical with the Spinozistic system as portrayed in the
Gespräche, viz. as an intra-deical world which the theist too has to
admit, and which the pantheist refuses to recognise as real outside
God.[23] Against Spinoza's denial of God's freedom Mendelssohn,
again, uses the interpretation he had offered in the Gespräche.
Spinoza's objection to freedom is valid only if we identify freedom
with perfect equilibrium. It does not affect the affirmation of
freedom by the determinists, viz. the freedom to choose the
morally best.[24] It is remarkable indeed that thirty years after he
had written his first work he resorted to the very ideas he had
expressed there.

Can these ideas stand the test of scrutiny? Mendelssohn bases
his notion of the identity of Spinoza's system with Leibniz'
world as it existed in God's mind on two textual comparisons.
In both instances he quotes not Leibniz himself, but 'the Leibnizians', and his one and only direct reference is to Wolff's
Theologia naturalis. The text quoted (II, #92) is supposed to
express the same notion as found in Spinoza's statement (Ethics,

I, 25, cor.) that the *res particulares* are but the modes expressing the divine attributes in a certain limited way (*certo et determinato modo*). What Wolff does in fact say bears, however, a different connotation. He distinguishes the in-existence in God of the 'first possibles' (*possibilia prima*), or 'unlimited realities' (*realitates illimitatae*), from the 'second possibles' (*primitiva secunda*) or 'first principles of finite things' (*prima entium finitorum principia essendi*), which arise from the first possibles by way of limitation and are known by God but do not exist in Him. The point Wolff makes in the paragraph quoted by Mendelssohn is based on this distinction (found in #87, 88, 91–93). It relates to God's knowledge of the second possibles: *Patet adeo Deum omnia possibilia primitiva secunda sive a primis orta quam distinctissime cognoscere* (#92). This is also the meaning of the sentence quoted by Mendelssohn: *Deus possibilia prima omni possibili modo limitat, & omnes eorundem limitationes quam distinctissime ac simul cognoscit*. The stress is on God's knowing (*cognoscit*) the second possibles which arise by the limitation of the first. Although God is the *ens perfectissimum* in whom all reality exists *in gradu absoluto summo* (#93), He knows the second possibles because they arise from the first by limitation (#92). These second possibles are, however, the principles of finite things, and not – as Mendelssohn seems to assume – particular things as such. The 'possibility of contingent things' of which, in Mendelssohn's phrase, the Leibnizians speak is something entirely different from the 'particular things' which he finds discussed by Spinoza. Nor is it correct to describe the second possibles as the divine ideas which constitute the 'possibility of the contingent things'. It would be more correct to define the second possibles as the principles of finite things. At any rate, Spinoza speaks of particular things as modes of the attributes, while Wolff deals with the principles of finite things. What is even more decisive, Spinoza conceives of the particular things or modes as being in God, whereas Wolff differentiates the unlimited realities which are in God from the second possibilities of which God knows. Mendelssohn's identification of Spinoza's system with the Leibnizians' world in God's mind breaks down. While for Spinoza the modes

18

are intra-deical, for Wolff the second possibilities are clearly not.

The second comparison is less fraught with ambiguity but is still unconvincing. Mendelssohn quotes Spinoza's statement (*Ethics*, II, 9) which explains the possibility of the infinite having a knowledge of the finite. Directly, the idea of each individual thing has for its cause the idea of another individual thing, and so on *ad infinitum*. God is the cause of these individual ideas in so far only as they form an infinite whole.[25] The same notion, Mendelssohn asserts, is found in almost identical words in the Leibnizians. He quotes no *locus probans* but might have pointed to Leibniz' *Monadology*, #36 where the sufficient reason for the contingent truths of fact is found in an infinite sequence of causes. The point Mendelssohn wants to bring out is the recognition by both the Leibnizians and Spinoza of contingent things as possible objects of God's knowledge, and the definition, by both, of contingent things in terms of an infinite number of causes. But does this help to prove Mendelssohn's main thesis, which equates Spinoza's system with Leibniz' world *antecedenter ad decretum*? Does it imply that the meaning of the infinite series of causes is the same for Spinoza and Leibniz? The answer is in the negative. For Spinoza, every contingent fact is not only determined but also necessary.[26] For Leibniz, a contingent fact is determined but not necessary.[27] In his commentary on Wachter's *Elucidarius Cabalisticus* (1706), where he criticises Spinoza *via* Wachter, he makes the point (against *Ethics*, I, 7 and 10, *scholium*) that while essence and existence are one and the same thing in necessary things, this is not the case in individual or contingent things. The latter have no necessary connection with God but are freely produced. *Dieu a été incliné vers eux par une raison déterminée, il n'y a point été nécessité.*[28] Moreover, Spinoza's God is the cause of an infinite series of causes within Himself, whereas Leibniz' God is a transitive, not an immanent cause.[29] In the light of these fundamental differences it is hard to see Mendelssohn's justification for trying to approximate the two thinkers. The distance between them was not as small as Mendelssohn suggested.

Nor can one easily approve of Mendelssohn's effort at explaining Spinoza's denial of God's freedom as an error due to a faulty definition of 'genuine freedom'. It follows, in the first place, from his definition of the will as 'a certain mode of thought, like the intellect' (*Ethics*, I, 32) and from his basic notion of the immanence of all things in God: *quare nihil extra ipsum esse potest, a quo ad agendum determinetur, vel cogatur, atque adeo Deus ex solis suae naturae legibus, & a nemine coactus agit* (I, 17). It is this concept of the necessity from which God acts which constitutes the essential difference between Spinoza and Leibniz. That God acts *sub ratione boni* is a proposition sternly rejected by Spinoza (I, 33, *scholium* 2) and firmly embraced by Leibniz: 'The reason why the best of all possible worlds is the world which exists, is that God's wisdom makes him know, his goodness makes him choose, and his power makes him produce, the best possible'. (*Monadology*, #55).[30] In Spinoza's view there is no distinction between a world in the mind of God before the *decretum* and an actual world after God's choice of the best possible world. *At cum in aeterno non detur quando, ante, nec post: hinc, ex sola scilicet Dei perfectione, sequitur, Deum aliud decernere nunquam posse, nec unquam potuisse; sive Deum ante sua decreta non fuisse, nec sine ipsis esse posse* (*Ethics*, I, 33, *scholium* 2). Leibniz' distinction between the infinite possibilities *antecedenter ad decretum* and the reality of the world chosen by God is the very antithesis of Spinoza's doctrine. No doubt, Mendelssohn was fully aware of this, and yet he tried to present Leibniz as having 'happily' dispelled Spinoza's error by re-defining the concept of freedom.

We now turn to the other proposition, *viz.* the one offered in the first dialogue of the *Gespräche*. It is built up skilfully and with dramatic effect. From an unguarded remark of Neophil's Philopon concludes that in his friend's view Leibniz was not the 'inventor' of the doctrine of the pre-established harmony. When pressed to declare himself, Neophil admits that this is indeed his considered opinion. Philopon challenges him to prove what seems an odd proposition since, in Neophil's own words, 'no one has as yet contested the fame he [*sc.* Leibniz] has earned on this score, and that Bayle himself offered him congratulations on this great

discovery on behalf of the scholarly world.'[31] Neophil is ready
with his proof but first defines more clearly the nature of his
proposition. All he means to say is that the 'essential core' (*das
Wesentliche*) of this particular doctrine was discovered first by
another philosopher (whose identity remains as yet undis-
closed). He admits, moreover, that Leibniz was the first to desig-
nate this doctrine by the name 'pre-established harmony'.[32]
After some bantering talk about the trifling nature of this latter
point the discussion becomes more serious. What is meant by the
pre-established harmony? Philopon offers an account which is
carefully designed to fit Mendelssohn's notion of an 'essential
core' of the doctrine which Leibniz could have taken over from
Spinoza. In the ensuing debate the point is made that Leibniz did
in fact present his doctrine in two different ways, *viz.* with and
without its monadological aspect, and that Wolff adopted it in the
latter sense. This, then, represents the 'essential core' of Leibniz'
theory, which he is said to have borrowed from another philosopher. Who is that other philosopher? Neophil still refuses to
name him, but the quotation of a passage from Spinoza's *Ethics*
gives him away. 'Unless I am mistaken, I believe to be recognising Spinoza in these words,' says Philopon. We are now in the
full swing of philosophical argument and more of Spinoza's
passages are adduced in proof of the point at issue. The line of
argument proceeds roughly as follows: Spinoza (like the Cartesians and Leibniz) assumes that body and soul cannot determine
each other; the body follows the natural laws of corporeal
motion, and the actions of the soul can arise only from its adequate ideas. How, then, does Spinoza explain the accord between
body and soul? The occasionalist theory of the Cartesians could
not have been his answer since it presupposes the attribution of
free will to God, which he denies. We are driven to the conclusion that he assumed a pre-established harmony between the
two realms. This is what, in fact, he says in clear terms: 'The
order and connection of ideas is the same as the order and connection of things' (*Ethics*, II, 7). Mendelssohn feels he has achieved
the rehabilitation of Spinoza. 'You have shown me yesterday
with much acumen,' Philopon attests in the second dialogue,

'that Spinoza asserted the pre-established harmony.' As a result of the discussion in the first dialogue both friends agree that, notwithstanding the difference of principles, Leibniz and Spinoza arrived at almost the same view; that Spinoza's propositions are incomplete rather than false; and that by the correct principles contained in his system he was able to discover many other truths. The dialogue ends with an apology on behalf of Leibniz, who for reasons of prudence considered it necessary to conceal his source. He would have courted disaster had he revealed it.

Before we proceed to a closer inspection of Mendelssohn's main thesis, viz. the assertion of the Spinozistic origin of the doctrine under discussion, a minor point has to be cleared up. Mendelssohn presents his view of Leibniz' indebtness to Spinoza as a brand-new theory. No one, Neophil declares, has ever before contested Leibniz' title to fame as the author of this doctrine. This statement is, of course, historically incorrect. Already in Leibniz' own lifetime the Dutchman Ruardus Andala accused him of having plagiarised Spinoza in putting forward the doctrine of the pre-established harmony as his own.[33] The charge was later renewed with a great deal of venom by Joachim Lange in his attacks against Christian Wolff. Lange sought to discredit Wolff by labelling his and Leibniz' systems as Spinozistic. His *Causa Dei* (Halle, 1723) describes the notion of the pre-established harmony as *adoptatus pseudo-philosophiae Spinozianae foetus, novo potius nomine insignatum* [sic] *quam alio habitu indutus.*[34] The memorandum written by him as Dean of the Theological Faculty at Halle accuses Wolff, *inter alia*, of propounding a doctrine, *viz.* the one of the pre-established harmony, which amounted to Stoic and Spinozistic fatalism.[35] Wolff defended himself in his *Erinnerungen wieder diejenigen, die in seiner Metaphysick den Spinozisinum entdecket zu haben vermeinen*[36] and in other writings of his.[37] Mendelssohn might have been unaware of Andala's dissertation, but he could not have been ignorant of the Lange-Wolff controversy and the charge levelled against Leibniz. It has been suggested that he actually took his point of Leibniz' dependence on Spinoza from either Lange or Wolff's defence.[38] Whatever the merits of this

22

suggestion, there can be no doubt that he knew about the accusation of plagiarism laid at Leibniz' door. This knowledge on his part is reflected in his apology (at the end of the first dialogue) for Leibniz' failure to acknowledge his debt to Spinoza: 'Let it suffice to say that there are people who judge even truths according to a certain genealogy. In order to condemn a doctrine, they only need to know that it occurred in this or that author in bad company with other doctrines. . . . Tell me, would those people not have believed to find the refutation of this doctrine in the very name of Spinoza, had Leibniz freely confessed that he had borrowed the essential core of his harmony from Spinoza?' There is a subtle irony in Mendelssohn's defence of Leibniz' silence on his source. He presents his caution as if it had achieved its purpose. Those who know history, he implies, know of course that it availed him nothing. Far from obliterating the memory of the Lange-Wolff controversy which centred around Leibniz, the dialogue presupposes it. The denunciation of Leibniz' doctrine as Spinozistic, which is portrayed as merely hypothetical, actually took place. It is, therefore, obvious that Mendelssohn deliberately uses an element of fiction in what is otherwise a straight philosophical dialogue. This insight into his working method enables us to understand the inaccuracy of his statement that no one had ever before contested Leibniz' title to fame. In the first place, it is in league with the point just discussed. The irony of Mendelssohn's apology for Leibniz could not be expressed unless the historical charge of plagiarism was suppressed. Neophil had to present himself as the first to suggest such a connection, which in the changed intellectual climate of the attempted rehabilitation of Spinoza no longer incriminated Leibniz. In the second place, the disclosure of Leibniz' indebtedness to Spinoza achieves a heightened dramatic effect by its claim to be something entirely novel and daring. We have to make allowance for these fictional ingredients, which Mendelssohn could safely assume to be understood by his readers.[39]

Mendelssohn develops his thesis in two stages. In the first, he defines the meaning of what he described as the 'essential core' of Leibniz' doctrine of the pre-established harmony. In the second, he offers his arguments in proof of his assertion that this doctrine, in its essential form, derives from Spinoza. His procedure at both stages calls for some closer inspection.

1   Philopon gives the following account of Leibniz' doctrine of the pre-established harmony:

> A doctrine according to which everything that happens in our soul arises therein, in compliance with the body, by its own original power, and not as the effect caused by another substance; precisely as everything that happens in our body is produced therein, in compliance with the soul, by no other than corporeal, mechanical powers. Should one, then, ask a Leibnizian by which means the union of the body and soul is achieved, he will answer: God has, from eternity, arranged such a harmony between them that certain representations in the soul give rise to certain motions in the body, which have their sufficient reason simultaneously in both; *viz.* the reason *by which* they arise they have in the mechanical powers of the body, and the reason *why* or *to what end* they arise they have in the state of our soul. Conversely, certain motions in our body give rise to certain corresponding representations in our soul, which have their reason *by which* they arise in the original power of our soul and in its preceding state, while they have the reason *why* they arise in the motions of our body. The Leibnizian simile of the two clocks is well known.

This account contains no reference to the monadological concept with which the doctrine of the pre-established harmony is interwoven.[40] In the course of the discussion Neophil suggests that Leibniz was anxious to show the validity of his new theory, irrespective of the acceptability or otherwise of his monadological view. For this reason, he further suggests, Leibniz made no use of the monadology in his first presentation of the pre-established harmony nor in his replies to Bayle's criticisms in the *Journal des Savans*.[41] Moreover, he says, the pre-established harmony was accepted by Wolff in the simplified form only in which Leibniz had defended it against Bayle.[42] All this is clearly designed to make plausible Mendelssohn's suggestion that the 'essential core' (*das Wesentliche*) of this doctrine can be traced to Spinoza. Mendelssohn is obviously intent upon isolating such an essential element not merely by a logical process of abstraction but by the display of textual evidence. He wants to show that Leibniz himself offered his doctrine in its reduced form also, and that it therefore makes sense to link this particular form with Spinoza. He admits, on the other hand, that the pre-established harmony is, for Leibniz, inseparable from the monadic system: 'In the *Monadology* he showed it as following from his system of monads. It is here that it is revealed in its full splendour.'[43] The question, then, arises whether Leibniz did in fact present a simplified version of his doctrine, *viz.* one shorn of the monado-logical concept. According to Mendelssohn he did so in his essay *Système Nouveau* and in his subsequent *Éclaircissements* in the *Journal des Savans*. Do the texts bear out his contention? We shall deal with the essay first.

It starts from the notion of simple substances endowed with force analogous to feeling and desire and after the manner of souls. This concept is applied to the bodies of animals and other corporeal substances. The rational souls are said to follow much higher laws. The term *monad* is not used, but its meaning is clearly present. Thus, it is said that each of these substances represents the whole universe in its own way and from a certain point of view. Yet Leibniz himself obscures the relevance of this concept for the doctrine of the pre-established harmony by not using it straight as proof for it. For after the initial presentation of his notion of simple substances he continues: 'Having settled these things, I thought I had gained my haven, but when I set myself to meditate upon the union of soul and body I was as it were driven back into the deep sea. For I found no way of explaining how the body transmits anything to the soul or *vice versa*.'[44] It could, therefore, have appeared to Mendelssohn that Leibniz' subsequent discussion of the pre-established harmony was not meant to follow from the notion of substance or monad. He was, however, mistaken and, moreover, was simply ignoring Leibniz' own statement in his first reply to Foucher: 'With laudable candour you recognise that my hypothesis of harmony or concomitance is possible. But you still have a certain repugnance to it; doubtless because you think that it is purely arbitrary; through not being aware that *it follows from my view regarding unities; for everything in my theory is connected together*.'[45] Jacobi already drew attention to this statement when questioning the accuracy of Mendelssohn's contention that in the *Journal des Savans* Leibniz did not proceed from a monadological position.[46] He added the remark: 'And so I see indeed no material difference between the first essay and the *Principes sur* [sic] *la nature & la grâce* or the *Principia philosophiae*[47]; only a difference, according to the author's own remark,[48] in accommodation and way of presentation.'[49] This sweeping statement does not, however, correspond to fact. There is a material difference between the view of the monads presented in the essay and the one offered in the *Monadology*. Only in the latter work does Leibniz go as far as to reduce the difference between bodies and souls to one of degree, and thereby establish the harmony between them.[50] Mendelssohn's statement nevertheless remains open to criticism. The monadic concept plays a decisive part in the presentation of the doctrine in the essay.

In the three *éclaircissements* published in the *Journal des Savans* in reply to Foucher, Leibniz makes but sparing use of the monadology. The first of these refers to it as the premise from which the view of the pre-established harmony necessarily follows.[51] It mentions the notion of substances *douées d'une véritable unité*[52] and, with special reference to the harmony, the endowment of substances with 'forces' (*efforts*),[53] but it does so merely in order to clarify, not to prove the doctrine. The second and third *éclaircissements* do not mention the monadic concept at all but introduce, for the first time, the analogy of the two clocks.[54] Mendelssohn was, therefore, right in suggesting that in the *Journal des Savans* Leibniz defended the doctrine with 'only such weapons as common philosophy put into his hands'. He was, however, mistaken in applying this characterisation to Leibniz' defence of it against Bayle. The three *éclaircissements* published in the *Journal des Savans* were in reply to Foucher, not to Bayle. Leibniz' answers to Bayle, on the other hand, are far from conforming to Mendelssohn's description. For both the *Éclaircisse-ment* of 1698 (Gerhardt, IV, 517 ff.) and the *Réponse* of 1712 (Gerhardt, IV, 554 ff.) are steeped in the monadological theory, as even the most cursory glance will reveal. Mendelssohn knew at least the first of these replies, since he quotes Bayle's argument from the transition from pleasure to pain which occurs in it. He does not, however, mention the *Histoire des ouvrages des scavans* where the *Éclaircissement* appeared, and it may, therefore, be inferred that all he really meant to to say was that in the *Journal des Savans* Leibniz defended his theory on grounds other than monadological. His argumentation is, however, anything but a model of accuracy.

Even though Leibniz did make use of his monadology both in the *Système Nouveau* and in his replies to Bayle, the fact remains that this concept could be neglected by him in his defence against Foucher, and that Wolff adopted the doctrine of the pre-estab-lished harmony in a form divorced from Leibniz' understanding of the monads.[55] There was, then, some justification for Mendels-sohn's attempt to differentiate between an 'essential core' of the doctrine and its fully-fledged form. The question still to be dis-cussed is whether he succeeded in proving his thesis asserting the Spinozistic origin of the essential form of Leibniz' doctrine.

2   In building up his proof, Mendelssohn first shows that the problem of explaining how body and soul can act upon one another was as acute for Spinoza as it was for Leibniz, since both started out from the Cartesian dualism of extension and thought. He quotes Spinoza's proposition (*Ethics*, III, 2) which states that 'The body cannot determine the mind[56] to thought, neither can the mind determine the body to motion or rest or to anything else (if there be anything else).' Two further quotations are offered in corroboration of this point. The first is from the *scholium* on the proposition just cited, and the second from proposition 3 which follows it. In the *scholium* Spinoza points out that 'what the body can do no one has hitherto determined, that is to say, experience has taught no one hitherto what the body, without being determined by the mind, can do and what it cannot do

from the laws of Nature alone, in so far as nature is considered merely as corporeal.' He adds that 'no one as yet has understood the structure of the body so accurately as to be able to explain all its functions, not to mention the fact that many things are observed in brutes which far surpass human sagacity, and that sleepwalkers in their sleep do very many things which they dare not do when awake – all this showing that the body itself can do many things, from the laws of its own nature alone, at which the mind belonging to that body is amazed.'[57] In proposition 3 Spinoza says that: 'The actions of the mind arise from adequate ideas alone, but the passive states depend upon those alone which are inadequate.'[58] Mendelssohn adds:

He demonstrates this proposition by reference to the fact that the essence of the soul consists in its thoughts. Now, all thoughts are composed of adequate and inadequate ideas. Hence that which follows from the nature of the soul, i.e. that which has the soul for its proximate cause by which it can be explained, must follow from either an adequate or an inadequate idea. Since, however, it has been demonstrated in the third part of the *Ethics* that from inadequate ideas nothing but passions can arise, he draws the conclusion that the actions of the soul can arise from its adequate ideas only.[59]

The radical dichotomy between body and soul having been thus established as Spinoza's view, Mendelssohn shows that for Spinoza the problem of the accord between body and soul could not be solved by invoking God's constant intervention as suggested by the occasionalist theory ('the system of occasional causes'). 'Nothing can be more contrary to Spinoza's philosophy than the system of occasional causes. The protagonists of this view must, of necessity, attribute free will to the Being by whose intervention body and soul are connected; and how could Spinoza have admitted this? He who considered intellect and will to be one and the same?'[60] Moreover, he argues, Spinoza stated that all changes that occur in the body can be explained from purely mechanical causes, a view not acceptable to the occasionalists. Finally, he recalls the close similarity between Spinoza's description of the feats which the human body can perform *per se* and the Leibnizians' statements on this subject. 'Spinoza even employs all the argumentation resorted to by the Leibnizians. Like them, he invokes our ignorance of the inner structure of our body, and, finally, the fact that no one has as yet shown the impossibility of a machine capable of producing mechanically all those performances which are allotted to this or that individual body.' Mendelssohn is obviously referring to Leibniz' discussion of the artfulness of the human body and the possible accomplishments of a superbly constructed automaton, in his *Réponse* to Bayle (Gerhardt, IV, 555–557).

Since the occasionalist theory was of no avail to Spinoza, we are led to assume that, in his view, the accord between body and soul must be due to an exact correspondence between the two systems. The sequence of ideas in the soul must be an exact pre-established parallel to the sequence of the motions of the body. This is what Spinoza says in effect: 'The order and connection of ideas is the same as the order and connection of things' (*Ethics*, II, 7). Mendelssohn considers this proposition as decidedly expressive of the same notion as Leibniz':

Do you now recall what Leibniz had to say in his defence against Bayle's objection that, without our assuming the action of another substance upon the soul, it would be incomprehensible how the soul can pass on occasion immediately from pleasure to displeasure and from sadness to joy? Did not he too suggest that the changes in the soul can be explained by the very same reason by which the changes in the visible world can be understood? That the states of the soul succeed each other in the very same way in which there is succession in the nexus of things? What else does this amount to than what Spinoza says in the words we have quoted: 'The order and connection of ideas is the same as the order and connection of things.'

This, then, is Mendelssohn's proof for his thesis that the doctrine of the pre-established harmony is found in essence, though not in name nor in its full expression, in the much-maligned Spinoza, and that Leibniz took it from there.

The validity of this proof does not seem to have been questioned by the reviewers of Mendelssohn's *Gespräche*. 'I am surprised', Lessing wrote to Mendelssohn in a letter dated 17th April, 1763, eight years after the publication of these dialogues, 'that no one has as yet spoken up for Leibniz and against you'.[61] This omission was now being made good by Lessing himself. 'I must confess to you that for some time past I have not been too happy with your first dialogue. I believe you were a little of a sophist at the time you wrote it.' The gist of his objections is as follows: Spinoza assumed that body and soul are one and the same substance, which is considered now under the attribute of extension and now under that of thought (*Ethics*, II, 7, *scholium*). What kind of harmony had to be established between them? A harmony which the thing has with itself? Is this not playing with words? Leibniz wants to solve by his harmony the riddle of the union between two entities as diverse as body and soul. Spinoza, on the other hand, sees no diverse things, no union, therefore, and no riddle to be solved. Lessing, in other words, denies that the problem which Leibniz wished to solve ever existed for Spinoza. The need for the hypothesis of the pre-established harmony did not arise for him. Lessing quotes Spinoza's proposition (II, 21) which he understands to mean that the soul is united with the body in the same way as the idea of the soul which it has of itself is united to the soul. Now, the idea which the soul has of itself belongs to the essence of the soul, and is inseparable from it. Hence the body too is inseparable from the soul, and it is by virtue of this inseparability or identity that they are united. Lessing admits that the key-passage quoted by Mendelssohn ('The order and connection of ideas is the same as the order and connection of things') and a similar one (V, 1) do have a Leibnizian ring. This, however, he does not consider decisive:

> If, then, both use the same words, do they, at the same time, associate identical concepts with them? Impossible. Spinoza only means to say thereby that everything that follows formally from the nature of God and, hence, from the nature of an individual thing, follows also objectively in the same order

and connection. According to his view, the sequence and connection of ideas in the soul agrees with the sequence and connection of the changes of the body merely because the body is the object of the soul; because the soul is nothing but the body thinking itself, and the body is nothing but the soul that extends itself. But Leibniz?

Fortunately, we possess Mendelssohn's reply to his friend's criticism.[62] Far from disowning his youthful dialogue and its argumentation, he firmly upholds them. His so-called 'sophistry' can, he thinks, be justified. Notwithstanding the fact that for Spinoza body and soul are modifications of one and the same substance, extension and thought are still two different attributes. Each of them is conceived by itself without involving the other (II, 6). Hence motion cannot be understood by reference to thought, nor thought by reference to motion. Ideas follow from ideas and motions follow from motions. Yet they harmonise with each other, i.e., in Spinoza's language, the ideas invariably express *per modum cognitionis* what the motions express *per modum extensionis*. It follows that Spinoza regards body and soul as different attributes between which a harmony exists. The fact that they are one substance – in the unusual sense in which he uses the term, there being for him only one single substance – and one individual, does not obliterate the distinctiveness of the attributes. What matters, he sums up, is not this or that expression used by Spinoza nor the concept of substance, but whether or not Spinoza subscribed to the following propositions, which constitute the essence[63] of the doctrine of the harmony: (*a*) motion and thought are different things; (*b*) *cognitio* can never be *causa efficiens mutationis extensi*, nor can *extensio* be *causa mutationis cogitationis*; (*c*) *cogitatio* invariably follows *ex cogitatione*, and *motus ex motu*; (*d*) at the same time, the series *motuum et cogitationum* are always in harmony.

Mendelssohn affirms that these propositions, which are the essential elements of the doctrine of the pre-established harmony, were held by Spinoza before Leibniz, who merely fitted them into his system. One may admit that the proposition which reads

'The order and connection of ideas is the same as the order and connection of things' is demonstrated in different ways by Spinoza and Leibniz. This, however, Mendelssohn suggests, is irrelevant to our point. What is important is not the systematic framework in which a sentence is embedded but the meaning of the sentence. 'Has the proposition as such', he asks, 'one meaning in Spinoza and another in Leibniz? Does the latter explain the words differently? Is his understanding of the terms 'things', 'ideas', and 'order' different from that of any one else? Not at all. The meaning of the proposition is thoroughly Leibnizian.' This is, clearly, a restatement of the claim made in the *Gespräche*: the 'essential core' of Leibniz' doctrine is found in Spinoza. Mendelssohn adds, however, a further thought in this letter:

You say: 'According to his [*sc*. Spinoza's] view, the sequence and connection of ideas in the soul agrees with the sequence and connection of the changes in the body merely because the body is the object of the soul; because the soul is nothing but the body thinking itself, and the body is nothing but the soul that extends itself. But Leibniz?' . . . I must confess to you that to me Leibniz does not seem to be very far from these thoughts. According to him, the ideas and representations are but the changes of the simple things [*viz*. the monads] *as they are*, and the motions are but the changes of the simple things *as they appear*. The same modifications of the simple things constitute thought on the one hand, when considered as realities, and extension and motion on the other, when considered as phenomena. The soul has representations of the world, i.e. of all changes in the simple things, in accordance with the position of its body in it. Spinoza expresses this by saying: the body is the object of the soul, and the body itself is but the totality of changes occurring in certain simple things and perceived by me as phenomena. This being the case, it is inevitable that the series of phenomena be in harmony with the series of realities, i.e. that the motions of the body harmonise with the ideas in the soul.

Mendelssohn's view may be restated as follows: Spinoza held that the body is the object of the idea constituting the human mind (*Ethics*, II, 12–13, 21), and that the object of our mind is a body existing, and nothing else (II, 13). Spinoza, moreover, considered the body to be nothing but the totality of changes occurring in certain simple things and perceived as phenomena. Similarly, Leibniz saw in the body and all that appertains to it (extension, motion) but *phenomena bene fundata* reflecting the viewpoint of the monad, which alone is real.[64] Hence the difference between the two systems is even further reduced. It seems, however, that Mendelssohn wrongly attributed to Spinoza the view that the body is but the totality of changes in certain simple things (?) perceived as phenomena. For Spinoza, the body is not a phenomenon in the Leibnizian sense. He defines 'body' as 'a mode which expresses in a certain and determinate manner the essence of God in so far as He is considered as the thing extended' (*Ethics*, II, *Def.* 1). He says that 'The mind does not know itself except in so far as it perceives the ideas of the modifications of the body' (II, 23). The relation between body and soul cannot be described, therefore, as one between phenomena and reality. Both equally express reality. Mendelssohn's argumentation for a closer resemblance of the two systems than originally suggested by him thus falls to the ground.

Interestingly enough, Lessing's point was restated with even greater emphasis twenty-six years later by Karl Heinrich Heydenreich, an admirer of Jacobi's, in his brilliantly written *Natur und Gott nach Spinoza* (Vol. I, Leipzig, 1789, 90–102).[65] The author develops his critique of Mendelssohn (who had died three years earlier) in a dialogue between two philosophers, called rather anachronistically Parmenides and Xenophanes. Parmenides admits not having read a single line of Spinoza's nor having derived any clear view of his system from the accounts of it by Bayle, Lamy and many others. He gratefully acknowledges, however, the help he had received from the most recent writers on the subject, *viz.* Mendelssohn (in the *Morgenstunden*, 1785) and Herder (in *Gott*, 1787). They had indeed attracted him, and he was convinced that Spinoza, were he to rise again, would accept the revisions suggested by them. Xenophanes is not of this opinion. In order to understand the Spinozistic doctrine one ought to read, above all, Jacobi's *Über die Lehre des Spinoza, in Briefen an den Herrn Moses Mendelssohn* (1785). In the ensuing discussion Parmenides recalls Mendelssohn's early *Philosophische Gespräche* in which the agreement of Spinoza's system, if shorn of some unessential points, with the Leibniz-Wolffian philosophy is shown with a delicacy which defies criticism, provided his interpretation of Spinozism is correct. He adds: 'It seems to me also highly probable that Leibniz borrowed the basic concept (*den Grund*) of his pre-established harmony from Spinoza, as he [i.e. Mendelssohn] has already shown many years ago.' Xenophanes reacts rather sharply to this reminiscence. 'It is true, Mendelssohn asserted this, and he did so with such a degree of confidence that one seemed to have done enough for Leibniz' honour if one covered his theft with a few lame excuses. I believe, however, that this philosopher [i.e. Mendelssohn] committed here the same mistake as was made by another long before him.' 'Was, then, Mendelssohn not the first to offer this particular suggestion?' asks Parmenides. Xenophanes is hesitant to accuse Mendelssohn of plagiarism but his reply tends that way. 'I do not know whether he himself knew that this had been done before. I should, however, almost assume that, since he took such a great interest in Wolff's philosophy, he turned one day, from curiosity, the pages of Joachim Lange's book against Wolff.' In that book, *viz.* in the *Modesta disquisitio*,[66] Xenophanes relates, proof is offered to the effect that Leibniz took the pre-established harmony from Spinoza. The startling fact is disclosed that the very same passages from Spinoza quoted as evidence by Lange re-appear in Mendelssohn's argumentation. Lange had cited, *inter alia*, the passage (*Ethics*, III, 2): *nec corpus mentem ad cogitandum, nec mens corpus ad motum neque ad quietem . . . determinare potest* (which is the very same passage which Mendelssohn adduces as the basis of his proof). Xenophanes challenges, however, the validity of the argument, and he does so on grounds familiar to us from Lessing's objection: Matter and thought are, strictly speaking, one and the same thing according to Spinoza.

Hence there are no things requiring harmonisation, and there is no scope for the notion of a pre-established harmony. It is different in the case of Leibniz, whose system, both in its dualistic and monadological form, poses a plurality of substances in need of harmonisation. In other words, Leibniz could not have taken his doctrine from Spinoza for the simple reason that in Spinoza's system the problem of explaining the accord between body and soul does not even arise. Xenophanes shows with a wealth of quotations that this point had already been made by Wolff in his *De differentia nexus rerum sapientis et fatalis necessitatis nec non systematis harmoniae praestabilitae et hypothesium Spinozae* (1724).[67] He assumes that both Lange and Mendelssohn had but a superficial knowledge of Spinoza's system. The former sought to discredit the Leibniz-Wolffian philosophy by labelling it as Spinozistic, while the latter was led into error by the outward resemblance between certain of Spinoza's propositions and the principles which underlie Leibniz' doctrine. Mendelssohn might, however, have considered the possibility that Leibniz was sufficiently capable of producing his doctrine on his own, and sufficiently honest to admit his source had there been one. 'But what does one not put out of sight when the possibility of exhibiting oneself as a discoverer is at stake!'[68]

Mendelssohn could no longer reply to these charges. He might have admitted that he had read Lange or – as suggested by Jacobi[69] – found Lange's proof in Wolff. As we have ventured to suggest, his presentation of the theory asserting Leibniz' indebtedness to Spinoza contains a deliberate fictional element. What matters, however, is not the (still open) question as to whether or not he had met this theory in Lange or Wolff, but the fact that he made it so thoroughly his own and defended it vigorously against Lessing's objections long after he had first expressed it. If he knew Wolff's rejection of Lange's proof, he certainly disregarded it when writing his *Gespräche* and when replying to Lessing. The impression one gets is that he was unaware of Wolff's line of reasoning. Otherwise, he might have mentioned Wolff's precedence to Lessing. He may have read Lange, but the way he presents the theory is much subtler and interwoven with the point made in the second dialogue. Above all, he offers it from an entirely new viewpoint, *viz.* that of deep respect for Leibniz and, coupled with it, a desire to rehabilitate Spinoza. The courage which he evinced by taking his stand was not without effect. The change of attitude toward Spinoza which became noticeable in the eighties of his century can be traced back to his little *opus* and the influence which it then began to exercise. Lessing was probably first introduced to an appreciation of Spinoza by Mendelssohn.[70] Jacobi, who had the lion's share in the renaissance of Spinoza starting in Germany, was well aware of Mendelssohn's *Gespräche*. He referred to this work in his historic discussion with Lessing in 1780: 'Mendelssohn has publicly shown that the *Harmonia praestabilita* is found in Spinoza.'[71] Heydenreich's book gives further evidence of the attention which Mendelssohn's first *opus* commanded in the last decade of his life.

It seems futile to discuss the validity of Mendelssohn's reply to the objections raised by his friend Lessing and, after his death, by Heydenreich, who had discovered them in Wolff's refutation of Lange. For even assuming that Mendelssohn's interpretation of Spinoza was correct, *viz.* that the two attributes of the one substance involve two distinct orders of existence and, therefore, call for an explanation of their harmony,[72] we would still be far from proving that Leibniz took his doctrine from Spinoza, unless it could be shown that this was also Leibniz' interpretation of Spinoza. In other words: the issue at stake is not, as Mendelssohn asserted, the identity of meaning of certain propositions in the two systems (which represents a purely semantic problem), but whether or not Leibniz actually understood Spinoza after the manner suggested by Mendelssohn (which is a historical question). This historical question admits of an answer in the light of a number of documents which were not available to Mendelssohn since they were published only after his time. All of them make it plain that Leibniz considered Spinozism a monistic system in which the harmonisation of the body and soul did not even arise. In his annotations in the margin of his copy of Spinoza's *Oeuvres posthumes* (written *ca.* 1678), which were first published in 1830, he comments on the words of the *scholium* to *Ethics* II, 21 (*hoc est Mentem et Corpus unum et idem esse Individuum*, etc.): *Ergo revera non differunt mens et corpus, non magis quam urbs diversimode inspecta a se ipsa, sequitur et extensionem a cogitatione revera non differe* (Gerhardt, I, 151).[73] He clearly understands Spinoza's words to mean that body and soul are the same reality conceived under two different attributes, but not differing more from one another than a town viewed from here and there differs in itself. This view of Spinoza's doctrine is restated in his *Animadversiones* on Johann Georg Wachter's *Elucidarius Cabalisticus* (1706)[74]:

Spinoza dit (*Eth.*, p. 3, *schol.*, prop. 2) que l'esprit et le corps sont la même chose, mais seulement exprimée de deux manières, et (*Eth.*, p. 2, *schol.* 5, prop. 7) que la substance pensante et la substance étendue sont une seul et même substance, que l'on conçoit tantôt sous l'attribut de la pensée, tantôt sous celui de l'étendue. . . . Je blame tout ceci. L'esprit et le corps n'est pas même chose, pas plus que le principe de l'action et celui de la passion. . . .

Leibniz' interpretation of Spinoza's two attributes as *la même chose* accords with his understanding of Spinoza's *mens idea corporis* as implying a concept of soul as mere idea, devoid of force. In his annotations on the *Oeuvres posthumes* (Gerhardt, I, 150–151) he wrote, *à propos* of proposition 12 of part II: *ideae non agunt. Mens agit. Totus mundus revera est objectum cujusque mentis.* . . .[75] An oversimplified version of Spinoza's concept of *mens idea corporis* is offered by Leibniz in his *Elementa rationis* (*ca.* 1686) along the same lines. According to him, Spinoza considers the soul as bereft of all activity of power since 'l'âme n'est rien d'autre que l'idée ou, si vous préférez, la figure abstraite ou la forme mécanique de son corps de même que le cube géometrique est la forme du cube matériel.'[76] This is, of course, a misreading of Spinoza, who did attribute concrete reality and power to the soul.[77] The fact, however, remains that in Leibniz' view the soul was but the idea of the body and both were the same reality, a view which precludes the possibility

37

of assuming that he took the notion of the pre-established harmony from Spinoza. Wolff's, Lessing's and Heydenreich's interpretations of Spinoza agreed with Leibniz'. Mendelssohn's thesis has, therefore, no *locus standi*, and would most probably not have been proposed had Mendelssohn known of Leibniz' observations on Spinoza.

The question of Spinoza's influence on Leibniz, which Mendelssohn's *Philosophische Gespräche* had set afloat, was not settled by the late eighteenth-century reaction to the claim that had been put forward. Jacobi, who endorsed Heydenreich's critique of Mendelssohn, left the question in abeyance: 'How much or how little Leibniz owed to Spinoza – I have no opinion on this nor do I seek to have one.'[78] The issue claimed a great deal of attention in the nineteenth century and has not ceased to be debated even today. It was no longer confined to the doctrine of the pre-established harmony but took in the whole range of Leibniz' monadology and other areas as well.[79] Ludwig Stein placed the discussion on a new basis by investigating in great detail and with a wealth of fresh documentary evidence the stages of Leibniz' development. He believed that he had shown, among other things, that Leibniz passed through a Spinozistic phase.[80] This view has, however, since been discarded. Ernst Cassirer rejected it as ill-founded,[81] and Georges Friedmann disproved it more recently in convincing fashion.[82] While Cassirer admits Spinoza's possible influence on Leibniz' moral theory,[83] Friedmann makes the point that Spinoza had no share in the formation of Leibniz' system,[84] and that Leibniz' *Système Nouveau* was offered in radical opposition to previous systems.[85] Leon Roth, to whose memory the present study is respectfully dedicated, expressed a different point of view[86]:

All that Leibniz says about his many individual things is the same as what Spinoza says about one thing. . . . Nor is there any reason why Leibniz should not have made his own use of Spinoza. What he ought not to have done, however, was to go out of his way at every opportunity to discredit the source from which he drew. And he drew and adapted much. His theory of soul, of the pre-established harmony, of liberty, of perfection, depend closely on specific points in Spinoza's doctrine; while his central concept of the fundamental place of activity (*esse = agere*) is one of the most important, although usually neglected, sides of Spinoza's general point of view. . . .

It is interesting to find that Leon Roth resumed, on a far larger scale and in far sterner accents, the thesis which the young Mendelssohn had propounded *sine ira*, albeit *cum studio*. Roth was obviously not aware of Mendelssohn's early *opus*, since he quotes only his *Morgenstunden*.[87] His rather sweeping claim is supported by but one single reference, *viz.* to Stein's 'very thorough discussion'.[88] In view of the shakiness of Stein's theory, his claim does not stand on firm ground, and one cannot withhold sympathy from Herbert Wildon Carr's angry rejection of the charge of plagiarism so repeatedly levelled against Leibniz.[89] Mendelssohn's *opus* 1, we may sum up, made history, and it has its place in the protracted debate on the issue it raised long after Lange's rancorous attack had occurred and fallen into oblivion. It also made history in Mendelssohn's own life, and did so in rather a poignant way. The figure of Spinoza, which his very first dialogue had raised from the shades, was to haunt him almost like a ghost when, towards the end of his life, Jacobi's disclosure about Lessing's Spinozism upset him in uncommon degree and forced him to re-examine his own relationship with Spinoza. It may well be true, as many of his contemporaries felt to be the case, that the anguish over his shattered peace was a contributory factor to his death. Spinoza had been his first thought as a young writer. Spinoza was also his last.

NOTES

1 Published anonymously by Christian Friedrich Voss, Berlin, 1755. A revised edition appeared in *Moses Mendelssohns Philosophische Schriften*, Erster Theil, Berlin 1761 (reprinted in 1771). Both editions are reproduced in Moses Mendelssohn, *Gesammelte Schriften*, Jubiläumsausgabe, I, Berlin, 1929 (JubA), 1–39; 335–77. The second edition is contained also in *Moses Mendelssohn's gesammelte Schriften*, I, Leipzig, 1843 (GS), 191–231.

2　See Leo Strauss' introduction to this essay in JubA, II, 1931, xv–xx.

3　JubA, I, 64 (Sechster Brief). The letters are republished in Mendelssohn's *Philosophische Schriften* of 1761 (1771), where, however, Palemon is replaced by Theokles. For the passage quoted see JubA, I, 256–7.

4　JubA, I, 11, 12, 14 (346, 349).

5　JubA, I, 9, 10, (344, 345); 15 (350). Christian Wolff's critique of Spinoza is found in his *Theologia Naturalis*, Pars Posterior, #672 ff., pp. 346 ff. in the Verona edition of 1738. Mendelssohn is particularly impressed with Wolff's argument that an infinite number of finite perfections cannot produce an infinite perfection. He quotes this argument in the *Gespräche*, JubA, I, 16 (351); *Morgenstunden*, GS, II, 346–7. In his *Erinnerungen an Herrn Jacobi* (published by Friedrich Heinrich Jacobi in his *Über die Lehre des Spinoza in Briefen an den Herrn Moses Mendelssohn*, Neue Vermehrte Ausgabe, Breslau, 1789, 78–96) he says: 'Die grösste Schwierigkeit aber, die ich in dem System des Spinoza finde, liegt mir darin, dass er aus dem Zusammennehmen des Eingeschränkten das Uneingeschränkte will entstehen lassen' (94–5).

6　JubA, I, 14 (349).

7　JubA, I, 14–15 (349–50).

8　See Georges Friedmann, *Leibniz et Spinoza*, 1962, 133.

9　JubA, I, 16 (351).

10　JubA, I, 18 (354).

11　JubA, I, 14 (349); 15 (350).

12　In the course of his discussions of the *Trauerspiel* with Friedrich Nicolai in the summer of 1756, Mendelssohn suggested that the tragic hero is not necessarily a virtuous man who is destroyed through an error he has committed; even a rogue who bears a certain semblance of virtue may be a tragic figure. See JubA, XI, 59, and Bruno Strauss' note, p. 409. For a full appraisal of Mendelssohn's theory of tragedy see Robert Petsch, *Lessings Briefwechsel mit Mendelssohn und Nicolai über das Trauerspiel*, Leipzig, 1910.

13　JubA, I, 11–12 (346–7).

14　JubA, I, 17 (352); see also 10 (344).

15　In the second edition Mendelssohn quotes Wolff's *Theologia Naturalis*, Part II, #92: *Deus possibilia prima omni possibili modo limitat, & omnes eorundem limitationes quam distinctissime ac simul cognoscit.*

16　Mendelssohn gives no reference. Fritz Bamberger, who edited and annotated JubA, suggests that he was possibly referring to *Ethics*, I, 25, corollary: *Res particulares nihil sunt nisi Dei attributa certo et determinato* [in the sense of *limitato*] *modo exprimuntur.*

17　No reference is given. Wolff's *Theologia Naturalis*, II, #154–6 discusses the knowledge of God as embracing the *singularia*, which are said to be determined by the *entire* nexus of causes (unknown to us). The term *'infinite* series of causes' does not, however, occur.

18 *Ethics*, II, 9: *Idea rei singularis, actu existentis, Deum pro causa habet, non quatenus infinitus est, sed quatenus alia rei singularis actu existentis idea affectus consideratur, cujus etiam Deus est causa, quatenus alia tertia affectus est, & sic in infinitum.* Mendelssohn translates *affectus consideratur* imprecisely by *in ihm . . . anzutreffen ist.*

19 JubA, I, 18 (353–4). Mendelssohn interprets Spinoza's notion of *mens idea corporis* (*Ethics*, II, 12–13) to imply that the soul is devoid of a force of its own. Leibniz understood it in the same way. This was, however, not Spinoza's meaning. See below, p. 37.

20 JubA, I, 18 (354); cf. 9 (343).

21 JubA, I, 18–19 (354–5); Spinoza, *Ethics*, I, 17, *scholium.*

22 *Morgenstunden*, chs. XIII–XIV, GS, II, 340 ff.

23 GS, II, 352.

24 GS, II, 345.

25 Cf. Harry A. Wolfson, *The Philosophy of Spinoza*, Cambridge, Mass., 1934, II, 32.

26 Cf. Wolfson, *op. cit.*, I, 188 ff., 398–9.

27 Cf. Herbert Wildon Carr, *The Monadology of Leibniz*, London, 1930, 75.

28 See A. Foucher de Careil, *Leibniz, Descartes et Spinoza*, Paris, 1862, 197. The text of Leibniz' comments on Wachter appears there (pp. 185–220) under the title 'Remarques critiques de Leibniz d'après le manuscrit original de la Bibliothèque de Hanovre'. It was published first by Foucher de Careil under the title, *Réfutation inédite de Spinoza par Leibniz*, Paris, 1854. The full reference of the book commented on by Leibniz is: *Elucidarius Cabalisticus sive reconditae Hebraeorum philosophiae Brevis et succincta recensio*, Epitomatore Joh. Georgio Wachterio, philos. Prof., Romae, 1706.

29 Cf. Friedmann, *op. cit.* (note 8), 167.

30 See also Leibniz, *Essais de Théodicée*, I, 8, 173 (Gerhardt, VI, 107, 217). Cf. Friedmann, *op. cit.*, 101.

31 JubA, I, 4 (337–8). The point is taken up again later in the discussion, p. 11 (346). It introduces a slightly fictional element into the presentation of the facts surrounding Leibniz, since nothing is known about any 'congratulations' offered by Bayle. Cf. Bamberger's note, JubA, I, 615.

32 JubA, I, 4 (338). Mendelssohn quotes [Johann Christoph Gottsched's] German translation of Bayle's *Dictionaire historique et critique*, 1702, art. Rorarius, note L, [Gottsched's] note A, which

41

records Leibniz' refutation of Bayle's remark attributing the invention of the term to Dom François Lamy. The term was used by Lamy in his *La Connaissance de soi-même*, II, 1699, 226. Leibniz replied in his 'Extrait du Dictionnaire de M. Bayle article Rorarius . . . avec mes remarques' (Gerhardt, IV, 534): 'Je luy avois déja donné ce nom dans ma réponse a M. l'Abbé Foucher mise dans le Journal des savans du 9 Avril de l'an 1696, et le R. P. Lami l'a trouvé convenable'. The original text of Leibniz' 'Extrait' was first published in C. I. Gerhardt's edition of Leibniz' philosophical writings (1880). A German translation of it appeared, however, as early as 1720 in Heinrich Köhler's *Des Hn. Gottfried Wilh. von Leibnitz Lehr-Sätze über die Monadologie . . . wie auch Dessen letzte Vertheidigung seines Systematis Harmoniae praestabilitae wider die Einwürffe des Herrn Bayle* (Jena, 1720). The relevant clause reads in Köhler's version: 'Ich hatte dem Systemati diesen Namen schon in meiner Antwort an den Herrn Abt Foucher gegeben . . . und der P. Lamy hat ihn für bequem gefunden.' Gottsched copied this sentence *verbatim* from Köhler.

33 In his *Dissertatio de unione mentis et corporis physica*, which forms part of his *Pentas dissertationum philosophicarum*, Franecker, 1712. Cf. Ludwig Stein, *Leibniz und Spinoza*, Berlin, 1890, 3. Andala attacked Leibniz also in his *Dissertatio philosophica*, etc., which likewise appeared in the *Pentas*. See Carl Günther Ludovici, *Ausführlicher Entwurff einer vollständigen Historie der Leibnitzischen Philosophie*, Leipzig, 1737, #362, p. 393. His attacks on Leibniz were continued by his pupil Bernhardus Jorna. See Stein, *loc. cit.*, 3.

34 Quoted by Stein, *loc. cit.*, 4. He uses similar terms in his *Modesta disquisitio novi philosophiae systematis de deo mundo et homine et praesertim de harmonia praestabilita*, Halle, 1733, 127, 138.

35 See C. G. Ludovici, *Ausführlicher Entwurff einer vollständigen Historie der Wolffischen Philosophie*, Leipzig, 1737, #252, pp. 196–7; #260, pp. 200–1.

36 Published in *Leipziger gelehrte Zeitungen*, 1723, 527 ff.; see Ludovici in the work quoted in note 35, #254, p. 198.

37 See Ludovici, *ibid.*, #57, pp. 44–5; #58, p. 45.

38 See above, pp. 34–5.

39 It is possibly the dramatic quality of the *Gespräche* which gave the reviewer in *Göttingische Anzeigen von gelehrten Sachen*, 1755, 586–8 (Johann David Michaelis) the impression that Lessing was the author.

40 It is based on Leibniz' doctrine as presented first in the essay entitled 'Système nouveau pour expliquer la nature des substances et leur communication entre elles, aussi bien que l'union de l'âme

avec le corps', and published in the *Journal des Savans*, June, 1695 (reprinted in J. E. Erdmann's edition of Leibniz' *Opera Philosophica* I, Berlin, 1840, 118 ff.). The original draft and a version revised and altered by Leibniz appear in Gerhardt's edition (IV, 471 ff.; 477 ff.).

The distinction between the reason 'by which', and the reason 'why' (in other words, between the efficient and the final causes) does not occur in the essay. It appears in the *Monadology* (#79) and in the *Théodicée* (I, #62, Gerhardt, VI, 137), where, however, acting according to final causes is said to belong exclusively to the soul, and acting according to efficient causes is attributed exclusively to bodies. See also Leibniz' essay of 1705 (Gerhardt, VI, 539 ff.). Mendelssohn's presentation of Leibniz' view is, therefore, incorrect, as far as this particular aspect is concerned.

41 JubA, I, 5–7 (339–41).

42 Mendelssohn quotes Wolff's 'Latin Cosmology' [*viz*. his *Cosmologia Generalis*, Frankfurt-Leipzig, 1737], #206, 213. As already noted by Bamberger (JubA, I, 617), the paragraphs referred to do not discuss the subject. Bamberger substitutes a reference to the 'German Metaphysics' [*viz*. Wolff's *Vernünfftige Gedanken von Gott, der Welt und der Seele des Menschen*, Frankfurt-Leipzig], 1720, #765. See, however, *Cosmologia Generalis*, #294, and also *Vernünfftige Gedanken*, #215–19. Mendelssohn seems to have conflated the two references. Jacobi (*Über die Lehre des Spinoza*, etc., 392, note) quotes both. He likewise describes Wolff as never having adopted Leibniz' monadology 'totally and expressly' (p. 380, note). For a similar view see Robert Latta, *Leibniz*, London, 1898 (and many reprints), 166 ff.

43 JubA, I, 6 (340). Mendelssohn refers to [Michael Gottlieb] Hansch's discussion of the doctrine in his *Principia philosophiae Leibnitzii geometrico modo demonstrata* (Frankfurt, 1728), which work was based on the Latin version of the *Monadology* published in the *Acta eruditorum Lipsiensium* (Suppl. Vol. VII, 1721, Sect. 11, 500–14).

44 Erdmann, I, 121; Gerhardt, IV, 483. The English translation is Latta's (*op. cit.*, 311).

45 Gerhardt, IV, 494 (Latta, 322). The italics are mine.

46 *Über die Lehre des Spinoza*, etc., 389–91, note.

47 I.e., the writings which, in Jacobi's assumption, represented the French original and the Latin version respectively of what the German translation called the *Monadology*. See *Über die Lehre des Spinoza*, etc., 387–9. In this assumption he was, however, mistaken. The discovery of the original manuscript of the *Monadology* proved that this work was different from the *Principes de la nature et de la*

grâce. Cf. Robert Zimmermann, *Leibnitz' Monadologie*, Vienna, 1847, 7–8; cf. Bamberger, JubA, I, 616–17.

48 JubA, I, 6 (340).

49 This is a misreading of Mendelssohn, who speaks of *verschiedene Gestalten* in the sense of two variants of the doctrine, *viz.* one based on the monadological concept and one divorced from this base.

50 Cf. Latta, *op. cit.* (note 42), 263, note 126; 324, note 16.

51 Cf. the passage quoted above and note 45.

52 Gerhardt, IV, 493–4.

53 Gerhardt, IV, 496.

54 For a discussion of this simile see Latta, *op. cit.*, 46 ff.; for the question whether Leibniz borrowed it from Geulincx see the references in Latta, *loc. cit.*, 43–4. Mendelssohn unquestioningly takes it to be Leibniz' invention.

55 Cf. above, note 42.

56 Mendelssohn translates Spinoza's term *mens* by 'soul'. There is some justification for this, since for Spinoza *mens* includes such *modi cogitandi* as *amor, cupiditas,* etc. (*Ethics*, II, *axiomata*, 3). Cf. Heinrich Christoph Wilhelm Sigwart, *Der Spinozismus historisch und philosophisch erläutert*, Tübingen, 1839, 122.

57 Mendelssohn's German translation is not altogether precise. The English translation quoted above is taken from James Guttmann's edition of the *Ethics*, New York, 1949, 130–1.

58 Mendelssohn translates simply: *Die Wirkungen der Seele entspringen aus ausführlichen (ideis adequatis) und die Leidenschaften aus unausführlichen Begriffen* (JubA, I, 8, 342–3).

59 This is a fair restatement of Spinoza's demonstration.

60 See above, p. 20.

61 GS, V, 168–70.

62 GS, V, 174–7. Mendelssohn's letter is undated.

63 *Das Wesen der Harmonie* (p. 175); *die wesentlichen Sätze der vorherbestimmten Harmonie* (p. 176). We have here a restatement of the term *das Wesentliche dieser Meinung* in the *Gespräche* (JubA, I, 4; see also 8).

64 See Leibniz' *Éclaircissement* in answer to Bayle, Gerhardt, IV, 523, and his *Réponse*, IV, 562; Latta, *op. cit.* (note 42), 98 ff.

65 Heydenreich does not seem to have had any knowledge of the objection raised by Lessing in his letter to Mendelssohn. The letter, as well as Mendelssohn's reply, is included in *Gelehrter Briefwechsel zwischen D. Johann Jacob Reiske, Moses Mendelssohn und Gotthold Ephraim Lessing* (I, 290–5; 301–7), which appeared in 1789, the year of the publication of Heydenreich's book. In an earlier treatise entitled *Animadversiones in Mosis Mendelii Filii Refutationem Placitorum Spinotzae* (Leipsig, 1787), Heydenreich had already

taken issue with Mendelssohn's interpretation of Spinoza as offered in the *Morgenstunden* (1785).

66   See above, note 34.

67   Heydenreich, *op. cit.*, 96–100. We quote some of Wolff's statements cited here: *Spinoza non admittit duplicem substantiam, adeoque nullum statuit inter mentem et corpus commercium, consequenter iuxta ipsius hypothesin vana quaestio: quomodo commercium illud obtineatur, seu quaenam sit eius causa. . . . Vide itaque, quam absonum sit, systema harmoniae praestabilitae in Spinosa quaerere, qui nullo prorsus opus habet. . . .*

68   Heydenreich, *op. cit.*, 96.

69   *Über die Lehre des Spinoza*, etc., 385–6. Jacobi more or less endorses Heydenreich's critique of Mendelssohn.

70   Cf. Erich Schmidt, *Lessing* (Berlin, 1884), I, 297.

71   *Über die Lehre des Spinoza*, etc., 34.

72   Sigwart, *op. cit.* (note 56), 123, 139, 154, interprets Spinoza in this sense.

73   Cf. Friedmann, *op. cit.* (note 8), 102, 298 (note 1 *ad* p. 101).

74   Foucher de Careil, *op. cit.* (note 28), 200.

75   Cf. Friedmann, *op. cit.*, 103, 172.

76   Cf. Friedmann, *op. cit.*, 134.

77   Cf. Friedmann, *op. cit.*, 134.

78   *Über die Lehre des Spinoza*, etc., 394.

79   For a survey of the debate up to 1890 see Stein, *op. cit.* (note 33), 1–16.

80   *Loc. cit.*, 60–110.

81   Ernst Cassirer, *Leibniz' System*, Marburg, 1902 (Hildesheim, 1962), 519.

82   Friedmann, *op. cit.*, 225, 273, ff.

83   Cassirer, *op. cit.*, 520.

84   Friedmann, *op. cit.*, 218.

85   Friedmann, *op. cit.*, 137.

86   Leon Roth, *Spinoza*, London, 1929, 205.

87   See p. 210.

88   See p. 205, note 1.

89   Carr, *loc. cit.* (note 27), 206 ff. Carr's book appeared in 1930, one year after Roth's, but his strictures do not seem to be directed particularly against Roth's claims. It may be noted that Leibniz himself rejected the charge of plagiarism in his letter to Bourguet quoted by Jacobi, *op. cit.* (note 5), 363–4, and by Friedmann, *op. cit.*, 188.

2

Israel
and the *Oikoumenē**

SAMUEL HUGO BERGMAN

The intention of the following remarks is to investigate the theological difficulties to which the tension between the narrowness
imposed by confessional religion and the amplitude envisaged by
ecumenism gives rise, with particular reference to the example
afforded by the religion of Israel. In this connection, it becomes
immediately necessary to define the sense in which the word
Oikoumenē is here to be understood: for it has two meanings, the
one completely different from the other. If what is meant by
Oikoumenē is the Church of Christ united within itself, then
Israel has nothing whatsoever to say on the subject. If, however,
it is to mean 'the realm in which the expectation of God obtains',
or 'moving off from a hitherto static position to meet God'
(*Aufbruch dem Herrn entgegen*) – phrases taken from the
relevant article in Herder's *Bildungsbuch*, 1958, pp. 1425f. – the
conception of *Oikoumenē* becomes a central one for Jewish
religious thinking. It is in the latter sense that ecumenism will
be used here.

It is still true today that anyone who wishes to succeed in
representing accurately the ecumenical tendency at play within

the various religious communities must take cognisance of the dialectical antithesis that exists between the centripetal force which, directed inward, emphasises what is particular and divisive, and the centrifugal force, directed outwards and universalistic, which stresses that which the various religions have in common. How dour the struggle of these two forces is is shown, perhaps more clearly than anywhere else, by the example of Israel, since here both tendencies – the election of Israel and the messianic ideal of a united mankind – are anchored deep down in religious consciousness: so deep, indeed, that neither of the two contrasting tendencies may be repressed without what is characteristically peculiar to the Jewish religion being lost. How, then, are these two hostile powers to be brought together? The spiritual task of Israel is nothing more nor less than achieving unison between the two of them – a task reassigned to Israel generation after generation, throughout the age-long history of the Jewish people.

The very beginning of Israel's history is rooted in a symbol of severance. God bids Abram – not yet Abraham (*Gen.* 12: 1) – break asunder all the bonds that tie him to his father's house and his homeland, to leave his country and to betake himself into the land that He would show him. Jewish tradition is very much alive to the contrast between Abraham and the world of his environment – to what Hegel terms the *Austritt aus der Natürlichkeit* – and can even represent God as saying, in connection with Abraham, 'I am unique in My world even as he is unique in his.'[1] Nevertheless, following immediately on the verse that commands this separation God says, 'thou shalt be a blessing. . . . and in thee shall all the families of the earth be blessed.' Severance is thus for the sake of ultimate unification.

This separatist tendency of the Jewish religious consciousness finds its classical expression in the story of the curse, turned to a blessing, wherewith the heathen prophet Balaam, summoned by the king of Moab, sought to curse Israel in the wilderness (*Num.* 22 f). His vision of the tented dwellings of Israel, stretching as far as the eye could see, found expression in the immortal words, 'Behold, it is a people that dwelleth apart, and doth not reckon itself amongst the nations' (*goyim*) – a verse (*Num.* 23: 9) which has rightly been quoted time and again as giving epigrammatic expression to Jewish self-consciousness. As Franz Rosenzweig put it, 'The Jew knows that he is loved and chosen by God – what does he want to worry about the world for?' Or, in the words of Rilke, 'the assuredness of the reality of God, which runs *a priori* in the blood of the Jew,' and the assuredness of being close to God his father, produces in him something akin to compassion for the Gentiles, who cannot know the bliss of being a Jew and of having, in God, at once a king and a father.

This self-awareness founded on 'election', this look directed so completely inwards, and the blissfulness of knowing oneself to be a Jew, find expression likewise in the Jewish prayer-book – that most faithful of mirrors of the Jewish soul. In his morning prayers, the Jew thanks God 'who hast not made me a Gentile' (*goy*) – to which the prayer-book issued by the Israeli Ministry of Religions has seen fit to add the footnote, 'This expression refers to the idolaters of ancient times.' And again, when the Sabbath comes to an end, and the Jew makes the blessing of 'Division' (*Habdalah*), he says, 'Blessed art Thou, O Lord our God, King of the Universe, who makest a distinction between "holy" and "secular", between light and darkness, between Israel and the peoples.'

And yet, this separatist tendency is but one side only of Jewish religious self-consciousness. To the blessing quoted above that is recited at the outgoing of Sabbath, there is attached the prayer, 'Soon may there come to us Elijah the Prophet, together with Messiah, the son of David.' At the end of Sabbath and the beginning of the working week with all its hazards, reference to division and distinctiveness is appropriate. But the fissure between the holy Sabbath day and the workaday world of the week is not the last word. That is accorded to the Messiah, who will introduce unity in place of separation and divisiveness. Franz Rosenzweig put it thus in his *Der Stern der Erlösung* (Part iii, Book 1, p. 386): 'No one knows better than the Jew that to be

49

God's favoured son is but a beginning and that mankind remains unredeemed so long as it is merely this beginning that has been realised. Over against Israel, ever beloved of God, ever faithful, and ever complete, there stands the Messiah, ever still to come, ever full of expectation, ever wandering, and ever growing in stature.'

This expectation of the Messiah is always, for the Jew, something of immediate meaningfulness in the here-and-now. In the articles of belief by which, in the twelfth century, Maimonides attempted to establish the dogmatic content of Judaism, there is stated as article no. 12, 'I believe with perfect faith in the coming of the Messiah, and, though he tarry, I will daily wait for his coming.' For modern times we may refer to the late Chief Rabbi A. I. Kook of Jerusalem, whose religious poem 'The beacon of Messiah flashes forth' I have translated into German (*Freiburger Rundbrief*, 49, 1960). It is the expectation of the Messiah which gives Judaism its almost exclusive orientation on the future – an orientation that lends its character likewise to the attitudes in matters secular that are almost second nature to so many Jews.

The polarity of an introspective seclusion and a desire for an extroverted accessibility – this 'jumble of contradictions' as Rosenzweig calls it – is accurately reflected in the liturgy. The daily morning service has, at its beginning, the blessing of God quoted above, 'Who hast not made me a Gentile'; but, like the afternoon and evening services, it concludes with the *Alenu*-prayer – a credal statement embodying an impassioned messianic hope[2]: 'We therefore hope in Thee, O Lord our God, that we may speedily behold the glory of Thy might . . . let all the inhabitants of the world perceive and know . . . let them all accept the yoke of Thy kingdom. . . .' In this *gewaltigem Gebete*, in Hermann Cohen's words, with which every Jewish service concludes, 'it is the foundation of the kingdom of God that constitutes the highlight, and which twines itself like a tendril around everything else.'

To a certain extent, this messianic future is something which the Jew experiences by anticipation in the Sabbath that crowns each week. The Sabbath – so utterly different from the Christian

Sunday – is, in those circles where it is still celebrated in its
genuine spirit, the precursor of redemption in the midst of an
unredeemed world. It is a complete setting oneself free from the
workaday world: but even here a flat note is struck which evokes
consciousness of the tension obtaining between the Jew and the
gentile peoples. The morning prayer for the Sabbath contains
the following passage:[3] 'But Thou didst not give it (*sc.* the
Sabbath) unto the nations of other lands, nor didst Thou, O our
King, make it the heritage of worshippers of idols, nor do the
uncircumcised dwell in its rest; but unto Thy people Israel Thou
didst give it in love, unto the seed of Jacob whom thou didst
choose.' One might have expected, at this point, a prayer that
looked forward to the time when all peoples might have a share
in the Sabbath: but we shall look for it in vain.

It is the inner dialectic of election that is responsible for these
symptoms of onesidedness and contradiction. For it is in the notion
of election, as an axiom, that there is rooted that magnificent
God-awareness of Jewry of which history can show so many an
example. But the tendency towards isolationism has its roots in
the same place. To be sure, this Jewish trait of character has its
historical reasons as well: a minority, subject to persecution,
looks to a seclusion turned in on itself for its protection against
the hostility of its environment, and its 'pride' and contempt
for that environment is but a compensation for the humiliations
to which it must perforce submit. But historical and sociological
explanations ought not to lead us into forgetting that it is religious
considerations that are here operative in the first instance.
Even Jesus himself did not send forth his apostles to the heathen
or to the Samaritans, but to the lost sheep of the house of Israel:
'It is not right to take the children's bread and throw it to the
dogs' (*Matt.* 10: 5; 15: 26, *New English Bible*).

The terms of this internal dialectic are as follows. The election
of Israel is an event that took place for the sake of messianic hope,
even as Abraham was constrained to leave his homeland in order
that through him all the peoples of the earth might be blessed.
That election is, indeed, but the means to an end is a view

unanimously endorsed by all Jewish thinkers. But it would appear that the means themselves may work adversely to the end – that *Apartheid* becomes an object in itself, and frustrates messianic expectation and endeavour. Judaism itself perceives this dialectical problem, and struggles to come to terms with it. Two attempts in particular to master the contradiction need to be noticed here, *viz.* (1) the concept of the 'Descendants of Noah', and (2) that of the 'Righteous among the Peoples of the World'.

The first of these attempted solutions begins by insisting that, despite its national character, Judaism is a basically universalistic phenomenon – an all-embracing religion catholic in the truest sense of the word. The theoretical foundation for this universalism is then discovered in the distinction between the manifold commands and prohibitions – the so-called '613 Commandments' enjoined upon the Jew – and the seven only which are incumbent upon the remainder of peoples – the so-called 'Seven Command-ments of the Sons of Noah'.[4] These are: the prohibition of (1) idolatry, (2) murder, (3) blasphemy, (4) incest, and (5) theft, the commandment (6) to establish courts of law, that is to say a regular system for the administration of justice, and the prohibi-tion (7) of eating a limb from a living animal, i.e. before the flesh of an animal is used for food the animal is itself to be killed.

It has recently been stated[5] that Judaism combines in itself the seeming contrasts of a particularist, national religion, and a universalistic faith. The Torah, i.e. the Instruction comprised by the Pentateuch, is addressed to Israel and not to the gentile peoples. It is none the less stated therein that 'all the earth is Mine', as well as saying that God chose Israel from all peoples (*Ex.* 19: 5; *Deut.* 7: 6–8; 10: 14–15). The national character of Torah evinces itself likewise in the content of the commandments. A small proportion of them are of general human relevance – for the most part they refer to the history of Israel or to institutions connected with the Land of Israel. These commands and prohibi-tions are obligatory on the Jew – and on the Jew alone – in virtue of the covenant which God contracted with Israel, and which is expressly stated to be binding upon all their subsequent generations (*Deut.* 29: 14). In implementing those commandments, and in so taking upon itself the 'yoke of the kingdom of heaven', Israel is fulfilling within the context of humanity a function analogous to that exercised, within Israel itself, by the priestly descendants of Aaron. Israel is enjoined to become a 'kingdom of priests' and a 'holy nation' in the service of mankind at large, who constitute, so to speak, the laity of this universal religion.

Israel is, however, not some closed priestly class: it is open to every man to take upon himself the 'yoke of the commandments', and so to become an Israelite. Nevertheless Jews have not interested themselves in active missionising, since the gentile peoples are under no obligation to make all the commandments their pursuit but merely to fulfil the terms of the Noachide covenant. In nineteenth-century Judaism it was Elie Benamozegh (died 1900), the rabbi of Leghorn, in particular who represented the view that the so-called Noachide provisions could form the basis of a universalist religion, in the work of his old age entitled *Israël et Humanité: Étude sur le Problème de la Religion Universelle et sa Solution*. The book was published posthumously (Paris, 1914) by Benamozegh's pupil Aimé Pallière, of whom a word must here be said. Pallière was born and bred a Catholic; and after a long religious quest which even led him through the Salvation Army, he arrived at the decision to become a Jew and thus adopt the original faith which lay at the basis of Christianity. He applied to Benamozegh in Leghorn, but the Rabbi indicated to him that the original religion behind Christianity was not Judaism in its full-blooded form, but rather the Noachide provisions: and he consequently advised Pallière against taking the formal step of conversion to Judaism.

Benamozegh wrote to him as follows:

. . . In order to adhere to the true religion, in order to become, as you wish to do, our brother, it is in no sense necessary for you to adopt Judaism – that is to say, to subject yourself to the Law. We, who are Jews, have ourselves at our disposal the religion intended for the whole human race – the one religion, that is, to which the nations have to subject themselves and through which they may be redeemed and come to stand within God's grace, exactly as did our own Patriarchs before the revelation of the Law at Sinai. Can you possibly conceive that the true religion which God had intended for the whole of mankind dates no earlier than Moses, and bears upon itself the stamp of one particular people? What an inconsistency that would be! God's plan is something much further-reaching. The religion of mankind is *Noachism*. . . . It is that religion that Judaism has preserved, in order to transmit it to the peoples. Noachism is the road which opens itself before each individual, if he can believe in revelation at all,[6] without it becoming necessary for him to adopt in consequence either Mosaism, which is the specific statute relative to Israel, or Christianity or Islam, both of which purport to abrogate the Law for Jews as well.

Benamozegh here sees in Noachism a middle way. Peter was wrong in wanting to impose the Law of Israel on the pagan world, and Paul was wrong in wishing to set the Jew free from it. The solution is – *Mosaism* for the Jew and for those who, of their own free will, wish to adhere to it (without themselves being of Jewish birth): and *Noachism*, that is to say the religion of the Patriarchs Abraham, Isaac, and Jacob, the religion for all peoples. It is this Noachist faith of which the prophet predicted the triumph in messianic times; and it was for Noachism that Benamozegh won the young Pallière as a convert. His own religious struggles thus ended without a formal adoption of Judaism, but he did exercise, in the liberal Jewish synagogue of Paris, 'Noachide' functions. Pallière has himself related the story of his religious pilgrimage in his book *Le Sanctuaire inconnu. Ma Conversion au Judaisme*, which has been translated into German and Hebrew.

Amongst Jewish thinkers of the twentieth century, it has been Hermann Cohen who has emphasised the importance of these speculative essays in 'Noachism'. The point of view from which he proceeded was that belief in the Jewish God is not something that is demanded of Noachides[7]; so that the bonds of particularist religion have here been burst, and a standpoint beyond them achieved. Whether – and, if so, how far – that is really the case, will be considered below. But first we have to discuss the second of the two concepts by means of which Judaism has attempted to shatter its own confines and to build a road out into the vast expanses of ecumenism. The concept here referred to is that of the 'Righteous amongst the Gentile Peoples'. It is not a concept that is either sharply defined, or of a single, constant meaning. The title is given, as a mark of respect, to those non-Jews who, in one way or another, have stood at the side of Judaism in its struggle for existence. The 'righteousness' of the individuals concerned here signifies really the steadfastness with which they have thrown themselves against the waves of hostility to Jewry, and have made the cause of the persecuted their own.

Whereas the concept of the Noachides is something that derives from a scholastic mode of thinking, the concept of the 'Righteous amongst the Gentiles' is one which, right up to today, has been very much alive in the popular Jewish consciousness; and indeed, as a result of the catastrophes brought about by the second World War, it has emerged into an even more lusty stage of life as a symbol, being applied to the activities of individual non-Jews who often exposed their own persons to risk in order to save Jewish lives.

In his *Religion der Vernunft aus den Quellen des Judentums* (1919), Hermann Cohen devoted a good deal of space to the discussion of this concept. Of particular importance for him was the religious, i.e. halakhic (canonical) ruling of Maimonides[8] to the effect that 'the righteous of the gentile nations have a portion in the world to come.' The nations of the world, Cohen comments, do not possess the Torah: nevertheless, righteousness can arise amongst them. It is here that he sees (p. 389) a stark contrast with Christianity in all its forms. 'In Christianity, Christ is the indispensable condition of redemption. By the present assertion of principle, on the other hand, blissfulness is assured to man *qua* man; and the conditions of humanism are found to be determined exclusively within terms of a purely humanistic morality. Belief in the sole God is not required.'[7]

The concept of the 'Righteous amongst the Peoples of the World', like that of the Noachides, is an attempt – made within the confines of a specific faith – to discover a springboard into the wide tracts of an all-embracing ecumenism: or, to put it into Jewish terms, to find the means of breaking through from the notion of the election of Israel into that of a single, messianic mankind.

For all this, it cannot (as it seems to me) be said that, in the postulation of the two theoretical entities which have been discussed above, Judaism has discovered a means of reconciling the two dialectically opposed principles which formed our starting-point. Recognition is certainly due to the earnest endeavours made from within the framework of particularist Judaism to overcome particularism, and to achieve a standpoint in which the concept of a universal, ecumenical religion for all mankind might be comprehensible: but we cannot assert that the attempt has proved successful. The notion of the 'Righteous amongst the Gentiles', noble a notion though it is, suffers under the disadvantage that, at least as popularly understood (though not, perhaps, as its scope is defined by Maimonides),[9] the canon governing the portion of Gentiles in the 'world to come' is a specific attitude and mode of behaviour on the part of those Gentiles towards the Jewish people itself: so that attention has been focussed back again on particularism. Neither can 'Noachism' fulfil the expectations which Benamozegh attached to it, as the merest glance at the content of the seven Noachide provisions will make clear. The formulation of the concept of the 'Sons of Noah' as a religio-political entity is one of outstanding juridical importance – an importance to which, as far back as the seventeenth century, Grotius drew attention – in that it laid down the conditions under which a foreign minority might enjoy a domicile in ancient Israel without participation in the 'state' religion. But as viewed from the strictly religious angle, the seven commandments lack both life and substance. Are we to say that all the yearning of mankind for God, and for the love of God, is to be comprised within the range of such precepts as that which

56

enjoins the establishment of courts of law (to cite but the most positively impressive of the seven Noachide commandments)? Would not a universal religion, such as that to which Benamozegh aspired, if constructed round so meagre a framework as this, be but a travesty, or rather a crying scandal? Are such commands as that regarding loving one's neighbour, or that which bids us love God with all our heart, soul, and might, to be commandments reserved for the Jewish people alone? If that were so, the abyss separating the religion of Judaism from the religion for mankind would be an intolerable one.

Let us remind ourselves of the problem that has led to the construction, on the basis of the Noachide provisions, of this remarkable concept of a universal religion for all mankind. Like many other Jews, Benamozegh felt uncomfortable about the alleged election of his own people. He saw in it, to a certain extent, an injury inflicted on the remainder of mankind; and he wished to put this divine act of 'injustice' right by means of the religion of the patriarchs that had preceded the revelation at Sinai. It is this feeling of 'injustice' that has occasioned the move by which a significant trend within contemporary American Jewry, the Reconstructionism of which Professor Mordecai Kaplan is the spokesman, has given expression to the hope that Jews may come to abdicate the doctrine of their particular election.[10] This rationalist position of extreme positivism may be understood as a reaction against another extreme. That is to say, if the concept of election is construed in an entirely passive and static sense, in such terms that every human being who is born a Jew is deemed automatically to have within him a portion of that election, the danger lies near at hand of coming to speak about a special Jewish soul which is allotted to the elect. Just such a doctrine was developed in the sixteenth century by the well-known rabbi Judah b. Bezalel Löw, the 'Maharal' of Prague: and it has exercised great influence, especially on certain trends within Hasidism (the so-called Ḥabad-ḥasidhim).

But even when these extremes are disregarded, the doctrine of 'election', if incorrectly understood in some unduly narrow sense, carries within itself the danger that all other religions are to be measured against Judaism, as being the religion *par excellence*, instead of each being evaluated in its own right. Such an approach is exemplified by an attitude towards Christianity and Islam that sees in them 'daughter-religions' of Judaism, that are intended to lead the heathen world towards the true religion, *viz.* Judaism itself. That is to say, that Christianity and Islam themselves act as missionary forces for Judaism without realising it. It was Judah Hallevi, poet and philosopher, born in Castile in 1085, who gave classical expression to this attitude in his great religio-philosophical dialogue the *Cuzari*[11]:

> . . . God has a secret and wise design concerning us, which should be compared to the wisdom hidden in the seed which falls into the ground, where it undergoes an external transformation into earth, water, and dirt, without leaving a trace for him who looks down upon it. It is, however, the seed itself which transforms earth and water into its own substance, carries it from one degree to another, until it refines the elements and transfers them into something like itself, casting off husks, leaves, etc., and allowing the pure core to appear, capable of bearing the Divine Influence. The original seed produced the tree bearing fruit resembling that from which it had been produced. In the same manner the law of Moses transforms each one who honestly follows it, though it may externally repel him. The nations merely serve to introduce and pave the way for the expected Messiah, who is the fruition, and they will all become His fruit. Then, if they acknowledge Him, they will become one tree. Then they will revere the origin which they formerly despised. . . .

Maimonides likewise sees in Christianity and in Islam intermediate stages that are to lead mankind towards the messianic age.[12] There is no doubt that such an attitude was, in the twelfth century, witness to a spiritual magnanimity and to a substantial meed of tolerance. But that ought not to blind us today to the circumstance that Judaism is here treated as being the only true religion, of which the 'daughter-religions' are but incomplete imitations.[13] No real position of ecumenical universalism in religion is thereby achieved.

A brief glance is here necessary at relativism, the reproach of which lies near to hand and might, it seems, easily be advanced against us. Does the circumstance of our opposing the thesis that one of the historical religions is the sole, absolute, and uniquely true religion force us into admitting that we are rejecting all absolute truth? By no means.[14] Historical religion is true in virtue of its having been revealed by God: but He who revealed it has spoken at sundry times and in diverse manners, according to the nature of each recipient of revelation. Schuon cites a parable from Al Ghazali. Some blind men who have never heard anything whatsoever about an elephant chance one day to meet one and begin to feel him, each one handling a different limb – one a leg, another the tusks. When they come to describe to each other the beast that they have encountered, each describes the particulars in a different manner; to one, it resembles a column, the second a stake, and so on. Each of them is right in regard to what he is describing, but should he contest the veracity of the others' description, he at once falls into error. The eternal and absolute cannot be comprehended in fragmentary aspects, and each of the religions of man can be but a fragmentary aspect. The fact that there is a plethora of aspects, and consequently a plethora of religions, does not mean that not all these various aspects can be true alongside one another. Indeed, even in cases of direct 'contradiction', it ought not be asserted that one only of the mutually contradictory attitudes and perspectives of what is eternal can be true, and that the others are necessarily false. We are here at a stage that transcends the finite and leaves formal logic and the laws of epistemology behind it. That is why, whereas conversations between religions can be fruitful, disputations between them conducted on the plane of a semblance of logic can never be so.

All the attempts which we have so far examined, which endeavour to maintain, as being simultaneously justifiable, the doctrine of

Israel's election and that of a messianic hope of ecumenical dimensions, have in common one element that renders the success of each of them dubious, to say the least. All of them hold fast to the exclusive claims of Judaism to constitute the one and only religious doctrine that is true. It was here, at the heart of the problem, that Franz Rosenzweig took a decisive step forward in his *Der Stern der Erlösung* (1921). We cannot now enter into the details of his thesis, and indeed it is the basic idea only that concerns us here. For Rosenzweig, Christianity is no longer the ancillary 'daughter-religion' of Israel. Judaism and Christianity stand rather in a coordinated relation of parallelism. Side by side they make their several ways across history, each of them towards its own destiny. The revelational character of Judaism, and its claims to comprise still a fully valid revelation, are maintained unimpaired; and yet, at the same time, Christianity is acknowledged in its own right, and its own specific religious claim is likewise recognised.

Before God, both Jew and Christian are co-workers in the same field, with neither of whom He can dispense. Between the two of them He has set enmity for all time, and yet He has bound them to one another by the closest of reciprocal ties. To us Jews He has given eternal life by kindling the fire of the Star of His truth in our hearts: the Christian has been set by Him upon an eternal Way, being compelled to advance until the end of time onward, ever onward, towards the light that radiates from that Star of God's truth. . . . Truth – that is to say the whole truth – is the property neither of Christians nor of ourselves. . . . It is no derogation of either truth or of ourselves if we acknowledge that truth is ours in a limited measure only. An uninterrupted view of truth in its entirety is possible for him only who can view truth in God; but that is an angle of viewing that lies beyond this life.[15]

Rosenzweig was fully aware of the magnitude of the revolution, in regard to the relationship of Judaism to Christianity, which the conceptual system adopted in his religious thinking signified. Three years after the publication of the *Stern der*

Erlösung, on 18th September, 1924, he wrote in a letter to Ernst Simon 'and so I am indeed a "Jewish fanatic", and at the same time I have (so far as I am aware) written the first non-fanatical Jewish book – that is to say, a book that is Jewish and certainly non-fanatical, non-fanatical and yet at the same time Jewish.'[16]

The *Stern der Erlösung* is, in very truth, a 'non-fanatical' book in its approach to Christianity, and viewed from this angle it certainly constitutes one of the highlights of Jewish religious thinking. At the same time, it cannot be said that the *Stern* has really won through to the stratosphere of an all-embracing ecumenism for which, from its earliest beginnings, prophetic Judaism has been looking in its vision of mankind messianically welded into one. 'For all the peoples will walk every one in the name of his god, and we will walk in the name of the Lord our God for ever and ever' – such is the great vision of the end of time entertained by the Prophet Micah (4: 5). Rosenzweig never succeeded in swinging himself on to the lofty plane at which it was possible for Nicholas of Cusa to say *una est religio in rituum varietate*. Great as his understanding for Christianity was, it is balanced by his lack of understanding for the far eastern religions, and by the 'fanaticism' of the position adopted by him *vis-à-vis* Islam.

And so it would seem that Jewish religious thought has fallen down in its endeavours to resolve the dilemma posed by the narrowness of particularism and the expansiveness of ecumenism, and so to bridge the gap between election and messianism. When all is said and done, there remains, on the one side a concretism that takes full account of the biological facts and sees election as something 'according to the flesh', transmitted not by persuasion but by procreation, or, as expressed more felicitously in the German formula coined by Rosenzweig, *durch Zeugung, nicht durch Überzeugung*: and on the other, the complete renunciation of the idea of election, and so (together with it) the renunciation also of one of the most deep-seated ideas in the religious development of mankind, *viz.* that of the love of God so gloriously portrayed (according to traditional Jewish exegesis) in the *Song of Songs*.

It was Hermann Cohen who found a way out of the wood, and gave the problem a completely new orientation in his well-known work *Religion der Vernunft aus den Quellen des Judentums*. Cohen sensed, more, perhaps, than anyone else, the inner conflict that must confront a Jew who finds some contradiction of the divine justice in the notion of Israel's being a Chosen People. If the closing words of the Psalter are 'Let every thing that hath breath praise the Lord', how can there be such a thing as the election of any particular people?

> God will surely not always cling fast to his love for Israel, which comprises a phenomenon whose starting-point is linked to a specific moment in history. He must, surely, love humanity *qua* human universality . . . the relevant point of correspondence (*Korrelation*) consists, for God, in its infinity (p. 173). It is necessary to free God's love for Israel from the suspicion of its constituting an anomaly, incompatible with the universal love of God for man that is without any exceptions. God does not love Israel more, or in any other way from that in which He loves mankind in general, let alone any possibility of His love for Israel's restricting or compromising His love for the human race as a whole. God loves Israel in precisely the same way as He loves the whole human race, *Israel being His peculiar possession merely as a model and as a symbol for the whole of mankind* (italics mine). It is a misconception to understand Jewish messianic hopes for mankind as if they were but a means of forwarding the glorification of Israel. The election of Israel constitutes in no sense an exception: it is rather the symbolic confirmation of the love of God for the whole race of man.

It is the introduction of the notion of *symbol* that points the way forward. Cohen writes as a platonist. The relationship of Israel to God, and *vice versa*, as represented by the prophets, has to be divested of its concrete materialism and translated into the language of ideas (in the platonic sense) and of symbolism.

The idea of a 'correspondence' (*Korrelation*) between God and His beloved, chosen community has found a concrete realisation in ancient Israel, but 'the beloved people turns into a beloved mankind' (p. 496). Israel itself becomes a symbol: 'Man and people are capable of being symbols; it is only the uniquely one God who is not' (*ibid*). Cohen speaks of a '*self*-transformation of the beloved people of God into a messianic humanity.'

This is to give the whole problem we have been discussing here a completely new complexion. Alongside Israel in the concrete, physical sense there marches also the invisible Israel; and it is the latter which is portrayed as God's beloved in the *Song of Songs*. The concept of election or (to use Cohen's favourite expression) *Korrelation* remains entirely unimpaired; but just as platonic ideas may experience a plethora of embodiments, even so there can be a plethora of 'elect' groups within mankind. It was Israel after the flesh (I here elaborate somewhat Cohen's own explicit presentation of his thinking) to whom the prediction was vouchsafed through the prophet Isaiah (59: 21) that 'as for me, this is my covenant with them, saith the Lord; my spirit that is upon thee, and my words which I have put in thy mouth, shall not depart out of thy mouth, nor out of the mouth of thy seed, nor out of the mouth of thy seed's seed, saith the Lord, from hence-forth and for ever.' But this promise which has fulfilled itself down the centuries, does not mean that there cannot be other 'elect' groups in the midst of mankind, other 'religions'. Whether any individual or any particular religious group has been elected by God, God Himself alone knows; for man, election comprises an aim towards which he strives and a task wherewith he feels himself commissioned. God, and only God, knows who belongs to the *corpus mysticum* of the elect. According to an earlier conception, it was the Jewish people who fulfilled a priestly function *vis-à-vis* mankind; in place of that function fulfilled by concrete Israel alone, there is now the service of the invisible community of God, the growing divine kingdom, still orientated on mankind as a whole. It is this invisible community that is the Suffering Servant of whom Isaiah (*chap.* 53) speaks, the servant who must suffer for God's sake in the struggle through which

God's kingdom becomes extended ever wider. Israel's long tale of suffering is thereby transformed into a symbol – a symbol that itself becomes truth and ideal reality. Such ecumenical endeavour as we may observe going on – inter-faith conversations, congresses etc. – thus becomes symbolic of true reality; symbolic, that is, of the struggle for the extension of God's kingdom that goes on invisibly in the heart of every man and in the life of the community – or, to put it into Jewish terms, symbolic of the fight for the Redeemer's coming: 'and though he tarry, I will wait daily for his coming.'

NOTES

* Translated by the Editor from the original German text, which has now appeared in a volume devoted to ecumenism entitled *Konfession und Ökumene. Aspekte, Probleme, Aufgaben*, edited by Helmut Ristow and Helmuth Burgert, Evangelischen Verlagsanstalt, Berlin-Charlottenburg, East Germany [1966], pp. 567–78.

1 Babylonian Talmud, *Pesaḥim* 118a, *infra*.

2 The full text of this paragraph is cited in K. D. Wilhelm's article, *infra*, p. 301. Cf. also A. Neher's reference to it, *infra*, pp. 191 f.

3 S. Singer, *Authorised Daily Prayer Book*, p. 139.

4 For further treatment of the seven Noachide commandments and the concept of the 'Sons of Noah' see R. Loewe's article, *infra*, pp. 125 f.

5 E.g. by Ḥayyim Rambani in the religious bi-monthly *Prozdor* (Hebrew), 1962, no. 3. English version, p. 7.

6 This proviso should be noted; it derives from the insistence by Maimonides (*Hilekhoth Melakhim* 8, end) that those who implement the seven Noachide commandments out of considerations of purely humanistic ethics are not be reckoned 'Sons of Noah'.

7 But cf. note 6, *supra*.

8 *Loc. cit.* (see note 6). On this ruling by Maimonides see J. Katz in *Zion* (Hebrew), 1958–9, pp. 174 f., and more briefly L. Roth, *Judaism: A Portrait* (1960), p. 95.

9 Cf. note 8; Maimonides' formulation, at any rate, is not exposed to the charge that it is basically Jewish self-interest that determines who is, and who is not a 'Son of Noah'.

10 *Questions Jews Ask: Reconstructionist Answers*, by M. M. Kaplan, 1956. See index, *s.v. Chosen People*.

11 iv, 23; I cite the English translation, made from the original Arabic, by H. Hirschfeld (2nd ed., 1931), p. 200. Cf. I. Maybaum, *infra*, p. 155.

12 Maimonides' positive appreciation should not, however, be exaggerated; for his very low rating of Islam, see *'Iggereth Teman*, ed. S. Goldman, 1950, pp. 27, 31; Christianity, though its exegesis may be misconceived, does at least affirm the authenticity of the Torah (*Responsa*, ed. A. Freimann, 1934, no. 364, p. 331 f.). See R. Loewe's article, *infra*, pp. 139, notes 50–52.

13 Cf. S. H. Bergman, *The Problem of Christianity in Jewish Thought* (discussing Jacob Fleischmann's Hebrew book), *Prozdor* (Hebrew), 1965, no. 9–10, English version, p. 20.

14 Reference may be made here to the extended treatment of this question by Frithiof Schuon, *De l' Unité transcendante des Religions*, 1948, English translation, 1953.

15 Part iii, book 3, p. 521 (1921 ed.).

16 *Briefe*, p. 510.

3

Paul a
Hellenistic Schoolmaster*?

DAVID DAUBE

In the First *Epistle to the Corinthians* (4: 21) the apostle assures
the quarrelsome factions that he will come, and it is up to them
whether it will be 'with a rod or with love'. A few sentences
before[1] he contrasts himself, the one father of the Corinthian
church, with its thousands of schoolmasters or attendants
(παιδαγωγοί). Hence, when he threatens 'the rod' he may have
in mind either the punishing role that a father must sometimes assume,[2] or the punishing role of a schoolmaster or
attendant as opposed to the loving one of a father[3] – or, indeed, as
I incline to believe, both and neither, the metaphor being used
in a general indeterminate sense. Schneider holds[4] that Paul is
referring to a schoolmaster or attendant; and since in Jewish
schools (he states) it was not the rod but the strap (*rᵉṣuʿah*) that
was employed, he reaches the conclusion that the passage
clearly reflects Hellenistic life. It may be worth while entering a
protest before this establishes itself as one of the many fanciful
arguments surrounding Paul's background and mode of thought.

For his distinction between Jewish and Hellenistic instruments
of school discipline Schneider quotes Klostermann.[5] Unless I have

G
67

overlooked a paragraph or sentence, however, Klostermann does not deal with this question at all. In any case, to start with the Hellenistic schoolroom, we have only to look at vases and other pictorial representations of educational scenes to discover that the rod was far from being the only weapon wielded. As regards literary sources, it is sufficient to draw attention to a piece by Herodas entitled *The Schoolmaster*, in which the teacher is depicted as being in possession of a selection of straps and the pupil as being well acquainted with their respective characteristics. The young miscreant is to suffer the δριμὺ σκῦτος, the 'sharp leather thong', i.e. a kind of 'scorpion' on which bones were strung, also described as βοὸς κέρκος, 'the ox-tail', and he begs for the milder kind of punishment without the bones.[6] His petition is not granted. It may be noted that our word 'belt' is the same as the Latin *balteus*: in Juvenal[7] slaves get it, and there is no reason to suppose that bad boys did not.

How Schneider reaches the view that the rod was unknown in Jewish schools I am unable to guess. (Though it could soon be true of Berkeley.[8]) Possibly it has something to do with Krauss,[9] who in his *ex professo* discussion of punishment in talmudic schools mentions the strap only. In the section dealing with punishment by parents, however, the rod does appear, as it also does in that on the punishment of slaves.[10] Differences of course there are. The slipper, used in the home by the mother, will play no part at school; nor, at the other extreme, will the *maghlabh*, a stick with metal barbs, the mere sight of which made slaves quail. But it is difficult to see why both strap and rod should not have been plied by both father and teacher.

Strack-Billerbeck's commentary[11] rightly treats rod and strap as interchangeable. Of the parallels cited, one is particularly appropriate: according to Rabbi Simeon b. Yoḥai, in the middle of the second century C.E., God gives Israel the choice between bread, if they are obedient, and the rod (*maggel*) if they are not.[12]

Paul's word for 'rod' is ῥάβδος. The following occurrences of the word in the Septuagint are here relevant. *Ex.* 21: 20 (a master beats his slave): *I Sam.* (*Kings*) 17: 43 (the rod appropriate for subduing a dog): *II Sam.* (*Kings*) 7: 14 (God will chastise Solomon as a father does his son): *Job* 9: 34 (sufferings inflicted by God are described as 'His rod'): *Ps.* 89 (88): 33, echoing *II Sam.* 7: 14 (God, whom David calls his father, will chastise David's sons): *Prov.* 10: 13 (punishment of a fool): 22: 15 (a foolish lad is improved by correction): 23: 13 f. (a father procures his son's salvation by timely beating): 26: 3 (a fool needs to be beaten): *Isa.* 10: 5 (God describes the Assyrian, sent against His people, as 'the rod of My anger'): 10: 15 and 24 (the rod is an instrument of punishment): *Lam.* 3: 1 (punishment inflicted by God is described as 'the rod of His wrath'): *Ezek.* 20: 37 (God uses the rod by way of punishment and education).

In view of this role of ῥάβδος in the Greek Old Testament, coupled with the fact that the strap – r^esu'ah – appears in post-biblical Hebrew literature only, one might almost make out a case for the latter being a Hellenistic addition to the arsenal of the Jewish pedagogue. One of the fundamental weaknesses of a theory like Schneider's is that it takes for granted a clear-cut division between Jewish and Hellenistic institutions which no longer prevailed by the time of Paul. However, to postulate Jewish borrowing in this matter would likewise be rash. For the present, at any rate, we have too little information for any such deductions. What is surely undeniable is that Paul's picture is in good old traditional style. That did not make it unintelligible to a gentile public – the rod is a universal aid to discipline.

Although there is but a remote connection between corporal correction in the course of education and the official penalty of scourging, it may be of interest here to recall a possible change of instrument for the infliction of the latter – the rod giving way to the strap. Under talmudic law flogging is administered by means of a specifically described r^esu'ah, i.e. a strip of calf-hide with multiple folds.[13] This was very likely the recognised instrument already in New Testament times. The general consensus of opinion, however, seems to be[14] that the regulations laid down in *Deut.* 25: 1 ff. for flogging indicate the bastinado, administered with a stick, and that the strap was substituted much later under Greek and Roman influence. There is much to be said for this theory. To be sure, the existence of ancient oriental laws which prescribe the strap for official scourging[15] is an argument against it and in favour of there having been no change between Old Testament times and the Talmud; but it is by no means conclusive. We know that, as far as capital punishment is concerned, the biblical methods of execution were drastically reformed at the beginning of the present era[16]; stoning, for example, in the literal sense was replaced by pushing the condemned person down from a height. This latter method is in itself extremely old, yet within the Jewish penal system – or at any rate within one strand of it – it represents a second and relatively late stage.

NOTES

* Leon Roth was ever appreciative of the efforts of colleagues less gifted than he, and engaged on work of only indirect relevance to the crucial ethical and spiritual problems to which he devoted his energy. The following short note may, therefore, be acceptable in a volume dedicated to the memory of a great and generous man.

1 *I Cor.* 4: 15.

2 This is how it is taken e.g. by Parry, *The First Epistle to the Corinthians*, Cambridge Greek Testament, 1937, p. 85.

3 Thus, e.g. Craig, *The First Epistle to the Corinthians*, Interpreter's Bible, 10, 1953, p. 59.

4 *Art. ῥάβδος* in *Theologisches Wörterbuch zum Neuen Testament*, ed. Friedrich, 6, 1958, 968.

5 'Das Schulwesen im alten Israel', in *Theologische Studien*, Zahn Festschrift, 1908, pp. 193 ff.

6 *Didaskolos* 68, 73. See *The Mimes of Herodas*, ed. Nairn, 1904, p. 40, and *Herodas*, ed. Knox, 1922, pp. 114 f.

7 9, 112.

8 According to the *San Francisco Chronicle* of 16th June, 1965, p. 5, the disciplinary manual discussed at a meeting of the Board of Education 'approved . . . strapping, but specifically outlawed . . . the use of a ruler'.

9 *Talmudische Archäologie*, 3, 1912, pp. 225 f.

10 *Op. cit.*, 2, 1911, pp. 19 f., 95 f.

11 *Kommentar zum Neuen Testament aus Talmud und Midrasch*, 3, 1926, pp. 341 f.

12 *Siphrē, Deuteronomy* 40, on *Deut.* 11: 12, ed. L. Finkelstein, 1940, p. 83, l. 16.

13 Mishnah, *Makkoth*, 3, 12, H. Danby's translation, p. 407.
14 See S. R. Driver, *Deuteronomy*, International Critical Commentary, 1903, p. 279; Benzinger, *art. Law and Justice* in *Encyclopaedia Biblica*, ed. Cheyne and Black, 3, 1902, col. 2722; Levesque, *art. Bastonnade* in *Dictionnaire de la Bible*, ed. Vigoroux, 1, part 2, 1912, col. 1500; Beurlier, *art. Flagellation, ibid.*, 2, part 2, 1912, col. 2281.
15 E.g. Code of Hammurabi, 202. The Assyrian laws have rods, e.g. 18.
16 See A. Büchler, *Die Todesstrafen der Bibel und der jüdisch-nach-biblischen Zeit*, in *Monatsschrift für die Geschichte und Wissenschaft des Judentums*, 50, 1906, pp. 539 ff., 664 ff.; also Daube, *The New Testament and Rabbinic Judaism*, 1956, pp. 304 ff. and in *Studia Patristica* ii (= *Texte und Untersuchungen* 64), 1957, pp. 109 f.

4

'Knowest Thou . . . ?'

Notes on the Book of *Job*

NAHUM N. GLATZER

[1]

With chapter 31, Job concludes his challenge to God. 'Here is my
mark, let the Almighty answer me. . . . I will declare unto Him
the number of my steps, as a prince I will enter His presence'
(31: 35, 37). In the course of his argument Job has spoken of 'the
terrors of God' that 'set themselves in array' against him (6: 4);
he has pointed to God as the cause of evil ('While Thine eyes
are upon me, I am gone', 7: 8); and he has portrayed God as
having set a watch over Job, as scaring him with dreams (7: 12,
14). God is said to be the cause of destruction of innocent and
wicked alike; it is He who handed over the earth into the hands
of the wicked (9: 22, 24); He oppresses and despises His creatures,
and shines 'upon the counsel of the wick*d*' (10: 3). Even if man
be righteous, he cannot lift up his head (10: 15). God 'shutteth
up a man and there can be no opening'; He controls 'the deceived
and the deceiver' (12: 14, 16). He makes judges fools and the men
of trust He deprives of speech (12: 17, 20). He hides his face and
holds Job for His enemy; he puts Job's feet in the stocks and

73

watches all his paths, so that 'man wastes away like a rotten thing' (13: 24, 27); He destroys the hope of man (14: 19). In His wrath He has torn Job, hated him, gnashing at him with His teeth. He has cast him into the hands of the wicked and broken him asunder; He runs upon him like a warrior (16: 9, 11, 12). Job cries out, 'Violence', but 'there is no justice'. God has kindled His wrath against Job and counted him 'as one of His adversaries' (19: 7, 11). He has estranged Job from his kinsfolk and his friends, even from his servants (19: 13 ff.). God's presence inspires terror and dread (23: 15); He has deprived Job of his right (27: 2); his cry receives no answer from God, who has 'turned to be cruel' to him and who persecutes him with His mighty hand (30: 20 f.). Towards the end of his argument Job speaks of the 'destruction from God' that threatens him, and 'by reason of His fear I could do nothing' (31: 23).

In this argument, God and Job appear as antagonists. God exists and He has brought Job into being. But in the situation in which Job finds himself there is no breakthrough to this hostile, estranged divinity. The issue at stake does not seem to be Job's affliction; his personal calamity is but a part of a general picture: a world without order and justice, a society in which the wicked rule, unchallenged from above. The divine care and concern with man, posited and defended by Job's friends, is rejected by him as contrary to his experience. Though both parties live in the same world, he sees what they fail to see. The friends' judgment of events is rooted in the firm basis of tradition, of concepts established by religion as true, whereas Job speaks from a radically different background. This essay will attempt, however tentatively, to inquire into the background of Job's rebellious utterances, in which God and world appear in such sharp opposition to man and which express his utter isolation.

To find the clue to the motif behind Job's defiant stand we may do well to examine the key terms employed by the author in the presentation of his subject.

Elihu, introduced by the author (or the editor of the final version of the book) after Job had concluded his argument, appeals to 'men of understanding' who will agree with him that

'Job speaketh without knowledge' (34: 35). He accuses Job of multiplying words 'without knowledge' (35: 16). He himself, Elihu, will fetch his knowledge from afar (or, with Tur Sinai, will carry his knowledge far away), while disobedient men 'shall die without knowledge' (36: 3, 12). God is great 'beyond our knowledge' (36: 26); His deeds in the realm of nature (in the description of which Elihu anticipates God's own revelation in chapters 38 et seq.) are great, but we cannot 'know' (comprehend) them (37: 5).[1] He bids Job consider the wondrous works of God 'who is perfect in knowledge', taunting him twice with the question of whether he had knowledge in the field of nature (37: 15, 16), adding ironically: 'Let us know what we shall say unto Him' (or, according to Tur Sinai, 'unto it', sc. the dark clouds) (37: 19). Elihu's speech concludes on the note that God rejects the 'wise at heart' among men (37: 24).

It seems, therefore, that it was the proud affirmation of knowledge on the part of Job that provoked the divine anger and became the barrier between creator and creature. A closer reading of Job's own speeches suggests that Job's claims were indeed based upon the assumed possession of knowledge, whereas the friends disputed his possession of it, holding that knowledge is with God, not with man.

In the first cycle of speeches, Bildad's resigned insight, 'For we are but of yesterday, and know nothing' (8: 9) while God is eternally just (8: 3), is countered by Job: 'I know that it is so, – how can man be just with God?' (9: 2) Here the doubter and rebel gives an ironical twist to the pious man's faith; the former says what he does because he 'knows'.[2] And what is yet unknown to him, he demands to know: 'Make me know why Thou dost contend with me' (10: 2).[3] He reminds God of His creation and life-granting action, adding, proudly, 'I know that this is with Thee' (10: 13). Zophar tries to make Job aware of the 'deep things' and the 'purpose of the Almighty' which leave man impotent to 'do' or to 'know'; it is God who 'knows' (11: 7, 8, 10). Job counters: 'Who knoweth not such things as these?' (12: 3),[4] and 'What ye know, do I know also' (13: 2). But this equality of knowledge is but in appearance; it is only Job's knowledge that

75

drives him 'to reason with God' and to argue his ways before Him (13: 3, 15). He is sure of his ways: 'I know that I shall be justified' (13: 18).

At the start of the second cycle of speeches, Eliphaz accuses Job of 'windy knowledge' (15: 2) and rejects the notion that Job possesses wisdom acquired in the secret council of God, a knowledge unattained by the friends (15: 8 f.). Bildad adds a description of the downfall of the wicked: 'This is the place of him that knoweth not God' (18: 21). In answer, Job wishes his friends to 'know' that God has wronged him (19: 6). As for himself – 'I know that my vindicator liveth' (19: 25); Job's deepest hope, like his innocence and his notion of evil in the world, is a matter of knowledge.[5]

Zophar's conviction of just retribution is conveyed to Job as a matter of sound 'knowledge' (20: 4). Job rejects the dogma of the misfortunes of the wicked, pointing to the prosperity of those who 'desire not the knowledge of God's ways' (21: 14). The enigmatic verse, 'Will any teach God knowledge' (21: 22) is either Job's quotation of an argument of the friends who discuss his claim to knowledge (F. Hitzig, Tur Sinai) or it means: Can any man explain on behalf of God the injustice meted out to human kind, depicted in the following verses (B. Duhm, Ehrlich). In either case, the key word is *knowledge*.

In the third cycle of speeches Eliphaz unjustly attributes to Job, the knower, the notion that God does not know ('What doth God know?', 22: 13; comp. *Ps.* 73: 11). His friend's admonition to return to God evokes in Job the image of a God who conceals Himself, who eludes man: 'Oh that I knew where I might find Him' (23: 3); if he indeed would reach His presence, he 'would know the words which He would answer me' (23: 5). But though 'He knoweth the way I take' (23: 10), i.e. although He is aware of my innocence, He prevents those 'that know Him' from seeing His days (24: 1) – if it is exegetically possible to read chapter 24 as a continuation of 23.

Thus it appears that underlying the argument of the dialogue is the question of whether Job has knowledge of the ways of God – for only on the basis of such knowledge could he have uttered his invective and made his passionate pleas – or whether such knowledge is not accessible to man, the latter being the position held by the friends.

The cycles of the discourses of Job and the friends are appropriately followed by the poem on wisdom (28). This chapter, which 'contains no single *obvious* connection with the stage of the debate now reached',[6] has been conceived by some interpreters to be a later addition to the book of *Job*. But if our suggestion of the knowledge-motif in the discourses is correct, the poem on wisdom, regardless of its literary origin, is in its right place. It refers both back to these discourses, which raise the problem of human knowledge, and forward, subtly presaging the answer announced in the speeches of Elihu and finally given by the voice from the whirlwind. Many are man's achievements in the material world, the poem declares. But as to 'wisdom' – a term which to the author denotes not prudence, practical, or applied sagacity, but true wisdom, 'knowledge' – 'man knoweth not the price thereof' (28: 13; Greek: *the way thereof*), only 'God understandeth the way thereof, and he knoweth the place thereof' (28: 23). Such wisdom remains with God; it is not communicated to man. Man's wisdom is no more than 'the fear of the Lord – and to depart from evil' (28: 28), traits that characterised Job in the happy days (1: 1), before he had met with adversity and realised the unjust order in the world, and had rebelled in reliance on his own possession of 'knowledge', and had thus encountered as his antagonist Him 'who is perfect in knowledge' (37: 16).

When the Lord appears to answer Job, the text again uses 'knowledge' as a central motif. The divine speeches unfold the wonders of creation. However, the literary form chosen by the author is not that of an objective presentation, but a series of questions addressed to Job, disputing his ability to know and to act. Divine justice is not argued or interpreted; rather, man's access to knowledge is denied by implication. Apparently, then, this is what is at stake: it is the claim to knowledge that has been at the base of Job's rebellion.

The key word is placed at the very outset of the speeches: 'Who is this that darkeneth counsel by words without knowledge?'

(38: 2). Continuing on the note of Elihu's concluding statement (37: 24), Job is asked about the earth's foundation, if indeed he has 'understanding,' if he 'knows' (38: 4 f.). He is asked about the 'recesses of the deep' 'if thou knowest it all' (38: 18). About light and darkness – 'thou knowest, for thou wast then born' (38: 21), a reproach reminiscent of 15: 7 and 20: 4. Pointing to the stars, God asks: 'Knowest thou the ordinances of the heavens?' (38: 33), and turning to the animal kingdom: 'Knowest thou the time when the wild goats . . . bring forth? Does the hawk soar by thy wisdom?' (39: 1, 2, 26). Man's inability to know is related to the limits set upon his ability to act (38: 12, 16, 20, 22, 31–35, 39; 39: 1 f., 9–12, 19 f., 27; 40: 9, 25–32).

The issue of human knowledge *versus* divine knowledge is now settled. The fourfold[7] use of the key word in Job's answer to the Lord's speeches reveals the author's intention to have his hero realise that 'knowledge' is the true issue between him and his God. By now, Job's knowledge is but an awareness of his own limitations. 'I know that Thou canst do everything' (42: 2). It is man who, 'without knowledge', attempted to obscure the purpose of God (42: 3) and who 'uttered that . . . which he knew not' (42: 4). Knowledge is with God; Job who, out of presumption, attributed to himself the possession of knowledge, can now but pray that God grant him knowledge: 'I will ask Thee and do Thou make me know' (42: 4) – thus turning God's taunting question (40: 7) into a humble quest addressed to Him.

[II]

Some commentators have suggested that the book of *Job* contains allusions to the Adam story in *Genesis* or, possibly, in some ancient poetic version of the Pentateuch. *Job* 12: 7–10 seems to refer to an ancient legend about Adam's conversation with the animals.[8] The expression 'first man' in 15: 7 is interpreted by some as a reference to the myth of a primeval man.[9] The phrase *ke-'adham* in 31: 33 may mean 'like (ordinary) men' or may allude to Adam's concealment of his transgression. Less probable is Tur Sinai's proposal to see in the conclusion of the poem on wisdom (28: 28) a reference to Adam – plausible only in the context into which the commentator places the poem.[10]

Can it be maintained that, beyond these probable references, the author (or the final redactor) of the book of *Job* as a whole wished to allude to the story of Adam's daring appropriation of knowledge of good and evil, by which he antagonised divinity and incurred trouble and, finally, death? The parallels in both the story of Adam and the drama of Job point in that direction. Eve's prompting of Adam to disobey the divine command is paralleled by the suggestion of Job's wife that he 'blaspheme God and die' (2: 9). The serpent of *Gen.* 3 reappears as Satan in *Job*. The change in Job's fate once his afflictions evoked in him the ability to 'know' evil around him, which in turn aggravated his misfortune, corresponds to the change in Adam's lot caused by his acquisition of 'knowledge'; granting the obvious differences between the two stories, in both instances the loss of innocence, 'knowledge', and estrangement from God are interrelated. Adam (and Eve) receive the announcement of God's wrath; Job experiences this wrath throughout the poem. 'To dust thou shalt return' (*Gen.* 3: 19) is paralleled by Job's reference to 'dust and ashes' in his final confession (42: 6). The motif of death in the Adam story recurs numerous times as a central element throughout Job's speeches, from the curse of the day of his birth (chapter 3) to his final cognition, 'I know that Thou wilt bring me to death' (30: 23). Commencing his answer to Job, God asks, 'Where wast thou . . .?' (38: 2), echoing His question to Adam, 'Where art thou' (*Gen.* 3: 9). The panorama of the created world, spread out before Job's eyes, yet excluding man from the picture, corresponds to Adam's exclusion from the paradisiac world, originally created for his sake.

If these parallels and references are not merely coincidental, it may be surmised that the author of the book of *Job* (or its final redactor) wished his readers to notice the correspondence between the heroes of the two stories. In the internal history of the Bible, Adam, man, expelled from Paradise, is progressively recalled into the presence of the divine, in Noah, in Abraham, in Moses; and 'the knowledge that is forbidden' and death-causing is reformed into a knowledge that is revealed, granted, and life-giving. As against this theory of man, the author of Job presented his hero as the man who remained 'Adam', the being who by arrogating 'knowledge' became fully man, and who upon that knowledge based his judgments, expectations, and claims. Like Adam, whose fate it was to undergo suffering as a consequence of knowledge, Job experiences the interdependence of the two factors up to the point when a divine revelation teaches him to see himself in the context of a wider, extra-human, universe, and to recognise the limits of his knowledge before God, who, in spite of Adam's deed, still remains the Lord of knowledge.

[III]

The medieval Jewish bible-exegetes and religious thinkers interpreted the book of *Job* primarily as an argument about providence and God's concern with individual man, His goodness, and man's central position in the world.[11] However, among the other themes recognised by the interpreters as germane to the book, is the theme of knowledge. This is especially true of the conception formulated by Moses Maimonides (1135–1204), who discussed Job in his *Guide* III, 23–24. Maimonides finds it noteworthy that the text speaks of Job's ethical conduct but makes no mention of wisdom. 'Had he been wise he would not have been in doubt about the cause of his suffering'.[12] Only after 'he had acquired a true knowledge of God' (*yedi'ah 'amittith*) did he realise that 'there is true happiness in the knowledge of God' (*yedi'ath ha-Shem*), attainable by all 'who know Him' (*she-yeda'o*), a condition that cannot be upset by earthly affliction.[13] Thus, according to Maimonides, the book of *Job* demonstrates man's progress from ignorance and the wrong type of knowledge ('imagining God's knowledge to be similar to ours'[14]) to the stage of knowing God, a knowledge which leads to the love of God.[15]

Man's limited knowledge is also an aspect of the *Job* interpretation by Joseph Kara (11th–12th century). Human understanding 'is like nothing compared with His wisdom.' Though God's ways are intended for the welfare of man, they are, nevertheless, beyond human comprehension. It is man's error to approach the problem of divine rule as if 'he were God's partner in the work of creation.'[16]

In his commentary on *Job*, Abraham ibn Ezra (1092–1167) singled out the recurrent phrase 'knowest thou?' as the main point in the divine speeches and as the argument that brought about Job's submission and helped him to overcome his rebellious self-pride (*gobhahh libbo*).[17] Similarly, Samuel ben Nissim Maṣnuṭ of Aleppo (13th century), in his *Midrash Sefer 'Iyyobh Maʿayan Gannim*, interpreted chapters 38 *seq.* as having the aim of making Job 'realise that he has no knowledge and that he is unable to fathom the ways of God'. He found peace only after 'he has been made to know what he has not known'.[18] Baḥya ben Asher ibn Ḥalawa (Spain, *d.* 1340) likewise traced Job's rebellious assertions back to his lack of knowledge, maintaining at the same time that Elihu's observations are rooted in wisdom. In the end Job, in Baḥya's view, realises that he is unable to know the wondrous ways of God 'unless He, in His mercy, makes them known to him'. Now, Job says, 'I have attained to prophecy and I know that You exist and know. . . .'[19]

Levi ben Gerson (Gersonides, 1288–1344), in his classical commentary on *Job*, ascribes chapter 28 to Job. In so doing, he makes Job the spokesman for the high value of wisdom and for the notion that only God 'knows the complete essence of wisdom' – an understanding that Job reaches only towards the end of the stormy disputes.[20] Somewhat weaker is the argumentation of Joseph Albo (*ca.* 1380–*ca.* 1445), whose Job arrives at the idea of God's supreme knowledge by way of logical deduction from His power as it is displayed in creation.[21]

These references (and more could be added) indicate that the tradition of medieval Jewish bible-interpretation was aware, though not centrally, of the motif of knowledge in the book of *Job*. The book was interpreted as reaching its culmination in the demonstration of the perfect knowledge that is God's, which, by more or less evident implication, serves as a radical correction of man's ability to 'know'. Maimonides is alone in using the concept

81

of knowledge as the key to the interpretation of the entire *Job* complex.

[IV]

Like the motif of knowledge, so the motif of the Adam-Job correspondence did not escape the attention of some readers of the book, Jewish, Christian, and Moslem. The emphasis varies according to the observer's religious tradition and theological tendency. Yet even an exposition that points to a *contrast* between Adam and Job is of interest. What is significant is that the exploration of either of the stories has evoked a reference to the other.

In the course of its multifarious discussion of the book of *Job*, the Midrash in interpreting *Job* 9: 35, makes Job argue that he has not followed the example of Adam 'who listened to the words of his wife'.[22] The Targum to *Job*, in its original version, saw in *Job* 28: 7 an allusion to Eve and the serpent, an observation that the later reviser eliminated from his text.

In his *Expositions on the Book of Psalms*, St Augustine (354–430), refers to Satan who 'took away everything' from Job but left him his wife. 'Merciful do ye deem the devil, that he left him a wife? He knew through whom he had deceived Adam.'[23] Similarly, St Chrysostom (*ca.* 344–407) interpreted the role of Job's wife as an accomplice of Satan, whom he quotes as saying: 'For if even out of paradise I cast mankind by her means, much more shall I be able to trip him (Job) up on the dunghill.'[24] The examples of Adam and Job serve Chrysostom as indication that Satan 'both accuseth God to man and us to God'.[25]

In a homily 'on the power of man to resist the devil',[26] Chrysostom compared the temptation of Adam, whom the devil 'attacked by means of mere words', to the trial of Job, who was 'attacked by means of deeds', i.e., by the calamities that befell him. Adam was deceived and conquered by a serpent; Job's tempter was a woman, his wife, who 'was far more persuasive' than the serpent, and yet she did not prevail. The preacher exhorted his audience to avoid imitating Adam, whose indolence

82

caused him many ills, and to 'imitate the piety of Job' who emerged 'the conqueror throughout': in the course of his dispute with the Deity Job overcame the notion that 'the just God who had in every way been served by him, was at war with him'. Similarly, in a homily 'concerning the statues',[27] Chrysostom compared Adam in paradise and Job on the dunghill; the former had provoked God and lost his paradisiac state, the latter had risen in piety and 'all things reverted to him with greater glory than before'. In another connection both Adam and Job appear as 'enjoying great dignity and proclaimed by the God of all', and because of this honour are ready targets for Satan.[28]

In a Moslem version of the folktale of Job,[29] which goes back to Wahb (d. A.H. 110, = 728–9 C.E.) and Ka'b-el-aḥbar (d. A.H. 32, = 652–3), Satan (*Iblīs*) boasts about the power given him over Job's possessions and declares that only once before had he enjoyed such power, namely, when he expelled Adam from paradise.[30] When Job's trial was over, the angel Gabriel gave him a fruit from paradise and Allah clothed him in garments taken from paradise.[31] In the Moslem legend of Job, related in Tha'labi's *Book of the Stories of the Prophets*, and discussed by D. B. Macdonald, Satan is counselled to apply to Job the technique he used in enticing Adam.[32]

The *Zohar* reads *Job* 1: 21 ('Naked came I out of my mother's womb, etc.') as a parallel to Adam's and Eve's 'knowledge' of their nakedness (*Gen.* 3: 7); the garments in which a man ascends to the other world are made out of 'those days in which he acted virtuously and did not sin'; both Adam and Eve's and Job's 'nakedness', therefore, refer to their sinful state.[33] Shemtob ben Joseph Falaquera (13th century), in his commentary on Maimonides' *Guide*, quotes the saying of Rabbi Simeon ben Laqish[34] who identifies Satan with the Evil Inclination and the Angel of Death in this form: 'Satan, the Evil Inclination and the tempter of Eve are all one.'[35] Zeraḥiah ben Isaac ben She'alti'el of Barcelona (13th century), in his commentary on *Job*,[36] drew a parallel between the book of *Genesis* and the book of *Job*. Both fall into two parts. To the story of Adam, Eve, and the serpent corresponds to the story of Job and Satan; both stories are followed by a second part which deals with issues of faith, providence, understanding, and right behaviour. At the base of this observation is the talmudic notion that Moses was the author of both 'his book and the book of *Job*'[37]; to Zeraḥiah, however, this notion suggested a deeper, thematic relationship between the two works. The above-mentioned Baḥya ben Asher ibn Ḥalawa also assumed that there was a correspondence between the book of *Job* and *Genesis*. Both books, he postulated, concern themselves with the creation of the world, with the issue of divine providence and retribution; and both the story of creation and the book of *Job* avoid the tetragrammaton and use instead the name *'elohim*, which denotes the quality of divine justice.[38]

The suggestion advanced in this article, that the author of the book of *Job* wished to turn the reader's attention to the motif of knowledge (human knowledge *versus* divine knowledge) is not founded upon the references to it in later literature; to an even lesser degree is the tentative note, that the book of *Job* alludes to the story of Adam, dependent on such references, significant as these are. Our reading of the *Job* text is based on a form-critical approach, or more specifically, on the guide provided by the text in its use of the key term *yada'*, *know*, and its synonyms. And if the assumption is permissible that the author of the book of *Job* was conscious of the story in *Gen.* 3, the implication is not that 'knowledge' in both *Job* and *Gen.* 3 mean in reality one and the same thing; but merely that the author of *Job* read *Gen.* 3 in the light of his own problem, and that he intended to resolve in his book the issue raised by the Adam story. Adam, who was made to believe that, by eating from the Tree of Knowledge, he would become 'as God, knowing good and evil', is here, in Job, led to the realisation that he does not know: that knowledge belongs to God. If at all correct, the reading of the book suggested here would help to underline its character as a work that is at once genuinely Hebraic and universally human.

NOTES

1 'That all men may know it' (37: 7) is obscure.
2 On the problem of similarity between 9: 2 and 4: 17–19 (Eliphaz), see Tur Sinai's comments on both passages. See also F. Stier, *Das Buch Ijjob*, Munich, 1954, p. 282.
3 Cf. 13: 23: 'Make me know my transgression.'
4 Cf. also 12: 9.
5 But the Ugaritic phrase, 'And I know that the powerful baal liveth' (C. H. Gordon, *Ugaritic Handbook*, Rome, 1947, p. 138) suggests that a liturgical formula underlies 19: 25a.
6 S. R. Driver and G. B. Gray, *The Book of Job* (International Critical Commentary), Edinburgh, 1921, p. 233.
7 Or threefold, if we exclude 42: 3a as a variant of 38: 2.
8 Tur Sinai *ad loc.*
9 Cf. Driver and Gray, *op. cit.*, p. 134.
10 Tur Sinai *ad loc.*
11 On this subject, see the present writer's 'The Book of *Job* and Its Interpreters' in *Studies and Texts* (ed. A. Altmann), vol. III, Philip W. Lown Institute of Advanced Judaic Studies, Brandeis University (Harvard University Press), 1966, p. 197f.
12 *Guide to the Perplexed*, III, 22.
13 *Ibid.*, III, 23.
14 *Ibid.*
15 *Ibid.*
16 Kara's *Job* commentary was published in the *Monatsschrift für Geschichte und Wissenschaft des Judentums* V–VII (1856–8). See comments on *Job* 37: 18 and 24; 36: 26 and 29.
17 Appendix to the commentary on *Job*, towards the end.
18 *Majan-Gannim, Commentar zu Job*, ed. by Solomon Buber, Berlin, 1889, comments on *Job* 38: 1 and 42: 2.
19 *Kad ha-Qemah*, ed. by Ḥayyim Breit, Lemberg, 1880, 74a and 76b.
20 Commentary on *Job*, *ad loc.*, especially 'the Discourse as a Whole'.
21 *'Iqqarim* IV, 10.
22 *Gen. Rabbah*, 19, 12, ed. Theodor-Albeck, p. 181, l. 4 f., ed. Wilna f. 44a col. ii, quoted also by Samuel ben Nissim Maṣnuṭ in his *Job* commentary, *Ma'ayan Gannim, ad loc.*
23 *P. L.* 36, 660; *A Select Library of the Nicene and Post-Nicene Fathers of the Christian Church*, vol. VIII, ed. by A. Cleveland Coxe, New York, 1888, p. 224, comment on *Ps.* 56.
24 *Homilies on First Corinthians, op. cit.*, vol. XII, ed. by T. W. Chambers, New York, 1889, p. 166. *P.G.L.* 61, 237, *supra.*
25 *Homilies on Second Corinthians, loc. cit.*, p. 284. *P.G.L.* 61, 402, *med.*

26 *A Select Library of the Nicene and Post-Nicene Fathers of the Christian Church*, vol. IX, New York, 1889, pp. 191–7, especially 194 (translated by T. P. Brandram). *P.G.L.*, 49, 269, *supra*.

27 *Ibid.*, p. 369. *P.G.L.*, 49, 66. Another juxtaposition of Adam and Job appears in the author's treatise 'To Prove that No One Can Harm the Man Who Does Not Injure Others', *ibid.*, p. 273.

28 *Homilies on the Gospel of St Matthew*, *op. cit.*, vol. X, New York, 1888, p. 80. *P.G.L.*, 57, 209, *supra*.

29 Naftali Apt, *Die Hiobserzählung in der arabischen Literatur*. Erster Teil. Kirchhain, N.L., 1913. University of Heidelberg Dissertation.

30 *Op. cit.*, p. 38; German tr., p. 15. Comp. also Duncan B. Macdonald, 'The Original Form of the Legend of Job', *American Journal of Semitic Languages and Literatures*, XIV, 1898, p. 146.

31 Apt, *op. cit.*, p. 65; German tr., p. 28.

32 Macdonald, *op. cit.*, p. 157.

33 *Zohar* I, 224a, on *Gen.* 47: 30. English tr., by H. Sperling & M. Simon (Soncino Press), ii, 1932, p. 319.

34 Babylonian Talmud, *Babha Bathra* 16a.

35 Commentary on the *Guide* III, 22.

36 Published by Israel Schwarz in his *Tikvath 'Enosh*, Berlin, 1868, pp. 167–293.

37 T.B. *Babha Bathra* 14b.

38 *Kad ha-Qemah*, ed. Ḥayyim Breit, Lemberg, 1880, 68a.

5

The Doctrine of
the 'Divine Spark'
in Man in Jewish Sources

LOUIS JACOBS

The belief that there is a special mystical 'spark' in every human
breast can be traced back, in western mysticism, at least to
Jerome in the fourth century. Both Bonaventura and Bernard
of Clairvaux speak of this mystical organ; the latter, calling it
scintillula, a small spark of the soul,[1] and speaking of the nearness
of God, said: 'Angels and archangels are within us, but He is
more truly our own who is not only *with us* but *in us*.'[2] However,
both these mystics are anxious to prevent an identification of this
mystical spark with the divine. Eckhart, on the other hand,
embraces the identification, calling the spark, among other
endearing names, *das Kleidhaus Gottes*,[3] 'the house in which God
attires Himself'. This and other pantheistic tendencies in Eckhart's
thought were condemned in the papal Bull of 1329.[4]
In Eastern mysticism the identification of the mystical spark
with the divine is frequent. In the Upanishads *Atman* is *Brahman*,
the soul of man is identical with the universal principle, *tat tvam
asi*, 'That art thou'. 'This my spirit within my heart is greater
than the earth, greater than the sky, greater than the heavens,

greater than all worlds. The all-working, all-wishing, all-smelling, all-tasting one, that embraces the universe, that is silent, untroubled – that is my spirit within my heart; that is Brahman. Thereunto, when I go hence, shall I attain. Who knoweth this, he, sooth, hath no more doubts.'[5] Sankara (c. 788–820), the famous Hindu mystic, describes the identification in these terms:

That same highest Brahman constitutes – as we know from such passages as 'That art thou' – the real nature of the individual soul, while its second nature, i.e. that aspect of it which depends on fictitious limiting conditions, is not its real nature. For as long as the individual soul does not free itself from Nescience in the form of duality – which Nescience may be compared to the mistake of him who in the twilight mistakes a post for a man – and does not rise to the knowledge of the Self, whose nature is unchangeable, eternal Cognition – which expresses itself in the form 'I am Brahman' – so long it remains the individual soul. But when, after disregarding the aggregate of body, sense-organs and mind, it arrives, by means of Scripture, at the knowledge that it is not itself that aggregate, that it does not form part of transmigratory existence, but is the True, the Real, the Self, whose nature is pure intelligence; then knowing itself to be of the nature of unchangeable, eternal Cognition, it lifts itself above the vain conceit of being one with this body, and itself becomes the Self, whose nature is unchanging, eternal Cognition.[6]

In Islamic mysticism the idea appears, from Ḥallaj, with his *Ana 'l-Ḥaqq*, 'I am the Truth [which is God]', to Jalāl-ud-dīn Rumi's proclamation that the soul's love of God is God's love of the soul, and that in loving the soul God loves Himself, for He draws home to Himself that which is in its essence divine.[7] In an ode this poet says[8]:

> *O my soul, I searched from end to end: I saw*
> *in thee naught but the Beloved:*
> *Call me not infidel, O my soul, if I say that thou*
> *thyself art He.*

It is generally assumed that in every version of Judaism the distance between God and man is so vast that ideas such as the preceding can have no place in the Jewish faith. Salo Baron,[9] for instance, makes the following generalisation:

> But while Muslim fatalism tended to reduce greatly the distance between the Creator and the universe or man created by Him, thus opening the road to unrestrictedly pantheistic identification, Jews (even the Ṣufis among them) had retained enough of their traditional awe before the divine Holiness and its inherent transcendence to draw a sharp line of demarcation between them. Exclamations like that by Ḥallaj, 'I am He whom I love, and He Whom I love is I' – that is, 'I am God' – would have sounded as execrable blasphemies in the ears of the most confirmed Jewish followers of Ṣufism. This did not mean that they did not venture to argue with God about certain alleged injustices and imperfections in His world order. This had been done with perfect equanimity by Job and many aggadic homilies. But in their most daring dialogues and visions they never forgot the chasm which separated the Infinite from all His creatures, even those belonging to the highest emanations, which alone the 'Descenders of the Chariot' dared to approach. In the ultimate sense, even these mystics resigned themselves in their diverse ways, to the acceptance of the inscrutable tortuousness of the divine guidance of man and history. Individually, too, they sought mere communion, not actual union, with the Deity.

It should be made clear that Baron is correct only if his observation is limited to the *Merkabhah* ('*Chariot*') mysticism with which he deals. The categorical statement that Judaism, in any of its forms, knows nothing of the identification of the 'divine spark' with the divine can be maintained only by ignoring a considerable portion of the evidence we shall here adduce. Consequently, R. C. Zaehner's remarks are true only of 'normative' Judaism, not of Judaism in all its manifestations:

> It can be maintained that the strictly monotheistic religions do not naturally lend themselves to mysticism: and there is

much to be said for this view. Christianity is the exception because it introduces into a monotheistic system an idea that is wholly foreign to it, namely, the Incarnation. . . . Such an idea is as repulsive to the strict monotheism of Islam as it is to that of the Jews. Judaism, on its side, never developed a mystical tradition comparable to that of the other great religions because it held that union with a transcendental God who manifests himself in history could not be possible to a finite creature.[10]

Zaehner quotes Scholem[11] as his authority: 'The Creator and His creatures remain apart, and nowhere is an attempt made to bridge the gulf between them or to blur the distinction.' But Scholem, too, is here speaking of 'Chariot' mysticism alone. Our evidence prevents us applying the rule to every type of Jewish mystical thought.

David Baumgardt[12] is on surer ground in remarking with regard to the 'divine spark' idea:

The way in which similar ideas about an inner well of mystical religious life emerge in movements which had hardly any contact with Christian religious thought, may be inferred from the sayings of the founder of the Habad Society or Lubovitcher Hasidim, Shneur Zalman of Ladi in Lithuania[13] (1745–1813), who was called the 'Rav of Reussen' or 'alter Rebbe' (the old Rabbi). He taught in his *Sefer Tanya* that in every Jew there is a spark of divinity (according to popular Jewish thought 'a small point of Jewish faith' [*dos pintele Yid*] by which religious Jewishness can, on principle, always be rekindled, no matter how hidden it may be or how dead it may appear to the eye of the observer).

We shall see that Baumgardt is certainly right in finding this idea in *Habad*. But it has its antecedents in earlier Jewish thought. It is the purpose of this essay to consider the doctrine of the 'divine spark' in the form it assumes in a number of important Jewish sources and to demonstrate that its prominence in *Habad* comes at the end of a long process.

It is hardly necessary to state that there is no hint of the idea in the Bible. The verse: 'Then the Lord God formed man of the dust of the ground, and breathed into his nostrils the breath of life' (*Gen.* 2: 7), though used as a proof-text for the notion of the 'divine spark' by Philo and others, really means no more than that God blew the spirit into Adam.[14] 'The spirit of man is the candle of the Lord' (*Prov.* 20: 27) means, of course, a candle *kindled* by the Lord. 'And the dust returneth to the earth as it was, and the spirit returneth unto God who gave it' (*Eccl.* 12: 7) similarly means no more than that God *gave* man his soul, not that it is a part of God.

Philo, writing at the beginning of the first century C.E., was the first Jew, so far as we know, to teach that there is something divine in the human soul.

> For the essence or substance of that other soul is divine spirit, a truth vouched for by Moses especially, who in his story of the creation says that God breathed a breath of life upon the first man, the founder of our race, into the lordliest part of his body, the face, where the senses are stationed like bodyguards to the great king, the mind. And clearly what was then thus breathed was ethereal spirit, even an effulgence of the blessed, thrice blessed nature of the Godhead.[15]

Philo reverts to the idea of the soul as an 'effulgence of the blessed nature of the Godhead' in a number of passages in his works. Thus in his comment to *Gen.* 2: 7 he says[16]:

> 'Breathed into', we note, is equivalent to 'inspired' or 'besouled' the soulless; for God forbid that we should be infected with such monstrous folly as to think that God employs for inbreathing organs such as mouth and nostrils; for God is not only not in the form of a man, but belongs to no class or kind. Yet the expression clearly brings out something that accords with nature. For it implies of necessity three things, that which inbreathes, that which receives, that which is inbreathed: that which inbreathes is God, that which receives is the mind, that which is inbreathed is the spirit or breath. What, then, do we infer from these premises? A union of the three comes

91

about, as God projects the power that proceeds from Himself through the mediant breath till it reaches the subject. And for what purpose save that we may obtain a conception of Him? For how could the soul have conceived of God, had He not breathed into it and mightily laid hold of it? For the mind of man would never have ventured to soar so high as to grasp the nature of God, had not God Himself drawn it up to Himself, so far as it was possible that the mind of man should be drawn up, and stamped it with the impress of the powers that are within the scope of its understanding.

Thus, according to Philo, the human mind would be incapable of knowing God were it not that God had permitted the abyss to be crossed by infusing the mind with something of Himself. Elsewhere[17] Philo states that the gift of a divine part of the soul to Adam is shared by his descendants, albeit in fainter form. Every man, he says, in respect of his mind, is allied to the divine Reason, having come into being as a copy or fragment or ray of that blessed nature. In the later literature the 'divine spark' is frequently limited to Israel. In Philo the more universalistic tendency prevails. All Adam's descendants share in his nature and have something of the divine within them.

If we turn to the rabbinic literature[18] we find references to the purity of the soul[19] and its heavenly origin.[20] Just as the woman of royal lineage who marries a villager is never satisfied with all that her husband provides because she is accustomed to life in the royal palace, so the soul's immortal longings are never satisfied because it derives from 'those above' (ha-'elyonim).[21] In a famous passage[22] it is stated that the soul resembles God in that it is invisible, it sustains the body as God sustains the world, it is pure, it fills the body as God fills the world, and, like God, it dwells in the innermost chambers. In all this there is not the slightest hint at any identification of the soul with God. The nearest we get to such identification in the whole of the rabbinic literature is the saying of R. Eleazar[23] (third century) that a man should consider himself as if the Holy One dwells within him: but even if this is what R. Eleazar really means (and this is by no means certain[24]), it is clear from the context that he is simply stating in picturesque fashion the need for man to take care of himself, since his bodily needs are also God-given. It would be exceedingly precarious to deduce from this isolated saying that there are rabbinic echoes of the Philonic idea.

Nor is there any clear attempt at the identification of the soul and God in the classical medieval philosophers. These agree that the soul is not material, and the Aristotelian three-fold division of the soul into vegetative, animal and rational is frequently found. Under the influence of the Arabic Aristotelians the doctrine of the Active Intellect was adopted by thinkers like Abraham Ibn Da'ud, Maimonides, Gersonides and Crescas. By means of the Active Intellect, which emanates from God, man can gain an acquired intellect through the exercise of his mind in study and comprehension of metaphysical truth. This alone is the immortal part of man.[25] All this has little to do with the doctrine that there is a divine spark hidden in the recesses of the human *psyche*. However, a neo-platonist like Gabirol (*d.* 1058) can refer to the soul as a pure radiance from God's glory[26]:

> *Who can contain Thy might when from the abundance*
> *of Thy glory Thou didst create a pure*
> *radiance, hewn from the quarry of the Rock,*
> *and dug from the mine of Purity?*
> *And on it Thou didst set a spirit of wisdom, and*
> *Thou didst call it the Soul.*
> *Thou didst fashion it from the flames of fire of*
> *the Intelligence, and its spirit is as a fire*
> *burning in it.*
> *Thou didst send it into the body to serve it and to*
> *guard it, and it is as a fire within, and yet*
> *it does not burn it.*

It is in the teaching of the *Qabbalah*, with its strong neo-platonic influences, that the doctrine of the 'divine spark' comes into full prominence in Jewish thought. The zoharic teachings on the nature of the soul are exceedingly complex[27] but at least in one passage[28] it is clearly stated that the highest part of the soul – *neshamah* – comes from the sephirotic realm, from the 'body' of *'Adham Qadhmon*, Primordial Man, the world of the *Sephiroth* – the 'qualities' or 'attributes' which emanate from *'Eyn Soph*, the Infinite: God as He is in Himself.

> R. Judah began his discourse by quoting the verse: 'Let every soul praise the Lord' (*Ps.* 150: 6). We have been taught that all souls are derived from that Holy Body and they animate human beings. From which place are they derived? From the place that is called *Yah*. Which place is that? Said R. Judah: It is written: 'How manifold are thy works, O Lord! In wisdom hast Thou made them all' (*Ps.* 104: 24). We have been taught that all things are contained in that wisdom the spring of which flows into thirty-two paths, all things above and below are contained within it.

In the zoharic scheme the highest *Sephiroth* are: *Kether*, 'Crown', the divine Will; *Hokhmah*, the divine Wisdom; and *Binah*, the divine Understanding. In the above passage the soul is said to derive ultimately from the divine Wisdom. This means much more than that God in His wisdom created the soul. The *Sephirah* of Wisdom is in zoharic thought an aspect of the Deity. Consequently, the soul comes from God Himself. In other zoharic sources it is suggested that the soul comes from the *Sephirah* of Understanding.[29] The author of the *Zohar*, remarks Professor Scholem,[30] on the whole holds the view that only the *nephesh*, the natural soul, is capable of sin. The *neshamah*, the spark of the divine in man, is beyond sin. Indeed, Moses de Leon, identified with good reason by Scholem as the author of the *Zohar*, discusses in other works of his how it is possible for the soul to suffer in Hell since *neshamah* is substantially the same as God!

Nahmanides (1195–1270), in his Commentary to the Pentateuch, on the verse: 'Then the Lord God formed man of the dust of the ground, and breathed into his nostrils the breath of life; and man became a living soul' (*Gen.* 2: 7) gives an interpretation in the spirit of the *Qabbalah*, which bears remarkable affinities with Philo's interpretation of the same verse. Nahmanides observes[31] that the verse provides us with a hint of the soul's most elevated nature by using the complete divine name – 'the Lord God'. By stating that God 'breathed' the soul 'into his nostrils' the verse teaches that the soul has its origin neither in the four elements nor as an emanation from the disembodied intelligences, the angels, but is from the very 'mouth' of God. In support, Nahmanides quotes for his purpose: 'Out of His mouth cometh knowledge and discernment' (*Prov.* 2: 6). The soul is thus a spirit which comes from God Himself. For when one blows into the face of another it is of his own breath which he blows.[32] Quoting 'But it is a spirit in man and the breath of the Almighty that giveth them understanding' (*Job* 32: 8), Nahmanides refers to the cabbalistic doctrine that the soul comes from the divine Understanding, i.e. from the *Sephirah* of that name. He then goes on to discuss the different parts of the soul under the conventional medieval categories. At all events, according to this author, there is a portion of the divine in the soul of man.

Nahmanides was the first bible-commentator to make use of the *Qabbalah* for exegetical purposes. In this he was followed by Bahya Ibn Asher (*d.* 1340) of Saragossa. After a lengthy exposition of the different views on the nature of the soul held by the philosophers, Bahya[33] turns, in his comment to the *locus classicus* on the question, *Gen.* 2: 7, to the views of the *Qabbalah*.

That the soul, after its departure from the body, is immortal is stated in this verse which calls it the 'soul of life' (*nishmath hayyim*), namely, a soul hewn out of the Source of life, for the soul is hewn out of the Source of the divine Wisdom (i.e. the *Sephirah* of *Hokhmah*, as in the above-quoted zoharic passage). . . . If you will grasp the significance of the verse uttered by Solomon in his wisdom you will understand the soul's lofty and elevated degree, its foundation and its mystery. Solomon says: 'Man's pre-eminence above the beast is nothing' (*Eccl.* 3: 19). He states that the pre-eminence of man over the beast is by virtue of that which is called 'Nothing', that is to say, by virtue of man's rational soul which derives from Wisdom, represented by the letter *yodh*, united with the divine Will, represented by the letter *'aleph*. Understand this thoroughly. (Baḥya here follows the cabbalistic representation of the *Sephiroth* by the letters of the Hebrew alphabet. The letter *yodh* represents the *Sephirah Ḥokhmah*, the divine Wisdom. The letter *'aleph* represents the highest of the *Sephiroth*, *Kether* (Crown) the divine Will. The first two letters of the Hebrew word for 'nothing' – *'ayin* – are *'aleph* and *yodh*. Hence the human soul derives from the first divine impulse to create, allied to the potential wisdom manifested in creation.) Hence the verse speaks of God as breathing into his nostrils that we might understand the foundation of the soul and its most elevated state, since it emanates from the Holy Spirit. It is for this reason that the soul is compared to the Holy One, blessed be He, in five matters.[34] The soul resembles God in all its qualities and is greater than the angels. . . . The conclusion of the matter is that whatever the mouth can utter in precise praise of the qualities of the Holy One, blessed be He, in His role as Creator of all things, can be included in the qualities of the soul as a created thing. The Sage observes: 'Know yourselves and you will know God.'[35] Consider all this!

The ideas of both Naḥmanides and Baḥya were drawn upon by Manasseh ben Israel (*d.* Middleburg, Holland, 1657) in his treatise on the soul.[36] Referring to the verse quoted by the previous authors he observes[37] that this calls attention to the spiritual and elevated nature of the soul which emanates from the Holy Spirit – the very words used by Baḥya. It is as if 'the Holy One, blessed be He, as it were, touched the formless lump of Adam and blew the soul into it, thereby imparting to man some of the divine wisdom'. The souls of all other animals were created together with their bodies, but man's soul, being divine, was infused into him after his body had been created from the dust. Those 'who prepare savouries' (i.e. rather fanciful comments to Scripture) are quoted by the author in pointing out that the letters of the word for soul, *neshamah*, are largely the same as those in the word for heaven, *shamayim*, to hint at the divine origin of the original soul.

The cabbalist Ḥayyim Vital (1543–1620) elaborates on the theme of the divine soul in his *Sha'arē Qedushah*,[38] 'Gates of Holiness'. The true man, states Vital, is not the body, for this is known in Scripture as the 'flesh of man'. The soul is the real man, using the body as its garment. At death the soul divests itself of the coarse garment of the body to become clothed with pure, refined, spiritual vestments. As a result of Adam's sin there came about a mixture of good and evil in all things so that even the divine soul, hewn from the four divine elements represented by the four letters of the tetragrammaton, became surrounded by an evil soul, deriving from the forces of impurity and known as the Evil Inclination. The limbs of the physical body are garments to the spiritual 'limbs' of the unclean soul and these are, in turn, garments to the 'limbs' of the pure soul, the true man. When man uses his bodily limbs for sin he adds fuel to the forces of the impure soul. When he uses them to perform good deeds these nourish and sustain the divine soul, enabling it to get the upper hand of the unclean soul. In later parts of the work[39] Vital describes in detail the whole scheme by which man's psychic nature is linked to the 'upper worlds'. One passage, in particular,[40] deserves a passing notice:

> The soul's greatness has been described, for it is a great light born of the light of the *Sephiroth* themselves, without any intermediary. This is the meaning of: 'Ye are children of the Lord your God' (*Deut.* 14: 1) for they are in the category of a son who is completely attached to the father from whom he is descended. This is the mystery behind the saying that the Patriarchs are the Heavenly Chariot[41] to the light of the *Sephiroth* which rides above them without the mediation of any other light. . . . And this is the mystery of: 'But ye that cleave unto the Lord your God' (*Deut.* 4: 4), with real attachment to the light of the *Ten Sephiroth*: but it is otherwise with regard to all other creatures. This is the meaning of the

97

verse: 'For as the girdle cleaveth to the loins of a man, so have I caused to cleave unto Me the whole house of Israel' (*Jer.* 13: 11).

It will be seen that for Vital, as for the majority of the cabbalists, the elevated role of divine kinship is reserved for Israel, and is really based on the notion that Israel on earth mirrors the heavenly pattern.

Vital was the pupil of the famous Safed cabbalist Isaac Luria (1534–72). An earlier leader of the Safed mystical school was Moses Cordovero[42] (1522–70). Elijah de Vidas, Cordovero's pupil, published his own *Reshith Hokhmah*[43] (*The Beginning of Wisdom*), as an ethical guide for the mystical adept, in the spirit of his master. Here the doctrine of the divine spark in man is treated in elaborate detail[44] and, like much of de Vidas' work, owes a great deal to Cordovero. Claiming that his ideas are based on the *Zohar*,[45] though it is only through considerable homiletical ingenuity that the passage quoted can be made to yield the thought, de Vidas states that an actual spark (*niṣuṣ*) of the Holy One, blessed be He, and His *Shekhinah* (Divine Presence) is contained within man.

De Vidas writes: 'Souls are flaming threads drawn below from on high, their vitality stemming constantly from their Source.' In his view death is caused by God drawing up to Himself the thread by which the soul is bound to Him, just as the scent of an apple is drawn away when one smells its fragrance. This is why Scripture says: 'For the portion of the Lord is His people, Jacob the lot of His inheritance' (*Deut.* 32: 9). The soul of an Israelite is an actual portion of the Deity (taking the word 'portion' not in the sense of a part *belonging* to God but to mean a part *of* God). This does not mean, however, that there is any kind of separateness or division in God but rather that the source of the soul on high is a part of God. Souls inhabiting individual bodies are naturally separate entities but in their source in God they are one with Him. 'For the portion of the Lord is His people' can be read as 'For the portion of the Lord is with Him' (*'immo* for *'ammo*), i.e. God's portion of the soul, the part that is divine, is 'with' Him as part of His being with its branches here below. Hence the verse speaks, too, of Jacob as the 'rope' (*hebhel* can mean 'rope' as well as 'lot') of His inheritance; for the soul and God are united like the strands of which a rope is composed. Furthermore, the illustration of a rope is given to denote that the soul, even after its descent into the body, is still attached to God, so that one end of the 'rope' is in God's hands while the other inhabits the body. 'The meaning of the love of God and "cleaving" to Him is that man attaches himself to God by means of this link, binding himself to the root of his soul which is attached to God, blessed be He.' Just as man's soul loves his body to which it is joined and the body the soul as the source of its life, so should man love God with whom his soul is united.

Shabbethai Sheftel Horowitz the Elder (*b. ca.* 1565, *d.* 1619) flourished in Prague and was the author of the famous cabbalistic book *Shepha' Tal*.[46] At the beginning of the work[47] Horowitz writes: 'It is known that the souls of the people of Israel are a "portion of God from above"[48] (*Job* 31: 2). The verse: "For the portion of the Lord is His people" (*Deut.* 32: 9) hints at this. The term "portion" is to be taken literally. A portion separated from some thing is in every way like the thing from which it has been taken, the thing being the whole and the total, which is naturally greater than the part separated thereof. But in essence the whole and the part are identical. In the same way there is no difference or distinction between the soul and God, may He be exalted and may His name be blessed, except that God, may He be exalted and may His name be blessed, is the whole. He is the all-embracing light, the infinite, unending, great light, whereas the soul is a portion and a spark separated from the great light, blessed be He and blessed be His name. As king Solomon, on whom be peace, says: "The spirit of man is the candle of the Lord" (*Prov.* 20: 27). He means to say that man's soul is a candle, a spark deriving from God's light. He takes particular care to speak of the "candle (*ner*) of the Lord" rather than the "light of the Lord" in order to hint at the truth that all three degrees of *nephesh*, *ruah* and *neshamah* in the soul are a portion and a spark of God's light. This is hinted at by the use of the expression the *"ner* of God" since the word *"ner"* has the initial letters of *nephesh* and *ruaḥ*.[49] The meaning is that *nephesh, ruaḥ* and *neshamah*, the three degrees of the soul, are all holy sparks which come from God's light. Hence the verse says: "The *neshamah* of man is the *ner* of God." ' It can be seen that Horowitz draws almost entirely on his predecessors. He is extraordinary only in giving such prominence to the doctrine of the divine spark, placing it right at the beginning of his lengthy treatise.

Horowitz was not unaware of the offence-giving nature of his contention. No sooner had he written this first paragraph than he added a cautionary note which reads:

O student of this work, be not astonished at this idea; for my master and teacher, Rabbi Moses Cordovero has written even more than this is his holy *Pardes*,[50] Gate of *Hēkhaloth*, Chapter 13, where he remarks: 'The Patriarchs are more elevated than the *Sephiroth* for they are not "limbs" but they are Divinity Itself in Its extension to creatures here below.' You see that he states explicitly that the Patriarchs are Divinity Itself. His words there and ours here will become perfectly intelligible to you when you reach the Gate of *nephesh, ruaḥ* and *neshamah* of this work. But I request the student to study this treatise in the order of its Gates and Chapters, for each Gate and each Chapter is the key, introduction and commentary to the Gate and Chapter which follows it. Do not, therefore, permit your thoughts to skip immediately to the middle of the work, for this will be of no advantage to you. But if you study the work in the order we have mentioned the gates of light will be revealed to you without mental fatigue. However, as a preliminary thought and first postulate you may grasp this idea and understand it.

Horowitz's *Shepha‘ Ṭal* was no sooner off the press than it was widely acclaimed as a basic cabbalistic text-book; but the fears of the author, that his notion of the divine character of the soul would give offence, were not unfounded. It appears, indeed, that so fierce were the protests that it evoked that the author resolved to write a special work of defence against his critics. This little book, entitled *Nishmath Shabbethai Ha-Levi*[51] (*The Soul of Shabbethai the Levite*), has the avowed aim of removing the misconceptions to which his formulation in the *Shepha' Tal* had given rise.

In the preface to his apology Horowitz states that the work deals with the mysteries of the holy soul which were revealed as a result of the difficulties raised by his sons, pupils, colleagues and teachers – a formidable list. The author claims, in his introduction, that mysteries still left concealed in his *Shepha' Tal* are now revealed so that the new work must be seen as an appendix to the earlier one. In fact, he remarks, he has now decided to give a new name to both books so that they can be treated as one. The new title, significantly enough, is *Galē Razayya* (*Revealer of Mysteries*). Horowitz claims further that, so far from being in any way original in his notions concerning the divine character of the soul, he has four great authorities – he calls them 'pillars' – on whom he relies, four earlier teachers of the highest renown who had taught the same truth. The first of these is none other than Moses himself, the second Rabbi Simeon ben Yohai, the traditionally reputed author of the *Zohar*, the third Nahmanides, the fourth Elijah de Vidas. The last two references are, of course, to the works we have mentioned previously. The book is divided into thirteen brief chapters corresponding, the author informs us, to Maimonides' thirteen principles of the Jewish faith. They provide the reader with the basic principles concerning his psychic life.

In a special introduction to the 'Gates' of the treatise Horowitz proceeds to describe its purpose. His pupils and teachers, he observes, raised a 'tremendous objection' to the ideas on the nature of the soul contained in the *Shepha' Tal*. Sure of the value of the latter work, and perhaps being sensitive about the criticism it had inspired, he calls it 'a holy work, holy in all its parts, containing words of truth and uprightness, words of the living God, without any blemish'. The objections raised are then stated fairly. How can it be maintained that the soul is an actual part of God since this would mean that there are as many parts in God as the total

101

number of Jewish souls, thus compromising traditional Jewish monotheism? All the cabbalists agree that the Infinite – *'Eyn Soph* – has neither parts nor divisions. Furthermore, every Jewish child is taught to praise God for *creating* his soul, and the Rabbis speak of God *creating* the souls of Israel before the creation of the world. If the soul is *created* how can it be a portion of the Creator?[52] After a general introduction to the basic cabbalistic principles regarding the relationship between *'Eyn Soph* (God as He is in Himself) and the *Sephiroth* – God in the process of re-vealing Himself to others – the author begins his reply in Gate 4. He first calls attention to the note of warning inserted at the beginning of the *Shepha' Tal*. Here he has reminded the reader of the dangers inherent in a superficial understanding of the notion of the divine spark. Denying emphatically that he is in any way recanting, he goes on to say that all along he had meant to say that the soul was a portion of the sephirotic realm – God in His aspect of self-disclosure – not a portion of *'Eyn Soph*. *'Eyn Soph* is God as He is known to Himself alone. Of this aspect of Deity nothing whatsoever can be postulated. It is not men-tioned in the Bible, it is utterly beyond all human comprehension, of it nothing can be said, it is entirely remote from the slightest attempt at comprehension. It follows that it is quite improper to speak of the soul as a portion of *'Eyn Soph*, since it is really improper to speak of *'Eyn Soph* at all. How then can one speak of a 'portion' of *'Eyn Soph*? Horowitz denies that he had ever suggested that one could. Of the *Sephiroth*, however, one can speak. Moreover these are ten in number. Here there is division, for God, as He reveals Himself to others, has varying attributes and aspects. Consequently, it is quite proper to speak of the soul as a portion of the sephirotic realm, for here there is division; and there can be no harm in extending the divisions to include the totality of souls.

This possibly lessens the difficulty. It does not abolish it. It is true that in the *Qabbalah* the distinction between *'Eyn Soph* and the *Sephiroth* is made, but the cabbalists felt bound to demon-strate that somehow there is no degeneration into dualism. Consequently, various illustrations are used by them in their attempt to convey the thought that there is a basic unity of *'Eyn Soph* and the *Sephiroth*. Among these illustrations are those of water poured into bottles of different colours, which partakes of the colour of the bottles without really suffering change; or of the human soul which is one and yet which possesses different characteristics; or of the multi-coloured flames proceeding from the one glowing coal. It follows that the doctrine of the divine spark – even if it comes from the sephirotic realm – is still exceedingly bold. Hence Horowitz, in the next three chapters, quotes his four 'pillars' in support of his radical viewpoint. Gate 5 gives an account of Naḥmanides' views to which we have referred. In chapter 6 the second 'pillar', Elijah de Vidas, is quoted. Chapter 7 relies on the zoharic passage quoted by de Vidas. As we have seen, the idea of the soul as a portion of God is far from explicit in this passage, although, since Horowitz now admits that he is thinking only of the sephirotic realm, it is rather strange that he does not quote the zoharic passages in which it is stated clearly that the soul comes from either the *Sephirah* of Wisdom or that of Understanding. Finally, the strongest proof of all, Moses himself is asserted to have referred to the doctrine in the *Shemaʿ*, Israel's declaration of faith: *'Hear O Israel, the Lord our God the Lord is One'* (*Deut.* 6: 4). Horowitz is here somewhat obscure, but, if my reading of what he says is correct, he appears to interpret the verse with a boldness bordering on blasphemy, as some of his critics would surely say, in this way: 'Hear! Israel and the Lord our God are one Lord'! 'Israel', observes Horowitz, 'are united with God in the upper worlds.'

In the sources mentioned hitherto the doctrine of the divine spark in the soul is accepted, occasionally with qualifications, and it forms a more or less significant part in the spiritual outlook of the various authors. Nowhere, however, do we find such a highly developed metaphysical system based on the idea as we do in the writings of Schneor Zalman of Liady, mentioned above, the founder of the *Ḥabad* group in Hasidism. Schneor Zalman relies mainly on the cabbalists of the Lurianic school, Ḥayyim

Vital in particular.[53] Following Vital, Schneor Zalman speaks of the two souls which every Jew possesses. The first, the 'animal soul', is the vital force by which man lives. It is the source of all his desires and appetites. It is constantly at war with the 'divine soul', the portion of God within man. Here is Schneor Zalman's description of the divine soul[54]: 'The second soul of Israel is an actual portion of God from above, as it is said: "And He breathed into his nostrils the *neshamah* of life" (*Gen.* 2: 7), and "Thou didst breathe it into me."[55] As the *Zohar*[56] comments: "When one blows it is from himself that he blows", that is to say, from his most inward essence, for man ejects his most inner vitality when he blows powerfully. In the same way the souls of Israel ascended in God's thought, as it is written: "Israel is My son, My first-born" (*Ex.* 4: 22), "Ye are the children of the Lord your God" (*Deut.* 14: 1). This means that as the child derives from the brain of the father[57] so, as it were, the soul of every Jew is derived from God's thought and wisdom. . . . Even though there are myriads of different degrees of soul, one higher than the other, for instance, the most elevated state of soul of the Patriarchs and of Moses above the souls of these generations of the "heels (i.e. harbingers) of the Messiah", which are in the category of the "heel" in comparison with the brain and the head. So, too, in each generation there are the heads of Israel, whose souls belong in the category of "head" and "brain" in comparison with the souls of the masses and the ignorant, and there are, too, divisions among souls into *nephesh, ruah* and *neshamah.* For all that, the root of every *nephesh, ruah* and *neshamah,* from the highest of all degrees to the lowest, in which the soul is clothed by the body of the ignorant man and the lowest of the low, derives from the Supernal Mind, the Supernal Wisdom, as in the illustration (if it is permitted to say this) of the child who stems from the brain of his father. Even the child's finger and toe nails are formed from the actual drop of semen which remains in the mother's womb for nine months, there descending from stage to stage until it changes so much that nails are formed, and yet, nonetheless, it is still bound to and united with, in marvellous fashion, its first essence when it was part of the brain of the father. . . .'

Prominent in Ḥabad thought is the idea of *biṭṭul hay-yesh* – 'annihilation of the self'. From one point of view God is the only true Being – *yesh* ('somethingness') – whereas all creatures, including man, are nothing – *'ayin* ('nothingness'). But from another point of view it is God who can be referred to as 'Nothing', because He is so far above all human comprehension that of Him nothing can adequately be said, whereas man can be referred to as *yesh*, 'that which is', that which is evident to the senses. Since the human soul is a part of God it longs to return to its source in Him, but the human *ego* in its separateness creates a barrier between the soul and its source in God. In technical Ḥabad terms, man's *yesh*, his 'somethingness', acts as a screen before the divine 'Nothingness', *'ayin*. The screen can only be removed by self-abnegation or self-annihilation. When man's *ego* is set at naught, when he attains to *biṭṭul hay-yesh*, complete abandonment of his 'somethingness' as a being apart from God, he becomes *'ayin*, 'nothingness', and he is then able to achieve contact with the divine 'Nothingness' that is God.[58] The veils of the senses and the *ego* are then stripped away and the soul in its naked 'nothingness' is in touch with its source in God. This is a tendency to be observed in much mystical thought, 'that the spark of the divine cannot be described because it contains nothing but the All, that the vacuum is the richest fullness, the negative the highest degree of positivity.'[59] As the *Tao-teh King* puts it[60]:

Thirty spokes meet together in a single hub.
The waggon's usefulness depends on their
     nothingness;
         (sc. on the empty space between them);
Clay is moulded into vessels;
The vessels' utility depends on their
     nothingness.
To build a house, holes are made in the walls
     for doors and windows;

On their nothingness depends the usefulness of
the house.
Hence: Being yields possession, but Non-being
utility.

It is well known that hasidism found its strongest opponent in
Elijah the Ga'on of Wilna (1720–97). The opposition was on
various grounds, not least of them the pantheistic viewpoint of
Hasidism. The divine was seen by the adherents of the new sect
in the most mundane matters. The famous disciple of the Ga'on,
Hayyim of Volozhin (1749–1821), treats of cabbalistic matters in
his *Nephesh Ha-hayyim*.[61] The mystical ideas of this work are
not very different from those of Schneor Zalman whose writings
were certainly familiar to Hayyim, but, for obvious reasons,
greater caution is used in such an anti-hasidic work. The
author accepts, for instance, the idea of the divine spark in the
soul but is far more qualified than Schneor Zalman in his acceptance. Hayyim admits that the 'essence' of the soul is divine,
but he states that this 'essence' never enters man's body. Before
Adam sinned he did, indeed, possess this 'essence' but when he
ate of the fruit of the tree it was taken from him, remaining
only in a state of suspension over him. Moses alone had the great
merit of possessing the 'essence' of the divine soul while still in
the body, hence he is called 'the man of God' (*Deut.* 33: 1). No
other human being is in possession of it, but sparks flash from it
over the heads of the saints, each according to the spiritual
degree he occupies and according to his spiritual capacities.[62]
Thus, for Hayyim, the divine spark has become a spark from the
soul, not a spark of God, and even this is not a basic part of every
man but is earned through saintly endeavour. A far cry this from
the categorical statements of *Habad*, that there is an actual
portion of God in every Jewish soul.

If the opponents of hasidism gave only a grudging recognition
to the doctrine of the divine spark, the followers of Schneor
Zalman of Liady furthered the powerful and influential *Habad*
movement with the doctrine as a central plank in its platform.

One of the most remarkable mystical testimonies in the whole literature of mysticism is that of Schneor Zalman's son and successor, Dobh Baer of Lubavitch (1773–1827). This work, entitled *Qunteros Ha-hithpa'aluth* (*Tract on Ecstasy*), is in the form of a long letter, sent by the master to his followers soon after his assumption of the leadership of the sect, offering them the guidance they had sought on the role of ecstasy in prayer.[63] Dobh Baer teaches that two types of ecstasy are possible in prayer. There is the power of man's two souls, the 'animal' or 'natural' and the 'divine', in his prayer life. The force of the 'divine soul' is strong or weak according to man's nearness to God in his daily life and the amount of divine grace granted to him. Dobh Baer describes the difference between the manifestations of the two souls in prayer as the difference between the 'essential' and the 'separate'. This means that an experience by the divine soul, though it is expressed through the normal channels of human will, thought and emotions, is, in reality, an experience of the divine by the divine, as it were. It is an 'essential' experience – divine essence responding to divine essence, the spark drawing near to the flame. An experience of the 'natural soul', on the other hand, through the channels of human will, thought and emotions, is a 'separate' experience. It involves an encounter with the divine by something not itself divine. Ecstasy induced by the divine grace extending to awaken the 'divine soul' is referred to as 'serving the Lord with the soul', whereas ecstasy induced by contemplation through the channels of the 'natural soul' is called 'serving the Lord with the body'. The whole tract is a profound analysis of ecstatic states, spurious and authentic, but its detailed investigation does not belong here.[64]

We have tried to trace the doctrine of the divine spark in the soul from its beginnings in Philo, through the cabbalists, and down to its significant place in the Ḥabad system. Admittedly, the doctrine is a highly unconventional one for Jewish religious thinkers, but the evidence we have adduced in this essay demonstrates convincingly that there were subterranean currents in Jewish thought on the soul which occasionally burst to the surface. For all the emphasis in normative Jewish teaching on the impassible gulf between God and His creatures, these currents carried across the centuries the daring idea that in the soul of man the abyss had been bridged.

NOTES

1 *V*. David Baumgardt: *Great Western Mystics*, New York, Columbia University Press, 1961, p. 34 and p. 81 note 74. The references, given by Baumgardt, are: to Jerome, Commentary to *Ezekiel*, *liber* I, *vers*. 6, 7 (*P.L.* 25, 22B (*scintilla conscientiae*)); to Saint Bernard, *Opera* (1781), *tom*. IV, p. 521b, *In Cantica Canticorum*, *sermo* 18, 6; to St Bonaventura's *Opera omnia*, Quaracchi, Vol. V (1891), *Itinerarium mentis in Deum*, Chapter II, 13.

2 *V*. Evelyn Underhill: *Mysticism*, London, Methuen, 1930, p. 304.

3 *V*. Baumgardt, *op. cit.*, p. 82 note 78 where a full list of the sources in Eckhart is given.

4 Baumgardt, *op. cit.*, p. 34 and p. 83 note 79. Cf. Jeanne Ancelet-Hustache: *Master Eckhart*, in the 'Men of Wisdom' series, London, Longmans, 1957, trans. Hilda Graef, who says: 'He (Eckhart) also calls it "the ground" (*der grunt*), the "little castle" (*bürgelin*), above all "the spark of the soul" (*scintilla animae, das fünkelin der séle*), an expression that comes from Peter Lombard who borrowed it from St Jerome; but it has so often been cited with reference to Eckhart that it has almost become his special property' (pp. 65–6).

5 The Chandogya-Upanishad (III, 14) quoted by George Foot Moore: *History of Religions*, Vol. I, Edinburgh, T. and T. Clark, 1914, p. 273 f.

6 C. Hartshorne and William L. Reese: *Philosophers Speak of God*, University of Chicago Press, 1953, p. 171, from *The Sacred Books of the East*, trans. George Thibaut, ed. F. Max Müller, Oxford, Clarendon Press, 1890, XXXIV, 14–15, pp. 185–6. Cf. Chapter VII, 'Some Hindu Approaches' in R. C. Zaehner's: *Mysticism Sacred and Profane*, Oxford, Clarendon Press, 1957, pp. 129–52. Aldous Huxley in his *The Perennial Philosophy*, Fontana Books (London), Collins, 1958, Chapter I, pp. 14–33, gives some interesting illustrations from mystical writers of various ages on this theme, though it is doubtful, to say the least, if his interpretation of Hillel's famous saying, quoted on p. 28, is correct. A useful translation of the Upanishads dealing with the theme is: *The Upanishads Breath of the Eternal*, trans. by Swami Prabhavananda and Frederick Manchester in the 'Mentor Religious Classics', New York, 1957. However, Rudolph Otto's comparative study of Sankara and Eckhart in his: *Mysticism East and West*, trans. by Bertha L. Bracey and

Richenda C. Payne, Meridian Books, 1957, reminds us that not all mystical statements regarding the *scintilla animae* and its identification with the Ground of being mean the same thing.

7   *V*. R. A. Nicholson: *The Mystics of Islam*, London, G. Bell and Sons, 1914, Chapter IV, pp. 102–19, and Chapter VI, pp. 148–68.

8   Nicholson, *op. cit.*, p. 119.

9   *A Social and Religious History of the Jews*, 2nd ed., Vol. VIII, New York, Columbia University Press, 1958, pp. 112–13.

10   R. C. Zaehner: *Hindu and Muslim Mysticism*, University of London, Athlone Press, 1960, p. 2.

11   *Major Trends in Jewish Mysticism*, 3rd ed., London, Thames and Hudson, 1955, pp. 55–6.

12   *Op. cit.* (note 1), p. 83.

13   There are a number of solecisms in this note of Baumgardt. Ladi or Liady is in Russia, not in Lithuania; the town is Lübavitch, not Lubovitch; the work is known as *Liqquṭe 'Amarim* or *Tanya*, after the opening word, not *Sefer Tanya*, which simply means 'The book "*Tanya*"'. Baumgardt quotes the later chapters of the work but, in fact, there is a detailed exposition of the 'divine soul' at the beginning of the book, Chapter 2, ed. Wilna, 1930, pp. 11 f.

14   Cf. J. Skinner: *Genesis* in *I.C.C.*, pp. 56–7.

15   *De Specialibus Legibus*, IV, 24, Eng. Trans., F. H. Coulson and G. H. Whitaker, Loeb Classical Library, p. 85. For Philo's views on the nature of the soul, cf. H. A. Wolfson: *Philo*, Vol. I, Harvard University Press, 1948, pp. 389–95.

16   *De Legum Allegoria*, I, 13, Loeb Classical Library, p. 171.

17   *De Opificio Mundi*, 51, Loeb Classical Library, p. 115.

18   *V*. I. Broyde in *Jewish Encyclopedia*, Vol. XI, pp. 472–6; Julius Guttmann in *Universal Jewish Encyclopedia*, Vol. IX, pp. 653–4; George Foot Moore, *Judaism*, Harvard University Press, Vol. II, Index, *s.v.* 'Soul', 1927, pp. 448–9; K. Kohler: *Jewish Theology*, New York, Macmillan, 1928, pp. 212 f.

19   T.B. *Sabb.* 152b.

20   *Siphrē, Deut.* 306.

21   *Midrash Qoheleth Rabbah*, on *Eccl.* 6: 6, ed. Wilna f. 17a, vol. ii.

22   T.B. *Ber.* 10a. Cf. Baḥya, 'Duties of the Heart', *Sha'ar Ha-Yiḥudh*, Chapter 10, ed. Warsaw, 1875, p. 87. English translation by M. Hyamson, New York, 1925, p. 51.

23   T.B. *Ta'an.* 11a–b.

24   *V*. Rashi *s.v. ke'ilu*, and *Tosaphoth*. The note of Samuel Edels (*Maharsha*) *ad loc.* is, of course, homiletical.

25   *V*. Isaac Husik: *A History of Mediaeval Jewish Philosophy*, Jewish Publication Society of America, Philadelphia, 1940, pp. xlv–xlvii. A good popular account of mediaeval thought on the soul is Ahad

Ha'am's essay on Maimonides entitled *Shilṭon Ha-Sekhel*, Collected Essays, Berlin, 1921, Vol. IV, pp. 2–11.

26 *Kether Malkhuth*, XXIX, trans. by Bernard Lewis, Vallentine, Mitchell, London, 1961, p. 49.

27 *V.* Hillel Zeitlin: *Maphteaḥ Le-sepher Ha-Zohar*, in *Ha-Tequphah*, Vol. IX, Warsaw, 1921, pp. 287 f., and I. Tishbi: *Mishnath Ha-Zohar*, Vol. II, Jerusalem, 1961, pp. 3–124.

28 *Zohar* II, 174a.

29 *V.* G. Scholem, *op. cit.* (note 11), p. 241 and notes.

30 *Op. cit., ibid.* Cf. R. J. Z. Werblowsky: 'Philo and the *Zohar*', *Journal of Jewish Studies*, Vol. X, 1959, pp. 38–9.

31 Ed. C. B. Chavel, Mosad Ha-Rav Kook, Jer. 1959, pp. 33–4.

32 This saying with reference to the divine origin of the soul and its identification with the divine is frequently quoted in the later literature in its semi-Aramaic form – *man de-naphaḥ mi-tokho naphaḥ*. Schneor Zalman of Liady in his *Tanya*, Wilna, ed. 1930, Chapter II, p. 11, quotes it as a saying of the *Zohar*, but there is no such passage in the *Zohar*. Chavel in his notes to this section of Naḥmanides (p. 33) gives the source as the *Sepher Ha-Qanah* but fails to give the reference.

33 Commentary to the Pentateuch, Amsterdam, 1726, f. 12b.

34 T.B. *Ber.* 10a. Cf. *supra*, pp. 92, 109, note 22.

35 Cf. A. Altmann: 'God and the Self in Jewish Mysticism' in *Judaism*, Vol. III, 1954, pp. 142–6 and the same author's 'The Delphic Maxim in Mediaeval Islam and Judaism' in *Biblical and other Studies*, ed. A. Altmann, Harvard University Press, 1963, pp. 196–232.

36 *Sepher Nishmath Ḥayyim*, Stettin, 1851.

37 *Ma'amar* I, f. 2b.

38 Sulzbach, 1758, Part I, *Sha'ar* 1, ff. 3a–4a.

39 Part III, *Sha'ar* 2 and 3, ff. 25b–29b.

40 Part III, *Sha'ar* 2, f. 27b.

41 *Genesis Rabbah*, 82, 6, ed. Theodor-Albeck, Berlin, 1913, Vol. 2, p. 983, ed. Wilna f. 154b, vol. ii.

42 On Cordovero *v.* my trans. with an introduction and notes of his *Palm Tree of Deborah*, London, Vallentine, Mitchell, 1960. On the Safed circle *v.* Solomon Schechter: *Studies in Judaism*, Second Series, Philadelphia, 1908, pp. 148–81. Cordovero's views on the soul are exceedingly complex. In his *'Elimah Rabbathi*, Brody, 1881, III, part 4, Chapter 62, p. 131, he states that the *neshamah* is the result of the 'copulation' of the 'Holy One, blessed be He' (=the *Sephirah 'Tiph'ereth'*) with the *Shekhinah* (=the *Sephirah 'Malkhuth'*) but this is further qualified to suggest an even 'higher' source for the soul. Elsewhere (*Pardes Rimmonim*, Koretz, 1786,

Sha'ar I, Chapter 7, f. 8a) he writes that souls are hewn out from under the Throne of Glory although they actually come from a 'higher' source. (On the medieval development of the 'Throne of Glory' as the *source* of the soul from the rabbinic notion of the 'Throne' as the soul's *destiny*, v. R. J. Z. Werblowsky, *op. cit.* (note 30), p. 39, note 75.) Cf. *Pardes, Sha'ar* VIII, Chapter 22, pp. 52a–53a and the whole of *Sha'ar* XXXI, pp. 162b f.

43 Amsterdam, 1717.

44 'The Gate of Love' (*Sha'ar Ha-'Ahabhah*), Chapter 3, pp. 67–9.

45 *Zohar* III, 68a.

46 Hanover, 1612, Frankfurt, 1719.

47 Introduction, par. 1.

48 So far as I have been able to discover Horowitz is the first author to use the verse in *Job* to denote the idea that the soul is a portion of God. In *Ḥabad* literature this quotation is very frequent.

49 These are the two lowest degrees of the soul; obviously the highest stage of *neshamah* is included as well.

50 I.e. *Pardes Rimmonim (op. cit.*, note 42).

51 Prague 1616, during the author's lifetime, and Jerusalem, 1850(?) (the only two editions of the book). I am grateful to Rabbi Solomon David Sassoon for calling this fascinating little book to my attention.

52 In Chapter 8, in the reply to his critics, Horowitz records a further objection to his theory which his colleagues had put to him (Prague ed., p. 12a). This is that if every Jewish soul is a part of God it must follow that God has numerous parts, and this is an even greater offence against pure Jewish monotheism than the Christian doctrine of the Trinity – 'for believers in the Trinity, even though they speak of the three, say at the same time that there is one', i.e. whereas in the author's view there allegedly are in actuality as many parts of God as there are Jewish souls. Horowitz replies by softening still further the boldness of his concept. (It should be noted that the cabbalists frequently have cause to defend their central notion of the *Sephiroth* against the charge of 'decatheism'. It is clear from their apologies that the charge was often made by their opponents in connection with the Christian doctrine, v. *Responsa* of R. Isaac b. Shesheth (*Ribash*), no. 157. Cf. M. H. Luzzatto's famous dialogue: '*Ḥoqeru-mequbbal*', ed. A. Abi-Oded, Jerusalem, Mosad Ha-Rav Kook, 1952, Part I, *init.*, p. 8. Cf. the distinction made by Leon de Modena between the doctrine of the *Sephiroth*, which are *attributes*, and that of the Trinity, which is comprised of *persons*, in his: '*Maghen Wa-ḥerebh*', ed. S. Simonsohn, Jerusalem, 1960, Part II, 1, p. 21.)

53 E.g. in *Tanya*, ed. Wilna, 1930, Part I, Chapter 1, pp. 10–11 and

Chapter V, p. 19. Cf. M. Teitelbaum: 'Ha-Rabh Mi-Ladi', Vol. 2, Warsaw, 1913, Chapter 6, pp. 127–33.

54   *Tanya*, Part I, Chapter 2, pp. 11 f.

55   T.B. *Ber*. 60b, where it is said that man on rising in the morning should say: 'My God, the soul (*neshamah*) which Thou hast placed in me is pure. Thou hast fashioned it in me, Thou didst breathe it into me, and Thou preservest it within me and Thou wilt one day take it from me and restore it to me in time to come. So long as the soul is within me I give thanks unto Thee, O Lord, my God, and the God of my fathers, Sovereign of all worlds, Lord of all souls. Blessed art Thou, O Lord, who restorest souls to dead corpses.' This declaration was adapted as part of the morning service, *v.* Singer's *Authorised Daily Prayer Book*, p. 5, new ed. p. 6. *V*. Baer's note (*Siddur 'Abhodath Yisra'el*, Rödelheim, 1868, p. 39) to the effect that one should pause after the words 'My God' in order to avoid the suggestion that the soul is God! David Abudarham (14th century) in his commentary to the Prayer Book, Lisbon, 1489, Jerusalem, 1959, p. 39, had made the same point centuries before Baer.

56   Actually there is no such passage in the *Zohar*, *v. supra*, note 32.

57   I.e. the semen is drawn from the brain.

58   *V*. Schneor Zalman's *Liqquṭe Torah, Genesis*, Wilna, 1884, p. 2, where he remarks that in 'external' contemplation the thought in the mind is that God created the world out of nothing – the world is *yesh* and is created out of *'ayin*. This leads to 'inner' contemplation, in which the thought is reversed – God is the true *yesh* and He created the world which is really *'ayin*. Cf. *Liqquṭe Torah, Deuteronomy*, Wilna, 1878, *Shir*, p. 64, *Tanya*, *'Iggereth Ha-Qodesh*, 20, p. 258, and H. J. Bunim's *'Mishnēh Ḥabad'*, Warsaw, 1936, Chapter IV, pp. 104–35. In *Liqquṭe Torah, Gen.*, p. 98, Schneor Zalman writes: 'The many waters of concern regarding one's livelihood and of worldly thoughts cannot quench the love that is in the category of hidden love in the soul of every Jew by nature. This is the category of the divine soul whose nature it is to ascend and be consumed upwards as the flame flies upwards of its own accord.' Cf. *Liqquṭe Torah, Numbers*, Zhitomer, 1866, p. 59 and p. 89. A vivid account of the origin of the divine soul is given in *Tanya*, *'Iggereth Ha-Teshubhah*, Chapters 4 and 5, pp. 186–90. Horowitz, as we have seen, denies that he had ever said that the soul is a portion of *'Eyn Soph*; but here (though he does not actually go so far as to say that the soul is a portion of *'Eyn Soph*) Schneor Zalman speaks, none the less, of 'the soul of man which derives directly from the category of the inner vitality and influence which *'Eyn Soph*, blessed be He, pours out' (p. 187). The divine soul is situated in the brain whence it is diffused through the rest of the body, *Tanya*, Part I, Chapter IX, pp. 26 f.

In *Liqquṭē Torah, Deut.*, pp. 75–6, there occurs Schneor Zalman's homily to *Deut.* 21: 15 concerning the man who has two wives. The 'two wives' are man's two souls, the 'divine' and the 'natural'. These are rivals and they engage in war, particularly at the time of prayer when the divine soul yearns for God and the natural soul seeks distraction in worldly thoughts. If man emerges victorious from the struggle, the first-born 'child' is that of the 'hated wife', i.e. the love and fear of God which stem from the struggle within are far greater than they could have been were it not for the opposition of the natural soul and the need for the divine soul to fight temptation. The love and fear are far more powerful when the natural soul is also coerced into loving God and fearing Him. On the doctrine of the two souls in *Ḥabad* cf. the elaborate homily of Menahem Mendel of Lubavitch, the third leader of *Ḥabad* and Schneor Zalman's grandson, in his *Derekh Miṣwotheykha*, Poltava, 1911, 'On the Command to be fruitful and multiply', pp. 1–8.

59   G. Van der Leeuw: *Religion in Essence and Manifestation*, London, George Allen and Unwin, 1938, Chapter 43, pp. 299–307.

60   *Tao-teh King*, 11, quoted by Van der Leeuw, *loc. cit.* On this theme in the mystic life *v.* Evelyn Underhill, *op. cit.* (note 2), pp. 347 f., who quotes the following from Rumi's *Divan* (quoted, too, by Nicholson, *op. cit.*, note 7, p. 116):

> *This is Love; to fly heaven-ward,*
> *To rend, every instant, a hundred veils.*
> *The first moment, to renounce life;*
> *The last step, to fare without feet.*
> *To regard this world as invisible,*
> *Not to see what appears to oneself.*

61   Wilna and Grodno, 1824.

62   *Nephesh Ha-ḥayyim*, Gate I, Chapters 15–16, pp. 13 f. Another non-hasidic nineteenth-century author who accepts (without qualification) the doctrine of the divine spark is Israel Lipschütz (1782–1860) in his homily, *Derush 'Or Ha-ḥayyim*, printed at the end of Vol. IV of his famous Commentary to the Mishnah, the *Tiph'ereth Yisra'el*, Wilna, 1911, pp. 279 f. Lipschütz gives the rather crude illustration of a balloon which receives its shape from the breath of the man who blows it up. Cf. his curious observation, in his Commentary to *'Abhoth*, f. 264b, that only Jews possess this divine spark, and this is the real reason for the so-called 'Jewish' appearance: since the face is the soul's window.

63   See my English translation of the *Tract on Ecstasy*, with an Introduction and notes, Vallentine, Mitchell, London, 1963. The best

Hebrew text is the rare Warsaw ed., 1868, with notes by the author's pupil, Hillel ben Me'ir of Poritch.

64 For similar descriptions of mystical prayer v. F. Heiler: *Prayer*, trans. and ed. by Samuel McComb with the assistance of J. Edgar Park, London, Oxford University Press, 1958, pp. 190–1.

6

Potentialities and Limitations
of Universalism in
the *Halakhah*

RAPHAEL LOEWE

It is but a truism to observe that universalistic thinking in the
Hebrew Bible stands in constant tension with Israel's preoccupation with itself, and that the explicitly universalist matter
is, quantitatively speaking, slight. Its paucity does not necessarily
impugn its significance, an awareness of which was writ large
on the mind of Leon Roth. As regards post-biblical Judaism and
its treatment of the Bible, Roth perceived – and helped others to
perceive – how Jewish exegesis can sometimes take what seems
an unpromising text, and deftly read into it a universalist moral
that arrests attention and compels assent.[1] 'I do call to witness
heaven and earth that whether one be Gentile or Israelite, man
or woman, slave or handmaid, the Holy Spirit will rest upon each
in accordance with his own deeds.' That such a sentiment should
emanate from a rabbinical source[2] may be a matter of satisfaction to Jewish apologists; and for those of us who would claim, or
at least endeavour, to eschew apologetics it may be a matter
worthy at least of attention. But the significance of the remark
for the purposes of the present discussion lies, as it seems to me,

in the subtlety of its exegetical framework. An occasion for the unqualified assertion that the divine gift of prophecy is available to all who merit it has been discovered in the bald scriptural description of Deborah as 'a woman, a prophetess' (*Judges* 4: 4) and as 'the wife of Lapidoth' – Lapidoth, according to the rabbinical source, having been a mere boor who was induced by his wife to make wicks for the sanctuary lights, and thus come to rub shoulders with folk whose piety might prove an inspiration to him. It is therefore not unfitting that the present survey of the halakhic potentialities and limitations of universalism should be offered as a tribute to Leon Roth's memory, since it is to his perceptiveness as a student of rabbinic texts such as the foregoing that many of us owe an enhanced understanding of what I may term the 'ethical syntax' of Jewish scriptural exegesis.

For the rabbis, the universalism of the Hebrew Bible is contrapuntal, the main theme being domestic. The pattern is determined by Jewish conviction that the Bible is addressed to Israel and communicates sundry matters arising directly out of God's will, for the implementation of which Israel consequently carries a peculiar responsibility. The psalmist, aware of God's providential care for His creation, could praise Him for 'showing His word to Jacob, His statutes and judgments to Israel', whilst being in no doubt at all that 'He hath not dealt so with any other nation, and as for His judgments, they have not known them' (*Ps.* 147: 19–20). The essential fabric of the rabbis' biblical exegesis is consequently an attempt to carry out, in Jewish institutional life, certain matters adumbrated in Scripture or suggested by intimate familiarity with it; and thus the Talmud takes its place alongside Plato's *Republic* as a search for the ideal constitution, with the difference that the rabbinic blueprint can never be but an academic exercise – 'thou shalt observe *and do* these statutes' (*Deut.* 16: 12).

This Jewish conviction of a special vocation, and of the particular relevance of the Bible to Israel alone, might prompt the conclusion that universalist sentiment of the kind cited above is but peripheral, and that it cannot go beyond pious platitude;

there being, supposedly, no room for any practical application of such an outlook when it comes to the positive ordinances (and their negative corollaries) within the framework of institutional Judaism. Universalism, it might be contended, is innocuous – and indeed to be applauded – when restricted to the sphere of *'Aggadha*, i.e. of edificatory legend, etc., embroidered round the Bible: but if it intrudes into the sphere of *Halakhah* – the legal and institutional component of Judaism as based on the Pentateuch, its exegetical cocoon, and the codes of the jurists – universalism is an irrelevant, alien, and possibly even an insidious force. If considered from the viewpoint of a phenomenologist, there is certainly enough social exclusiveness about Jewish institutional existence to give such an assertion some plausibility: and it might be a matter of some importance to show whether it is an accurate presentation of all the relevant facts, or but an over-simplification.

We shall best begin by defining *Halakhah* a little more closely. Its world is one of down-to-earth practicalities in which decisions are required that shall be simultaneously feasible socially, defensible jurisprudentially, and maintainable ethically. And yet the rabbinic sources that handle halakhic matters such as criminal law occasionally raise issues that must strike the modern reader as being not realistic ones, and of academic interest only. Probably the best known example is the inclusion in the mishnaic tractate *Sanhedrin* (which deals with criminal and constitutional law) of a discussion concerning qualifications for and disqualification from the future life.[3] The practical administration of the World to Come is not a responsibility with which, at any rate in their terrestrial life, the rabbis were charged, and we may be tempted to ask why they dealt with the problem where they did. Is the discussion, in fact, a halakhic matter at all, or rather a piece of *'Aggadha* – edificatory lore, allegedly without any binding force as dogma – that has been allowed to stray into an halakhic context for the sake of literary variety? It would seem that it is correctly classified as *Halakhah*, inasmuch as it deals with a matter of stark reality, and of fundamental concern, to those circles from which the Mishnah emanates – a matter the burning importance of which would have been appreciated readily enough by the generation for which Marlowe's *Faustus* was written, even though it is difficult for the modern student to grasp. The rabbis consequently felt called upon to thrash the matter out and to determine an 'official' ruling on the subject, even though few practical consequences patient of implementation might flow from it. The situation is analogous to the rabbinic attitude towards those delinquents for whose offences the penalty was in Jewish law not within the competence of a rabbinical court, but was reserved to heavenly judgment. Since to ignore such cases entirely might give the impression of condoning them, the rabbis signalised their disapproval by stating that the offenders were liable to scourging.[4] The sensitivity, then, of the rabbis and of their early public to the issues involved may justify us in using their treatment of 'academic' matters like the eligibility for resurrection, as evidence of the scope allowed to universalistic thinking in the sphere of *Halakhah*: and *Halakhah* will consequently be defined, for present purposes, as the rabbinic control of practical matters concerning the individual and society, and the rabbinic treatment of other matters which have no obvious practical aspects or consequences, but which have, notwithstanding, been considered to be matters of vital concern to the Jewish people as a corporate entity.

The universalistic presuppositions of the Hebrew Bible are clearly enunciated in the schematic history of the Pentateuch and also in a few shorter texts, e.g. *Psalm* 78. The divine plan unfolds itself in a series of covenants, either explicit or implicit, established with or imposed upon a series of contracting concentric circles: beginning with the cosmos (cf. *Jer.* 33: 25), and proceeding *via* Noah (i.e. humanity in general) through Abraham, to Israel. Within the 'Israel' circle fall two others, not concentrically arranged, *viz.* the covenant with the Aaronic priesthood and that with the Davidic dynasty. These, however, are not to be regarded as a further restriction of the human contracting party, in view of the markedness in Israel of the psychological phenomenon sometimes described as oscillation between individual and group personality. Granted ideal conditions of inner harmony and mutually complementing cohesiveness, Israel is capable of becoming an entire 'kingdom of priests' (*Ex.* 14: 6). And possibly a rabbinic homily (occurring, however, in a non-halakhic context)[5] hints that the process need not be halted at that point, and implies something like a theology of a continually expanding universe. Using recognised hermeneutical methods, the comment forges a link between the Deity's self-assertive use of the first person in *Isa.* 46: 4 – '*I* am he – 'tis *I* have made, *I* will carry, *I* will bear and deliver' – and the exordium to the Decalogue – '*I* am the Lord thy God' (*Ex.* 20: 2). A syncopated world-history is then set forth: God, who had *made* mankind, had to *bear* with the failure, first of Adam, and then of Noah's descendants at Babel, and in each case He rejected them; but He *delivered* Abraham, and so Israel, only to be confronted by failure on Israel's part in the sin of the Golden Calf – traditionally Israel's darkest hour: and yet, God was Himself constrained by Moses' plea (*Num.* 14: 18 f.) to deliver Israel by extending to them His forgiveness. The passage occurs as a comment on the Ten Commandments, and it is of course possible to construe it as finding its climax in the circumstance that it is Israel alone that is privileged to be granted the divine pardon. But, as the commentator David Luria points out, integral to the homilist's argument is the forbearance by which God refrained from utterly exterminating the men of Babel, although their fault merited annihilation. It may, therefore, be a shade too facile to read the comment as but a blunt assertion to the effect that *extra ecclesiam nulla salus*. We may consequently take the risk of being too subtle instead. Perhaps what the homilist saw in Israel's acceptance of the Ten Commandments, and in their response to the "*I*" which introduces (and may symbolise) them, was rather a redemptive act, of ecumenical significance. All post-Sinaitic generations of Israel are deemed to have shared the spiritual experience of those who stood beneath the mountain to receive the Torah; and analogously, the figures of Adam, Noah, and the builders of the Tower of Babel must typify and subsume all their future descendants (here, of course, excluding Israel itself). The letter *'aleph*, therefore, the initial letter of *'Anokhi* = *I* (which comes often to symbolise in itself the entire Decalogue), is here being as it were superimposed on to the three concentric circles that correspond respectively to Israel/Abraham, the men of Babel/Noah, and Adam: and in virtue of its superimposition it may be thought to effect, theologically, the organic unity and ultimate coherence of the whole pattern.

But the history of salvation concerns us in so far only as it can be shown to be reflected in halakhic thinking, and we must therefore begin by enquiring whether any patterns parallel to those in the foregoing homily occur in *Halakhah* at all. Does the 'political philosophy' of the juridical authorities, as embodied in the codes, reflect anything of the sort, and do their rulings on specific cases that were brought before them ever argue an outlook that reaches beyond Jewry? It is, of course, a fallacy to speak of "the" *Halakhah*, *tout court*. Halakhic Judaism is a process of growth, development, and endeavour to keep social changes under control; and if we wish to trace out its treatment of universalism, we shall not have fulfilled the requirements of scholarship until we have reconstructed the picture as it appeared in successive historical periods and environmental settings, whilst maintaining a carefully disciplined methodology such as that exemplified in the pioneer study of Dr Jacob Katz.[6] Space precludes so elaborate an investigation on this occasion, and any generalisations which are here made are therefore to be regarded as tentative only. That some cautious generalisation is nevertheless in order seems to be suggested by the following circumstance. The main period of Jewish code-making (if we exclude the Bible) comprises some 1500 years, from the last decades of the Temple, destroyed in 70 C.E., to Joseph Caro's *Shulḥan 'Arukh*. The latter was completed, but not published, in 1555 – the very year in which Paul IV's Bull, *cum nimis absurdum*, radically circumscribed Jewish activity and imposed containment within the Ghetto. Between these two *termini* sociological conditions to some extent forced upon Jews the obligation to consider the implications of their own contacts with Gentiles, whether these were in any given case relatively free and easy or were restricted to an essential minimum. Whichever was the case, Jews – or at any rate some Jews – could not easily, or with intellectual integrity, evade their own confrontation by gentile society in general; or, more precisely, confrontation by the basic social presuppositions of imperial Rome, Christianity, and Islam, as each of these were meaningful (albeit in an elementary or oversimplified way) to the broad masses of their respective adherents. Later Jewish-Gentile confrontation, which begins in any demographically or statistically significant sense with the French Revolution, may here be ignored. For although opportunities for interaction have almost certainly been greater in this period than in any earlier one, and although several social philosophers of primary significance in the modern west have themselves been Jews, the latter have owed little or nothing to Jewish speculative thinking; it was the popular ethic of the Jewish proletariat that influenced them, whether positively or negatively. On the other hand, halakhically conscious Jewry has been content in the modern age to tinker with the problem of Jewish-Gentile confrontation where it could not completely ignore it; it has shirked any comprehensive re-examination of the basic issues. Such Jewish thinkers as have, during the last century or more, essayed a philosophy of Judaism or of Jewry, have not chosen the idiom of *Halakhah* for their approach (including even Krochmal), but in most cases the idiom of Jewish national self-identification in modern political terms; and they, for the most part, have either tacitly assumed, or else have emphatically insisted, that the issues raised by Jewish-Gentile confrontation are but phantoms – at most accidental and insignificant issues, which will disappear with the solution of the so-called Jewish problem and the so-called normalisation of the Jewish people.

It is, effectively, questions regarding status which will require the halakhist to orientate his views regarding Judaism, Jewry, and the gentile world – questions, that is, of establishing the personal status of given individuals; questions regarding the feasibility, desirability, or dangers of recognising sundry changes of status; and questions of authorisation of such contacts as might lead to the blurring, or even the *de facto* frustration, of the distinctions between classes postulated by the *Halakhah*. What those classes are may best be set forth diagrammatically, after which the composition of each, and its relation to its neighbours, may be considered. In the interests of clarity, two classes known to the *Halakhah* are here ignored, *viz. women*, and *Jewish slaves*: the former because, for present purposes, sex distinctions are not significant save for priestly marriages, which we shall touch upon, and the latter because the slavery of a Jew to a fellow-Jew is not, or need not be, other than a temporary status in *Halakhah*, analogous to that of minority.

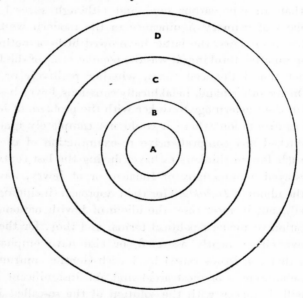

A Priesthood, of Aaronic genealogy
B Israel
C 'Descendants of Noah'
D Mankind – described variously as 'creatures' (*beriyyoth*), 'those who come into the world' (*ba'ey 'olam*), 'the sons of man' (*beney 'adham*), 'nations' (i.e. gentiles, *goyim*), 'strangers' (*nokhrim*), 'idolaters' (*'obhedhey 'abhodhah zarah, 'obhedhey gelilim, 'obhedhey kokhabhim u-mazzaloth*, commonly abbreviated to *'akkum*)

We shall find it instructive to begin by examining the situation as it obtains between *A*, those of priestly genealogy, and *B*, the main body of Israel. 'Priesthood', in other words, is to be understood in the particular sense of membership of the stock which furnished the hierarchy in temple times; and the *Halakhah* is concerned not merely to preserve that stock from any indelible compromise, but probably also to see to it that male Jews of authentic Aaronic descent shall be available, and fit, to resume their functions in the restored Temple of the messianic era.[8] Now although priests' daughters have at all times freely intermarried within the main body of Jewry, biblical law places certain restrictions upon the matrimonial choice open to a male descendant of Aaron: and rabbinic jurisprudence had to take account of cases of priests choosing to defy these biblical limitations. The offender himself forfeits neither his status nor his priestly privileges, but the issue of such disapproved unions is classified as 'desecrated' (*ḥalal*), and in turn passes on that status, irremediably so in the male line. A daughter of a *ḥalal*, however, if she marries a Jew of non-priestly descent, could herself produce a daughter nubile to an Aaronic descendant whose own priestly status was intact; and thus the great-grandson, in the female line, of the original delinquent party may recover his ancestor's privileges and status. Whereas in temple times priestly privileges carried substantial emoluments in kind, with the destruction of the Temple these virtually disappeared at once, and in the Synagogue Aaronic descent has since been distinguished by certain courtesies of rank only, together with the residual right and duty to pronounce the priestly benediction. It will be obvious that these residual privileges are too tenuous to exercise much counterpoise to the strong temptations to those of priestly stock to disregard the matrimonial restrictions which put them at a disadvantage compared with their fellow-Jews. Inevitably, there have been many occasions when the Synagogue has been under pressure, from individuals or from groups, to abandon the position of pentateuchal law in the matter and to countenance, as being legally acceptable, some or all of the marriages which the Bible prohibits to the priesthood. Yet traditional Judaism has made no attempt to find a casuistic means of legitimising such proposed unions halakhically – indeed, since a negative commandment is involved, it is doubtful if such casuistic argument would be feasible. While reform Judaism has felt able to jettison all Aaronic privilege and its corollary obligations, traditional Judaism has insisted that these, as being status-linked, are inalienable. The *Halakhah* will therefore neither promote nor countenance their voluntary surrender, nor will it condone their being ignored, disdained, or repudiated by those genealogically affected by them.

The same considerations govern the halakhic view of the line dividing circle *B*, Israel in general, from *C* – the so-called Descendants of Noah, to whom we shall revert below (pp. 125 f.) and who form a category intermediate between Israel and circle *D*, or mankind at large. We have here a tripartite arrangement, the (albeit inexact) analogy of which to the Roman jurisprudential concept of *ius civile* and *ius gentium*, as these were influenced by the Aristotelian and Stoic notion of *ius naturale*, has been remarked since the time of Selden and Grotius.[9] The *Halakhah* disposes of various administrative sanctions for penalising the Jew who sees fit to defy its requirements. It has no power to 'expel' the recalcitrant from the Jewish community; but its powers include, *in extremis*, a ban of excommunication which can ensure his complete social ostracism by the Jewish community, both in life and in death, should he die without prior submission or retraction. Lack of Jewish executive power may sometimes frustrate halakhic control of a situation in which a Jew chooses to defy or ignore the rabbinical courts. But the *Halakhah* cannot compromise over the principle that, as a matter of personal status, Jewishness is an inalienable affair, not patient of being abdicated at will – equally so whether it is derived through birth, or through a conversion effected by a competent Jewish authority. 'Escape' from circle *B* to *C* is not legally recognisable: and indeed, should circumstantial evidence raise the presumption that an individual who regards himself as a Gentile is, in point of fact, of authentic Jewish ancestry, a rabbinical court may feel obliged to investigate the facts, should the person concerned happen to come before it. Movement inwards, however, from C to B is possible by conversion, similarly to the movement inwards from B (Israel) to A (the priesthood) of wives of the priests and their resultant offspring. A non-Jew seeking to become a Jew, i.e. to secure from a duly constituted rabbinical authority the formal conferment of Jewish status, will have to convince that authority of his acceptance of certain elementary dogmatic propositions and of his preparedness to observe the institutions, both positive and negative, of Judaism: or, at the very least, he must so conduct himself as to give rise to the inference that such propositions are accepted by him. In addition, certain ritual formalities are requisite. The degree of responsiveness that a would-be proselyte will evoke from a rabbinical court is, in the nature of things, an inconstant reaction, determined by psychological and other factors. Acceptance, however, once it has been formally accorded, cannot with propriety be withdrawn, any more than recognition can ever be withheld of the Jewishness of those who possess it by right of birth.

It is, in effect, around the question of the frontier dividing circle C – the so-called Descendants of Noah – from circle D – the remainder of gentile humanity – that the problem central to this essay revolves. Let us therefore proceed further by indicating, in summary form, the assumptions underlying the postulation by the rabbis of such a category as Noachides and the social function of distinguishing its membership as forming a class of their own. This will lead us to the consideration of the various terms by which the remainder of gentile humanity is collectively described; and thereafter to enquire whether the *Halakhah* ever exhibits any theoretical tendency towards a notional expansion – either of the Noachides themselves, so as to embrace a larger segment of humanity, or even perhaps on the part of Israel, as an encroachment upon the Noachides as forming its nearest gentile 'cocoon'.

The recognition in the Descendants of Noah of an entity with its own social and legal dimensions rests upon rabbinic presuppositions that reach beyond the flood to Adam himself, whose capacity for response to God's address to him is taken for granted in *Genesis*, and is not regarded by the rabbis as having been invalidated or compromised by his sin. Into the words of *Gen.* 2: 16 – 'the Lord God commanded the man' – they read a picture which makes Adam the recipient of five specific prohibitions not mentioned in the text, directed respectively against idolatry, blasphemy, murder, unchastity (as defined slightly less rigorously than in the code applicable to Jews),[10] and robbery; and also of a sixth, positive command, namely to establish courts of justice. They moreover envisaged these six injunctions as having been divinely promulgated afresh after the flood, with the addition of a seventh, allegedly discoverable within the terms of *Gen.* 9: 4 – *viz.* the prohibition of consumption of flesh taken from a living animal. These together make up the 'Seven Commandments of the Sons of Noah'[11]; but the source material contains variant items, such as the prohibition of sorcery, of the emasculation of animals, and of cross-breeding, and one passage[12] actually refers to as many as thirty laws (deducible from the seven general categories mentioned) without, however, specifying them. It is possible that as early as talmudic times some advantage was sensed in leaving the list imprecisely identified, in that it might, in such a state, afford the basis for a rudimentary Jewish social theory of the non-Jewish world. At the very least, it can be shown that the relationship of the post-diluvian code to the Sinaitic one, i.e. the question of any continuing obligations still incumbent upon Noachides after Israel's own receipt of a more elaborate legal system, was a matter of concern to some talmudic rabbis.[13] And such a concern may suggest that they felt some obligation to reach out, even if incoherently, towards a social theory into which they might fit, tentatively at least, that portion of the gentile world with which they were, *de facto*, in some positive contact. The rabbis consequently sketched out some elements of a criminal law as supposedly applicable to Noachides – in part as theoretically to be adopted by them in their own non-Jewish courts of law and being, broadly speaking, more lenient than the Jewish criminal law; and in part as relative to their standing before rabbinical courts, where they were deemed to be entitled to fewer safeguards of procedure than were available to protect the interest of a Jewish accused party, but were on the other hand not exposed to many of the detailed charges that a Jew might be called upon to answer.

'The Descendants of Noah', then, is a formula for a positive, if indeed a guardedly positive attitude on the part of Judaism towards the remainder of mankind. A natural conclusion might be that the other terms by which the non-Jewish world is referred to in rabbinic Hebrew represent the reverse side of the coin. We may therefore examine their usage, and consider whether the attitude that they reflect is invariably negative. There are, I fancy, seven expressions, falling into two main groups; I describe the first of these (a) as *comprehensive* terms (nos. 1–4), and the second (b) as *exclusive* terms. The latter breaks down into two sub-groups, (i) comprising *neutral* terms (nos. 5–6), and (ii) a *disparaging* term (no. 7).

(a) Comprehensive terms

1 *Beney 'Adham* (Sons of man) may be quickly disposed of. In early rabbinic and medieval Hebrew it is used quite generally ('people', 'the man in the street'), mostly with reference to social habit, and indiscriminately applied to Jews and non-Jews. In a few talmudic passages, indeed, it must mean specifically Jews, the social setting being taken for granted.[14]

2 *Basar wa-dham* (Flesh and blood) merely contrasts humanity, in all its frailty or pusillanimous inconstancy, with the invariable reliability of God. It is not a halakhic term and need not concern us further.

3 *Beriyyoth* (Creatures) is most frequently used, like *beney 'adham*, of mankind in general – the average man.[15] The universalistic potentialities of this term are underscored by the circumstance that rabbinic texts make God speak of 'My creatures', and it is used, correspondingly, to distinguish humanity from Deity.[16] 'The honour of creatures' corresponds, in rabbinic parlance, to human dignity,[17] and *beriyyoth* is in most cases of

general reference – Jewry being, by implication, subsumed in it.
It is sometimes, however, contrasted to Israel, as e.g. in the
variation of formula for blessing at the sight of Jewish and gentile
scholars respectively,[18] while to make a proselyte is described as
'introducing a *biryah* beneath the wings of the divine Presence.'[19] The term is, however, non-halakhic.

4 *Kol Ba'ey 'Olam* (All who come into the world). This expression, although not particularly common, is possibly of some
significance. It seems to occur predominantly in tannaitic
literature, i.e. prior to *c.* 200 C.E., especially in the *Siphrē*.[20] In
some cases[21] the context is general and tells us little. In others,
although all mankind is intended, the emphasis is on the gentile
world.[22] Of some importance, as it seems to me, are the passages
where the context does, indeed, evince a consciousness of the
actuality of the distinction between Jew and Gentile, but nevertheless claims (or implies) that a responsiveness to God's approach
to man is, in principle, to be expected from both. Thus Rabbi
Simeon b. Yoḥai, commenting on *Ps.* 50: 7, 'I am God, even thy
God', paraphrases thus: 'God am I over all who come into the
world, but nevertheless I have uniquely associated My Name
(*yiḥadti shemi*) with My people Israel alone.'[23] Again, we have
the mishnaic statement[24] that the world is 'judged' on four
annual occasions, three of which relate to the water supply and
agricultural prospects; on the fourth one, i.e. 1st Tishri commonly
regarded as the Jewish New Year's Day, 'all those who come into
the world pass before Him [in review] like a military unit.'[25]
The picture, to the modern reader but a mythological conceit,
was and is a matter of stark enough realism to those to whom the
idiom of myth was, or is still, a natural idiom. This assertion may
hold, in spite of the demurrer advanced already in the Talmud
itself[26] to the effect that man is judged every day, indeed every
minute. It is therefore, perhaps, legitimate to assess the myth of
an annual, universal judgment as bearing a significance parallel
to halakhic decisions on the 'unrealistic' question of qualification
for the resurrection (see *supra*, p. 117). It should further be noted
that the term *ba'ey 'olam* was still being used in halakhic
contexts by Maimonides (see *infra*, p. 136).

(b) *Exclusive terms*

   (i) *neutral*

5   *Goyim* (Nations). Little need be said here. The biblical Hebrew *goi* = nation is a colourless term, used frequently of Israel as well as of gentile peoples. From the plural *goyim* = [totality of gentile] nations, rabbinic Hebrew has reminted the singular, so that *goi* means an individual gentile and *goyim* the totality of gentiles *qua individuals*. For the concept of peoplehood post-biblical Hebrew employs *'ummah*, plural *'ummoth* (see *infra*, no. 6.). It is to be emphasised that *goi*, in its new meaning, is still essentially a neutral term of differentiation, unlike no. 7; so that any pejorative overtones with which it has come to be infected are accidental ones.

   The term *nokhri*, stranger, does not call for separate examination and may be regarded as a synonym of *goi*.

6   *'Ummoth ha-'olam* (The peoples of the world). This term indicates the gentile world, as a collectivity, in its confrontation of and by Jewry; and the foregoing observation regarding *goi* is likewise applicable here. Estimates of the *'Ummoth ha-'olam* are frequently unfavourable, but favourable ones are occasionally found. Unlike *goi*, however, which is a frequent halakhic term, *'ummoth ha-'olam* is infrequent in halakhic contexts. One passage only calls for notice, because it may throw into relief a rabbinic understanding of the circumstance that Jewish-gentile confrontation has to be envisaged, halakhically, on two different levels. The text,[27] which is itself a non-halakhic excursus, deals with the penultimate stage of world history when, it is declared, the nations of the world will be so attracted by the flowering of Israel's fortunes that they will declare themselves to be proselytes – only to become disaffected and relapse at the onset of the eschatological war.[28] The narrative is interrupted with an halakhic objection, to the effect that there is a long-standing principle that 'in messianic times, as in the times of David and Solomon, proselytes will not be received into Judaism'; and the apparent contradiction is resolved by the explanation that the nations will be merely self-declared proselytes, adopting the

practical institutions of Judaism but not being officially recognised as proselytes. It would seem that this picture is the result of a not very satisfactory harmonisation of two different sets of convictions, relative to individual and collective confrontation respectively. Jewry is ready, where it is essential, to meet the individual Gentile positively, and it can, where appropriate, accord him acceptance as a proselyte. Within the framework of historical time, to face the collective gentile world in the same manner is held to be impracticable – perhaps, indeed, undesirable – and certainly unnecessary. It is nevertheless recognised that the tinkering methods of individual proselytisation will not fit the conditions of the messianic age, which for Judaism falls within terrestrial time, albeit at its culmination. In other words, a messianic solution of the 'gentile problem' will be forthcoming – either eliminating the Gentiles or absorbing them. If the latter is the case, absorption will be on lines different from those appropriate under current, historical conditions, where positive confrontation will never, on the gentile side, develop into an appreciation of Judaism by the non-Jewish masses so positive as to induce them to adopt it themselves. Indeed, one (non-halakhic) source makes God declare (on the basis of *Zephaniah* 3: 9) that in the world to come it will be He himself – and not the righteous of Israel, as in this world – who will effect proselytisation of Gentiles.[29]

(ii) *Disparaging*

7 *'Obhedhey 'Abhodhah Zarah* and variant expressions (Worshippers of a strange cult, of images, of the constellations). These terms are extremely common in halakhic texts, but can be dealt with summarily. The opprobrium in which Judaism holds idolatry and everything connected therewith inevitably colours the view taken of those who, as a general class, are deemed to subscribe to it or to condone it. Since the term cannot be neutral, wherever Jewish thinkers have for mercantile, social, apologetic, or philosophical reasons found it an embarrassment, their answer has been not to attempt to water its meaning down, but to circumvent it altogether (see *infra*, pp. 138 f.).

We may sum up these seven descriptive titles applied to non-

Jewish humanity as follows. The commonest (nos. 5, 6, 7) emphasise the barriers between Jew and Gentile; but of these no. 6, *'ummoth ha-'olam*, is more conscious that such barriers are an historical accident, in that there is (or may be) common to Jew and Gentile alike some element of potential response to the divine challenge. The recognition of the existence of an area of common religious experience is conveyed more pointedly by nos. 1, 2, 3, and 4; but in view of the natural tendency of everyone to think primarily in terms of his own environment, these four titles may sometimes unconsciously substitute the microcosm of Jewry for mankind in general – the 'man in the street' being unthinkingly identified with 'the Jew in the street'.

Having now reached the outermost circle, we may retrace our steps and ask just how sharp the inner dividing lines were for the Jewish jurists. Could they entertain the notion that the fringes of circle B (Israel) might overlap into the gentile world, instead of being tidily circumscribed? And what were their views regarding a possible expansiveness of C (the Descendants of Noah) at the expense of D ('outer' humanity)? And in considering these questions, we had best safeguard ourselves against taking a wrong turning at the outset. By and large, the rabbis' practical assumptions regarding Gentiles reflect a low estimate of their moral standards: indeed, there often seems to be a tacit assumption that they have none, and this despite the theory of the seven commandments incumbent upon Noachides (see *supra*, pp. 125 f. and *infra*, pp. 137 f.). There are clearly jurisprudential advantages in assuming that the only alternative to one's own ethico-legal religious system is social anarchy; the involvement of members of one's own community with outsiders, in matters for which they would be answerable to the law of the community itself (e.g. adultery), may be more easily dealt with (or, if desirable, by-passed), where it is presumed that the alien party is activated purely by personal interest, and has no moral norms of his own by which his delinquency can be measured. It scarcely needs stating that the above thesis is not consistently pursued to its logical conclusion. Quite apart from the positive theory of the Noachides' obligations (however much Noachides might in fact neglect them, see *infra*, p. 137), the relationship of certain rabbis with Gentiles – e.g. that of Judah the Patriarch to 'Antoninus' – could not have developed on the basis of an entirely negative attitude of the Jew to the ethics of the other party. Since, however, the predominant attitude of much of the older source-material is pragmatically negative, one might be tempted to conclude that when, occasionally, we do find evidence of a greater openness on the Jewish side towards *rapprochement*, it reflects an improvement in the moral climate of the environment. At the most, such putative improvements constitute a secondary cause; the primary one derives, as we shall see, from domestic needs and considerations of the Jewish community itself. When the rabbis generalised about gentile ethical standards they expressed themselves not as moralists but as lawyers; and lawyers will discharge their tasks the more effectively if they assume that they are dealing not with saints, but with people whose personal interests can easily persuade them to stoop to actions beneath their own better selves. The rabbis' attitude to the *'am ha-'areṣ*, or member of the non-pharisaic proletariat within Jewry, is not dissimilar from their estimate of gentile morality[30]: his standards – sexual and otherwise – are reputedly such that close contact with him is, if at all possible, to be avoided. And although it is certainly true that the rabbis, rightly or wrongly, presuppose the prevalence of a higher ethical standard and sexual morality amongst their own followers, it is nevertheless the case that, in their casuistry, they show themselves aware enough that the average halakhically-conforming Jew is not to be unrealistically credited with a high-mindedness such as to render all pernicketiness on the rabbis' own part superfluous.

A universalistically-minded halakhist is limited in his scope by his own axioms. To accept the notion of the divine choice of Israel, and of Israel's corollary obligations, carries with it certain consequences of ethnic demarcation between Jew and non-Jew. There may be room for debate as to the exact social implications of such demarcation; but about the propriety of ethnical separation itself there can be no argument, unless the terms *Israel* and

Jew – for rabbinic purposes of course synonymous – are to be redefined. Redefinition was the Pauline answer, endorsed by the Church and rejected by the Synagogue as misconceived. Moreover, on the ideological level, Judaism hinges round the distinction between the recognition of God and the acknowledgment of false gods, and round the superiority – inherent and consequential – of those who, like Abraham, 'recognise their Creator' over those who, as idolaters, do not. Any Jewish theoretical basis for a more positive appreciation of the gentile world must circumnavigate this rock, and it will in effect have to avoid a *de facto* compromise of its own principles, by redefining not Jews or Israel, but the Gentiles. Finally, it should be noted that the issue will be but rarely approached, from the Jewish side, at the abstract level. It will be met pragmatically, by finding solutions to such problems as whether selling a Christian the wherewithal to celebrate a saint's day involves a Jewish vendor in endorsing, by implication, the hagiological doctrines of the Catholic Church.[31]

The ethnic distinction between Jew and Gentile has occasionally been slightly obscured by political, geographical and demographic factors. We may disregard the first, which here refers to confused situations that have been brought about by decisions of an external authority, e.g. the early insistence of Rome that ex-pagans converting directly to Christianity were, from the government's point of view, Jews. Such problems as this were for the rabbis merely phantoms to be ignored. But what of persons coming as strangers to a local Jewish community and claiming to be Jews, either by birth or by formal conversion? And what of localities where, in addition to a clearly identifiable Jewish community, there may also be (as a result of long Jewish settlement) a substantial element of Jewish stock amongst the general population – can there ever be grounds for according to members of the latter a recognition of presumptive Jewish status? These are practical problems, upon which the rabbis were called to give decisions.[32] In the case of the stranger from without, a minority of jurists declare that the onus of proving his Jewish status rests upon himself; the general view, however, is that he is to be taken at his word,[33] on the grounds of his being a member of a Jewish family – all Jewish families being presumed to enjoy authentic Jewish status. The self-confessed proselyte, however, has no parents in Jewish law; and his eligibility for marriage under the auspices of a Jewish community where he is unknown has consequently to be considered.[34] It is held that, under current (i.e. post-temple) conditions, he is required for such a purpose to adduce evidence of his formal conversion. For purposes other than marriage, the authenticity of a self-declared proselyte may be presumed without corroborative evidence, in the light of conformity on his (or her) part to Jewish institutional practice as it affects the respective sexes.

The same consideration governs the talmudic ruling with regard to regions where the general population allegedly contained many persons of presumptively Jewish origins, among the areas mentioned being Palmyra[35] and those parts of Mesopotamia and Media to which, according to *II Kings* 18: 11, the ten northern tribes of Israel had been transplanted in the eighth century B.C.E. There is a slight but significant difference of treatment accorded to these two areas. Regarding the Palmyrenes, the issue revolves round their eligibility as proselytes. No problem arises if their general extraction is presumed to be purely gentile; but, if Jewish folk-tradition is assumed to be correct in asserting that there had been a substantial degree of intermarriage with Jewish servile stock in Solomonic times, the inhabitants of Palmyra must be reckoned of Jewish, albeit illegitimate Jewish, birth – a status that cannot be remedied by 'conversion' (although other means of legitimising their subsequent progeny may be available). On the other hand, in places such as Adiabene, which were identified with the localities of northern Israelite exile mentioned in *II Kings*, the issue is not immediately raised by the question of potential proselytism, but revolves round that of a presumptive 'Jewish' status for the man in the street. R. Judah adduced a ruling of positive tendency, emanating from R. 'Assi: 'Account has nowadays to be taken of a betrothal effected between a "gentile" man and a Jewish woman, in case he is descended from the Ten Tribes' (and is consequently not, in point of fact, a 'Gentile' at all but of bastard Jewish origin). Samuel, however, is reported to have disposed of the arguments which would point to such a conclusion and to have simplified matters by ruling summarily that the local population was purely gentile.

The significance of each of these decisions seems to me to lie mainly in its negative corollary. The ruling that aspirant proselytes from Palmyra and a few other specified localities are unacceptable implies, by contrast, their general acceptibility from elsewhere; whilst the dismissal of claims to presumptive Jewish status on the grounds of remote Jewish ancestry in Mesopotamia possibly eases the situation of the persons concerned, by opening the door to their formal conversion. The dominant consideration in both cases is the rabbis' sense of Jewish responsibility, arising out of God's will as revealed in the Torah, for the scrupulous observance of those halakhic institutions and restrictions that are designed to ensure the transmission of Jewishness as an uncompromised, identifiable, and indeed attestable status. Before the paramountcy of that principle proselytism has to yield. That is not to say that the value set on the principle of extending Jewish status to the Gentile who genuinely seeks it is impugned. There is here an implicit understanding that the urge towards 'bringing Gentiles under the wings of the divine Presence' springs, in those who are at all responsive to its promptings, from motivations which in western categories would be described as ethical and not legal. Rabbinic thought struggles, indeed, against any rigid distinction between law and ethics; but it appreciates that certain things must be 'left to the heart' (i.e. conscience). Since, however, ethical endeavour, if it is to be authentically Jewish, must operate within the terms of reference of *Halakhah* and of the sociology that those terms reflect, the issue in hand is clear enough. A conflict between the obligation to protect Jewishness, as a status, from possible compromise, and the preparedness to welcome an outsider desirous of securing it either for merely matrimonial reasons or out of true theological conviction, may make a hard case. As such, it may in itself be regrettable; but it ought not to be reckoned as an ethical blindspot caused by legalistic pre-occupations.

Where genealogical considerations and potential proselytism do not arise, ideological confrontation may reveal itself – being raised for the most part quite incidentally, by practical questions arising out of day to day existence. It is, indeed, scarcely too much to claim that wherever Jewry has been a minority, it has owed to the perpetual 'environmental question-mark' the stimulus to be constantly examining the distinctive features of a Jewish ideology. The practical issues here involved are, effectively, all concerned with the legitimacy of various types of Jewish-Gentile contact.

The difficulty is thrown into focus by one of the major terms of the seven commandments incumbent on the Descendants of Noah, and by the notion, ascending, apparently, to tannaitic times (i.e. before *c.* 200 c.e.), that these seven injunctions, imprecise though they might be (see *supra*, p. 126) are something more than a mere legal fiction designed to account for the existence of a law-abiding society with its own code beyond the confines of Jewry. They were conceived rather to constitute a definite polity, imposed by God upon the non-Jewish world, the terms of which prohibited 'idolatry'. Its prescriptions were consequently taken seriously by Jews, and the Talmud records views[36] that for a Noachide to contravene certain of his own commandments, or possibly any one of the seven, is a capital offence. Maimonides was actually to infer[37] a Jewish obligation to enforce their observance – if necessary at the point of the sword – on humanity at large (his term here is *ba'ey 'olam*, cf. *supra*. p. 128) except those choosing to become proselytes to Judaism itself. It is scarcely necessary to point out the influence here of the Islamic theory of *Jehad*, or 'holy war'.[38] And even though Maimonides may have interpreted his talmudic sources somewhat more positively than they express themselves, it remains true that to his predecessors, no less than to himself, the cardinal issue was that of gentile idolatry. Unless this issue could be eliminated by redefinition, even the circumspectly positive relationships with Gentiles that were legitimate in the case of Descendants of Noah might not be countenanced. Once this obstacle was out of the way, R. Yoḥanan could go so far as to say,[39] on the basis of *Dan*. 3: 12 ('there are certain *Jews*, etc.'), that 'whosoever repudiates idolatry is called a Jew'. His remark is by way of explanation as to why Israelites of tribes other than Judah are called Jews; but he clearly means to say that one who disavows idolatry is reckoned a Jew by the gentile majority, or, in other words, he is from the Roman (or Christian) point of view guilty of 'judaising'.[40] Had R. Yoḥanan seriously meant that such a gesture is sufficient in order to constitute someone a proselyte to Judaism, his formulation would have been otherwise, and probably more precise. The same reservation is likewise, it seems, necessary for the correct understanding of the anonymous talmudic dictum that 'whosoever repudiates idolatry does something tantamount to acknowledging the whole Torah'[41] – a statement which Maimonides underscores[42] as including the totality of institutional Judaism ('everything in the Torah, all the prophets, and all that the prophets were commanded from Adam to the end of the world'). It is difficult, but not impossible, to harmonise what Maimonides here says with the rigorously enforced observation by the Gentiles of the Noachide commandments that he envisages elsewhere as it being a Jewish responsibility to secure.[43]

And yet, for all the seriousness with which the talmudic rabbis purport to have taken the seven commandments for Noachides as a polity binding upon Gentiles, they apparently cherished no illusions about the extent to which Gentiles in fact implemented it. Quite apart from the empirical evidence supplied by their *obiter dicta* concerning gentile morals (see *supra*, pp. 131 f.), we have, from the mouth of R. 'Abbahu, a piece of theorising[44] to account for the realities of social history, in the form of an interpretation of *Habbakuk* 3: 6: when God found the Noachide code being disregarded by Gentiles, he abrogated it, in the sense that, although its punitive sanctions still stood, the 'merit' contingent upon its fulfilment became but a voluntary matter. '*He beheld, and startled* (or, *released*) *the nations*' – this means

137

that He saw the seven commandments which the Descendants of Noah had accepted. Since they had not implemented them, *'He took His stand, and released'* their wealth to Israel (in the context this explains why gentile owners of goring oxen must pay full damages to Jewish farmers whose stock is wounded by theirs, whereas Jews are not required to compensate gentile farmers who sustain analogous damage).

Those who have, for various reasons, been concerned to find a means of by-passing the obstacle of gentile idolatry have approached the problem along one or more of three avenues. It was R. Yoḥanan himself who cut the Gordian knot by boldly asserting[45] that 'Gentiles beyond the confines of Palestine are not idolaters; [their practices are] merely ancestral customs.' This contention clearly lends itself to far-reaching conclusions, and it was to be maintained, with increasing emphasis, wherever the Jewish social situation demanded it or found it convenient, or where a liberal climate of opinion prompted more positive Jewish essays in social philosophy, sometimes indeed (overlapping with the last-mentioned case) for apologetic reasons. For example, it made trade with Gentiles possible in medieval France despite the mishnaic embargo on such dealings on, or around, pagan holidays; for since, as the Tosaphists observed,[46] every week contains at least one saint's day according to the Roman calendar, business would be well-nigh impossible were Christians reckoned idolaters within the meaning of the act. Similarly Ezekiel Landau, writing (somewhat apologetically, no doubt) in Prague in 1776, was concerned to emphasise in the preface to his *responsa* (*Noda' Biyhudhah*) that the terms Gentile (*goi*) and *idolater* were not applicable to the contemporary non-Jewish environment. In this he had been anticipated already by Menahem Me'iri, who at the turn of the thirteenth century had postulated a category of 'nations confined by the [ethical] ways of religions' (*dathoth*, i.e. religio-legal systems), to be distinguished from idolaters, and had thus found a way towards the appraisal of Christianity in positive, and not in mere negative, terms.[47] Me'iri's position gains in focus by comparison with that of Judah Hallevi,[48] who could concede a limited, preparational validity to

Christianity and Islam in the pre-messianic era. Maimonides, too, concedes readily enough[49] that some things – e.g. the temporal creation of the world – are common ground between Judaism, Christianity, and Islam. The latter he rates very low – a mere caricature of Judaism bent on imperial aggrandisement,[50] inferior to Christianity in that the latter, for all its wrong-headed exegesis, does at least affirm the authenticity and inspirational quality of the Torah.[51] Yet we should not over-estimate his appreciation of Christianity, in view of his assertion[52] that '[Jesus] misled the majority of the world into worshipping something other than the Deity'. It is therefore not altogether surprising that, in contrast to the Tosaphists, he rules[53] that Christians are idolaters, and that the talmudic laws restricting mercantile dealings with Gentiles consequently apply in their full rigour against Christians in Palestine: elsewhere, trade with them is to be prohibited on Sundays and saints' days, but not, as in Palestine, over the preceding three days. Islam, for all his contempt for it, does not (so far as I am aware) earn from Maimonides so explicit a repudiation; it does not, indeed, expose itself theologically to the objection cited above (note 52), and Maimonides and his family had at one time themselves been compelled to profess Islam outwardly as refugees from persecution. A defence of such crypto-Judaism, on the grounds that Islam does not call for idolatrous professions, is attributed to Maimonides,[54] but its authenticity may be a matter for doubt; and elsewhere[55] he asserts quite unequivocally that the innovation of any religio-legal system by Gentiles is illicit – their only legitimate alternatives are the adoption of Judaism, or observance of the seven Noachide commandments.

It would seem, then, that there is a slight ambivalence in his attitude, at any rate as far as concerns Christianity. But even if it could be shown that his attitude is in fact self-consistent, we have seen that he has quite arbitrarily extended R. Yoḥanan's distinction, so as to read into it a geographical discrimination regarding the question of how rigorously the law restricting trading with Gentiles is to be enforced. The fact that he (or his unidentified source) does so, although the cardinal issue of alleged Christian idolatry is unaffected by geographical considerations, itself hints at the possibilities of achieving, casuistically, a liberal solution of the basic problem.

The second argument revolves round the principle of *shittuph*, or 'partnership' – a term corresponding to the Arabic *ishrākh*, and probably its model[56] rather than its copy. By 'partnership' is meant the claim, or implication, that divinity extends associatively to some entity that is, by objective criteria, distinct from the Deity itself. There is no question but that from the Jewish point of view such attribution compromises monotheism, and the *Halakhah* consequently finds that it is prohibited to the Jew by the terms of Scripture itself (*Ex.* 20: 3).[57] At the same time, it is clearly a *petitio principii* to refer, in the foregoing definition of partnership, to 'objective criteria'; it invites the rejoinder, from parties charged with compromising monotheism through effecting a partnership, that an inextricable interpenetration obtains reciprocally as between the Deity and the alleged 'partner', so that the divine unity remains unimpaired. Since Jewish monotheism bases itself not on God's numerical unity but on His absolute and undifferentiated uniqueness, Judaism cannot seriously entertain such an argument; but, if the argument could be shown to be hypothetically plausible or at least logical, there might possibly be grounds for excluding those who advance it, in defence of their own theological position, from the category of idolatry. It is, however, typical of the world of the *Halakhah* that the problem is not formulated speculatively, but legalistically. Israel are specifically warned by the Bible that 'partnership' of this kind is prohibited: does this warning extend to Gentiles also, or are the terms by which idolatry is prohibited to the Descendants of Noah to be presumed to leave this aspect of the matter open? The earlier medieval Jewish jurists were definite that Gentiles do not fall within the scope of the prohibition, so that a Christian, for example, who swears by a saint is not to be regarded as thereby infringing the biblical law applicable to Noachides.[58] Certain of the later jurists attempted, it is true, to circumscribe this liberty, and alleged that the fact that Judaism might turn a blind eye to the terms of gentile oaths in order not to frustrate business contracts was not to be construed as implying a general condonation of the associative divinity attributed by Gentiles to non-divine entities. But the principle having once been granted, any restrictiveness in its application becomes a subjective matter. The *Halakhah* does, indeed, endorse Maimonides' view[59] that the seven commandments incumbent upon Noah's descendants include the prohibition of 'cursing God's Name': but the propriety of 'tolerating', in practice, a less exacting standard in such matters on the part of Noachides than the rigorousness expected of Jews, was already implicit in a pronouncement of R. 'Ammi, in the third century, concerning the correct construction of *Lev.* 22: 32.[60] From that text he deduced the absence of any obligation upon Gentiles (as opposed to Jews) to expose themselves to the risk of martyrdom rather than comply with pagan insistence that they abjure the sanctity of God's Name – 'it is among the *Children of Israel* that I am to be hallowed'.

Thirdly, there is the question of what constitutes 'idolatry', *stricto sensu*. In so far as Jews are themselves liable to be affected, halakhic literature attaches great importance to the scrupulous avoidance of anything that could be construed as a tacit condonation of idolatrous rites or approbation of idolatrous premises; and in order to safeguard the Jewish position, it enjoins a far-reaching meticulousness. At the same time, it evinces consciousness of the circumstance that a responsible Jewish leadership ought neither foster amongst its following a mania for martyrdom, nor encourage it invariably to make a test case over avoidable and insubstantial issues. It consequently recognises that extraneous demands for conformity by Jews with what they themselves may reckon to be substantive idolatrous rites may, in point of fact, sometimes be advanced not with the object of challenging the Jewish conscience, but from motives of administrative convenience, or in order to suit the private interests of some governmental official. The *Halakhah* grants that in such cases secluded and unpublicised Jewish compliance, under protest, may sometimes be permissible. Where, however, the element of publicity is even slightly involved (publicity here meaning within the Jewish community), it will frequently be necessary to regard the matter

141

as an issue of conscience even though it was not necessarily the clear intention of the non-Jewish party to raise one; and in such cases, what has been construed (even though perhaps perversely) as an implicit challenge, has to be resisted to the death. Rabbi 'Ammi's disavowal, already mentioned,[60] of any call for such resolute standards from Gentiles, is coherent with the pragmatic and common-sensible inconsistency in halakhic assessment of what it is that constitutes idolatry for a Gentile. Whereas a Jew can become constructively guilty of idolatry – e.g. by making an idol for another party – a Gentile cannot; in his case, a deliberate act of worship, proffered in due form, needs to be attested before any 'charge' of idolatry can be substantiated.[61]

These three avenues of approach to the problem seem all to lead to the same conclusion; and it is a conclusion which does not depend in any way on the validity of a supposition that favourable environmental conditions might, occasionally, give rise amongst Jews to an embarrassment at their own attribution to the average Gentile of the taint of idolatry. The motivation was, on the whole, far more self-interested. But Jewry had at its disposal a cumulative experience in regard to the avoidance of constructive apostasy, and it had developed an acute sensitiveness to the issue thanks to the perpetual presence of the environmental questionmark. These two factors had taught the Jew the relevant casuistic techniques necessary for the constant searching of his own conscience and conduct; and it was those factors that also made it intellectually acceptable to him to employ the same processes with the object of hypothetically effecting the relief of the Gentile's conscience. At the level of Jewish communal existence, mercantile relationships could thereby be facilitated and, to a limited extent, the amenities of positive social relationships could be countenanced. Those who, in addition, felt themselves compelled to come to speculative and theological terms with the problem, might possibly also consider that to approach it *via* a logically inconsistent pragmatism was but to emulate the example of the Deity Himself, who can, according to R. Simeon b. Laqish, in the light of man's penitence transform sins of deliberation into sins of negligent error.[62]

We seem to have reached the following results. The notion of the Descendants of Noah and their sevenfold obligations is intended by Judaism to go beyond mere ideological theorising about the nature of society, and is conceived to correspond, semi-realistically, to certain social facts. At the same time, there is no practical touchstone (such as ethnic origin or cultic practice) by which Noachides can be distinguished from 'non-Noachide' gentile humanity; and in the absence of such criterion, the Noachide circle can be expanded or contracted in the light of the experience of each observer and of his own philosophy, or rather (in the term which S. R. Hirsch adopted from Kant) his 'theonomy' of Judaism. Maimonides himself furnishes an example of both liberal expansiveness and doctrinaire restrictiveness. His liberalism is evinced in the fact that he does not hesitate to identify Noachides who are conscientious regarding their obligations with the 'righteous of the nations', and that he asserts that these, like Israel, have a part in the world to come.[63] Yet, in the same breath, he makes it clear that this identification is conditional upon a deliberate acknowledgment – not one merely to be constructively inferred – that ethical obligations derive from divinely ordained commandments. To blur the distinction between one who recognises in the Deity a force whose ethical requirements cannot be side-stepped, and one who does not, would be for Maimonides a compromise of intellectual clarity not justified by theological charity; inasmuch as the intellectual faculty is itself God-given, and is not to be betrayed by misuse. Every individual is required, in Maimonides' view, to maintain his intellectual capabilities at their maximum efficiency, in order to serve God by fulfilling the requirements of Torah and devoting the remainder of his intellectual energies, after such fulfilment, to religious philosophy. Maimonides therefore feels constrained explicitly to exclude from the circle of Noachides the 'scientific humanist' – one who does in fact comply with the obligations of the Descendants of Noah, but does so out of intellectual conviction that they constitute an acceptable, non-deistic social ethic. Such a one, says Maimonides, is to be reckoned not one of the righteous of the nations, but as one of their wise men.[64] Maimonides was here following earlier Jewish opinion: but it may be remarked that the question of the 'scientific humanist' was, for him, an academic one – his own world was peopled with Jews, Moslems, and Christians. Within the terms of these three religious societies, his liberalism could have fairly full rein; and it might even be taken, by those of less ruthless intellectual severity than himself, to point towards the possibility of an inferential identification of Gentiles as being all (or nearly all) Descendants of Noah – i.e., towards a claim that their social ethics argued a constructive acknowledgment by them of a theistic sanction for those ethics, so that their acknowledgment might be presumed rather than requiring demonstration.

The present survey, which has produced no very startling results, was undertaken primarily with the object of clarifying the issues involved. Its findings do not justify us in estimating as very substantial the extent to which halakhic ordinance has encouraged any practical application of universalistic thinking by Jews; it is nearer to the point to say that it has countenanced it, where necessary, as a means of obviating undue Jewish communal sacrifice or hardship. The evidence which we have cited shows, I think, that the halakhists possess a key wherewith to open the ideological door leading to the non-Jewish world, and that they are prepared to open it occasionally and even to make the key available to approved persons on application, so to speak; but that they feel inhibited – for reasons that are not, essentially, logical ones – from leaving the key in the lock. But when this has been said, the matter is not disposed of. Perspective is false if we picture *Halakhah* as a field of Jewish activity in which the institutional life of individual and community is planned in advance. Even if that were an ideal, it would be frustrated by historical vicissitude: and, in point of fact, the theory is rather the reverse, namely that the historical experiences of the Jewish people serve to actualise the potential that has always been available within *Halakhah*, in virtue of the divine establishment of *Halakhah* as one facet of Torah. That is, of course, a jurisprudential (or rather, a 'theonomical') formulation of the situation. A sociological formulation might put it rather that there is always present a tension between Jewry, as a social organism comparable in its behaviour with any other social organism, and the *Halakhah* formulated by the rabbis who strive to keep control of it. In other words, *Halakhah* does not plan Jewish life, but tries to keep pace with it – ratifying, authorising, discouraging, frustrating, or prohibiting trends, according to whether they appear to be compatible or not with established Jewish teaching and tradition. As regards the question of 'practical universalism', i.e. positive attitudes towards, and relations with, Gentiles, evidence is forthcoming to show, empirically, a greater prevalence of these than the foregoing summary of our findings might suggest; but that evidence has not been adduced here, precisely because this study has been orientated not sociologically, but halakhically.

The halakhist has necessarily to start from the presupposition that Judaism-Jewry, as an idiosyncratic form of society, possesses a certain validity; and most social philosophers (as opposed to sociologists) will have to make analogous assumptions of their own. Moreover, the halakhist will more often think of himself as charged with the responsibilities of the lawyer and jurist rather than those of the theologian, still less of the philosopher. But we have seen how, in spite of the limitation of his terms of reference, the halakhist can – thanks to his biblical basis – evolve a formula by means of which a 'near-Jewish' religious ethic can be deemed to enjoy, at any rate in theory, an ecumenical currency. If, in the event, his implementation of practical universalism is more potential than actual, it is because of his realisation that theory is belied by the facts: in ideal, or messianic circumstances, when (it is assumed by him) fact and theory will correspond, the circumstances that inhibit his allowing full rein to universalistic promptings will presumably no longer be operative.

It ought not, however, come as a surprise to us if it is but the occasional Jewish jurist, theologian, or mystic who evinces an awareness that universalism may be a question with immediately practical implications regarding the gentile world; nor ought we ascribe the rarity of its appearance as due to any obsessive particularism. The insistence that Jewry and its specific way of life must, for theological reasons, be preserved uncompromised, carries with it as a corollary a respect for the divine economy, evinced equally in the halakhic self-isolation of Israel and in the law against the agricultural mixing of diverse kinds (*Lev.* 19: 19); and just as in the former case, so in the latter, the halakhist's preoccupation is to respect the injunction whilst maintaining it as socially workable.[65] The negative aspects of Jewish isolation from the environment will consequently be taken by the halakhist in his stride, similarly to the matrimonial limitations affecting those of Aaronic descent (see *supra*, p. 123) or indeed the relative degree of self-isolation for each other expected in the parties to any marriage. The Jew who has passed the centuries immured, as it were, within what is idiomatically described as 'the four ells' of the *Halakhah*, has been absorbed in a fixed reflection upon his own obligations viewed in terms of a response to the will of God – as God has seen fit to communicate it to Israel, i.e. in terms of Torah. God's own universalistic relevance and concern is taken for granted, and the Torah has itself been divinely encoded in the historical pattern of the Bible, the arrangement of which enunciates its universalistic implications. The institutional programme of Judaism is consequently deemed to be a matter of universal pertinence; and if the Jew feels that the function of implementing that programme is a task that requires all his available energies, he may well feel that no explanation is called for from him for his frequently failing to focus on questions such as those which have been engaging us here. And so Jewry may feel that, in living its Judaism, it is discharging its obligations to humanity at large through fulfilment of its obligations to God – or, to put it in the more graphic language of R. Simeon b. Laqish, when God effected the creation of the world, He made the ordered balance of its cosmic forces specifically contingent upon Israel's accepting His Torah when, in due course, it should be offered to them at Sinai.[66]

NOTES

1 See e.g. his *Judaism, A Portrait*, p. 86; 'Moralization and Demoralization in Jewish Ethics', published in *Judaism*, 11, 4, Fall, 1962, p. 295.
2 *Sedher 'Eliyyahu Rabbah*, chap. 10 (9) ed. M. Friedmann, p. 48.
3 10, 3 f.; H. Danby's English translation, pp. 397 f.; see also the parallel passage in the *Tosephta*, 13, 2, ed. Zuckermandel p. 434, Danby's English *Sanhedrin, Mishnah and Tosefta*, 1919, p. 122, on which see C. G. Montefiore and H. Loewe, *A Rabbinic Anthology*, p. 604, *supra*, and Roth, *Judaism, A Portrait*, p. 95, referring to J. Katz in *Zion* (Hebrew), 1958–9, pp. 174 f.
4 T.B. *Makkoth* 13a–b, *infra*.
5 *Exodus Rabbah*, 29, 7, ed. Wilna 51b, col. i.
6 *Exclusiveness and Tolerance*. Studies in Jewish-Gentile Relations in Medieval and Modern Times (Scripta Judaica III), Oxford, 1961. References may also be made to M. Guttmann, *Das Judentum und seine Umwelt*, Berlin, 1927, and the articles by the late Dr K. D. Wilhelm and Prof. S. H. Bergman in the present volume, pp. 289 f., 47 f. The articles on 'Gentiles' by E. G. Hirsch and J. D. Eisenstein in the *Jewish Encyclopedia*, v, pp. 615 f., are well arranged historically but nevertheless somewhat apologetically orientated. The Hebrew *Encyclopaedia Talmudhith*, ed. S. Zevin, 1953, etc., articles *'Goi'* and *'Ben-Noah'*, may be consulted with profit.
7 On the importance of distinguishing categorically between Jewish status, Judaism and 'Judaicity' (i.e. a de-theologised Jewish ethic), see my article in *The Jewish Journal of Sociology*, 7, 2, 1965, pp. 153 f.
8 Cf. Maimonides, *Hilekhoth Keley Ha-Miqdash*, 4, 1.
9 J. Selden, *De Jure Naturali et Gentium iuxta Disciplinam Ebraeorum*, 1640. Cf. Guttmann, *op. cit.* (n. 6), p. 109, and N. Isaac in *The Legacy of Israel*, ed. E. R. Bevan and C. Singer, 1927, pp. 383 f., 386.
10 T.B. *Sanhedrin* 57b.
11 See *Jewish Encyclopedia*, viii, p. 648, *s.v. Laws, Noachian*, and *Encyclopaedia Talmudhith* (*supra*, n. 6).
12 T.B. *Ḥullin* 92a.
13 T.B. *Sanhedrin* 59a, fol. (R. Yosē b. Ḥanina). It may be remarked in passing that apologetic motives may have been involved here. Christian attempts to 'sequestrate' the Decalogue, by elevating its contents to a position superior to that of the remaining pentateuchal laws, evoked negative counter-demonstrations in the Jewish liturgy (see T.B. *Berakhoth* 12a, and Montefiore-Loewe, *op. cit.* (n. 3), pp. 641–2). Possibly Yosē b. Ḥanina, in third-century Palestine, was concerned to wrest back the Ten Commandments for

Jewry, even at the cost of thereby 'relieving' Noachides of items in their own, pre-sinaitic code that had not been expressly repromulgated in (or with) the Decalogue; such unrepeated commandments, he asserted, became after Sinai the responsibility of Israel alone (or alternatively, had had Israel alone in view from the (pre-Israelite) time of their promulgation). Cf. *infra*, p. 137, n. 44.

14 T.B. *'Abhodhah Zarah* 3b, *Shabbath* 151b, *Ḥaghighah* 16a, *Giṭṭin* 7a.

15 E.g., T.B. *Berakhoth* 17a. See also, for the background of the term *beriyyoth*, K. Wilhelm's article, *infra*, p. 306.

16 Mishnah, *Sheqalim* 3, 2, H. Danby's translation, p. 155 *supra*.

17 T.B. *Berakhoth* 19b, etc.

18 T.B. *Berakhoth* 58a. Modern liturgies (e.g. Baer and Singer, see below) substitute, for the talmudic *beriyyothaw* = His creatures, the phrase *basar wa-dham* = flesh and blood (see *supra*.) Although the meaning is not affected, the change calls for explanation. More significant is the modified applicability of these two blessings implicit in the rubrics to them in S. Singer's *Authorised Daily Prayer Book*, 1929 ed., p. 291, following S. Baer's *'Abhodhath Yisra'el*; this change constitutes a particularistic limitation not present in the talmudic source.

19 *Canticles Rabbah* (on *Song of Songs*, 1: 3), ed. Wilna, 6b, col. ii, 9 lines from foot.

20 References in E. Ben Yehudah's *Thesaurus*, 1959 reprint, vol. v, 4371, col. i, *infra*, *s.v.* *'olam*; vi, 5319, cols. i–ii, *s.v.* *pithḥon*.

21 E.g., T.B. *Babha Bathra* 16b, *Sanhedrin* 108a.

22 E.g., T.B. *Shabbath* 22b = *Menaḥoth* 86b.

23 *Mekhilta de-R. Yishma'el*, *Mishpaṭim* 20, ed. I. H. Weiss, f. 107b = *Exodus Rabbah* 29, 4, on *Ex.* 20: 2, ed. Wilna, 51a, col. ii, *supra*.

24 *Rosh Has-Shanah* 1, 2, Danby's translation, p. 188.

25 For this rendering, which follows the Kaufmann Codex in reading *kibhenumeron*, i.e. the Latin *numerum*, instead of the meaningless *kibheney maron* of the *Textus Receptus*, see S. Krauss, *Griechische und Lateinische Lehnwörter im Talmud*, ii, Vienna, 1899, p. 356.

26 T.B. *Rosh Has-Shanah* 16a (R. Yosē, R. Nathan).

27 T.B. *'Abhodhah Zarah* 3b, *Yebhamoth* 24b.

28 In the parallel in the Palestinian Talmud (*'Abhodhah Zarah* 2, 1, R. Hosha'yah) it is the *Descendants of Noah* who will subject themselves to all the commandments in the Torah and will thereafter relapse.

29 *Tanḥuma*, ed. Buber, *Genesis, Way-yera'* 38, f. 54b. The 'righteous', whom God there declares that He will bring near beneath His own Presence, are of course righteous Gentiles.

30 See especially T.B. *Pesaḥim* 49b.

31 *Tosaphoth* to T.B. '*Abhodhah Zarah* 2a, see *infra*, p. 138.

32 The halakhic treatment of the subject is summarised in the *Encyclopaedia Talmudhith* (see n. 6), v, 364 f., *s.v. sapheq-goi*.

33 See the *Maggidh Mishneh* by Vidal of Tolosa (late fourteenth century) on Maimonides, *Hilekhoth 'Issurey Bi'ah*, 20, 5. The *Encyclopaedia Talmudhith* further refers to *Sha'ar Ha-Melekh*, *in loc.*, and to the *Pithehey Teshubhah* on *'Ebhen Ha-'ezer* 100, 2, as being decisive on this point. Both these works are not at present accessible to me.

34 See Maimonides, *Hilekhoth 'Issurey Bi'ah*, 13, 10.

35 T.B. *Yebhamoth* 16a, foll., *Niddah* 56b.

36 T.B. *Sanhedrin* 57a.

37 *Hilekhoth Melakhim* 8, 10; cf. T.B. '*Abhodhah Zarah* 64b.

38 John Hyrcanus' forced conversion of the Edomites to Judaism (Josephus, *Antiqu.* xiii, 9, 1 (254)), could have been known to Maimonides from Yosippon, chap. 28 (ed. A. Kahana, Warsaw, 1898, 30b); but Hyrcanus' measures exceeded Maimonides' requirements, which parallel Islamic practice.

39 T.B. *Meghillah* 13a.

40 This term was to be applied by Eusebius, within 60 years of the death of R. Yoḥanan himself, to Christian heretics who denied the divinity of Jesus (*De ecclesiastica theologica* 2, 14, *P.G.L.* 932D).

41 T.B. *Qiddushin* 40a; cf. '*Abhodhah Zarah* 64b (R. Me'ir's view of what constitutes a *ger toshabh*).

42 *Hilekhoth 'Akkum* 2, 4, taking up T.B. *Horayoth* 8a, *infra*, and *Siphrē Numbers, Shelaḥ Lekha* 111 (on Num. 15: 22), ed. H. S. Horovitz, p. 116, *infra*.

43 See note 37.

44 T.B. *Babha Qamma* 38a.

45 T.B. *Ḥullin* 13b.

46 On T.B. '*Abhodhah Zarah* 2a, *s.v. 'asur*.

47 See Katz, *op. cit.* (note 6), pp. 115 f.

48 *Kuzari* iv, 23; English translation by H. Hirschfeld, 2nd ed., p. 200. Hallevi definitely asserts the repudiation [by Moslems and Christians] of idolatry, whilst not overstating the significance of this in view of other aspects of their respective theologies (*wa-la tultafitu 'ilâ ba'd ha'ula'i 'an al-'awṭani wa-ijtahidihim fi-t-tawḥid*, Hebrew version *we-'al tabbiṭ 'el roḥaq 'elleh min ha-'akkum we-histhtaddelutham bay-yiḥudh*). Cf. S. H. Bergman's remarks *supra*, p. 58.

49 *Guide to the Perplexed* i, 71; English translation by S. Pines, 1963, p. 178. See Katz, *op. cit.* (note 6), pp. 119 f. *Hilekhoth Melakhim*, cited below, note 52.

50 *'Iggereth Teman*, ed. S. Goldman, 1950, pp. xxv, 27, 31.

51 *Responsa*, ed. A. H. Freimann, 1934, no. 364, pp. 331 f.

52 *Hilekhoth Melakhim* 11, 4 (mutilated in some editions by censorship).

53 *Hilekhoth 'Akkum* 9, 4.

54 *'Iggereth Has-Shemadh*, published by A. Geiger, Breslau, 1850, and by M. D. Rabinowitz, *'Iggeroth Ha-Rambam*, Tel Aviv, 1951, pp. 29 f.

55 *Hilekhoth Melakhim* 10, 9.

56 Cf. T.B. *Sanhedrin* 63a, and Targum to *Ps.* 69: 10 and *Song of Songs* 1: 7.

57 Cf. *Mekhilta* (see note 23), *in loc.*, f. 74b.

58 *Tosaphoth* to T.B. *Sanhedrin* 63b, *s.v.* *'asur* (R. Tam). Fuller text in *Tosaphoth* to *Bekhoroth* 2b, *s.v.* *shemma*. Moses Isserles on *Shulḥan 'Arukh*, *'Oraḥ Ḥayyim* 156, end. Cf. Katz, *op. cit.* (note 6), pp. 34 f., 163 f.

59 *Hilekhoth Melakhim* 9, 1.

60 T.B. *Sanhedrin* 74b; T.J. *Shebhi'ith* 4, 2.

61 T.B. *Sanhedrin* 56b; Maimonides, *Hilekhoth Melakhim* 9, 2.

62 T.B. *Yoma* 86b, *supra*.

63 *Hilekhoth Melakhim* 8, 11.

64 *Ibid.* For the correct reading *'ella* (and not *we-lo*) *me-ḥakhmeyhem*, see Katz, *op. cit.* (note 6), p. 175.

65 See the mishnaic treatise *Kil'ayim*, H. Danby's translation pp. 28 f.; Maimonides, *Hilekhoth Kil'ayim*, especially 4, 16.

66 T.B. *'Abhodhah Zarah* 3a. As Rashi, *in loc.*, explains, the notion is derived exegetically through combining *Jer.* 33: 25 ('my covenant, *day and night*') with *Josh.* 1: 8 ('[in] this book of the Torah . . . thou shalt meditate, *day and night*') and *Gen.* 1: 31 (' . . . *evening and morning day the sixth*'), where the definite article is syntactically anomalous; R. Simeon b. Laqish therefore finds in it a pointer to the 6th day of Sivan, i.e. the date of Pentecost and therefore, in Jewish tradition, the anniversary of the Sinaitic revelation.

7

Jew, Christian and Muslim
in the Secular Age

IGNAZ MAYBAUM

[I]

LESSING'S PARABLE OF THE THREE RINGS

At the centre of Gotthold Ephraim Lessing's play *Nathan the Wise* stands the parable of the three rings. By means of this parable Lessing explains his attitude towards the three monotheistic religions – Judaism, Christianity and Islam. A father has three sons. In his possession is a precious ring. To which son is he to bequeath it? He loves his three sons equally. He finds a way out of the dilemma by asking a goldsmith to make two other rings in such a way that no human eye shall be able to discern any difference between the three rings. When the father died each of the sons inherited a ring and each could claim that his was the genuine one. The moral of the parable is that the question 'who possesses the genuine ring?' cannot be answered. But Lessing adds a postscript. It is only at the end of days that it will be known just what the whole truth is; and in the interim man, be he Jew, Christian or Muslim, must live according to what he

151

believes is the truth and, by his good deeds, must try to prove that he is on the right road. This means that he has no theoretical proof for the truth of his religion, but that he does have the practical solution of making it apparent that his life is guided throughout by the truth of God.

Franz Rosenzweig differs from Lessing. He likewise says that man can only prove the validity of his truth by testifying to it. But for Rosenzweig there are not three, but only two ways of testifying to the one truth – the way of Judaism and the way of Christianity. Rosenzweig will not acknowledge Islam as a monotheistic religion. To him, Islam is a religion of reason and duty, and it is without revelation. Rozenzweig was unfair to Islam, precisely as have been also many Christian theologians who have seen it as Semitic Hellenism or as a Christian heresy. Muḥammad was called the greatest plagiarist of world history. More to the point is Karl Becker, a German islamist who has called Islam a carrier of religions. Indeed, the Jewish and Christian elements in Islam cannot be overlooked. An attack on Islam is therefore often a boomerang which rebounds on Judaism or Christianity.

Rosenzweig's misconception of Islam has consequences for his own understanding of Judaism. The Jewish people has lived for centuries, indeed up to today, under the influence of islamic civilisation. In the Middle Ages, the Jewish people had, in its own cultural set-up, an Islamic way of life. Rosenzweig defends such forms of communal life as Jewish, although they have their origin in Islam. When he writes 'you can run away from the Law, but you cannot change it', he is not aware that what he is saying could well be a quotation from the *Sharia‘*. Since Muḥammad is regarded as the last of the prophets, prophecy as the continuous force of criticism and free enquiry are excluded from religious life, which is accorded recognition by men of piety in its character of unchanged tradition only. Rosenzweig's dictum about Jewish Law just quoted obliterates the difference between the Jewish and the Islamic doctrine of Law. Rosenzweig, who wished to be thought of as a liberal Jew, becomes rather the advocate of a Jewish *status quo* and the defender of the Jewish

Middle Ages – a thinker who, it is now even alleged, stands on the side of orthodox Jewish obscurantism.

The second consequence of this error regarding Islam is of wider relevance. The Christian theologian who does not understand Islam is not able to make sense of the european class founded on reason and law. That class, standing in the midst of Christendom but never acknowledged by Christian doctrine, was the *bourgeoisie*. A Christian rehabilitation of bourgeois life has never been forthcoming. The very word *bourgeois* has a derogatory meaning. Whereas in France the *citoyen* has the halo of citizen-soldier and patriot, the French *bourgeois* is without such glory; he represents nothing more than good living. In Germany the word *Bürger*, although imbued with respectability, carries the stigma of inferiority engendered through not belonging to the aristocracy. Above all, if a Christian becomes a bourgeois he ceases to be a Christian. Why? The world of today is divided into two halves, of which one half is called the bourgeois West. Is the West, then, in so far as it is bourgeois, not Christian?

Lessing's parable sees the three monotheistic religions as equals, but it does not draw any distinctions between them. But their equality need not be understood as identity; as between themselves they are different. Their difference becomes clear when we look at the Jewish, Christian and Mohammedan exegeses of *Gen.* 22. The great message of that chapter, according to the Jewish understanding of it, consists in exactly what the text says. God does not want Isaac to be sacrificed. God's love and mercy are available for man without having to be earned by sacrifice. Isaac returns home, marries, and himself becomes a father. That is the story of Abraham – a story dubbed by Kierkegaard a bourgeois idyll. But is it possible for God to be revealed in greater glory than in giving us life although we have done nothing to deserve it?

The Christian exegesis of *Gen.* 22 changes the story. Isaac *is* sacrificed. Someone has to suffer and to die, in order that man may live and be happy. Love is sacrificial love. The Koran has but a short extract of the story. Abraham is bidden 'sacrifice your son', and he obeys. That is all. The faith of the Muslim is the submission of his will to the will of God. He turns to God with a radical 'Thy will be done', and his obedience is his faith.

This threefold exegesis, although each motif is different, does not make it possible to say which one is more profound than the other two. We come back to Lessing's parable, with its emphasis on the undistinguishable equality of the three religions. Even though it is not possible to call any one of the three 'higher' or 'lower' than the others, their difference is apparent and must be carefully investigated.

[II]

JUDAH HALLEVI'S PARABLE OF THE SEED AND THE TREE

It was a Christian mystic, Angelus Silesius (1624–77), who transplanted the threefold form of the foregoing exegesis into the heart of Christianity itself. Just as we distinguish between Judaism, Christianity and Islam, so he saw three different forms within Christianity itself, explaining the doctrine of the Trinity not as three static ideas, but as referring to a process within the history of mankind.

> *First was the Father, now is the Son:*
> *The Spirit will be here on earth on the*
> *day of glory.*[1]

Accordingly Schelling – and after him, Rosenzweig – distinguished between the Petrine Church in the era of the Catholic Middle Ages and the Pauline Church which begins with the Protestant Reformation and lasts until the French Revolution. The Church which then enters history is the Johannine Church. The Petrine Church, like Islam, uses law to sanctify human order. Furthermore, it is a denominational imperialism: the Church militant aspires to make all infidels into believers. The Pauline Church christens the human soul; it converts the poet within man, transforming the ever-changing imagination into an ever-identical faith, into 'faith alone'. But with its 'naught but faith' this Church lets the world slip away, and the Johannine Church has to take over. The Johannine Church likewise christens man, but the whole of man – not only his political and social life, and not only his soul; man, endowed with body and soul and living his life in politics and society, is summoned to become a Christian.

How can Judaism fit into this philosophy of history? Here we have to set another parable at the side of Lessing's parable of the three rings and Angelus Silesius' vision of the three Churches. It is the parable of Judah Hallevi about the seed and the tree. He acknowledged Christianity and Islam as monotheistic civilisations, but saw them both as one tree with two mighty branches growing from a common seed. That seed is Judaism.[2]

Judah Hallevi's parable of the seed and the tree with its two branches puts Christianity and Islam, those two differing forms of monotheism, on an equal level. That equality consists in a fact which, although overlooked up till now, is nevertheless clearly visible in the two thousand years of Christian and fourteen hundred of Islamic history. Both Christianity and Islam created their own respective cultures and civilisations. The history of the West represents, for all to see, two civilisations – one Christian and one Islamic. Islam belongs to the West. The dialectic between love and law can be resolved neither within a single institution nor within a single civilisation. The civilisation of the West is based upon the two monotheistic civilisations, Christianity and Islam. To speak of a 'Jewish culture', or (the same thing) a 'Jewish civilisation' is a misconception. Insofar as Judaism holds fast to its prophetic element, it is debarred from the possibility of fulfilling itself in the sort of creativity that establishes states, cultures and civilisations. What is Jewish about the so-called 'Jewish intellectual'? With his uprootedness from reality, he has his habitat in the spiritual and intellectual sphere created by the Christian division between spirit and flesh, soul and body. What is Jewish about the so-called 'Jewish bourgeois'? With his trust in common-sensible reason, and his submission to the moral law, he has his habitat in a sphere which is a colony of Islam planted in the midst of the western world.[3]

155

Everyone agrees that the bourgeois era began with the French Revolution. When Shelley wrote a poem about it he gave it the title *The Revolt of Islam*. He castigates the zealotry of the demagogues, but does not disapprove of the aim of the Revolution itself, and can write 'the sympathies connected with that event extended to every bosom'. The words are quoted from the preface to his poem. Like others of his contemporaries, he found Islam more natural and more human than Christianity. Islam rejected a dualism that would exalt the soul above the body. Islam keeps faith with man, who is permitted to remain a whole man. At the same time as Shelley was calling the French Revolution the revolt of Islam, Goethe was writing his *West-östlicher Divan*. With the French Revolution there begins, according to Schelling and Rosenzweig, the Johannine era – a Christianity without dogma and, unlike Petrine Christianity, without a Christian law. In the present, Johannine, epoch intellectual and bourgeois become visible entities, and at long last justify themselves in the sense of finding their rightful place within a monotheistic civilisation. To move on from this point of our religio-sociological analysis, and to speak of a *Jewish* intellectual or of a *Jewish* bourgeois, involves us in an enquiry of some importance. In what way, we must ask, has Judaism been the leaven that has changed in the one case a Christian and in the other an Islamic character to such a degree that the attribute *Jewish* can be at all apposite?

That which appears, in institution and civilisation, as love and law in counterpoised opposition, as the contrast of mercy and justice, can live side by side within the man who is not shaped by civilisation but retains his human wholeness. No institution, no civilisation, no achievement of creative man can have the attribute 'Jewish'. There exists, of course, the Hebrew word '*Abhodhah*, which has a double meaning. It comprises two actions which are elsewhere generally thought of as contradictory to each other. '*Abhodhah* means both *work* and *worship*, worship of God and ordinary work, the work which man must needs perform in order to maintain himself. Promethean man – every creative man, that is – knows of a third activity; self-fulfilment in art and in politics, in culture and in civilisation. Christianity aligned art with worship and built the Church alongside the State. Christian civilisation is a superstructure by means of which promethean man has been christened. Marx condemned the Christian superstructure as a betrayal of the material world: and so did Islam. Islam turned aside from spiritual holiness, and worshipped instead terrestrial holiness: the world itself is the creation of God. Man can of himself, without any change effected by an inner conversion, turn to God.

Islam never came into contact with a polity in which man is free. Islamic Hellenism never encountered Athenian democracy, but only the tyranny of disappearing antiquity. It was not the state, but private society and the family that were sanctified by the *Sharia'*, the holy Law of Islam. Religion and Law became identical. Nothing whatsoever of the social and material world was to be excluded from sanctification through the legal supervision of the *Sharia'*, the Islamic Talmud. But neither was the material world itself intended to be raised to a spiritual level. Why should it be? 'The substance of the matter is obedience', said Simone Weil. That is, indeed, a statement begotten of piety, albeit not of Christian piety. Christianity and Islam, so close to each other because of their common origin in Judaism, are, as civilisations, divided by an unbridgeable gulf. The Jewish people had its history within Christian and Islamic civilisations and yet remained different from both of them. Seen from the standpoint of the Hebrew word '*Abhodhah*, the work-and-worship enjoined upon the Jew, Christian civilisation is but spiritual superstructure. What did the Jew contribute, then, to these two civilisations? He gave himself, and in so doing gave humanity. The Jew, as the word '*Abhodhah* implies, has no mission other than to work and pray. He must be a *Mensch* – he must be human. It is man's humanity which can combine love and law, mercy and justice. But in Christianity, love supreme, and in Islam, law supreme, constitute civilisations that are different from each other.

[III]

THE DISINTEGRATION OF THE MIDDLE AGES
AND THE NEW AGE

In our own nuclear age, which has set all established civilisations into a state of crisis, it is a consoling thought that man need not be identified with his own civilisation. Aloof from that civilisation, he is at once in the situation in which every biblical prophet found himself. The prophet was taken apart from the multitude, and had the task of telling others that in the destruction of the Temple not God, but man had suffered defeat. The work of man's hand, a civilisation, was being thrown into the melting-pot. The very word 'religion' has become discredited for many people, because it represents a civilisation in which a monotheistic religion appeared on the stage of past history. Bonhoefer demands a 'religionless Christianity'. Rosenzweig states, with satisfaction, that in the whole of his substantial work *Der Stern der Erlösung* the word *religion* does not occur once. Both Bonhoefer and Rosenzweig are expressing what Schelling, with reference to Angelus Silesius, called the Johannine age. Of these three witnesses of the coming age which has, indeed, already begun two are Protestants and one is a Jew. They are joined by Professor Heer, himself a Catholic historian. Heer demands that conversion should not be the first thought in the mind of a Christian when he meets a non-Christian. Rather, it should be his task to give himself to his fellow man as a Christian personality.[4] Jew, Christian and Muslim can enter into a true dialogue because they have to express what they stand for in their personal existence, and because they are no longer represented by a Jewish, Christian or Islamic civilisation styled the Jewish, Christian or Islamic 'religion'. The Jew has always been a human type. This now applies equally to the Christian and the Muslim because the two monotheistic civilisations which they represented so mightily in the Middle Ages no longer have any impact upon the world. The world today is divided into the democratic West and the communist East, and neither of the two can be fittingly identified with either Christianity or Islam. Both Christian and Muslim have entered a new era after the French Revolution. Progress has taken place: to put it in the words of Bonhoefer, 'the world has come of age', or to use the terminology of Angelus Silesius, 'the Johannine age is here'. Neither the Church nor the *Sharia'* makes our new age. It is neither a Christian civilisation in the West, nor an Islamic one in the East, that dominates our modern world. The world is one. East and West have met, and the world will be shaped anew through three types, the Christian, the Muslim and the Jew. In Christianity the sacrificial love of sons offering themselves for others, in Islam obedient submission to the authority of the fathers, and in Judaism the bliss in which fathers and sons are united – here is a trinity in which Christian, Muslim and Jew can cooperate, and can collectively enter into a dialogue with a party that has never, hitherto, belonged to their own family: the Bhuddist. Prophetic Judaism is needed to contradict Bhuddism. Asia wants, and is indeed entitled to retain her own civilisation. That circumstance will itself prevent Christian or Islamic civilisation from penetrating Asia. But to the Christian and Muslim who come to her as Christian and Muslim persons, Asia is wide open. And where the Christian and the Muslim can live, the Jew can also live.

There is no disintegration here, amounting to an end; but rather a regrouping. Medieval Christianity and medieval Islam break up, and a Jewish, a Christian, and a Muslim form of personal existence are set free. The 'Johannine age', the Christianity without law and dogma which Schelling and Rosenzweig saw as entering our life after the French Revolution, does not involve an abolition of what Petrine and Pauline civilisation, the Christianities of law and dogma, have contributed. What is truly new does not destroy the old, but revives it. Freemasonry misinterprets the Johannine age as being disrupted from the past. The well-known nineteenth-century Viennese preacher, Dr A. Jellinek, was influenced by this misinterpretation when he said, 'Judaism is now called upon to build on the ruins of religions its Third Temple, of the true religion.'[5] The Austrian rabbi, in the days of that virulent antisemitism which preceded Hitlerism, could place no hope in the Church which he observed participating in anti-semitism. Probably unknowingly, he was preaching Freemasonry and not Judaism. Lessing was interested in the Freemasons but never joined them. It seems that in the days of classical Enlighten-ment Freemasonry was not yet what it is today – a travesty of monotheistic religion. The Johannine age of which Schelling and Rosenzweig hopefully spoke does not rest upon the 'ruins' of the two preceding ages. In the regrouping that takes place intel-lectual and bourgeois come forward anew, as far as their manifest presence on the scene is concerned: but they were in fact born and bred in the preceding Christian-Islamic civilisation.

[IV]

INTELLECTUAL, BOURGEOIS AND SOLDIER

Beside the intellectual and the bourgeois there stands the soldier. War as a crusade, as the 'holy war' of the Muslim, did not end with the Christian and Islamic Middle Ages; it merely transformed national wars into 'zoological' wars. Among the types of human character to which our civilisation has given birth the soldier must not be forgotten. Citizen-soldiers of the two world wars suffered as did those who died in Auschwitz. We may observe these soldiers in their obedience to authority – the great virtue of the Muslim. We must also view them in the setting of the sacri-fice through which they died so that others might live. The tomb of the Unknown Warrior revives the symbol of the Cross; no one can pass a war memorial without being reminded of the Golgotha of our own time. The inhumanity of Auschwitz began with the inhumanity of the trench warfare of 1914–18. The youth that died in Flanders died in Auschwitz. The genocide of Auschwitz began in Verdun, which a German general called his blood-pump; and the French commander who opposed him was no less subaltern mentally in allowing himself to accept a method of fighting which made of genocide an instrument of war.

The two thousand years of Christianity have been two thousand years of war. The 'holy war' which Muḥammad taught the Muslim to fight was a Christian conception. In the China of Confucius the soldier has no status – he is on a par with the brigand. In Christendom it is different: here the principle of 'Render unto Caesar the things which are Caesar's' is no less important than is the second half of the verse. It is a principle which makes of the soldier who sheds his own blood for his country a Christian figure; and it makes the state, though it be different from the Church, its equal. The state is a secular institution, but a secular institution that exists because the Church exists. The secular realm stands bathed in the light that proceeds from the Church. The secular element in it itself has its origin in the Church. Bhuddist civilisation is not secular in the way that Christian civilisation is: Bhuddist civilisation is *Bhuddist* – not secular.

Bhuddist civilisation has no concept of history, and presupposes a reality which is not yet purged of gods and spirits as is western civilisation. Asian 'reality' is like a dreamland, as we see it in the drawings of Japanese and Chinese artists. In the tender lines and flourishes of these drawings, neither trees, stones, mountains, rivers nor the human figures among them have any contours. They have no existence of their own, but flow into each other to make up something which is really nothing at all, like the hub in the middle of a wheel. A wheel cannot be imagined without a hub, but the hub is merely the nothing without which the spokes of a wheel could not exist. In the Bhuddist cosmos, sustained by the nothing as the spokes of the wheel are sustained by the hub, things and living beings are nothing in themselves; actions do not have a real purpose, everything is according to an aesthetically strict form, and everything in the social sphere is conduct and etiquette without moral justification. No one ought to cry out against cruelty perpetrated upon himself or upon others. Pain is unredeemable: and it has to be sustained without reproach and bitterness. One cannot, here, love one's neighbour in the way in which the Hebrew Bible bids us love him, because one's neighbour is not discovered as a neighbour. Your fellow man is not 'like you',[6] as the Bible says of one's neighbour; he is *tat tvam asi* –

identical with you, even as a grain of sand in a heap is identical with other grains of sand. It is this world about which the Mona Lisa smiles with an expression so successfully caught by Leonardo da Vinci: it is a cold, disinterested smile, outwardly friendly, but in truth cruel. It is the smile of the Buddha. Westerners, too, can of course learn to smile like that: but the moment that smile steals over their faces they cease to be westerners. How near to each other, Judaism, Christianity, and Islam are, when viewed from the background of Buddhist civilisation – because there is in it nothing at all of Judaism, Christianity, or Islam. Buddhist civilisation is Asia: Europe, western civilisation, is of Jewish, Christian and Islamic make.

Rosenzweig is aware of the Christian element in the secular civilisation of the West. In his youth, when he first encountered Zionism, he was afraid that a Jewish state might transform Jews into Jewish Christians. (It is rumoured that the Vatican cherishes as a hope what Rosenzweig perceived as a danger.) The Christian mission to Jewry has never had the slightest effect on the Jews. But a situation can arise – as it did arise in the early Church – in which Christianity grows out of Judaism. Christianity always grows out of Judaism: that is the glory of the Jew. The Hebrew Bible in the hands of Christians, the *opiniones judaicae* adopted by Gentiles, create Christianity. Whether Jews are present in the flesh or not, Judaism is an element in Western civilisation. A further probability arises when the Jew, deeming himself to be a faithful Jew, becomes in thought and action a Christian. Rosenzweig, realising that the state as a secular institution is still under the influence of the Church, pondered about a Jewish future in a Jewish state. Just as the Church is a state transformed by Judaism, so might not a Jewish state transform Judaism into elements of which one – the necessary spiritual opposition to power – becomes a Christian element?

In the Hebrew Bible the message for the servant of the Lord is a message for priest, teacher, preacher or prophet. It is the call to be ready for martyrdom. The soldier has the message of the Cross; in both instances it remains a message to the effect that someone must die in order that others may live. In the soldier's case the martyr's death is offered to a hero who, no longer like the Greek hero, dies for his own glory, but who dies for the glory of God. The message of the Cross makes of the soldier a Christian figure. The Jew of the Diaspora fought in two world wars and yet remained a Jew. A dilemma now begins to face the Jew who thinks about Judaism. The Jew who, with his own State of Israel, has now entered the realm of the *pólis*, faces something of which he is morally bound to take cognisance: the rise of a tension between teaching and governing, between persuasion and the application of power, between spiritual and temporal power. In Jewish existence – in the private existence of any person – such dualism does not come to the fore. As citizens of the Jewish state Jews will therefore be able step by step only, and in continuous watchfulness, to preserve their own Jewish existence. When everything in Rosenzweig's attitude towards Zionism is considered, it was not so much a Jewish state, but rather the deification of Jewish peoplehood against which he was uttering a warning. Einstein's telegram to Ben Gurion, 'curb Jewish nationalism', summarises the attitude of Rosenzweig.

[v]

THE WESTERN STATE

The Christian controversy between State and Church is today reappearing in Israeli affairs. In her forthcoming and unavoidable *Kulturkampf* Israel will have to learn from Church history how, in the european Middle Ages, the struggle between Church and State made western civilisation a fortress of the freedom of man. Christianity has also to be duly appraised for its faculty of paving the way for technological civilisation. The Jewish doctrine of creation, taken over into Islamic teaching, sees the world as 'very good' (*Gen.* 1: 31) and leaves man, as the creature of God, with his human status unchanged. Christian doctrine sees the world as not yet redeemed on its first day and as remaining unredeemed *ante Christum natum*. The Christian division between creation and redemption – redemption being the cosmic correction of creation – between flesh and spirit, can tell of a world which is material, neutral or even wicked, and at the silent disposal of man. The Christian view of man's status made it possible for him to become the subtle workman – technological man – who applies to his work one side only of his human existence, his mental faculties. Adam works on the land with his physical strength; but technological man is no longer Adam – he is 'second Adam'. He is man shaped by the division between spirit and flesh. The progress of technological civilisation has been bought at a price. Man has lost his wholeness – a unity undivided into spirit and flesh; and the world has lost its glory which the psalmist praises and has become instead but neutral matter. Man, the priestly father of his family – negatively assessed by Christianity as the bourgeois, but sedulously safeguarded by the Law of the Torah and by the *Sharia'*, the Law of Islam – is threatened with being edged out of the realm of technological civilisation altogether.

The Islamic countries realise perfectly well that they have to pay for their westernisation. The West has freedom. But Islam has equality, a brotherhood not compromised by any Christian division between the highly specialised scientist or technician on the one hand and, on the other, the masses who are to become cogs in a vast machine-civilisation. Islam was once capable of affording a dignity to the man of the Hellenistic mass age, and it has retained this capacity of making any impoverished beggar as much as a Muslim as the man who is independent, fearless, and a gentleman: it summons the pauper to worship at the mosque on equal terms at the side of prince and scholar. In the Middle Ages Islam and Christendom confronted each other as two civilisations – Islam, like Russian communism, offering equality without freedom, and Christianity, like American capitalism, torn asunder into rich and poor, offering freedom without social equality.

Whenever an Islamic state was established the ambition of the Islamic divines was the same as that which today fascinates the endeavour of Jewish orthodoxy in Israel – to have a western state as well as the Islamic way of life regulated by the laws of the

Sharia'. Israeli orthodoxy likewise wants it both ways: a western state *and* Jewish Law as interpreted in the Middle Ages. But an informed western observer of Islam has this to say (*The Times Literary Supplement*, 4th March, 1965): 'As the state formed on a western model comes increasingly to be the norm in Muslim countries, so the experience of the Muslim believer comes more closely to resemble that of the practising Christian in western states.' 'Talking of an Islamic system and thinking in terms of the western system (wrote a Pakistani in 1951) is an incongruity which is visible all around us. The spirit soars to the lofty heights reached in Omar's time, but the eyes are fastened on the spires of Westminster.' What Rosenzweig had to say about a 'Jewish' state Islamic theologians are now saying of an 'Islamic' state. Egypt, which in 1954 adopted a western constitution, thereby making the United Arab Republic a democratic socialist state, has in consequence of that decision abolished the *Sharia'* courts. Islam is, in Algeria (1963), the 'state religion'; Iraq is a 'democratic socialist state' 'in the spirit of Islam'. How can all this be possible? In fact, of course, it is not possible. The western state is of Christian origin and it remains a Christian institution. An 'Islamic' western state is embroiled in the same difficulties which must beset a 'Jewish' western state. Jews are happy to have achieved the State of Israel; but amid their enthusiastic joy the question has to be asked, 'whither goes the road for the Jew who knows himself to be shaped by the prophets and classical rabbis?'

In Israel, the rabbis of the Sephardic community are totally unaware that their own Sephardic way of life is influenced by Islamic civilisation. No intelligent statement of their difference from either the Ashkenazic community of Israel or from the Israeli political leaders has been forthcoming from the Sephardic rabbis; they merely defend their own vested interest as religious professionals. Something quite other has to be said of the rank and file of the Sephardic community. They form a valuable part of the Israeli people – rooted in the life of their family and, untouched by westernisation, dignified in their practical style of life. This will not, of course, remain so for long. The Israeli army is the great educational instrument of westernisation. Soon – and the sooner the better – the difference between the Sephardic community of Israel that comes straight from the Islamic Middle Ages, and the Ashkenazim who come straight from the civilisation of eastern and central Europe, will have disappeared.

The Islamic situation of the State of Israel was not introduced by the Sephardic Jew, but arises with an inner logic out of a peculiar political predicament. Owing to the electoral system, a socialist party group has to make some concessions to religious orthodoxy. It is for this most disreputable of reasons that religious Law has been made obligatory for the citizen of Israel. Identification of political law with religious law is Islam: and it is this which now governs the life of the Israeli citizen. A Jewish orthodoxy, established as 'state religion', is Islam, and something of which Jews cannot, with consistency, approve. A religious state is a caliphate. The fact that in Israel religious law is applied with the support of the state is a step back into the dark ages – into the Islamic Middle Ages. A Jew robbed of his freedom cannot live a Jewish life. We must opt for the West. In the century and a half since Mendelssohn, Jews have proved that they can be both westerners and Jews.

We see today that Christianity, Islam, and Judaism are disappearing as watertight groups, each separated from the others by their hitherto individual cultures and civilisations. Christian, Muslim, and Jew are all forced into a situation in which they have to assert themselves as three different types. To the Jew, there is nothing new in this situation. The Middle Ages had their two complementary civilisations, the Christian and the Mohammedan. Judaism, with its prophetic roots preserved, never represented a civilisation. If an architect were to reconstruct a model of the Herodian Temple, we would see the kind of building that stood everywhere around the Mediterranean world. The earlier Temple of Solomon was a work of Phoenician architecture. The Hebrew Bible itself has its Canaanite, Egyptian, and Babylonian elements. The Jew, as we have said, is a Jew in virtue of his being engaged in '*Abhodhah*, in worship of God and in work for his livelihood. He is not called upon to erect a 'Jewish' culture. It is only the apocalyptist who will condemn the superstructure over

Adam's field as an illusion, and as a quickly fading, sinful Babylon. The so-called superstructure, condemned by the apocalyptist and by the Marxist, is a home for man to live in. It lasts just so long as man can keep out the decay. This he can endeavour to do by his moral actions, by doing justly and by loving mercy. The Jew cooperates with the creators of culture and civilisation. But to speak of a 'Jewish culture' is to be misled by an ideological fallacy. We shall either establish western civilisation in Israel, or else, if we fail to do so, we shall become involved in Levantine disorder and corruption. By pursuing the phantom of a Jewish culture we cannot preserve our Jewish identity. We must either stand in the midst of western civilisation as God-worshipping Jews, or we must disappear.

As western civilisation becomes global civilisation, Christianity and Islam cease to stand each behind the 'cordon' once provided by their geographical separateness: they now permeate each other. The Christianity of the bourgeois West gains in non-spiritual humaneness; and Islam, adopting the western state, leaves terrestrial holiness behind and rises to a spiritual status that enables man to become the architect of the superstructure of art and of technical miracles. The Jewish people, divided in the Middle Ages into two groups, one Ashkenazi and the other Sephardi according to their respective habitation in either Christian or Islamic countries, is today losing the complexional differentiation conferred on it by these two different civilisations of the medieval past. After Auschwitz, and after the exodus from the Arab countries, the Jewish people has one cultural prospect only. What is to be mankind's prospect in this new world, in which Christians and Muslims will no longer exist as closed groups separated from each other, and in which the Jew can no longer maintain his distinctive medieval form of life? What is the human situation in an age described by Angelus Silesius, Schelling and Rosenzweig as the Johannine age? It is not the Christian of the Petrine Church, with its militant programme of converting non-western civilisation, who will survive; but rather the Johannine Christian, offering himself, as a Christian person, to the family of man. It is not the Muslim, dreaming behind the legalistic walls of his *Sharia'* of an eternity that stands still in human life, who will survive; but rather the Muslim as a God-believing humanist, united in equality with his fellow believer. It is not the Jew, integrated into a life of separation by his ritual codes, who will survive; but the Jew who meets God under the same conditions as those under which the biblical prophet met Him. It is the Jew, the Christian, the Muslim, without the support of their past Jewish, Christian and Islamic cultures, but as three different types of man meeting God in three different ways – these it is who will constitute the future.

NOTES

1 Der Vater war zuvor, der Sohn ist noch zur Zeit
   Der Geist wird endlich sein am Tag der Herrlichkeit.
2 *Kuzari*, iv, 23; H. Hirschfeld's English translation, 2nd ed., 1931, p. 200, quoted by S. H. Bergman, *supra*, p. 58, see R. Loewe, *supra*, pp. 138 f., note 48.
3 See also my *The Face of God after Auschwitz*, 1965, chap. vii.
4 *Offener Humanismus*, p. 359.
5 So ist das Judentum berufen, auf den Trümmern der Religion seinen Dritten Tempel der wahren Religion aufzubauen.
6 Cf. E. Ullendorff, *infra*, pp. 276 f.

8

Rabbinic Adumbrations of
Non-violence : Israel and Canaan*

ANDRÉ NEHER

A glance at some recent Christian literature on the subject of
non-violence is enough to reveal the urgent necessity for a
comprehensive investigation of the treatment of this theme in
Jewish thought. Writers who, with the best of intentions, carry
their investigations back to what they regard as the biblical
sources or the background of the New Testament, can evince a
distressing ignorance (or a no less distressing misconception) of
the immense, indeed decisive contribution brought by the
Pharisees and the rabbis – in both thought and action – to the
historical development of the concept of non-violence.[1] The
expansion of rabbinic theory and rabbinic practice alike is richly
documented in manifold midrashic texts: it crystallises out in the
legal rulings of the *Halakhah*, and it finds practical implementation both in the lives of leading figures of Jewish history and in
the reactions of the nameless masses, forming an unbroken
series that links Rabbi Yoḥanan ben Zakkai and Rabbi 'Aqiba
backwards, with their biblical masters – Jacob-Israel, Moses,
Isaiah and Jeremiah – and forwards, with their disciples down the
centuries of Jewish life in the Diaspora – the martyrs of the

169

Crusades, of Chmielnicki, and of Auschwitz. Both theory and practice have been brought into sharp focus by dint of allusion to the figure of *voice* and *hands* (*Gen.* 27: 22) – those *hands of violence* that are the constant, if incidental, feature of Esau, and the *voice of non-violence* that forms the heritage of Israel. In the midst of the twentieth century, a century that has witnessed Auschwitz, but also the Warsaw rising, and Lidice and Oradour-sur-Glane as well as Hiroshima, the conscience of humanity has the right – nay, perhaps the obligation – to turn in its perplexity towards the halakhic jurisprudence of Judaism, in which it may find the completest of all expositions of the principles whereon non-violence rests: and not least among them, the determination of the factors that must render illegitimate the resort to force in self-defence, as well as of those that dictate the limits beyond which non-violence may not be carried. For it may sometimes happen that non-violence is hemmed in round about by a violence that proclaims itself as being amply justified by considerations of self-defence, and indeed rendered by them unavoidable.

The present position is a paradoxical one. On the one hand, Torah and *Halakhah* (which Torah subsumes as being its own self-manifestation in social and legal practice) reaffirm their role – ancient, prophetic, and authentic – as ethical guardians of the absolute. It is on that basis that *Halakhah* lays down that obedience to non-moral orders is to be withheld, utterly condemns all notions of reprisal, and requires that one expose oneself to the supreme penalty rather than to kill a second party at the arbitrary command of a third.[2] It was by appeal to the spirit of the *Halakhah* that an Israeli court of justice could condemn officers and other ranks who had offended against it at Kibya, thereby furnishing a legal argument for the conviction of the soldiers of Oradour, the bomber-crew of Hiroshima, and the storm-troopers of Auschwitz. Proceeding from a sense of its responsibility for the moral health of the body politic, Jewish *Halakhah* – Jewish law – asserts, in unfaltering accents, its own competence to release (and to procure the release of) the spark of moral conscience that may illuminate for mankind the concrete situation or moment of drama in which it finds itself. And yet, it is still (apparently) possible for contemporary moralists to persist in ignoring the *Halakhah*, and in misunderstanding the springs and living forces from which it derives. Strange, too, is it that Jewish ethical thought (as opposed to Jewish halakhic regulation of society) should likewise be passed over, from this point of view, in silence, without its occurring to those concerned that the *'Aggadha* – Jewish legendary material with its rich moralising vein – might evince some echo of response to the high-minded courage of the *Halakhah* in its handling of this theme.

A comprehensive account of the Jewish aggadic material relative to non-violence – desirable though such an account certainly is – cannot be embarked upon here. In its place, but a fragment is presented; it has, however, been selected from one of the boldest and most challenging chapters of Jewish thought, *viz.* its treatment of the theme of the extermination of the seven peoples of Canaan enjoined upon the Hebrews in the Bible (*Num.* 31: 7, 15 f.; 33: 55; *Deut.* 7: 2; 20: 16 f., etc.). The theme is, it would seem, typical of that perspective of violence that so hypnotised (among others) Simone Weil, and led her to a wholesale condemnation of Jewish thought as reflected in the Bible.[3] Possibly a re-examination of it in the light of what the Jewish *'Aggadha* has to say on the subject might have helped her, conversely, towards a better appreciation of the spirit of the *'Aggadha* as a whole: and conceivably the small section to which, on the present occasion, we invite the reader's attention can contribute something towards a conception of the true proportions of the entire edifice.

The *'Aggadha* of the Pharisees did not have to wait for the twentieth century, nor, indeed, for the message of the Gospels, to enunciate a doctrine of non-violence. In enunciating it, moreover, it did not think of itself as furnishing either a corrective for the literal sense of the Bible or a surrogate for it, but rather as the key to the text - a key, the appreciation and application of which by the reader of the Bible, had been presupposed as a condition of the Scriptures' being put together, to say nothing of their being made a channel of revelation. The word of the Bible has never been, in rabbinic thought, the object of a communication in which both the originating and the receiving party each play a unilateral role, with the Deity in some sense dictating cut-and-dried commands in an apodeictic manner and man simply noting them down in a book of rules for his own conduct. The secret of the biblical notion of revelation is the covenant, a term which presupposes the simultaneous participation of two parties in a common undertaking, and their lasting cooperation in consideration of certain happenings that are not divulged to all and sundry. This notion finds its truest reflection in the treatment by Judah Löw b. Bezalel of Prague (generally known as the *Maharal*) of the traditional picture of midrashic legend regarding the handing over of the two tables of stone, two handbreadths' length being still held by God, two grasped by Moses, and the space of two handbreadths empty in the middle.[4] The essence of the biblical doctrine of revelation betrays itself in this image of the blank gap in the middle – it is here that we may catch a glimpse of revelation actually at work, in the movement which proceeds from the combined endeavour of God and man to transfer its content from the realm of potentiality into that of actuality: investing revelation with all the dynamism of the *creatio ex nihilo* with which *Genesis* begins, a dynamism that is not feasible (once the human level has been reached) without that element of collaboration. And indeed, the indispensability of such cooperation was enunciated for all time in the plural form of the cohortative mood in which, in *Gen.* 1: 26, the Deity was constrained to express itself – as if to say, 'Let *us* make, (0) man . . .'.[5]

What this means in regard to the word of Scripture itself is that biblical revelation is no mere monologue entrusted by God to man, but rather a continuing and open dialogue between the two of them: the progressive endeavour of each party to get to know the other better, and a process in which the fact of God's having reposed such infinite confidence in man as to create him a free agent confers on man, from the outset, the advantage of having far greater opportunity than is available to God Himself. The definitive pronouncements of the Torah — *Thou shalt* and *Thou shalt not* — are, in the last resort, nothing else than what the unending, restless challenge of this dialogue succeeds in getting inscribed on to those two middle handbreadths on the tables that are still blank. The day when the space is filled up, and one will be in a position actually to read words that have never, in point of fact, been published in the same way as the rest of the text was originally promulgated — that day will be the Messiah's. In the meantime, matter that was never promulgated for man to hear nor published for him to read keeps creating itself, is erased, detached, and reborn within a tireless dialogue that is nothing other than the essential substance of the biblical text itself. It is a text in which everything is question, hypothesis, trial-and-error — the address, almost the button-holing of man by a God who needs man as much, and more, than man needs God.[6] For the world to survive and for God's hope to be realised that, with an equipoise of mercy and justice, it may succeed in surviving,[7] God must have an artisan to construct foundations for it: and so that nothing shall be overlooked in the selection of those foundations and the surveying of their adequacy, God needs a smith, prepared to hammer the metal and test its temper in the fire. It will come out either reduced to powder or duly cast for its purpose, as waste for the scrap-heap or as a masterpiece to crown the whole structure: but whichever it be, it will thus — and only thus — have authenticated its own value as a component of the whole design. Exactly so, the biblical dialogue is bespattered with regrets and fresh starts, defeats and victories, hesitations and decisions. Where evil is concerned, its boundaries have to be determined, obtruded at man by way of temptation, and left for him to discover through the oblique suggestions of hypothesis: let him learn to reject the hypothesis, resist the temptation, and, in overcoming evil, recover lost ground. Conversely, where good is at issue, perspectives have to be widened, obstacles strewn along the avenue by which it is approached, and the path barred by brambles: let man learn to uproot the weeds, sweep back the brambles, and march onward to extend his boundaries towards the infinite. Let man endeavour – he *can*, he *must* succeed. But whichever way it turns out, God accepts the fact of man's victory or man's defeat, smiling with delight when man can beat Him at His own game[8] and move further on towards the good than He can Himself, despondent and shedding tears when man allows himself to be ensnared by evil and fails to measure up to the heroes of his own history[9]: Himself earnestly desiring to be taught by man, so that Torah may prove to be in truth the fruit of the covenant between man and God and so improve, aye, complete the world that was itself the product of God's own, unaided act of creation.[10] In a pertinent rejoinder to Simone Weil's revulsion at the cruelties of the Bible, Emmanuel Lévinas writes that 'the rigid law of the Old Testament is not, perhaps, a *doctrine* of gentleness; what matters is that it is a *school* of gentleness.' A school indeed – but a school in which instruction was not simply given and translated into living experience solely in a past long since gone and done with, for 'the Oral Torah is eternally contemporaneous with the Written Torah'; and those who read the Bible are, by the invitation to walk into its school and sit in at the lessons, thereby set free from time.[11] If the Talmud can tell of Moses taking a back seat in the lecture-room of Rabbi 'Aqiba,[12] *per contra* Jewry constitutes an unbroken succession of students flocking for instruction to Moses himself: and it is their task, together with him, to help God translate His own message into historical actuality.

Let us set the problem of Israel and the seven nations of Canaan within this context of pre-messianic, uncompleted endeavour. We need to acknowledge that inherent therein we shall find a characteristically open question – a question that must always be essentially impatient of any summary solution, but which nonetheless poses itself to our conscience ever anew. It is not some academic exercise of the dim and distant past, the answer to which has been recorded finally, inexorably, and definitively in the chronologically governed annals of history; but a contemporary and abiding question to which we ourselves, in the here and now, are summoned to produce *some* solution. If we approach it in this way we shall be able to re-experience, with greater intensity, the dazzling illumination thrown on the problem by the *'Aggadha* of the rabbis, and shall find ourselves personally involved in the debates of conscience conducted by some of the heroic figures of Jewish history – Abraham, Moses, Joshua. Feebly supported by their associates, their inspiration obstructed by the hesitancy of their own scruples, and little aided, indeed, by circumstances, they did not, to be sure, succeed in 'solving' the problem: but their insistent endeavours at least to lift its implications on to an exemplary moral plane – and to ensure that it be retained on that plane – must command admiration. At the same time we shall be able to expose the dynamic character of the problem from within; for its energy is never frozen within some bleakly dogmatic formula, or within some categorical imperative that summons Israel to exterminate the Canaanites. Quite the contrary: the problem articulates itself across history in the manner of a crisis, with its troughs and its peaks, its quirks and its unpredictabilities. The controlling factor is that a clear-cut solution has never, at any time, been found for the problem. The issue, so far from being taken as read, clamours for constant and relentless resubmission to a scrutiny sufficiently subtle to satisfy the stringent insistence of ethical perceptiveness. It was never, for Israel, a matter of executing a judicial sentence, but of participating in a debate; God did not call upon the Jews to sit in judgment on Canaan, but to take up their role as party to a discussion of a question of principle, in which they happened also to be themselves materially involved. The meeting of Jew and Canaanite was to take place not in the impersonal atmosphere of the law-court, but rather amid all the intensity of a personal confrontation.

That the matter was ever destined to be one of paramount significance emerges from the fact that God saw fit to enshrine oblique reference to it in the opening words of the Bible, at the very first instant of creation – before, that is, either Canaanite or Jew enjoyed any physical existence. And yet, their moral existence was foreshadowed even in the prehistoric phase of the *cosmos*: for as Rashi (following the *Tanḥuma*)[13] recalls, it was the ethical problem of the co-existence of Israel and Canaan that dictated the radical modification in the logical lay-out of the Torah as this had been originally envisaged. For the Torah ought, logically, have opened with *Ex.* 12 and the preliminaries of Israel's exodus from Egypt at Passover; and if, instead, it begins with *Genesis* and creation, that is precisely because of the moral problem posed by the relationship of Israel towards the Canaanites whom they were destined to dispossess, the solution being discovered in God's absolute right of disposition of His own creation (*Ps.* 111: 6).

We are thus presented, at the very outset, with an astonishing *datum*, *viz.* that the whole problem was considered of sufficient significance to call for a modification of the divine plan. And it is natural to suppose that so daring a conception will not be limited in Jewish tradition simply to the textual architecture of the Torah, but that it will have been thought legitimate to extend it likewise to the sacred history which the Torah relates. If, at its very beginning, the Torah was constrained to jerk itself out of its own orbit in face of the (as yet) but *virtual* collision of Israel and Canaan, surely other moments of which the Torah tells will have experienced similarly asymmetrical diversions, in face of the *actual* collisions of the Israel and Canaan of history.

Even a cursory survey of Jewish tradition is sufficient to confirm the truth of this hypothesis, and to show that many commentators have seen in the problem of Israel and Canaan one of the factors that operate as a counter-current to the divine plan, imposing on it constant revisions—sometimes desirable ones, sometimes regrettable but necessary ones. Here we have one of the most pathetic features of the drama of the covenant, and round it there pile up misunderstandings as between God and man that render the authentic handling of the problem difficult and indeed, in extreme cases, impossible. Rarely can the Midrash have found occasion to express itself in terms more poignant than those in which it laments the failure of heroes of the Bible to measure up to the occasion when, amid circumstances as tremendous as they were unique, each in turn held in his hands the destiny of history; Abraham, Moses, and Joshua – the one a failure of faith, the second

176

of imagination, and the third of virtue. When Abraham confronted the king of Sodom, and for the first time Hebrew and Canaanite made contact with each other, he suffered what was, in effect, a failure of faith, and so caused history to take a wrong turning. The king of Sodom had made him an offer – 'Give me the persons (Hebrew *han-nephesh*: literally, *soul*(s)), and take the goods to thyself' (*Gen.* 14: 21). How was it, asks the Midrash in incredulous indignation, that Abraham could reply that he would take nothing that belonged to the king of Sodom? Surely he ought to have entered into the spirit of the Canaanite's own game, and merely have turned the proposition upside down! Ought he not to have laid claim to the 'souls' himself? For more than one decade he had been engaged, together with Sarah, in effecting conversions to the monotheistic faith by means of both teaching and example: was he now to deny the advantages of that faith to the men of Sodom? What a wonderful turning back of the course of history it would have been if, instead of sending those souls home to Sodom, he had led them to his tented home at Hebron, there to find refuge under the wings of the divine Presence, so that out of the hotbed of unspeakable vice, there had sprung forth good![14] Abraham did, no doubt, treat the king of Sodom to an impressive lesson in disinterestedness, but in so doing he missed his messianic *rendez-vous* – he would not take the risk of giving the one and only answer by means of which the Canaanite king would have been not merely edified, but converted.

It was that same *rendez-vous* which Moses, too, missed, when through his unduly hesitant changes of mind at the burning bush[15] he directly thwarted the wider, magnanimous intentions of the Deity; which had not solely in view the limited objective that was to be realised in the immediately ensuing chapter of history, *viz.* the exodus of Israel from Egypt, but which envisaged, even then, the exodus of *Egypt* as well from Egypt. 'This shall be a token unto thee, that I have sent thee: when thou hast brought forth *the people* out of Egypt, ye shall serve God upon this mountain' (*Ex.* 3: 12). *The* people (Heb. *ha-'am*) – not *My* people or *thy* people. *The* people, *par excellence*: a whole nation of persecutors, an executioner whose manacles are, for the

177

moment (it is true) beginning to slacken in order to permit one particular victim to go free. But it is destined to remain inscribed for ever as a nation of violence, lurking for yet other victims, if you – Moses – are going to miss your cue, if you are not going to undertake, here and now, the task of getting the monster itself away from the dominion of tyranny; if you are not prepared to lead out *two* peoples, executioner and victim hand in hand, and bring both Egypt and Israel together to the Mountain of God and to a messianic experience that shall beat swords into ploughshares, and that will transmute the Hebrew term *'abhodhah* from its meaning of *servitude* into the meaning of *worship*. But Moses could neither see the point nor take on the task. He was dubious enough about the prospects of success for Israel's own exodus – how could he even begin to contemplate the possibility of Egypt's exodus from Egypt? And as a result he constricted the divine plan within so narrow a perspective that in the end he was unable to recognise even his own intended role within it: 'Why is it that thou hast sent me?' (*Ex.* 5: 22). 'Why indeed?' we may picture God being constrained to rejoin in bitter irony, 'except for the fact that I no longer have an Abraham, an Isaac, or a Jacob available – men of heroic build whose kind is no more. They too, to be sure, made their mistakes; but at least they didn't lay them at anyone else's door. Whereas you can find nothing better to do than to cap all your own shortcomings by crediting them to – Me!'[16]

And Joshua? Nothing more nor less than a robber-baron – for it is as such, according to one almost buried strand of Jewish tradition,[17] that he strides into history, accoutred, it may perhaps be, with a soubriquet (Joshua *lista'a, the Pirate*) to characterise – with a devastating appropriateness – his whole manner of approach to Canaan, if the unadorned text of the Bible is alone to be our guide. The very reproach that God would fain have spared Israel from the aborigines ('you are nothing but brigands' (*listim*),[18] the possibility of which had indeed induced Him to modify the plan of His Torah so as to put Israel out of its range – it has to be precisely this reproach that sullies Israel in the person of their leader, at the very moment when their confrontation with Canaan is moving from potentiality on to the plane of concrete actuality. And so, as things turn out, the drastic rethinking of the architecture of the Torah seems to have been in vain. At every crucial moment the biblical heroes jib, and down goes the see-saw of history. The course of events is diverted into quite another plan – a plan that involves violence and massacre, and is radically different from that which God Himself regarded as being of such cardinal importance that He used it as the signature tune of His own Torah.

What, then, were the original main lines in the pattern of the divine plan? How was the problem of Israel and Canaan intended to unwind itself across the pages of history, as from the moment of the gesture by which God saw fit to inscribe it as (so to say) the legend on the medal of creation?

One preliminary observation is called for: and it is an observation that is prompted by rigorous attention to the letter of the text itself. There is not the slightest question of any extermination, execution, or massacre being enjoined throughout the 400-year long period of the 'Hebrew-Canaanite problem' that preceded a certain event which, from both the chronological and geographical points of view, is exactly fixed – the incident of the Spies. It is only after this episode that Israel is called upon to 'exterminate' the Canaanites. Previous to that, the terms employed as the controversy moves from stage to stage and through varying moods, first in the patriarchal age, then in Egypt, and thereafter during the first year of the exodus, are for the most part quite vague: they suggest at most a peaceful co-existence of Hebrew and Canaanite in the Land of Canaan. Where they are more precise, they indicate (without any equivocation) the idea of exile. The Hebrews are to be the agent by which the Canaanites will be driven out in rejection, even as Adam had been driven out of the Garden of Eden and as Israel knows that it must itself expect to be driven out, should it violate its covenant with God.

The divine plan thus comprises two clearly distinguished stages, hingeing on the affair of the Spies. The crisis brought about by the Spies' report was to leave its black mark on history

o   179

even more than did the crisis of the golden calf. The sin which precipitated the latter gave way to penitence and to reconciliation on the ensuing Day of Atonement, and the very individuals who had sinned themselves secured their forgiveness but a few weeks later.[19] But the Spies' crisis cuts deep into the living flesh of humanity: the individuals who, like the Spies themselves, have turned their back on Canaan are destined never to see the Land, and it is another, younger generation that will experience the confrontation with Land and people. And so a shattering rupture is effected between the exodus from Egypt and the entry into Canaan; and two events that had originally been intended to form twin episodes in a historical movement are set at loggerheads, each with its sights levelled at the other – lacking all link and harmony, like the surviving arches of some bridge whose decking has crashed into ruins. And the eve of the 9th of Ab, which witnessed this original collapse into the desert, haunts subsequent Jewish history with its sinister, nay, all but fatal reappearances. For this episode there is no Day of Atonement and reconciliation to staunch the cataract of tears that lasts for aye, their bitterness intensified as they splash their way across yet other calamities and convulsions that mark its anniversary[20]; the fall of the two Temples, the fall of Bethar, the expulsion of the Jews from Spain and so many happenings to recall, down the annals of history, each one its own 9th of Ab, intimately linked in its meaning to that first 9th of Ab of the Spies. For all of them are but sequels of that radical reorientation which the Spies made it necessary to impose on God's plan: and each one reawakens, across the spans of a still unfinished story, the memory of the stark sunderings which seared that first 9th of Ab on a desert night so long ago.

If, then, the trauma occasioned by that sundering has repercussions that run across the whole of subsequent history, could it have failed to leave its immediate traces on the period of the exodus, or have failed to affect Israel's then imminent confrontation with Canaan? Something had taken place to divert the world's course along a different road, and through it the dialectic of homeland and exile had been all but reversed. As from that fatal moment Israel, instead of preparing itself to become the people of the Land, had been reorientated, with exile as its condition of existence. The successive 'investitures' by which Israel's title to the land had been confirmed were thenceforth tied to a host of conditions, the effect of which was subtly to slide the connection between Israel and its Land out of the realm of the absolute, into the relative. Historically speaking, from that moment onwards Israel was able to survive in exile because it was, for the future, no longer bound to its own Land by a destiny that involved its very life and death. It is, moreover, this psychological tangle that forms the starting point for the whole midrashic concept of history. In the light of all this, one can scarcely do other than concede that the change in this dialectic, this terrestrial bond, and this historical self-consciousness which was brought about *on the spot* by the incident of the Spies, must itself have been an upheaval the decisiveness of which was inescapable. In point of fact, the result of the incident of the Spies was that Israel became 'canaanised'; henceforth there was to be a second Canaan in the Land. In place of an indissoluble 'marriage', Israel's settlement in the Land is to be an 'affair', with a thousand different nuances of relationship, ranging from a provisional faithfulness to treason, divorce, and whoredom. Israel having failed to respond to its call, Canaan, too, will fail in its own turn: Israel having refused to embrace the Land, Canaan will refuse to abandon it and embrace exile. But in the Land – one, unique Land – there is no room for two Canaans: and Israel's entry thereto henceforth becomes a rape.

To be sure, the generation of the exodus did not die in the desert in perpetuity. It will qualify for resurrection, as Rabbi Eliezer asserts despite the sustained objections of Rabbi 'Aqiba, and it, too, will share in the opportunity to make a reality – under messianic auspices – of that marriage with the Land that eluded so dramatically the generation of the conquest – not by might, nor by power, but by the spirit alone.[21] On the 9th of Ab, in the great moment of debate regarding the covenant, God had been defeated by man, who chose for himself the way of violence. Man thereby obliged God to take an oath not to re-establish peace

181

until man should himself desire it and implement it. Each day, God is on the look-out, waiting for man to have the courage to release Him from His own oath; and never, as He watches the march of history, does He abandon expectation.[22]

The line of that march is plotted by the Midrash, its eye quick to recognise the slightest delicacy of movement that can give it the chance to restage the debate more effectively, to focus the dialogue more accurately, and to flood the problem of non-violence with the most limpid of lights. In every biblical episode rabbinic analysis discovers some element of the problem, winning from the very sinews of the test a doctrine of non-violence which not even the frailty of man has been able to dull more than temporarily. Were one to take the trouble to collect and scrutinise all the relevant rabbinic material, it would be feasible to formulate a systematic *exposé* of that doctrine. On this occasion we shall examine but three fragments, all of them inextricably linked to the theme of the violent confrontation of Israel and Canaan: the War of Abraham and the Kings, the episode of Jacob's sons at Shechem, and Joshua on the eve of the Conquest of Canaan.

The problem of Abraham's War is analysed by the Midrash,[23] with a scrupulousness that refuses to leave obscured in the shadow any single point of major ethical significance in regard to a question so dramatic as that of violence or non-violence. On the one hand, surely, there can be no doubt at all about the legality of Abraham's act. In arming his liegemen he had nothing else in mind than to require them to take the field with him in a rescue operation completely justified by law and by morality, if the criterion is to be the 'rules' governing these things. After all, was it not a man's life that was at stake?

True enough. And yet, even in this context of legitimate defence and of rendering aid to those in danger – indeed, in such a context above all – these rules must be not merely recalled, but accepted in their underlying spirit and then applied. And so the Midrash proceeds to demonstrate how Abraham did, in point of fact, conscientiously discharge the task of applying the relevant ethical considerations that should govern any proposed resort to force; and it does so by offering (*inter alia*) three several interpretations of the words of *Gen.* 14: 14 which the Authorised Version renders 'he armed his trained servants' (Heb. *wayyareq 'eth ḥanikhaw*). The Hebrew means, quite literally, 'and he *emptied* out his initiated (i.e. trained) [men]', and the subtlety of the moralisation revolves round the various ways in which the roots *rwq = empty* and *ḥnk = initiate, educate,* may be understood. First, then, Rabbi 'Abba b. Zabda's explanation, which rests on a pun between the roots *rwq* and *yrq*: 'he equipped them with [well *burnished*] arms.' In other words, Abraham did not commit his soldiers to the hazards of war without having previously given them the means wherewith to protect themselves; he did not launch off into the adventure casually and without thoroughgoing preparation, as so many a *régime* has done in the course of history. Alternatively – and this is the exegesis of Rabbi Simeon b. Laqish, which glances at *Ps.* 68: 14 – 'he overlaid (i.e. endowed) them with [*burnished* gold, silver, and] precious stones', in order that their objective should be disembarrassed (purged, '*emptied*') of every spirit of booty-hunting, and might find its one and only proper motivation in the will to rescue those in danger. That is to say, Abraham was at pains to eliminate all lure of economic advantage – the factor that constitutes an accessory inducement to go to war as potent as it is criminal. Rabbi Nehemiah, however, perceived another dimension: 'Abraham set his face brazenly ("as if it were *burnished*") against [the reluctance of the men] whom he had himself *initiated* [into the rudiments of monotheism], saying, ["since it is my religious beliefs and evangelism that has earned me the hostility of these kings], I shall go forth [if necessary without you, despite your own, equal obligations in the matter, and if necessary] I am prepared to fall in sanctification of the Name of the Omnipresent."' A dictator will, often enough, throw his troops into battle whilst himself remaining comfortably in the rear, but Abraham's tactics were otherwise; in the true spirit of the Torah, he exposed his own person to the risks. Unlike so many a cloistered sage or ivory-towered intellectual who is ready enough to applaud – from a safe distance

– the courage displayed by those who fight in the streets for the ideals which they have proclaimed from the pulpit, Abraham can don his own armour on behalf of the cause that he has espoused, ready to hazard himself personally to all its dangers – once, that is, that he has arrived at the conviction of the complete congruence between the use of force that he is contemplating, and the ethical dictates of the Torah.

All this reflects a sensitivity that is scrupulous indeed regarding the responsibilities contingent upon a resort to force, even where that resort is legitimate: but is it the last word that the ethics of Torah have to say on the matter? It would seem that it is not, since, as has already been said, the Talmud[24] holds that the story betrays an aberration of faith on Abraham's part. Abraham could – perhaps, indeed, should – have essayed something more decisive still; inasmuch as it was not feasible for him to 'arm his trained men' at all, without at the same time playing traitor to the eirenic spirit of the Torah. As we have seen, the Hebrew means literally 'he *emptied* them'; and in *arming* his disciples he was necessarily *emptying* them of the content of the Torah in which he had for years been educating (training, *initiating*) them. In the crucial moment that he 'armed' his disciples he was *ipso facto* orientating them in a radically different direction. This latter interpretation of the text is that proposed recently by M. Emmanuel Lévine,[25] who shows himself here faithful to an exegetical tradition ascending to the Tosaphists in the middle ages – evidence enough of the extent to which Judaism has sensed the actuality (and the unabated urgency) of the whole problem.

It was, then, non-violence that constituted the radically new departure which, had he seen fit, Abraham might have embodied into his diplomatic gesture *vis-à-vis* the Canaanites. Could he not, ought he not, when his moment of destiny arrived, have attempted the impossible – to have armed his faithful band with nought but the Torah, nought but the spirit, and have pursued the kings of Sumer and force them to turn and face him, the radiance of that spirit his only weapon? Possibly the kings might have yielded to the assault of such 'radiational' warfare of the spirit;

they might have released both captives and looted property, and themselves have followed Abraham along his road of religion and morality. Perhaps . . . At any rate, Jewish tradition plays longingly with the dream that Abraham himself could not dream. Or, should we not rather say, *would* not dream? Abraham, we may feel sure, preferred to leave to his children the undecaying obligation of acknowledging that circumstances might yet arise in which this dream could be conceived anew, and be not merely dreamed, but find its practical implementation.

The episode of the sack of Shechem (*Gen.* 34) is the archetype of violence, the arrogance of its concluding words – 'Is he to be allowed to behave as he might towards a harlot, towards our sister?' – seeming actually to put forward a justification of resort to violence and its prosecution into the extravagant realm of reprisal; an outrageous escalation, in that it goes beyond all bounds of morality, the innocent being quite deliberately struck in place of the guilty. In point of fact, these parting words with all their *panache* prove to be a gesture of defiance on the part of Simeon and Levi towards their father Jacob, who had disapproved of their intervention and was, indeed, to maintain his disapproval until, still haunted on his very deathbed by the blameworthiness of his sons, he contrived to find sombre words of farewell in which to condemn their violence (*Gen.* 49: 5–7). It is quite clear that it is the Patriarch's unbroken maintenance of his condemnation for his sons' intervention which forms the key to the story as the Bible tells it: and Isaiah Leibowitz is entirely right in going back to the moral that it seeks to convey, in order to apply the lesson to Hiroshima and to Kibya.[26]

Once again, the Midrash takes soundings in the biblical account; and in exposing all the delicacy of mood and touch evinced therein, it is able to go further, and to construct around the incident of Shechem an archetypal analysis of the problem of violence as a whole. It will be remembered that, somewhat before he died, having execrated the deed of Simeon and Levi in what was practically his last breath, Jacob had mentioned the name of Shechem to his son Joseph. The context would seem at first to connect Jacob himself with the *sword* and *bow* by means of which the Canaanite city was captured – 'As for me, I have given thee an extra *Shechem* over and above thy brethren (Authorised Version, one portion above thy brethren) which I took out of the hand of the Amorite with my sword and with my bow' (*Gen.* 48: 22). Shechem, as nothing but a place-name, is grammatically very difficult if not impossible here; and since as a common noun it has the meaning of *shoulder*, Rabbi Judah in *Genesis Rabbah*,[27] 'Onqelos in his Aramaic translation of the Pentateuch, and (following them) Rashi in his commentary, offer the quasi-literal rendering of *portion* adopted by the Authorised Version (*ḥeleq*, *ḥullaq*), applying it to the birthright wrested by Jacob from the hands of Esau, 'whose way of life was that of the Amorite'. The same fair road of exegesis leads to the metamorphosis of *sword* and *bow* into instruments designed for something other than armed assault: according to Rabbi Judah, *fulfilment of the divine precepts* and *good deeds*, according to 'Onqelos (in some texts),[28] *prayer* and *supplication*; and according to Rashi, *wisdom* (i.e. scholarship in Torah) and *prayer*. It goes without saying that it is not mere grammatical concern that leads these interpreters to get rid of the name of *Shechem* from the verse entirely (Rabbi Judah and possibly 'Onqelos), or to bury it beneath exegetical superstructure (Rashi). What they are concerned to avoid is the ethically embarrassing association of Jacob's name and Jacob's achievements with an enterprise that was, from start to finish, one of violence. *Sword*, *bow*, and all mention (even though it be of but an allusive character) of any participation on the part of Jacob himself in the sack of Shechem must be eliminated. Everything suggestive of war and violence is to be stripped from him; and so, by dint of weeding the episode of Shechem right out of the text and linking the verse with the theme of the birthright, there is achieved one of the finest pieces of *pacifist transmutation* effected by Jewish exegetical alchemy. Jacob, the man of war, festooned with weapons from head to foot, becomes a hero of the spirit, decked in no armour other than that of philanthropy and prayer.

The foregoing piece of exegesis calls forth another; for it

emerges clearly from *Genesis Rabbah* that the construction of this verse of *Genesis* formed the subject of one of the many controversies – so profound in their implications – of Rabbi Judah and Rabbi Nehemiah. Behinds the names of these two controversialists there face each other two schools of pharisaic exegesis. One – that represented by Rabbi Judah – at a single stroke expunges the undertones of violence than run through the scoring of the verse; the other – that of Rabbi Nehemiah – retains them, but analyses the significance of the countenancing (here) of violence and defines its limits.

'*Shechem* here means *Shechem*' (*shekhem mammash*), is the unequivocal opening of Rabbi Nehemiah. Everything is to be understood absolutely literally; we are in truth dealing with Shechem the city, and by the Amorite is meant Hamor, her chief. But if that is so, then *sword* and *bow* have, equally, to be taken in the literal sense. Does this really mean, then, that we have here to deal with actual weapons that you can touch and see, instruments of physical violence, and that the patriarch Jacob, ancestor and symbol of the Jewish people, positively availed himself of them? Yes, says Rabbi Nehemiah, *sword* and *bow* are here intended in their most literal and concrete meaning; but it was not during the course of the Shechem episode that Jacob girded them on. With the incident itself – the stratagem, the attack and reprisals – Jacob himself would have nothing to do – not on any pretext whatsoever, either before or after the event. 'It was not with the acquiescence of Jacob our forefather that his sons perpetrated that dastardly deed.'[29] But afterwards? A new situation is created. The deed is done: though condemned by him and never to cease being condemned by him, it cannot be undone; and the circumstance of its having been done confronts Jacob with another problem, entirely new, which has no connection in ethics with the preceding one – *viz*., the danger to which his sons have become exposed by the threatened vengeance of the other Canaanite tribes. 'Can I abandon my own children to the native hordes?' Jacob asks; and it was then that he took up his sword and his bow and posted himself beside the gate of Shechem, saying, 'If the nations come to join battle with my sons, I shall fight against them myself.' And that, asserted Rabbi Nehemiah by way of definitive conclusion, was the only occasion in his whole life on which Jacob took up sword and bow.

A remarkable piece of exegesis, which puts its finger on the awesome limits that turn back non-violence – the frontier of feeling beyond which logic and reason abdicate their power, and nothing is left but that instinctive impulse by which, in a sympathy that knows nothing of things rational, human beings may be reciprocally bound one to another. In order to protect those to whom he is bound, in order to find means of expressing the mystic loyalty he feels towards his own which will brook no denial, man is ready in the last resort to defend them, if need be, by violence itself, and to die in battle for or with them. A problem is here, the fearful dimensions of which are thrown into stark focus by Albert Camus when he writes[30] that 'as between justice and his mother, he would choose his mother' – and dare any reader invert the answer, and declare that in order to vindicate the sacrosanctity of non-violence, he would be prepared to sacrifice his mother, or to allow her to be sacrificed, in the name of justice? Let each look deep into his conscience before he answers. And let him then appraise, at its true worth, the quality of greatness in rabbinic thought that can pose the problem dialectically, by way of the rival opinions of two rabbis, and so leave each individual conscience with the right – and also the obligation – of choosing as between Rabbi Judah and Rabbi Nehemiah; challenging him at the same time to exercise that choice in the full knowledge that, in the very moment of his exercising it, the consequences to which it will lead are severely practical ones and may also prove extreme. If you follow Rabbi Judah, it is not merely that the view changes, but everything changes with it. You yourself are not the same man, 'Esau' is no longer Esau nor 'Shechem' Shechem; the universe dissolves into nothing but allegory and myth. With Rabbi Nehemiah, it is creatures of flesh and blood, your own children, that you are called upon to defend. If you are going to hesitate to take up arms, reckon up your risks; it is not lifeless symbols or the archetypal figures of myth that are involved, but your own children and your mother.

At the gates of Canaan, on the eve of the decisive attack, Joshua – a very different Joshua from 'Joshua the Pirate' of one Jewish tradition (see *supra*, p. 178) – hesitates. Instead of flinging his troops forthwith against the enemy, he thinks out a plan: not a strategic plan, but rather one with an air of diplomacy about it. He draws up a proclamation, which he charges emissaries to bring to the knowledge of the Canaanites, boosted by all available means of publicity. The proclamation consists of three edicts (*prostágmata*), each of which places before the Canaanites a choice, expressed in brief and striking military terms: 'Let anyone who wishes to do so evacuate the country; those who wish to make peace should make peace with us, those who wish to fight with us should fight.'[31]

It is a strange appeal, not merely in its form – there being no hint in the biblical text that anyone ever suggested such a *démarche* to Joshua – but also in its content. Two of its clauses can be accounted for. Thus, one may take the view that in offering the Canaanites war, Joshua was in fact perfectly ready to carry out the letter of the law in all its rigour, and to implement all the prescriptions so insistently laid down in the Torah more than once after the episode of the Spies, regarding the confrontation of the Canaanites and their extermination by the sword. Again, one may gather that in offering them peace terms Joshua was doing no more than to put into practice the doctrine elaborated by Moses, and imposed by him on God in the course of a moving piece of dialogue,[32] *viz.* that the procedure laid down in *Deut.* 20: 10 for calling on an enemy city to make peace before laying siege to it should apply not only to possible wars of the distant future, but also forthwith, i.e. to the then imminent campaigns against the Canaanite nations themselves. But if each of the aforesaid proposals is consequently seen to place Joshua within the line of an identifiable tradition, that is no longer the case in regard to the third option given by him to the Canaanites, that of evacuation (*le-phannoth*; from the root *pnh*, *turn*). In this instance Joshua is exercising a strictly personal initiative. At the eleventh hour, in the very moment against which he has so long kept himself in readiness, Joshua makes a breathtaking attempt to lead history back on to its original path – he tries to reverse the course of events back to the period before the incident of the Spies, and, starting as if from there, he presumes to orientate the future along lines which that episode had twisted out of their own natural direction.

His whole life had been, in some way, a preparation for this crucial moment. He had never once been of the mind of the other, craven-hearted Spies, and his innocence of their knavery had served to promote the change of his name (*Num.* 13: 16) from *Hoshea* – approximating to a verb in the past, 'he has saved' – to *Joshua*, *'he who will yet save'*. It was *saving victory* that was now beckoning to him from the future, and one may observe Joshua looking in eager anticipation towards the hour that was to be his hour. Although he had been designated by Moses as his successor, he had taken no part in the conquest of the territory east of the Jordan – an operation carried out under Moses' own direction by Phineas. One gains the impression that, in his heart, Joshua disapproved of this campaign, and refused to have anything to do with it – unhappy that his own master and teacher should accept, without a murmur, the determinism of history and the inexorability of its cog-wheeled processes, meeting it instead with a fatalism that ran right athwart the protests whereby, on other occasions, he had prevailed in the very teeth of that determinism. So he bides his time, and his time comes on the morrow of his master's death. And then, in one magnificent bound, he revives – and makes his own – the original theme of Canaan's own exile from his Land: the theme that God had had in view when He created the world and when He made Israel His chosen people, but which, for well nigh forty years, has been discarded and completely forgotten by the world, by Israel, and by God Himself.

It is this last possibility of the three held open to the Canaanites by Joshua that carries the full weight of the decision that he had himself reached, and which enshrines his own secret hopes for the future – *viz.* that Canaan would reject equally a warlike solution and that of submitting peaceably to subjugation by Israel, and would instead adopt the solution of exile, with all its redemptive implications for Israel and Canaan alike. That the emphasis is in fact just as we have here represented it emerges from the evidence for another feature in Joshua's character as the Midrash sketches it. At the epoch-making moment of his own meeting Canaan face to face, he rounds off the diplomatic offensive which, by way of appeal to man, he has been conducting on the horizontal plane, complementing it by an appeal on the vertical plane addressed in prayer to God.[33]

For it was at the very gates of Canaan, no doubt whilst waiting in suspense for such reply as the Canaanites might see fit to make to his appeal, that Joshua composed (according to one Jewish tradition) the great prayer that begins with the words '*Alenu le-shabbeaḥ* – 'It is ours to praise the Lord of all.'[34] But whereas the first paragraph of this prayer is a categorical affirmation of monotheistic faith, the second[35] gives expression to ardent hope that God's kingdom may be established on earth and that the tearing down of idols may be brought about not by violence, but by a new dispensation (*tiqqun, le-taqqen*) – a moral resettlement of such a sort that 'all mankind shall call upon Thy Name . . . and all the inhabitants of the world shall so perceive as to make it integral to all their thinking, that it is to Thee that every knee must bend, etc.'; and, above all, that 'Thou mayest turn unto Thee all the wicked ones of the earth.' '*To make to turn to Thee*' – *le-haphnoth*: the very word (root *pnh*) that Joshua had allegedly employed in his proclamation calling upon the Canaanites to evacuate (*le-phannoth*) their territory, *turning* aside in order to vacate it for Israel. One may, indeed, raise the surmise that it may have been the occurrence of this same term in both the liturgical piece and the midrashic reconstruction of the language of Joshua's diplomacy that has given rise to the notion that both texts were inspired by, or drawn up by Joshua. Whether this be so or not, Joshua is revealed in the legend regarding the composition of the prayer as being one of those great souls who have impressed upon the problem of the encounter with human wickedness a characteristically – indeed eminently – Jewish stamp: the same company to which belong Beruriah, the wife of Rabbi Me'ir, with her celebrated exegesis of *Ps.* 104: 35,[36] and Rabbi Judah Löw b. Bezalel, the *Maharal* of Prague, who applied the same notion to the so-called 'test-benediction' of the Eighteen Blessings that was designed to exclude the leadership of sectarians in communal worship.[37] It is not for the extermination of the *wicked* that the Jew is called upon both to pray and to use his best endeavours, but the extirpation of *wickedness* – the conversion of evil into good, the return of the conscience of humanity to the purity from which it sprung, and the exile of evil with a view to its redemptive rehabilitation. Such redemption is not merely the object of prayer on the part of man: to steer man towards the point where he will himself desire to make that prayer his own – that is the prayer of . . . God.

Some there are who, dulled like Rabbah bar bar Ḥana,[38] pass the divine call by without comprehension. Others, like Rabbi Ishmael,[39] seize it on the wing, and in virtue of a responsiveness that is intuitive and also holds itself ever in readiness, are able to interpret it and so implement its directives. At those great cross-roads of history when – on two occasions now – the 'Return' of Israel to the Land has been set afoot, men of such calibre have been there, available and on the alert – as was Rabbi Ishmael – to raise up aloft (*qua* Jews) the banner of non-violence; and it is they who transmute the leaden import of the 'conquest' into a nobler metal, by their insistence that no matter what happened in the past, this time at least the conquest shall be no conquest, but rather – as befitting the harbinger of a messianic culmination – something peaceful, in which violence shall have no part. Such was the goodly fellowship of the prophets, including, at the time of the first return from exile, Zechariah – not by might, nor by power, but by My spirit alone; and such, amongst Jews throughout the world at the time of the second return, was Leon Roth, with the watchword *Berith shalom* – no covenant that is not founded on peace. Men of such a build do not wait passively for the Messiah to come and set the course of history aright; they prepare for the Messiah's coming themselves, by getting those things put right that cannot be allowed to be left uncorrected. Drawing their strength from the inexhaustible breast of the divine covenant, they give, instead of the wrong answer that men have been giving for so long, the right one – the answer for which God has Himself been tirelessly waiting down the ages, watching for it across the mighty movements of history as He muses, 'would only that men – would that men's ears – were but attuned to catch the whisperings of God Himself at prayer.'

NOTES

*Translated by the Editor from the Author's French.

1 The attitude of rabbinic Judaism to non-violence is completely ignored by William Robert Miller in *Non-Violence, A Christian Interpretation*, London, 1964, despite the occasion to notice it in connection with the treatment (pp. 24–32) of *Hindu and Biblical Concepts*. André Trocmé in *Jésus-Christ et la Révolution non-violente*, Geneva, 1961, gives an inadequate and indeed disfigured picture of the Jewish attitude; the texts chosen to illustrate chap. x, *Le courant de résistance non-violente*, insofar as they purport to represent the views of Jewish social groups or political parties, are taken exclusively from Josephus – the Talmud is not even mentioned.

2 The *locus classicus* for halakhic refusal to countenance obedience to commands that are contrary to ethical principle is to be found in the Babylonian Talmud, *Sanhedrin* 74a: 'A certain man came before Rabbah (more probably Rabha) and said, "The governor of my locality has bidden me 'Go and kill X – or else I shall have you killed yourself.' Rabha said to him, "You must let the governor kill you rather than committing murder yourself: who is able to say that your own blood is redder than his? Perhaps his is redder than yours?" ' Cf. D. Daube, *Collaboration with Tyranny in Rabbinic Law*, Oxford, 1965, pp. 26–7.

3 *Attente de Dieu*, p. 177: '. . . Les Hébreux se vantaient d'avoir entièrement exterminé quantité de cités et de peuples sur le territoire de Canaan, quand Josué les menait. Qui veut noyer son chien l'accuse de la rage. Qui l'a noyé plus encore. On ne reçoit pas contre la victime le témoignage du meurtier. . . . p. 189: '. . . Les Hébreux, conduits par Josué, purent massacrer sans peine et sans avoir besoin de beaucoup de miracles des populations sans défenseurs. . . . Pourtant le silence total d'Hérodote sur Israël reste très énigmatique. Il faut que ce peuple ait été regardé à cette époque comme sacrilège. . . .' The irony of the contrast between these passages and the title of the book from which they are extracts should be observed; its wryness is enhanced by the circum-

stance that the title is not even Simone Weil's own. It was chosen, long after her death, with sharp-eyed sedulousness by Father Perrin.

4 Maharal, *Neṣaḥ Yisra'el*, chap. 2.

5 Maharal, *Derekh Ḥayyim*, 5, 4.

6 *Genesis Rabbah*, 30, 10, ed. Wilna f. 63b, col. i, ed. Theodor-Albeck, p. 277, l. 5, and 97, 2, f. 188b, col. i, Theodor-Albeck, p. 1245, l. 5: 'commenting on *Gen*. 48: 15, *The God before whom my fathers did walk*, Rabbi Yoḥanan's view is that this means that we, like sheep, need a place near to Him, our shepherd; Resh Laqish's view is that God needs the glory which we, like elders attendant on a prince, can secure for Him.' Cf. the discussion of this theme by Abraham J. Heschel, *Theology of Ancient Judaism*, London-New York, 1962, 1, pp. 72–81.

7 *Genesis Rabbah*, 12, 15, ed. Wilna f. 32a, col. i, ed. Theodor-Albeck, pp. 112–13.

8 God exclaims, with a smile, 'My children have surpassed Me!', Babylonian Talmud, *Babha Meṣi'a* 59b. Cf. C. G. Montefiore-H. Loewe, *A Rabbinic Anthology*, pp. 340–1.

9 God laments, 'Alack for those who are perished and to be found no more', Babylonian Talmud, *Sanhedrin* 111a, cf. *infra*, p. 178, n. 16.

10 *Numbers Rabbah*, 19, 33, ed. Wilna, f. 83a, col. i.

11 Emmanuel Lévinas, *Difficile Liberté*, Paris, 1963, p. 167.

12 Babylonian Talmud, *Menaḥoth* 29b; L. Ginzberg, *The Legends of the Jews*, 3, p. 115, 6, p. 48, n. 250.

13 Rashi on *Gen*. 1: 1; *Tanḥuma*, ed. Buber, *Bere'shith* 11, f. 4a, n. 59, cf. A. Berliner's edition of Rashi (2nd ed., 1905), p. 424.

14 So Rabbi Yoḥanan, in Babylonian Talmud, *Nedharim* 32a *infra*; see R[abbi] N[athan] *in loc*.

15 This theme is developed – drawing on various sources – by Isaiah Horowitz in his *Sheney Luḥoth Hab-berith*, ii, 45d (6th homily on *Pesaḥim*).

16 *Exodus Rabbah*, 6, 4, ed. Wilna, f. 18a, col. i. Cf. *supra*, p. 174, n. 9.

17 There is some pointer to a reading 'Joshua the Brigand' having once stood in place of 'Phineas the Brigand' in Babylonian Talmud, *Sanhedrin* 106b; see Ginzberg, *op. cit*. (n. 12), 6, pp. 144 f., n. 855 and 177, n. 34, citing Procopius and Suidas; the relevant texts are assembled by W. Bacher in *Jewish Quarterly Review* (Old Series), 3, 1891, pp. 354 f.

18 Rashi on *Gen*. 1: 1; cf. *supra*, pp. 175 f., n. 13.

19 Babylonian Talmud, *Ta'anith* 30b, where see Rashi's explanation of the chronology.

20 *Numbers Rabbah*, 16, 20, ed. Wilna, f. 70a, col. ii.

21 Babylonian Talmud, *Sanhedrin* 110b (Mishnah, x, 3, H. Danby's translation, pp. 397–8).

22 Cf. Babylonian Talmud, *Babha Bathra* 74a, the gaffe of Rabbah bar bar Ḥana, who failed to grasp that what God was longing for was to be released from His oath whereby He had sent Israel into exile.

23 *Genesis Rabbah*, 43, 2, ed. Wilna, f. 87a, col. i, ed. Theodor-Albeck, p. 416. The matter enclosed in square brackets is implicit in the text, and is indeed elaborated by the commentators (especially Z. W. Einhorn) *in loc.*

24 Babylonian Talmud, *Nedarim* 32a (Rabbi Eleazar, reported by Rabbi 'Abbahu). The second explanation of R[abbi] N[athan] *in loc.* adduces the occurrence of *req = empty* in *Gen.* 37: 24 ('the well was empty').

25 E. Lévine has made use of the periodical *Tsédéq* (Paris) to put forward his thinking on the subject of non-violence.

26 Isaiah Leibowitz, *Torah u-miṣwoth baz-zeman haz-zeh*, Tel Aviv, 1954, pp. 168–73.

27 97, 6, ed. Wilna, f. 179b, col. i, ed. Theodor-Albeck, p. 1249.

28 The reading *bi-ṣelothi u-bhe-bhaʿuthi, my prayer and supplication*, is assumed without discussion in N. Adler's commentary *Nethinah Lag-ger*; but the Sabbioneta text of 1557 reproduced by A. Berliner, p. 56, retains the literal Hebrew. Cf. S. D. Luzzatto, *Philoxenus* (*'Ohebh Ger*), 1830, p. 46, no. 115.

29 *Genesis Rabbah*, 80, 10, ed. Wilna, f. 153a, col. i, ed. Theodor-Albeck, p. 965, l. 5, abbreviated at 97, 6 (see n. 27).

30 *Actuelles*, ii, 1953, p. 20.

31 *Leviticus Rabbah*, 17, 6, ed. Wilna, f. 24a, col. ii (Rabbi Ishmael b. Naḥman).

32 *Numbers Rabbah*, 19, 33 (see note 10). It will be remembered that the practical outcome of this 'pacifist' victory gained by Moses over God was codified by Maimonides as embodying the authentic position in *Halakhah* (*Mishneh Torah, Hilekhoth Melakhim*, 6, 4). In the following paragraph, Maimonides refers to – and thereby 'codifies', or endorses halakhically – the legend of Joshua's manifesto to the Canaanites. This is an example of aggadic source material contributing to the halakhic handling of the subject of non-violence.

33 W. R. Miller, *op. cit.* (n. 1), and Martin Luther King in recent publications emphasise the importance of prayer in both the theory and the practice of non-violence.

34 The first recorded mention of this legend seems to be by Aaron b. Jacob Cohen of Narbonne (early fourteenth century), *Kol Bo'*, i, 17; but the source may be assumed to be certainly an older aggadic one. See further L. Ginzberg, *The Legends of the Jews*, 6, p. 449, n. 58. The English translation of the second part, which will be

found in nearly all Jewish liturgies, is cited in K. D. Wilhelm's article, *infra*, p. 301. Cf. also S. H. Bergman, *supra*, p. 50; for the first part, see Singer (note 37), p. 76.

35 Strictly speaking, the legend locates Joshua's composition of the second paragraph after the invasion of Canaan had begun, on the occasion of Achan's confession of his sacrilegious act (*Joshua* 7: 19–20); but, as the conjunction '*al ken*, *therefore*, at the beginning of the second paragraph shows, it is organically a unity with the first and may, in the present context, legitimately be taken together with it.

36 Babylonian Talmud, *Berakhoth* 10a.

37 Maharal, *Be'er Hag-golah*, 7, on *Berakhoth* 10a; cf. A. Neher, *Le Puits de l'Exil*, Paris, 1966, pp. 96–7. For the English text of the benediction concerned see e.g. S. Singer, *Authorised Daily Prayer Book*, p. 48 ('And for slanderers . . .'), *Jewish Encyclopedia*, 11, p. 271, no. xii.

38 Cf. *supra*, p. 182, n. 22.

39 Babylonian Talmud, *Berakhoth* 7a, *supra*.

9

Rationalism in
Hobbes's Political Philosophy

DAVID D. RAPHAEL

Rationalism, if two senses of the term may be conflated, was a keynote in the work of Leon Roth. His distinguished studies in the history of philosophy were chiefly concentrated upon three thinkers, Maimonides, Descartes, and Spinoza, each of whom may be called a rationalist; and his last book (*Judaism, a Portrait*) is itself imbued with the spirit of Maimonidean rationalism. Rationalism in this latter sense is the attempt to give rational grounds for religious belief (or religious doubt), and is to be contrasted with a reliance on faith alone or on mysticism. Descartes and Spinoza are no less rationalist than Maimonides in this respect, though Spinoza's argument is designed to discredit the traditional theology and substitute a new one, while Descartes, like Maimonides, attempts to justify the creed of his forebears. Descartes and Spinoza, however, are also rationalists in a different sense, one that is used in discussion of the theory of knowledge. Here rationalism is contrasted with empiricism, the rationalist being a person who holds that knowledge proper is based on the intellectual grasp of self-evident truths and the deduction of further truths from these, while the empiricist is one who holds that knowledge of the real world is built upon the experience of the senses. For the epistemological rationalist, reason is contrasted with sense-experience; for the religious rationalist, it is contrasted with faith in revelation or with mystical experience. The religious rationalist need not be an epistemological rationalist (and neither Maimonides nor Roth himself was one), but the epistemological rationalist is likely to be a religious rationalist just because he places his trust in reason above all things.

I have said that Roth's work in the history of philosophy was concentrated on Maimonides, Descartes, and Spinoza. His very first book was a study of the influence upon Spinoza of the two earlier thinkers. Later he devoted a separate volume to each of these three philosophers. So far as I am aware, Roth did not give any special attention to Hobbes, and my excuse, such as it is, for contributing to this volume an essay on Hobbes is the fact that Hobbes exerted an important influence upon Spinoza. That influence may be seen in more ways than one, and notably in the actual content of their political theories. Here, however, I shall be concerned more with Hobbes's method, as a form of rationalism.

In calling Hobbes a rationalist, I am not thinking of epistemological rationalism proper. (Nor am I thinking particularly of religious rationalism, though Hobbes of course is a religious rationalist and, like Spinoza, one whose treatment of religion is disturbing to the orthodox.) Hobbes cannot be called an epistemological rationalist, because his theory of knowledge relies upon experience no less than upon deduction. The fact is that the division in the theory of knowledge between rationalism and empiricism had not yet hardened. Both rationalism and empiricism in the theory of knowledge, however, are attempts to follow what is taken to be the *method of science*. Rationalism fastens upon deductive reasoning, empiricism upon observation. Each of these is in fact a necessary ingredient in scientific method. Hobbes is true to science in including both, but he can be aligned to some extent with the rationalists in that he places inordinate trust in deductive reasoning, though not in allegedly self-evident premisses.

The garden path to rationalism was for Hobbes the usual one, the lure of mathematics. The major rationalist philosophers of this period – Descartes, Spinoza, and Leibniz – were eminently men with a talent for the mathematical style of thinking. Indeed, in the case of Descartes and Leibniz, it was the talent of genius. Descartes is the inventor of Analytic (or Co-ordinate) Geometry, the foundation of modern mathematics; and Leibniz shares with Newton the credit of having invented the Calculus. Hobbes unfortunately did not possess any special talent for mathematics, though he thought he did. He made a fool of himself by engaging in controversy with the Professor of Mathematics at Oxford on the old problem of squaring the circle, a problem which Hobbes thought he could solve. Hobbes knew practically nothing of mathematics until middle age. I quote a well-known passage from John Aubrey's 'Brief Life':

He was 40 yeares old before he looked on Geometry; which happened accidentally. Being in a Gentleman's Library, Euclid's Elements lay open, and 'twas the 47 *El. libri I.* He read the Proposition. *By* G—, sayd he (he would now and then sweare an emphaticall Oath by way of emphasis) *this is impossible!* So he reads the Demonstration of it, which referred him back to such a Proposition; which proposition he read. That referred him back to another, which he also read. *Et sic deinceps* that at last he was demonstratively convinced of that truth. This made him in love with Geometry.

It was not mathematics alone, however, that led the seventeenth-century rationalists to put their trust in deductive reasoning. It was rather the fact that mathematics had been used so successfully in physics. What is really distinctive about Hobbes's philosophy is the attempt to apply the methods and fundamental concepts of physics to the study of man, both as an individual and as a citizen. Although there had been previous theories of society and the state, Hobbes is the first to make a deliberate use, in social studies, of the tools of physical science. For this reason, it is, I think, possible to call him the inventor of social *science* in the modern sense of that term.

There are two ways in which Hobbes tries to make the study of society scientific. First, he uses the scientific method of causal explanation. Secondly – and this is more radical – he treats the sciences of man and society as themselves parts of physics. This second, more radical, point is the key to Hobbes's materialist metaphysics. Here I am concerned only with the first point, causal explanation; and since I propose to consider Hobbes's use of causal explanation in his political theory, I shall mainly confine myself to his most brilliant work, *Leviathan.*

In the seventeenth century, no distinction was commonly made between the terms 'science' and 'philosophy'. The one word was Latin, the other Greek, that was all. Both represented ordered inquiry. Such inquiry into the workings of the material world of nature was called Natural Philosophy (still retained as the name for physics in some Universities); inquiry into the workings of the mind was called Mental Philosophy (the old name for what we now call psychology); inquiry into human action was called Moral Philosophy. In the *Leviathan*, Hobbes is chiefly concerned with inquiry about human action in ordered society, Commonwealth or *Civitas*, and this he calls Civil Philosophy.

Hobbes requires of philosophy that it should pursue what he takes to be the correct method, of causal explanation, and also that it should be useful. At the beginning of Chapter 46 of *Leviathan*, he defines philosophy as follows:

> By PHILOSOPHY, is understood *the Knowledge acquired by Reasoning, from the Manner of the Generation of any thing, to the Properties; or from the Properties, to some possible Way of Generation of the same; to the end to bee able to produce, as far as matter, and humane force permit, such Effects, as humane life requireth.* So the Geometrician, from the Construction of Figures, findeth out many Properties thereof; and from the Properties, new Ways of their Construction, by Reasoning; to the end to be able to measure Land, and Water; and for infinite other uses.

Hobbes then attacks ancient philosophy on the ground that it has produced no useful results, and again refers to the value of geometry:

But what has been the Utility of those Schools? what Science is there at this day acquired by their Readings and Disputings? . . . The naturall Philosophy of those Schools, was rather a Dream than Science, and set forth in senselesse and insignificant Language; which cannot be avoided by those that will teach Philosophy, without having first attained great knowledge in Geometry. For Nature worketh by Motion; the Wayes, and Degrees whereof cannot be known, without the knowledge of the Proportions and Properties of Lines, and Figures.

It is true that the physicist applies geometry to his study of matter. But one may well wonder how geometry is supposed to consist of *causal* reasoning; and since the *Leviathan* is primarily concerned with civil philosophy, one may wonder still more what analogy there is between that and geometry. The answer to both queries depends on Hobbes's view of definitions. Hobbes holds that a good definition, in geometry or in anything else, states how the thing being defined is made up. It gives a method of generation or construction, a possible cause. For instance, you can define a circle as a plane figure bounded by a single line, called the circumference, which is everywhere equidistant from a point within it, called the centre; or alternatively, you can define a circle as the figure produced by one end of a straight line moving continuously while the other end remains fixed. Hobbes would prefer the second definition, because this explains how a circle is produced or generated, how it is caused. Now deductive reasoning proceeds from definitions; the reasoner sees what is implied by his definitions. And if his definitions describe the *causes* of what he is talking about, the consequences of those definitions describe the *effects* of the causes. So Hobbes does not mean that geometry itself can be used in studying human behaviour. He means that the method of reasoning used by the geometer is the proper scientific method, to be applied to any study that aims at being scientific. That method is reasoning from causes to effects, or from effects to possible causes. If you are reasoning from cause to effect, the cause must be described by a definition, and then the consequences of the definition will describe the effects. If you do not know the cause, but do know the effects, you can reason from the effects to a *possible* cause, by analysing the effects and seeing what could produce them. I have said that definition describes a cause. But if you do not know the cause, and have to start from the effects, you can only get to know these by experience. Then you can use reasoning to determine whether the definition of any suggested cause implies, as consequences, the effects which you know have occurred.

Hobbes's method is applied to civil philosophy in the following way. He has experience of two kinds of effects: civil strife or disorder, and stable or ordered society. He asks what are the causes of each, and he finds that human nature can be shown to be a possible cause in both cases. He therefore carefully defines the elements in human nature that can give rise to these effects, building up his definitions and relating them together in such a way as to show how strife or war between men may come about, and how ordered society may come about. The point of this inquiry is that a state of war is undesirable, and ordered society desirable. Hobbes must therefore show us also how the desirable thing can be maintained. This he does by making use of his causal explanations. Disorder or war is due to man's natural desire for power, his ambition or 'pride'. Organised society is due to man's desire for security, his fear of death. To obtain security, man needs protection from his fellows, protection that is afforded by the power of the state. But this protection can be exercised securely only if the state has absolute authority, i.e., only if the subjects give to the state their complete obedience. At the end of the *Leviathan*, Hobbes sums up his doctrine as showing 'the mutuall Relation between Protection and Obedience'. His philosophy, then, has demonstrated relations of cause and effect; and it is useful for human life, since it is intended to sustain obedience to the state, and so to sustain that protection which men need.

In the course of this scientific 'civil' or political philosophy, we are also given a scientific moral philosophy. The only true moral philosophy, says Hobbes, is the science of the Laws of Nature. Laws of nature, for Hobbes, are rational rules for self-preservation. They are rules which we can reason out as the only way to preserve our lives, the human condition being what it is. We reason out these rules when we see where our irrational human nature leads us, namely to a state of war, in which the life of no one is secure. It is the laws of nature that advise us to set up, or to keep in existence, an organised state, and to give to that state our complete obedience. A study of the laws of nature, therefore, is a scientific study. For it is a study of causal connexions between human nature and civil society; and it is a useful study, since it brings into a clearer light the reasons why we should obey the state.

Having outlined the way in which Hobbes's political theory conforms to his scientific method, I shall now set out the gist of the political theory itself in rather more detail. Hobbes's problem is this: how may we maintain a stable ordered society, and avoid anarchy or civil war? To deal with the problem scientifically, we must find the causes of each. Then we shall be in a position to consider how we may make it possible for the cause of ordered society to operate, and for the cause of anarchy to be overcome. The cause of ordered society is the desire for security; the cause of anarchy is the competitive nature of man. If security is to be maintained, and competitiveness restrained, there must be a power with absolute authority to repress competitiveness. This implies that men must *subject* themselves to a *sovereign* power. How can they be persuaded to do this? By showing them the reasons why they should obey the state. Hobbes is thus led to give us the grounds of political obligation.

In order to explain Hobbes's theory of obligation, and indeed his political theory as a whole, it is necessary to emphasise a distinction which is of key importance in his work, the distinction between the natural and the artificial. This distinction is drawn in the very first sentence of the *Leviathan*, and it runs throughout the work. Nature, or the natural, is what we find. Art, or the artificial, is what we make. The world of nature is not made by man; he just finds it, and it includes himself. For God, who has made the world, the world is artificial. Now art, human art, can to some degree imitate nature, the art of God.

For instance, Hobbes defines a living thing, an animal, as a piece of matter that has the power of moving itself. A man, or a dog, is a natural animal. But what of a piece of matter that has been artificially contrived to move itself? An automatic machine, such as a clockwork train, for instance? This answers to the definition of an animal, but it is artificial, not natural. It is an artificial animal, an imitation of a natural animal. Now Hobbes thinks of the state as an artificial animal, indeed an artificial man. It is artificial, not so much because it can be set up by a Social Contract (for that is not the only way whereby a state, in Hobbes's view, comes into existence). It is artificial because it needs to be kept in being *deliberately*, just as one has to keep winding up the clockwork train. If the train is just left to itself, if power is not deliberately applied when power is needed, the train will run down, it will 'die', i.e., it will cease to be an 'animal'. Similarly with the state. If it is left alone, it will drift into civil war or anarchy, it will cease to be an organised state. Hence Hobbes calls civil war the 'death' of the commonwealth. In this sense, therefore, anarchy or war is natural, while organised commonwealth is artificial. And just because the state is artificial, while anarchy is natural, men need to be told what they must do to keep the state in being.

We may say, then, that anarchy (the sort of thing that occurs in civil war, or any kind of war) is natural, while organised society is artificial. Let us now look with greater precision for possible causes of each. If anarchy or war between men is natural, it is likely, or at least possible, that the cause lies in human nature. Hobbes thinks we know by experience that human nature is predominantly, if not entirely, egoistic. Men are out for their own interests. This is why they compete and fight. But why is human nature egoistic? Because the natural tendency of any organism is to preserve its own life. In a state of nature, a man desires self-preservation and will do anything that seems to him a means to self-preservation. Furthermore, it does not make sense to say that he is obliged to refrain from any such actions. For what motive could he have to refrain? His fundamental motive is the desire for self-preservation, and so he cannot have an effective motive to act in ways that he thinks will militate against his own preservation. If he cannot have such a motive, it does not make sense to say that he has any obligation so to act. He has a right to do anything which he thinks will conduce to his preservation. To say that a man has a right to do something, is to say that he has no obligation to refrain. In a state of nature, every man has a right to all things. He may do whatever he chooses. This is his Natural Right.

The desire for self-preservation gives rise to a desire for pleasure, since pleasure is the appearance in consciousness of what conduces to life. Conversely there is an aversion from pain, pain being the mental appearance of what conduces to death. According to Hobbes, man's desire for continued preservation leads him to desire, not only pleasure now, but a store of pleasure for the future, since that means a store of continued life in the future. How can one lay up a store of future pleasure? By acquiring power. Power is the means to satisfy our desires. Therefore every man naturally desires power and more power, 'a perpetuall and restlesse desire of Power after power, that ceaseth onely in Death'. If one person had power so great that no one could resist him, he would be master of all. This is the position of God. God has irresistible power, in consequence of which we are obliged to obey Him. But among men in a natural state, none has the ability to attain for himself power so great that he can have dominion over all. Roughly speaking, all men are equal in their capacity to acquire power. One man may be physically stronger than another, but the second may be more cunning and so able to outwit the first by stratagem if not by physical strength. No man has enough power to compel all to do his will. All are roughly equal in power, and all can exercise their unlimited natural right.

What is the result? If no man is my master, equally no man is my slave. My neighbour is as strong as I, and as self-assertive as I. We fear each other, and we are liable to come into conflict with each other because we desire the same things. No one is strong enough to kill, or make himself master of, everyone else. So all go in mutual fear and suspicion, and from time to time there will be battles, in which any man is liable to lose his life. The natural state of mankind is a state of war, 'where every man is Enemy to every man'. There is 'continuall feare, and danger of violent death; And the life of man, solitary, poore, nasty, brutish, and short'. Here, then, is the state of anarchy, into which human society tends to drift if left to take its natural course. Hobbes has shown that its cause is human nature, the universal desire for power, deriving from the fundamental desire for self-preservation.

Fortunately, this situation carries within it its own remedy. The fundamental cause of the behaviour that leads to the state of war can also supply the cause of extrication from this predicament. For the fundamental cause is the desire for self-preservation, and the other side of that coin is aversion from death. But the state of war, into which men are led by their natural desires, is a condition in which life is nasty, brutal, and *short*. The result that is reached is the opposite of what was aimed at. Men aim at continued preservation of life, and find themselves in a situation where they are likely to lose their lives. They have a natural aversion from death, but are in a position where they are unlikely to avoid death for long. The fear of death, which arises in the state of war, supplies the cause of putting an end to the state of war.

Being moved to end the natural state of war, a rational man can see that he should seek the opposite, a state of peace. This piece of reasoning, which gives us advice on the means to secure our fundamental aim of self-preservation, Hobbes calls a 'precept', or 'general rule', or 'theorem', of reason. He also calls it the first Law of Nature. A law of nature differs from the right of nature. The right of nature is what we *may* do, what we are at liberty to do, in order to preserve our lives. A law of nature states an obligation or a precept or rule; it tells us what we *should* do, what we are obliged to do, in order to preserve our lives. In Kantian language, it is a hypothetical imperative; it prescribes a means to our own interest. The particular methods whereby we may carry out the first and fundamental law of nature, namely to seek peace, are listed by Hobbes as further laws of nature; they are means to peace, which is itself a means to self-preservation. Laws of nature, then, are hypothetical imperatives, prudential obligations. In the *De Cive*, Hobbes calls such obligation 'natural obligation'.

I should say at this point that there is dispute among scholars about the interpretation of Hobbes's theory of obligation. What I shall give is my own interpretation, with the warning that it is my own. In my view, Hobbes holds that there are two kinds of obligation. One is natural obligation, and this is a hypothetical imperative. The other I call artificial obligation, and I regard this as Hobbes's account of what Kant was later to call the categorical imperative. Hobbes himself does not anywhere use the expression 'artificial obligation', but he explicitly applies the adjective 'artificial' to covenants or promises, and he describes civil laws as 'artificial chains' or 'bonds'. According to my interpretation of Hobbes, an artificial obligation is a *verbal* obligation or bond, made by a promise. In Chapter 15 of *De Cive*, Hobbes contrasts this kind of obligation with natural obligation; and in all three statements of his political theory (*De Corpore Politico, De Cive,* and *Leviathan*), he brings out the linguistic character of the obligation of promises. If a man acts contrary to his promise, says Hobbes, he has in effect contradicted himself: for in promising, he has expressed in words a will to do what he promises; and then when he acts in breach of his promise, he wills an action which negates the will that he formerly expressed in words. Promise-breaking, therefore, is a kind of self-contradiction, a breach of obligation that is irrational, not in the sense that it is imprudent, but in the sense that it is illogical.

To go against a law of nature is irrational in the sense of being imprudent. It is irrational in that it goes against the hypothetical advice of prudential reasoning. To break a promise is not in itself imprudent, though it happens (often, but not always) to be imprudent as well, since it is usually in a man's interest to keep his promises. In itself, promise-breaking is not imprudent. It is sometimes to a man's advantage to break a promise, and in that case we cannot say that he is 'naturally' or hypothetically obliged to keep his promise. But he still has an artificial or verbal obligation to keep his promise, because it would be illogical or self-contradictory to break it. This artificial obligation has nothing to do with means to an end. The obligation depends entirely on the fact that one has promised. That is why I say that this represents Hobbes's version of what was later to be called the categorical imperative. To break a promise is wrong in itself, just because the promise has been made, not because of any end to which the action of keeping the promise is a means.

Since Hobbes gives the name of natural obligation to hypothetical imperatives, we may say that, for him, the obligation to keep a promise is, in a sense, 'non-natural'. But this does not imply that for Hobbes, as for Kant, there is a world of non-natural entities transcending the world of nature. Hobbes is an ethical naturalist. He is bound to be, since he is also a materialist. He explains ethics in terms of human nature, in terms of psychology. He has a form of non-natural obligation that does not imply anything *super*natural. Non-natural obligation is man-made; it is artificial.

What sort of thing is it? It is simply a contrivance of *language*. According to Hobbes, a natural obligation is a real motive force. A man who is naturally obliged is a man who is moved by fear or hope, by a real psychological force. This natural obligation, a real force, is simulated by that artificial 'obligation' of which we speak when a promise has been made. A man who makes a promise is said to 'bind' himself, by the words he utters, to the performance of an action. But the 'bond' is merely verbal or metaphorical. It is not a bond with any real force. As Hobbes says in *Leviathan*, Chapter 14, 'nothing is more easily broken than a man's word'; and again he says, in Chapter 18, that covenants or promises are 'but words, and breath,' that 'have no force to oblige, contain, constrain, or protect any man, but what it has from the publique Sword'. (In this quotation, 'oblige' means 'motivate'.) If a promise is to have a real force, an obligation in the sense in which natural obligations oblige, that is, a strong motivating power, it must be backed by 'the sword', by physical force that will cause a man to be afraid and to act from his fear. Nevertheless, there is this other kind of obligation that we talk about, and it also comes into Hobbes's theory.

If Hobbes is to persuade men to submit themselves to government, he must show them their *obligation* to do so. As I interpret him, he tells us that we have two kinds of obligation to obey the government. One is the prudential or natural obligation that results from our fear of the effects of anarchy. The other is the non-prudential or artificial obligation of promise-keeping. For he argues that any citizen of a state may be presumed to have promised obedience. This presumption is set out in Hobbes's theory of a Social Contract. Hobbes does not, however, suppose that states are normally set up by means of an explicit Social Contract. He speaks of two methods whereby a commonwealth can be set up, one being Social Contract, the other conquest; and Hobbes knows very well that most states come into existence by the second method. But he argues that, where a state has been set up by conquest, the subjects can be assumed to have given a tacit promise to obey the ruler in return for having their lives spared. This means that the subject has a double obligation to obey, the first being a prudential obligation depending on his fear of losing his life, the second being the artificial obligation to keep his promise. The point of the Social Contract theory in Hobbes is to bring out the logical implications of sovereignty and subjection, not to give a fanciful picture of how states may arise by agreement.

But, one may ask, why should Hobbes want to talk at all about an assumed promise in the case of a state that arises by conquest? Since the conqueror has the vanquished in his power, what need is there to speak of the obligation of a supposed promise? The subject will have a natural obligation to obey, just as a man is naturally obliged to hand over his money to a thug who points a revolver at him and says 'Your money or your life'. Hobbes is not satisfied with this, however. He draws a distinction between a subject or a servant on the one hand, and a captive or a slave on the other. A captive or a slave is in the power of his master, but he has no obligation other than natural obligation. If he can manage to run away, he is not obliged to refrain from doing so. By contrast, a subject or a servant has an *obligation to* his master (not just the natural obligation to do the best he can for himself). The master has not merely power over him, but also authority, i.e., a right to be obeyed. And if the subject or servant has an *obligation to* his master, that kind of obligation must be based on a promise.

The point of the distinction is this. The obligations of promises, if not backed by power, are merely verbal and have little force to act as a motive. But on the other hand, power by itself is not adequate either. Of course, the exercise of power goes a long way in getting people to obey their master's will. A captive or a slave simply has to do as he is told for the most part. But a state cannot be run on the lines of a prison. When the conqueror has the vanquished actually before him at the point of the sword, he can rely on the threat of force to get his wishes carried out. But he cannot be in this position all the time. When he is not on the spot, the other man may run away, just as a captive may run away if he is not kept locked up. Therefore something else besides the exercise of power is required for running a state. This something else is authority, whereby the sovereign has a *right* to be obeyed, and the subjects have an *obligation to him* to obey. In order to provide for this, Hobbes brings in the idea of a supposed covenant.

We now see the point of the Social Contract theory in Hobbes, and we can also see why he makes political obligation a combination of two kinds of obligation, natural and artificial. A man ought to obey the laws of the state for two reasons. The first reason is that it is in his interest to obey, i.e., he has a natural obligation; the state is intended to avoid the natural state of war, and however irksome the laws of the state may be, anything (save the instant threat of death) is better than the condition of war or anarchy, in which life is nasty, brutal, and short. Secondly, there is also an artificial obligation, depending upon a presumed promise to obey; the presumption is necessary for the relations of sovereignty and subjection, without which a state cannot work.

This, then, is Hobbes's political theory, his justification of political obedience. It has been carried out in accordance with his prescribed method, seeking relations of cause and effect, for the purpose of being useful to the life of man.

I now want to suggest a criticism of Hobbes's method as he

applies it to moral and political philosophy. In his procedure there appears to be a confusion between causes and reasons, between explaining and justifying. His avowed method is that of science, which aims at explaining phenomena by tracing their causes. This method can certainly be applied to the study of man and society, and when it is so applied, one is pursuing social science. Psychology, anthropology, sociology, economics, political science, are all attempts to study human behaviour scientifically, tracing causal connexions. When Hobbes looks for causal connexions between human nature (the psychology of motives) and civil war, he is doing social science; and there is no reason why he should not. But social science is not the same as social (including political) philosophy. Philosophy is not concerned with tracing causes. It is concerned (*a*) with the analysis of concepts, and (*b*) with the critical evaluation of beliefs in which those concepts are used. Now there is absolutely no reason why a man should not engage in both social science and social philosophy. Indeed there is every reason why he should combine social science with the first, analytic, function of social philosophy. A social science that does not go along with the logical analysis of key concepts is liable to be confused; and a social philosophy that takes no account of human behaviour and of existing institutions is liable to be a castle in the air. There need be no conflict or confusion between the tracing of causal connexions and the analysis of concepts. The trouble arises when the second function of philosophy, the normative function of giving justifying reasons for the acceptance or rejection of beliefs, becomes mixed up with the scientific task of tracing causes. There need not be a conflict between philosophical justification and scientific explanation, but the relation between them is rather obscure, and it is easy to confuse the two.

This is what Hobbes appears to do in his account of obligation. When he speaks of natural obligation playing upon the motive of fear, he thinks of obligation as a form of causal power. Similarly, when he speaks of artificial obligation as constituting only a weak bond, he again is thinking of the 'bond' as a causal factor that is too weak to be relied upon. At the same time, however, his theory of political obligation is an attempt to give us reasons why we *should* obey the state, rather than causes explaining why we *do*. The fact is that we don't, always; hence the need to give us reasons why we should.

To give a man reasons why he should do something is to presuppose that he has a choice, that he can rationally decide between alternatives. That is, it presupposes free will. Hobbes in fact holds that there is no free will, that everything we do is necessitated. This is because he thinks that everything can be causally explained, explained as following necessarily from causal laws. If he had seen clearly that to give justifying reasons is quite a different thing from setting out explanatory causes, he would have found his determinism less tractable.

The reason why he fails to distinguish adequately between explaining and justifying lies in his attachment to geometry. He thinks that causes are the same as logical grounds, in the way that the definitions of Euclid are grounds for the conclusions of theorems. Now the relation between causes and logical grounds is a difficult problem for the theory of knowledge. I cannot go into that here. In order to understand Hobbes's position, it is sufficient to note that the logical grounds of a theoretical conclusion constitute reasons for accepting that conclusion. So it was natural for Hobbes to suppose that reasons for a *practical* conclusion, which are indeed also grounds for that conclusion, are the same sort of thing as reasons or grounds for a theoretical conclusion. And since he identified geometrical reasoning with tracing the effects of causes, it was equally natural that he should confuse causal explanation with the giving of reasons for doing something.

It is easy enough to say that causal explanation is not the same as rational justification. But it is not at all easy to say just what the relation between them is. In criticising Hobbes for confusing the two, I am not complaining that he misleads us. On the contrary, I think we are indebted to him for enabling us to see that there is a difference. It is only when a result of mixing up causes and reasons comes out sharply, as it does in Hobbes's philosophy, that other philosophers can start trying to disentangle them. We should also remember that Hobbes is, as I said before, the first thinker to put forward explicitly the idea of social science in its modern sense. Social science cannot take the place of the normative function of social philosophy, but it can take and has taken the place of speculative ideas about the nature of man and society which once formed part of philosophy. It is understandable that the greater success of scientific methods than of the older philosophical methods in this latter field should lead men to think that scientific method can be applied successfully to the whole of the traditional province of philosophy. It is understandable, though it is not now excusable. It was excusable in Hobbes, since he was the first to make the attempt. Part of the point of studying the work of a philosopher like Hobbes is to enable us to see what scientific methods can do, and what they cannot do, and so to enable us to draw more clearly the distinction between the explanatory function of science and the analytic and normative functions of philosophy.

10

Torah and *Nomos* in Medieval Jewish Philosophy*

ERWIN I. J. ROSENTHAL

The blending of the Hebraic and the Hellenic mind was more than a subject for inquiry *more academico* for Leon Roth. The Jew who wrote on Maimonides and Spinoza and the Professor at the Hebrew University of Jerusalem who translated classical Greek philosophical works into Hebrew considered the twofold scholarly tradition in which he was reared as equally meaningful for our time. The universality of the Torah and the rationality of the *nómos* in their mutual penetration in affinity and contrast do not only form the central theme of medieval religious philosophy in Judaism, but do so in a special way, particularly in the thought of Abraham ibn Da'ud and Moses Maimonides. It may, therefore, not be inappropriate to discuss briefly the meeting-point of the two realms of faith and reason, as a tribute to a philosopher and friend whose untimely death has left not merely a gap in our lives, but also a challenging legacy to try to resolve the perpetual tension between the universal and the particular in the lives of those of us who are committed to Judaism.

Whereas Abraham ibn Da'ud speaks, in the introduction to his *'Emūnāh rāmāh*, of the difficulty of the co-existence of faith and philosophy, Maimonides in his *Moreh nebhūkhīm* (II, 40) expresses and in part resolves their conflict through his distinction between a divine and a human law, the law of revelation and the law of human reason. His identification of the latter with 'the laws of the Greeks' (*ibid.*, II, 39) not only gives us the source – Greek philosophy – but also the ultimate reason why the challenge of philosophy to religious tradition took the specific form of revealed *versus* human law. For this challenge would neither have been felt nor accepted if there had not existed some important common ground between revealed faith and human reason. Both have the same aim in regard to man as a *zŏon politikón*: to help him attain his highest good – *eudaimonía*, happiness or blessedness.[1] As far as philosophy is concerned, this task mainly falls to the share of practical philosophy (ethics, politics and economics), and to this end the philosopher has devised a *nómos*, a law guiding the citizen of the *pólis*. Religion uses the same means to enable the believer, as a member of a religious community, to reach his goal – in the case of the Jew the Torah. But here the affinity ends, and the contrast becomes apparent once the aim and the way to it are defined. The Jew starts from the fact of revelation, from God; but the Greek starts from man and his sovereign reason. The Torah shows the way to God; it is in the perception and love of God that the Jew attains happiness and bliss. Without obedience to the will of God expressed in the Torah there can be no happiness; for man is not only a rational being, he is also (and in the first place) a religious entity and a creature made in the image of God, whom to serve in love is his sole purpose. Why, then, does the medieval Jew stand in any need of a philosophy invented by the sovereign intellect of self-sufficient man? In point of fact, it is only a certain type of Jew who does need it – the Jew who looks out from the fortress of the Torah, and has come into contact with philosophy; not the fervent yet naive believer whose happiness and perfection is guaranteed by the spontaneous fulfilment of the *miṣwōth*. Every Jew is enjoined to study the Torah which is identical with *ḥokhmāh*, wisdom. He accepts this wisdom unquestioningly because it comes from God. For the intellectual *élite* wisdom has, however, also another connotation, which stems from the Greeks. Faith is no longer the only guide to the God whom to know and to love we are all, as Jews, commanded in the Torah. If practical philosophy constituted the totality of philosophy the Torah would, indeed, be entirely sufficient to lead rational man to his end. For according to Maimonides' definition, the divinely revealed law guarantees the religious human being twofold happiness, viz. wellbeing in this world as well as salvation, the bliss of the immortal soul, in the life everlasting. Practical philosophy guarantees the former only, through law and order in the *pólis*. But Plato demands more: for him, that man alone attains to perfection and happiness whose right doing springs from right beliefs and sound convictions. It is here that the conflict between faith and reason arises, but it is precisely here that this conflict – so the medieval religious thinkers hold – can be resolved. And yet, although divine and human law travel part of the way together in respect of what they have in common – the concern for man in this life on earth – it is theoretical philosophy (physics and metaphysics) alone that can help the believer to justify his right beliefs and convictions (i.e. the religious doctrines of the Torah), through demonstration. But demonstration is, ultimately, insufficient to solve the secrets of the Torah, commonly described in the twin concepts of *ma'asēh berē'shīth* and *ma'asēh merkābhāh*. For while the literal meaning of Scripture must be abandoned if incompatible with demonstrative proof, in the case where the metaphysician is unable to demonstrate his opinion – Maimonides means, of course, Aristotle's view of the eternity of matter – the believer is obliged to accept and to uphold the biblical account of the creation of the world *ex nihilo* as revealed truth. On the other hand, God's incorporality is established by philosophical proof, hence anthropomorphic language must be explained allegorically.[2] It is obvious that Jewish medieval thinkers started from the Torah; and while Bahya ibn Paqūda[3] sought to show – in his *Duties of the Heart* – that the Torah fully satisfies both the Jew's faith and his intellectual striving as well, Abraham ibn Da'ud[4] was equally convinced, as was Maimonides after him, that although the Torah was the best guide to man's *ḥaṣlāḥāh* (*eudaimonía*) – a better one than the practical philosophy of the Greeks – it is faith and its doctrines which must occupy first place in the intellectual study of the Torah in order to reach the highest perfection. Doctrines are only accessible to the inquirer trained in metaphysics, in so far as their deeper understanding is concerned. In this attitude Abraham ibn Da'ud is in agreement with both Plato and Aristotle. As we have seen, Plato demands right beliefs and sound convictions, and Aristotle sees in the intellectual virtues the highest that man can achieve. And yet, Abraham ibn Da'ud goes further, in his insistence that to know God is a religious duty as being a direct divine command.

It seems more correct, then, to speak of the *intellectualism* of Jewish medieval thinkers, and not of their rationalism; for intellectualism grants primacy to faith with its religious commandments, whereas rationalism insists on the primacy of sovereign reason. Intellectualism recognises frontiers in the endeavour of reason to unravel the secrets of God and His universe, and where reason fails the believer humbly accepts by faith even what he cannot fully grasp intellectually. Acceptance means, in this context, acceptance of the literal meaning. Only where the literal meaning runs counter to clear proof must it be abandoned for a rational explanation which aims at bringing out its inner, sometimes hidden meaning. For the out-and-out rationalist reason can, and must, plumb the deepest depths.

Abraham ibn Da'ud uses the Ten Commandments as a telling illustration of the difference between revelation in the form of the Torah and philosophy (in form of the *nómos*). Philosophy, he says, is silent about the first five commandments, which are concerned with our knowledge and worship of God. Nevertheless, as already stated, he considers philosophy necessary for the proper understanding of religious doctrines. It is only on this theoretical basis that ethics and politics are firmly established, and can fulfil their purpose: the good order of the world and the preservation of human civilisation. Hebraic and Greek ideas are so closely intertwined in his thought that he does not always present them in their right order or context. Thus, he declares the biblical commandment '*Thou shalt love thy neighbour . . .*' to be the first of the political laws and not one of the moral laws. This is, no doubt, due to the influence of Greek political philosophy which, together with its ethics, provided that link which was necessary to open the world of the Torah to the otherwise alien world of Hellas. There can be no doubt that Plato and Aristotle taught the medieval Muslim world and, in its wake, the Jewish thinkers the political character and significance of the divinely revealed law. For this reason, Abraham ibn Da'ud admits that the second half of the Ten Commandments is comprised also by practical philosophy – but, he adds, in a less comprehensive manner. Both the Decalogue and practical philosophy deal with inter-human relations in society and state; but human reason is bound to frame laws relative to time, place and economic and social circumstance, without the absolute, timeless perfection of the divine Lawgiver who made His law known through Moses, the greatest of the prophets. Naturally, practical philosophy is more concerned with personal and social interests and concerns in this world than with such religious demands as love of neighbour, abstemiousness and personal, inward piety. Piety is devotion to God in worship and good deeds towards our neighbour. Worship is more than prayer and fasting; it must permeate our entire daily life. We might at once point out that worship, i.e. the cult, is a Platonic demand equally, as being a civic duty. Nevertheless, Abraham ibn Da'ud's inward piety – like Bahya's 'duties of the heart' – is something much more than the civic duty of public worship, and goes beyond the prescribed measure of the law. It is precisely this *plus* of religious commandments which bestows upon the divine law its superiority over man-made laws. Through its addition of '*Love thy neighbour*' the Torah guarantees the best order for the world in a way which even the best *nómos* can never provide. In this context Abraham ibn Da'ud's religious interpretation of *sōphrosýne* is rather illuminating: to be content with what God has granted us without coveting what is our neighbour's. To repeat, man as the servant of God is a more perfect human being than is the *zóon politikón* of the *pólis* and its *nómos*. And yet, the very concept of perfection and happiness (or blessedness) is a

Greek concept, though it has been adapted to indigenous Islamic and Jewish concepts and has been transformed in the process. Even more important is another addition: the biblical command to *love* God. We have seen that for the Jewish disciple of Plato and Aristotle this is not possible without first *perceiving* the Creator and Ruler of the universe with man in it as a rational being. Man shows his love for God by serving his Master in obedience to His will as expressed in the Torah. Thus, man must at the same time love his neighbour by fulfilling his social and moral obligations under the Torah. The laws of revelation are a constant reminder to man to fear and to love God. With Plato, Abraham ibn Da'ud demands that the cogitative part of the soul must dominate and rule the other parts in order to guarantee justice, for the Greeks the foremost political virtue. Nevertheless, despite his recognition of the indispensability of the rational perception of God with the help of philosophy, Abraham ibn Da'ud classes the pious observer of the traditional commandments yet higher, even though such a pietist is not, or may not be intellectually capable of understanding their reasons. For the Jew's obedience is founded on, and grounded in a historical event which is prior to philosophy in both time and rank – the revelation of the Torah from Sinai in the presence of the whole people of Israel. This divine event is supported by the exemplary nature of Moses, the announcer of the law, and by the truth of his miracles performed in public sight. Abraham ibn Da'ud combines this traditional outlook with an intellectualism which maintains that there is nothing in the Torah which contradicts reason. Reason is therefore permitted full play in the interpretation of revelation. Such rational inquiry is, indeed, a religious duty. The fact that the Torah embodies teaching about God and contains religious doctrines and principles, clearly shows that it is concerned with the spiritual, inner well-being of the believer as the creature of God. This is something that philosophy does not do. Although the primacy of faith cannot be questioned and the significance of the ethical teaching of the Torah is continually stressed, the priorities of faith and philosophy are not always or consistently observed. This is due to the fact that the two realms are fundamentally different from each other even though they overlap and are complementary. This is a real dilemma: and it is one by no means confined to the Middle Ages. It was already present in Philo, who attempted a similar solution; but it meets us in its acutest form in Maimonides, and with him more concisely and sharply than in Abraham ibn Da'ud. Without Maimonides, there would be no modern Jewish philosophy in Spinoza, Moses Mendelssohn, Hermann Cohen and Franz Rosenzweig.

Needless to say, Sinai as the historical proof of God's existence no less than of the divine origin of the Torah of Moses, is as valid for Maimonides as for any other Jewish thinker. But the disciple of Aristotle felt bound to add to the incontrovertible proof of tradition the demonstrative argument of the metaphysician. He was convinced that the Torah did not teach anything which contradicted Aristotle's teaching, and he would not depart from the literal sense of Scripture unless Aristotle forced him to. Things were not always so clear cut – or, should we perhaps add, so obliging – as in the case of the creation. Since Aristotle's argument in favour of the eternity of matter did not convince Maimonides, he did not accept Aristotle in place of the plain sense of the creation story in *Genesis*. But how dangerous and precarious his position was between tradition and Aristotelian metaphysics is shown by his admission that, if Aristotle had been able to offer incontrovertible proof for his opinion, the Torah would have had to be abandoned. This would have disastrous consequences for the truth of the biblical prophets and the justification of miracles. Since I have discussed this problem elsewhere[5] and since it is moreover not directly relevant to the present theme, it must suffice here to emphasise that in order to uphold such fundamental biblical teachings as messianism and reward and punishment, Maimonides gave precedence to inherited religious principles over those of metaphysics (*Mōrēh* II, 40 and III, 54). Especially in the latter passage, Maimonides takes a decisive step further when he postulates that it is man's supreme duty to imitate the thirteen attributes of God, even though he emphasises – with Aristotle – intellectual perfection as man's greatest achievement. I would therefore hold that since the imitation of

God alone leads to the perception and love of God – the religious person's true fulfilment and attainment of the highest blessedness – Maimonides recognises the primacy of revelation.[6] God's attributes are, in his view, all attributes of action and not of the divine essence; and it is the Torah which conveys the perfect teaching of how to achieve that imitation.

Before recapitulating Maimonides' distinction between divine and human law, it is necessary briefly to digress. For the obvious objection must be met that the concept of the *Imitatio Dei* is also a philosophical postulate, defined in Plato's *Theaetetus* (176b) as 'becoming just, holy and wise'. When we remember that justice is the primary political virtue, we shall not be surprised to see Maimonides introduce his demand – justified by the *Siphrē* – by the following significant formula: 'His actions [i.e. the thirteen *middōth*] are necessary for the government of states' (I, 54).[7]

The importance of justice for state and society, which applies equally to Plato's ideal *Republic* and to the state of God with the Torah as its constitution and law, must not lead us to assume that medieval Jewish (and Muslim) thinkers identified their own ideal state with the Greek *pólis* as visualised by Plato. This is not only clear from what we found in Abraham ibn Da'ud – love of neighbour and inward piety – but even more apparent in Maimonides' distinction between the laws in force in the two states, in regard to their respective scope and ultimate purpose. Human law aims at the good order of the state and its affairs, and tries to keep injustice and strife away from it; to regulate inter-human relations, and to enable the citizens to attain what they consider to be their happiness. In contrast to the law in the philosopher's state, the divine law goes beyond it in extent as well as in content, for it aims at man's spiritual as well as his physical well-being and salvation. Its regulations are not only concerned with man's material interests and needs, but also (and in the first place) with right convictions and views about God, the angels, the divine order of the world, God's providence and reward and punishment. Its intention is to make man wise and give him insight so as to enable him to gain true knowledge of reality (II, 40). We note that Maimonides overlooks the fact that Plato, no less than he himself, demands right beliefs and convictions. But there is definitely more to the Torah than to the *nómos*, in virtue of the former's inclusion of purely religious matters. In another passage (III, 27) Maimonides emphasises that it is only the law of Moses, as being the divinely revealed law, that provides for our twofold blessedness in body and soul, in this world in the political community and in the life everlasting. The law announced by the prophet stems from God's unfathomable will; it reflects God's love, mercy, compassion and justice. But this does not mean that medieval thinkers denied the *relative* excellence of the philosopher's law, as is clear from their awareness of the political and social relevance of any and every law. Even Judah Hallevi who, like Ghazālī, recognised practical philosophy only, admitted this; and at the end of the period Albo found much of human law implied and included within divine law, as we shall see later on. It is not only Plato's *Republic*, but also Aristotle's *Nicomachean Ethics* with its ideas of equity, which impressed medieval religious thinkers. Nevertheless they were all convinced that equity, and not absolute justice, must be the norm wherever it is fallible man who makes laws; the divine law is by contrast immutable and absolutely just, not subject to changing times and varying circumstances, nor in need of improvement – only of clarification and interpretation.

The Torah was there at the beginning of all philosophical speculation and always remained in the centre, superior in its fundamental difference over the *nómos*. It served as a barrier between revelation and philosophy which no attempt at harmonisation, no esoteric interpretation could ultimately remove. And yet our picture would be incomplete and distorted if we simply confronted the ideas of Jewish medieval thinkers starting from the Torah, both written and oral, with the original Platonic and Aristotelian writings. For it was precisely the development and modification of Platonic and Aristotelian ideas among Neoplatonists and Stoics and the other Hellenistic schools which had made their reception by Jews and Muslims possible. The religious penetration and expansion of classical Greek ideas, especially among the commentators of Plato and Aristotle, played a decisive role: with the result that we cannot be dogmatic about the relative strength of 'religious' or 'philosophical' concepts, and the priority in every instance of their medieval reception and transformation.[8] The precise meaning of 'happiness' is not merely a question of semantic development of the term *eudaimonía*. Nowhere is this clearer than in the controversial question of the meaning and interpretation of prophecy, to be met with in Muslim and Jewish thinkers. Though very relevant to our question of Torah *versus nómos*, it cannot be even outlined here. I must content myself with the statement – substantiated in earlier studies[9] – that Maimonides explicitly exempts the prophecy of Moses, and thus the character of the Torah, from the psychological explanation of Fārābī (be its origin middle-platonic or Stoic). There is a profound difference between the prophet sent by God and the natural prophet.[10] Even in the case of the other prophets Maimonides would not allow that the gift of prophecy has to be automatic simply because its natural conditions – perfect imagination and perfect intellect – are extant in any given person; God has the power to withhold the actualisation of the prophetic nature, if He so wills.

To sum up what we have outlined so far it must, therefore, suffice to state that the law promulgated by the prophet, on divine instruction, is superior to the law devised by the philosopher. The same applies to the nature and degree of human happiness. Maimonides follows Fārābī in distinguishing between absolute – true – happiness, and relative – alleged, imaginary – happiness. True happiness is only attainable in the perfect state under the Torah; the other, inferior kinds of happiness are relegated to the states under the *nómos*, corresponding to Plato's imperfect constitutions.[11] This points to the primacy of revelation, the practical and political implications of which Maimonides stresses – clearly under Greek influence, in particular on the basis of Plato's *Republic* and Aristotle's *Nicomachean Ethics*. The Torah aims at the attainment of every person's happiness and perfection – though its degree is in proportion to the individual's intellectual level – and he says of it: 'only this law do we call divine, the other political constitutions as e.g. the *nómoi* of the

Greeks . . . are the work of statesmen (or, governors), but not of prophets' (II, 39). He also stresses another distinctive quality of the divinely revealed law: that it observes the right proportion, and is free from all exaggeration and excess. This not only reminds us of Aristotle's definition of virtue, but also seems to have a polemical significance, being possibly directed against both Christian monasticism and Muḥammad's sensuality (II, 36, 40).

In the wake of the battle that raged round the *Guide to the Perplexed* and the growing precariousness of the Jewish position, a decided swing back to the traditional outlook characterises the post-Maimonidean era, towards the end of the Middle Ages. Crescas[12] rejected the need for the philosophical justification of the biblical concept of God and of the relationship between God and man. The love of God is, for him also, man's highest good; but it can be achieved by the spontaneous fulfilment of the divine commandments of the Torah, and need not be preceded by the intellectual perception of God. He thus restored the undivided sovereignty and authority of revealed religion in a manner reminiscent of Judah Hallevi and Baḥya. His disciple Albo illustrates in his '*Iqqārīm* the self-sufficiency of religion with the help of philosophy, especially its practical part. Despite his dependence on Maimonides and Crescas, and consequently a marked absence of intellectual independence, his treatment of the Torah and its aim – the attainment of human happiness – is illuminating. Its main points may fittingly conclude our brief survey.

Albo's reduction of Maimonides' thirteen principles of faith to three 'root principles' is chiefly important in our context for its relegation of prophecy to the position of a secondary principle, derived from the revelation of the Torah. This not only avoids the dilemma posed by the psychological interpretation of prophecy; but it also reduces philosophy from its challenging position to one of illustration, in order the better to demonstrate (for throughout his theological treatise Albo uses the systematic methodology of philosophy) the superiority of revelation. His defence of Torah-religion is that of an unquestioning traditionalist who no longer feels the challenge of metaphysics to be dangerous. Thus, he can say: 'faith in God and His Torah leads man to eternal bliss and to the union with the spiritual'.[13] Such union in perfection is possible for the prophet only, not for the philosopher; experience attests this for Israel through tradition. Naturally, he agrees with the earlier Muslim and Jewish thinkers that prophecy is indispensable for man's attainment of his highest good. But, as stated, he derives prophecy from the Torah, for it is only the divine law that announces to man how he can attain his highest good, namely through his knowledge of the things that please God and through doing them. Man needs divine guidance – through the Torah – in order to learn what is true and good and what leads him to blessedness. Because of this need of divine guidance the Torah is a 'root principle'. In other words, Albo starts from God and His will and not from man and his desires and striving, just as do his predecessors; but for him tradition is sufficient, and it no longer requires philosophical justification and confirmation.

But philosophy, as already stated, is useful to spotlight this self-sufficiency of the Torah. Like Maimonides, Albo distinguishes between divine and human law, except that he subdivides the latter into natural and positive-conventional law, which together serve the same purpose as does that part of the divine law which, for Abraham ibn Da'ud, was contained in the latter five of the Ten Commandments. Albo is the first Jewish thinker who directly refers to Aristotle's *Politics*, either from direct knowledge or through Thomas Aquinas.[14] Natural law is common to all men, since it is necessary to maintain human life. We know that for the Stoa the law of nature (*lex naturae*) was identical with the divine law (*lex aeterna* or *lex divina*), but at the same time we remember that 'divine' in their case had nothing to do with the personal God of love, mercy and justice of the Bible. Jewish medieval thinkers derive the law of reason – which, for the Stoa, was identical with the law of nature – likewise from revelation, since all laws stem from the will of the one good God. They even assign the seven Noachide laws to revelation although they are common to all nations out of absolute necessity.

It is well known that they admit that reason would, after a long time had elapsed, have arrived at the laws of reason by its own effort, but only in their general outline, thus leaving man in the dark as to their particular application. This application we learn from the divine law which is, therefore, superior to human law. Moreover, the divine law not only commands what reason also postulates – justice, equity, truth and ethical conduct – and forbids what reason rules out – murder, theft, adultery and fornication. It also demands divine worship, religious feasts, purity and dietary laws. Whereas Sa'adya assigned the last group to laws of revelation (for he divided laws into those of revelation and those of reason) Maimonides recognises solely laws of revelation; and he distinguishes – with Aristotle – between general and specific laws, the reason for which man cannot always understand.

If we compare Jewish with Stoic law we realise that the revealed law comprises both natural and positive law, but denies man all power to promulgate any laws. Judaism would hence never acknowledge the ultimate validity of a *ius civile* issuing from some human legislator. But the very term 'rational laws' used by Sa'adya suggests that Islamic dialectical theology (*Kalām*) has mediated a Stoic concept to him. Nevertheless, he denies their independent existence, deriving them no less than what he calls laws of revelation – the ceremonial laws – from God.

This digression has been necessary in order to understand Albo's classification of laws. He avers that the principles of the divine law, like that law itself, are validated by experience – the historical experience of Sinai – and he rejects Aristotle's principles of positive or conventional law: choice and purpose ('*Iqqārīm* I, 93 ff.). He says,[15] in principle, the same as does Maimonides about the peculiar properties of the divinely revealed law which alone leads mankind (not only the Jew) to ultimate happiness and bliss. But his language is, naturally, that of his own age; it is conditioned as much by Thomas Aquinas, with his use and adaptation of Aristotelian legal philosophy, as by Maimonides and Crescas, with the additional flavour of rabbinic thought and expression in place of the philosophical superstructure as a justification of revelation.

The student of political thought in the Middle Ages will notice that, contrary to the main tradition of Greek-Hellenistic and Muslim-Jewish political philosophy, Albo – like Ibn Bājja – envisages the attainment of the highest good even in imperfect states based on bad constitutions. From the context – the Torah as the perfect guide to happiness – it would, however, appear that he was possibly thinking of the Jew in the Diaspora living according to the prescriptions of the Torah, and achieving the happiness of his soul and immortality by joyfully fulfilling the commandments. This is what he says:

> The purpose of the divine law is to lead men straight to the true blessedness which is spiritual happiness (*literally*, the happiness of the soul) and immortality. It shows them the ways they must follow to obtain it, teaches them the true good so that they strive to attain it, and teaches them true evil, too, so that they guard against it. It accustoms them to give up the kinds of imaginary happiness, so that they no longer crave for them nor are grieved at losing them. It also lays down ways of justice (*or*, equity) so that the political community may be ordered in a proper and perfect manner. As a result, the evil order of their community will not prevent them from attaining true blessedness, nor from striving to attain it and the ultimate aim of mankind which is the purpose of the divine law. Herein it goes beyond the conventional law.[16]

True and false, good and evil, what is done and not done – all these are contained in the divine law. Like Maimonides, Albo makes the divine law provide for true opinions and ethical action; but such provision is the function of the divine law alone. Just as we cannot rely on the human lawgiver in matters of what is seemly and unseemly, so we cannot trust him in matters of our deepest convictions, for example in the matter of the creation or the eternity of the world. For human reason is without certainty in this matter, nor can the observance of a human law that lacks all certainty fill the citizen with joy.[17] The rabbinic *simḥāh shel miṣwāh*, joy experienced through fulfilment of a commandment, is reserved for the Torah. This is the legacy of the Rabbis; and it was Crescas who brought it to the fore again.

NOTES

* This essay is a summary in English of parts of the first three chapters of my *Griechisches Erbe in der jüdischen Religionsphilosophie des Mittelalters* (*GE*), Stuttgart, 1960, and I am indebted to the publisher (W. Kohlhammer) for permission to use the book and quote from it. Lack of space forbids a full exposition with the necessary evidence *in extenso*; the reader may, therefore, be referred to the German publication for a justification of the views here expressed, especially the chapters entitled: '*Torah und Nomos I: Die Glückseligkeit als menschliches Ziel*' and '*Torah und Nomos II: Glaubenslehren, Herzensfrömmigkeit und praktische Philosophie*'. There will also be found the necessary references to the literature utilised, and to my earlier studies in problems of political philosophy in Islam and Judaism, from 1935 onwards.

1 Cf. Averroes' Commentary on Plato's *Republic*, ed. E. I. J. Rosenthal, p. 185.

2 Cf. *GE*, pp. 21 f., 56 with relevant notes. It is important to note that Maimonides links the question of creation with that of revelation and prophecy.

3 Cf. *K. al-hidāya*, ed. Yahuda, p. 5. The passage is reproduced and commented on in *GE*, p. 97, n. 5. Cf. also, for Baḥya's attitude generally, *ibid.*, pp. 41–4.

4 Cf. *GE*, pp. 44–9 and *passim* for a full account with reference to AbD's text (*S. ha-'emūnāh ha-rāmāh*, ed. S. Weil, pp. 98–104) and his indebtedness to Plato, Aristotle and Avicenna.

5 Cf. *GE*, pp. 22 f. with n. 18; *Mōreh* II, 25. Julius Guttmann's selection of the *Mōreh* – translated from the Arabic by C. Rabin – in *Philosophia Judaica* (East and West Library, London), especially his Introduction, is important. A rationalistic interpretation is given by Leo Strauss in his *Philosophie und Gesetz* and in *The Literary Character of the Guide for the Perplexed* (in *Essays on Maimonides*, ed. S. W. Baron). Cf. now also the new English translation of the *Guide* by S. Pines with an Introductory Essay by L. Strauss (Univ. of Chicago Press, 1963).

6 Cf. *GE*, chapter *Sendungsprophetie und Natürliche Prophetie*, especially pp. 55 f.

7 *Siphrē, Deut.*, 49 on 11: 22 (cf. 10: 12), ed. Finkelstein, p. 114. Cf. *GE*, pp. 28 f. with notes 4 and 5, and my *Political Thought in Medieval Islam* (*PT*), chapters 1, 5–7 and 9. The question of *eudai-*

monía is discussed in *GE, Exkurs I: Begriff und Bedeutungswandel der Eudämonie*, pp. 69–78 with notes, pp. 103 ff.

8 I have dealt with this problem briefly in *GE*, pp. 25 f. and at greater length in my *PT*.

9 Cf. my *Maimonides' Conception of State and Society* (in *Moses Maimonides*, ed. I. Epstein, 1935); *PT* for a similar view of Averroes as regards Muḥammad, and my studies mentioned there, dealing with Fārābī, Ibn Bājja (Avempace), Avicenna and Averroes, as also *GE, Exkurs I* and *II* (*Bemerkungen zur Theorie der Prophetie bei den mittelalterlichen islamischen und jüdischen Philosophen*), pp. 79–86, with notes pp. 105–7; also *GE*, pp. 32 f., especially note 22, p. 94.

10 Cf. *GE* as in note 6, above, the whole chapter.

11 Cf. *GE*, pp. 31 ff. with notes.

12 Cf. Julius Guttmann, *Die Philosophie des Judentums*, 1933, pp. 237 ff., whose interpretation I am following in *GE*, pp. 51 f. Hebrew version (*Ha-pīlōsōfīāh shel ha-Yahadūth* [2], 5713), pp. 205 f. English translation of the latter, by David M. Silverman, 1964, p. 224 f.

13 Cf. *Sēfer hā-'iqqārīm*, ed. I. Husik, 4 f., where the passage is translated (I, 173): 'and causes his soul to cleave to the spiritual substance (*dābhār ha-rūḥānī*)'.

14 Cf. *GE*, p. 53 with notes 18–22, which deal with Albo's attitude to Aristotle, citing the relevant passages in the *Nicomachean Ethics*. For want of space, I can here merely refer the reader to my treatment of Sa'adya in *GE*, pp. 34–40 and *passim*, with notes on pp. 95 f.

15 Cf. *GE*, p. 54, with notes 24–27, for a fuller treatment than is here possible.

16 Cf. *Sēfer hā-'iqqārīm*, I, 79 f. My translation differs slightly from Husik's. Cf. also *ibid.*, I, 146, 148, 152, 158; III, 59, 109, 230, 265 f. and my *GE*, n. 24, p. 99.

17 *Sēfer hā-'iqqārīm*, I, 80 f.; III, 46 f. and *GE*, n. 25, pp. 99 f.

11

Ethics and Education*

NATHAN ROTENSTREICH

[I]

The connection between education and ethics is obvious enough
and generally acknowledged to exist. It is immaterial whether we
define the concern of ethics as the field of man's actions or as
that of the character of man and his personal qualities: it is in
either case palpable that education constitutes one of the instruments available for the practical implementation of ethics. It is
education that is able both to attract its beneficiary to actions and
also to endow him with attributes reckoned to be ethical.
According to this approach, the place of education has to be
plotted as falling within the category of means that serve
some purpose, or promote some value, external to themselves –
ethical values, in this case. Or, to put it another way: in so far as
education promotes values external to itself, its justification will
lie in the values which it exists to serve. To the extent that education is reckoned an instrumental activity it cannot dispense with
such justification, inasmuch as every instrument is called upon
to prove its right to exist by reference to the action that it
accomplishes or the purpose for which it was invented. There is
no difference, from this point of view, between a mechanical
instrument and one consisting of a prolonged human enterprise

231

such as is educational endeavour. Thus regarded, education is in a position of some advantage in that it is ethical values which it exists to serve; for, by being able to confine itself humbly to the instrumental plane, it can derive from those values its own complete justification for existence.

But to state the relationship thus does not exhaust our subject, since it cannot be said that education serves to promote ethical values alone, inasmuch as *instruction* constitutes part of the educational process. In so far as the objective of education is to impart some sort of orientation in life, to provide some limited grasp of man's relationship to the world about him and of his present to his past, and (above all) in so far as it is concerned with providing the pupil with some definite corpus of factual information, education does indeed remain but a means instrumental to an end – without, however, being an instrument reserved by ethics for its own exclusive use. It is sometimes said nowadays that the hall-mark of any value is its capacity to evoke a 'pro-attitude'. If that is so, then every kind of education is concerned to engender a pro-attitude towards whatever may be reckoned by the educationist to constitute values, be they ethical, speculative, academic, aesthetic, or what you will. The ethical values in the service of which education is enlisted constitute but a rung in a ladder of values – or, let us rather say, in order to avoid giving the impression of passing hierarchically conceived value-judgments, they are but one fragment of a whole complex of values all of which education exists to serve, in virtue of its essentially instrumental nature: ethical values being no less, and no more entitled to its resources than are any others.

If, nevertheless, we insist on throwing into relief the special position occupied by ethical values, and on describing education by reference to its links with those values exclusively, then our whole conception of what education is will move out of the field of vision of whatever outlook we happen to maintain towards our system of values in general. It would seem that our consciousness assesses ethical values as being the primary ones, or at the very least sees them as possessed of greater weight than other values in the ordering of one's personal life. To the extent that education promotes certain values, or strives to make them the canons by which an educated person ought to conduct himself, it must concern itself, first and foremost, with those values that are held to be fundamental and of primary importance for human life, and for how one ought to react to its vicissitudes. The emphasis on the special connection between education and ethical values is not the outcome of any particular view as to the quality of education *per se*, since education itself falls within the category of things instrumental: it derives rather from the view taken of ethical values themselves, and of their supposedly peculiar position within the framework of human existence. The result of taking this attitude for granted in the daily round of common life is clear enough – 'it doesn't matter what you learn, the main thing is to be a decent person.' When we say that, we are coming down heavily on one side in regard to the various values in which man's actual, concrete existence is involved, and are assigning ethical values a position superior to that of all others. The trouble about taking sides in this way is that there are other values, not least the theoretical values, that can be regarded as relevant to a definition of what is meant by a 'decent person'. Where they are so regarded, the viewpoint remains within the field of ethical judgment, but of an ethical judgment much enlarged – for whatever reason – in respect of its scope and content. In other words, the answer to the question 'What qualities are to be considered as ranking high from an ethical point of view?' has been broadened.

[II]

It may be asserted that the more that education emphasises the role of man in society, and the well-being of the individual from the point of view of the integration of both his various potentialities and his own personal feeling of contentment, the more restricted is the range of values which education serves. That, in essence, is the way in which so-called 'modern education' sets about its various aims and objects. The idea of *adjustment* – one of the key concepts in modern educational theory – embraces two meanings, which usage confounds. The first of these meanings is that of *adaptation* to the world of reality, and particularly (as contained therein) to the world of social reality, by means of contact with other people, of facing up to the claims of society on the individual, and of a willingness and an ability to recognise also the claims of social existence in general: to recognise, that is, that social existence stands for a certain set of values, and is consequently entitled to elicit a pro-attitude in regard to itself. On the other hand, the concept of adjustment means also the integration of all the potentialities of the individual *psyche* – the achieving of a human harmony, a zest for life, an optimistic outlook, and all the other traits of a personality content in itself and affording contentment to others. The circumstance of these two meanings being both current in reciprocal confusion requires explanation: it would seem that the reason for this lies in the tacit assumption of the foregoing approach, to the effect that only he can achieve personal integration of character who is capable of recognising the system of values implicit in social life, and, conversely, that the achievement of a personal integration of character is a *sine qua non* for the attainment of an appreciation of the values implicit in social existence. We may remark that, as viewed from the angle of fundamentals, there has occurred within the frontiers acknowledged by modern education a marked incline here in favour of ethical values being those which it is a purpose of education to inculcate. Ethical values are here understood to fall within the field of the relationship of individual to society, in the very moment that that field of relationship is established upon the basis of integration – i.e. on the joy of meeting other individuals, alongside the respect of the individual's own right to maintain his privacy.

This is a truly paradoxical state of affairs, both historically and from the point of view of educational theory. To consider first the historical aspect, we may observe that the ideology and practice of 'modern education' were given formulation in a period of relativism, at a time when both the authority and the content of ethical values were under challenge. Perhaps, however, we need not after all detect a paradox in this inconsistency, if we are right in suggesting that this extra link between education and ethical values is, in essence, a kind of internal attempt by relativists to use education to surmount their own relativist assumptions. Because, in the last analysis, it is not the strict and practical amongst ethical values – values such as justice, purity, and self-dedication, etc. – that modern education professes to be attempting to impart to the pupil; instead, it substitutes for all of these a general notion of adjustment between individual and society, and assumes the existence of a connection between harmony in general as an ethical value and the particular harmony of individual and society which supposedly brings to that ethical value its practical realisation. But for all its emphasis on the connection between education and ethics, modern education nevertheless involves some degree of neutralisation of the ethical sphere, inasmuch as it plays down the rigidity of its claims. It takes as its starting-point the various potentialities of the human *psyche*, not any ethical commands of an objective quality; and it relies on those potentialities to resolve, in conjunction with each other, a problem that is fundamentally one of values and of ethics. This brings us to the node of the difficulty of this supposed particular link between modern education and the world of ethics as viewed from the standpoint of educational theory. For, in presupposing such a link, education is assuming the full weight of responsibility for providing answers to philosophical problems regarding the ethical sphere: for example, that of the relationship of individual rights to some course of action – whatever it may be – as viewed objectively, or the problem of spontaneity as against objective claims addressed to the *psyche* of man, etc. Modern education solves these complex questions in advance, by means of an assumption of a predetermined harmony obtaining between the various aspects of human existence, for example, the assumption that the development of personality is nothing but the taking root by the subject in society and a growing responsiveness on his part to its calls. No more need be said of the ingenuousness of such harmonistic presuppositions, to which we shall have to revert below. But in any event, if it once be granted that education occupies a position within the domain of ethical values, there devolves upon it the obligation of explaining ethical problems, to its own satisfaction at least, instead of merely passing the baby over to the concept of 'adjustment' (itself a term of manifold meaning), as if adjustment were some piece of automatic apparatus for answering questions.

[III]

Our description of the relationship of education and ethics has found itself caught up in the concepts of means and ends; and we must consequently face up to the responsibility of stating our position in regard to the complex subject of the relationship in general of means to ends, and in particular within the sphere of ethics. It would seem that two considerations make it possible to impugn the axiomatic assumption that the educational process stands to ethical values in a purely instrumental function.

(*a*) The first view may be labelled, for the sake of brevity, the Aristotelian. According to Aristotle's notion, ethics is a field of practical endeavour; and it is in virtue of a man's practical manifestation of ethical characteristics that he becomes an ethical entity. For example, *acts* of justice alone render a man a just man. A view of education that reckons it to be but an instrument in the hands of ethics would therefore push ethics off the centre of the pitch out into the deep field; reflecting thereby the status of ethics as but a distant aim, that can make no practical impression on the actualities of educational existence. Education, therefore, is not, as a functional means, capable of promoting ethical aims. It is only if education in practice comprises those qualities for the sake of which it was, in the last analysis, invented, that it both fulfils its task and finds its own justification. In other words, if we may say that the justification of education lies in the system of ethical values that has called it into existence, then education must itself bear the imprint of that system of values; otherwise it will both fail in its purpose and forfeit its justification. The justification of education forms a circle congruent with that of its content.

(*b*) The other consideration we may style Dewey's view.

Dewey spoke of a *continuum* of means and aims[1]; and he made this theme one of the cardinal features of his philosophy of values, in order to prove that in the last resort there is no real distinction between independent values and values which exist for the sake of other ones (*intrinsic* and *instrumental* values). Against the background of a system of thought concerned with the *continuum*, all values are, at one and the same time, both instrumental and intrinsic. This is to dispose of all difference in status as between ethical values and educational existence; and once again, we find that education has no option but to allow itself to be impregnated with those very values upon which its sights are set. Whether we follow Aristotle or Dewey, we reach the firm result that education is not feasible save with the help of the very qualities upon which education is itself orientated: and thus, at the basis of all education, there lies the axiomatic assumption that there can be no beginning *ab initio* – you cannot have an egg without a chicken. This is no isolated instance in the intellectual and speculative life of man: we elsewhere find that human activity likewise reveals its own circular character, as for example within the sphere of linguistics – language being a fund of expression acquired through speech, which is itself a linguistic activity. It is not possible, therefore, to give any ultimate description of how education, being itself an intellectual activity of such preponderant importance, might constitute an area constructed differently from the structure of the intellectual and speculative life of man in general. This leads, as far as concerns the educator, to a practical conclusion of far-reaching importance, *viz.* that an ethical system of values is something more than the mere horizon, within the limits of which the educator's business is to be prosecuted; it is rather part and parcel of the actual situation in which he actually finds himself. The educator simply cannot extrude all responsibility for taking ethical decisions right out of his own world, and dump it in the hands of the society which he exists, so to speak, to serve; and even if those who talk glibly about the sociological quality of education emphasise, in garish colours, the propriety of such a course of action, the educator who adopts it will fail in his own purpose. The supposedly distant horizon of values is, on the contrary, the immediate and intimate concern of the educational process itself, which is set directly face to face with ethical problematics, and not merely through its links with the *Weltanschauung* of the particular society in which its own practical undertakings take place.

To talk — as is so often done nowadays — about the purposefulness of education, is to contribute, in some degree, to the blurring of this presupposition regarding the nature of the educational process itself. When we use such language, what we are really concerned to establish is that the purposefulness of education is something imposed upon it in virtue of its bond with society, rather than being the product of its own character and therefore something independent. It is perfectly true that the values whose stamp education bears are values with a concrete content, and that they extend that concrete content over the course of generations through their link with the drift of society as a whole. At the same time, the transmission of those values down the generations, as also their original concrete embodiment, are processes that take place against the background of two fundamental assumptions: (i) the assumption that a belief in a system of values is in essence an established and abiding phenomenon, and (ii) the assumption that man's situation is, in essence, that of an agent by whom those values may be implemented. No matter what differences in the actual interpretation of those values may arise, both the values themselves are assumed to endure, and man likewise, to put them into practice. The character of education, *qua* itself constituting a value, has been impressed upon it and indeed derives from the very circumstance that education is an activity which takes place amongst people. One might formulate this idea somewhat differently, and say that every value-judgment is dependent on the recognition of certain boundaries to acceptable behaviour. The determination of what those boundaries may actually be consists in a variety of concepts concerning the forbidden, these concepts defining the frontier that is not to be crossed. The process of education comprises human intercourse, and particularly the meeting of persons from different stations in life, in point of age, accident of birth, etc., as well as in point of the educational content of such interchange; and it is the circumstance of its comprising such intercourse that will determine the limits of tolerable behaviour, and impose the requisite prohibitions. This whole aspect of education derives from its own inherent nature, and is in no sense something with which it is endowed by the vicissitudes of life or by the purpose of its parent society.

On the other hand, to recognise in the purposefulness of education a function or reflection of the purposefulness of society as a whole is bound up with the following presupposition, be it explicit or unavowed: *viz.*, that *all* social purposefulness has a built-in educational significance, and commands potential resources that are deliberately focussed on education and advance sundry claims in its name. That is not, however, the case. Education is bound up with the circumstance, fundamental to humanity, that throughout their lives people stand perpetually at some cross-road or other, i.e. that it is they who must themselves forge their own way ahead and determine the direction that it shall take. But the cross-roads of politics are not inevitably identical with those of man, and the latter kind of cross-roads symbolise a concept that is accorded greater priority than the former. There are, of course, occasions when politics can crystallise out into issues of ethical significance, i.e. they can spotlight decisions that have to be made, and which involve matters of principle: for example, the antinomy alleged often enough in the contemporary scene between freedom and equality. But the cross-roads of politics often unfortunately represent issues too complicated for us to be invariably able to set them exclusively against the background of ethical principle which happens to impinge upon them. To take an actual contemporary example: If one wishes to analyse the ideas basic to any political philosophy, one must determine what kind of Utopia it fundamentally presupposes; in other words, in what type of social philosophy the political ideas are involved. At this stage it becomes apparent that the ideas embodied in the writing of two (or more) given political philosophers, who may stand poles apart from each other, may well derive from one and the same utopian philosophy of human socialism. Thus, the late Lord Lindsay's conception of the nature of democracy,[2] and Lenin's[3] conception of communistic society, have in common the basic presupposition that human society is identical with the confrontation of man and his fellow – as far, that is, as a miniature society is concerned. From this common approach to a socialist philosophy of mankind, and the common acknowledgment of its essentially ethical foundation, Lenin and Lindsay can arrive at utterly different conceptions regarding the life of man in society and state. We are precluded, in discussion of these matters, from adopting so naive a line of argument as to assert that, since all great political struggles contain a grain of utopianism, *ergo* they all embody considerations of significance in terms of values. There are certain political movements that are the mere outcome of what goes on within the society concerned – the result of its interior mechanisms, of secondary causes, external factors and so on. It is thus a sheer confusion of categories, as well as a myopic view, to take it for granted that the various political struggles imply, by their very essence, things of significance in regard to educational purposefulness. In a nutshell: the purposefulness of education is an internal feature of education itself, not a mere transfer copy of the purposefulness of society at large.

[IV]

Before we turn to consider what it is that constitutes the ethical quality in the educational process, we may glance – by way of an example to illustrate the internal links between education and ethics – at the question of punishment, and its role in education. If we examine the various opinions in regard to this, we shall find that there is no difference of principle in regard to the problem surrounding punishment in education from that surrounding it in society in general. The differing approaches may be arranged schematically into those which see in punishment the reaction of an outraged society to an act regarded as wrongful, and those which view it as an attempt at reforming the agent of an act so regarded. We find that both these attitudes towards punishment are to be met with in education. It is sometimes the case that the reformatory motivation receives greater emphasis in the educational sphere than it does in that of the social environment, thanks to the ethical character of the whole educational process. If the concern of education is to impart ethical qualities and ethical modes of action, it may make use of something itself devoid of ethical significance in order to exploit its possibilities in an ethical direction: and punishment can consequently assume the role of the harbinger of a reformatory objective. Nevertheless, the essentially exact parallelism between the general sphere of social environment and the more restricted one presupposed by the educational process, is evidence of the fundamental closeness obtaining between the ethical convictions in the two respective spheres. It would seem that this fact occasions surprise precisely because of its being an example chosen from the problem of punishment. In the life of society punishment does not figure as a purely ethical category, but as a category of criminal law – i.e., it is tied to a plane defined, and indeed positively established by institutions that are a continuing feature of human life. In education, on the other hand, punishment figures also on planes free from the institutional aspects of the law – not merely in school or in the youth-movements in which it is possible, indeed, for the institutional and organisational aspects to attract most of the attention, but also within the domestic sphere, in which the formal categories of authority and reform have no place. Yet there is nevertheless operative an attitude of educational common-sense that happens also to coincide with 'ethical common-sense'. The foregoing example may thus furnish useful evidence of the complex of problems, human and ethical, that evince themselves within spheres diverse from each other in point of practical action, but which are nevertheless close in respect of the ethical element common to them all.

Furthermore, it is just this difference as between the spheres of education and society in general in the matter of punishment that may underline the ethical *plus* inherent in education. Punishment in education, in contrast to punishment in society, is – or at any rate ought always to be – directed at one, specific, concrete individual. Educational punishment is something personal, imposed by an educator (himself possessed of the characteristics of personality), who is obliged to accept practical responsibility for the punishment which he imposes, and not to pass it on to anonymous and abstract notions of character-reformation. Within education, punishment is retained within the framework of human relationships as between fellow creatures. It may be that, in this particular instance, those relationships find expression in a tension contingent upon punishment; but the circumstance that we do, nevertheless, remain within the realm of personal relationships makes evident the fact of ethical significance being the hall-mark of the whole educational process – assuming always that ethical significance is something that we associate with the immediate contact between man and man, uninterrupted by any rigid and established interposing factor. All the same, the educational process is not, in this respect, a monolithic unity; and the institutional basis is less prominent within the family than it is in school or in the youth-movements. The sort of education that emerges from personal contacts needs, for that contact, an institutional background, and it is conceivable that it has no feasible alternative. Nevertheless, one must regard its inevitable dependence on an institutional basis as an eccentric swerve outside its own sphere – a kind of tribute that has to be paid to the genius of organisation, a necessary evil perhaps, but none the less an evil. Every educational consideration has therefore to regard itself as being always placed within a quasi-magnetic field between two (so to say) poles: one of them, that of personal relationships, providing the background for the ethical significance of education, and the other being the institutional one that may well not be a bad thing within the context of society at large, but which is always liable to qualify as something undesirable within the particular context of educational existence.

When all has been said, the problem of punishment constitutes but a detail taken out of the general problem of the individual's responsibility for his actions and the authority of the social community, or of those of its representative members who may, as guardians of principle, summon the individual to take his responsibilities seriously. And it is this situation that gives expression to the difference – a small difference, perhaps, but still an important one – between the ethical view taken of social life in general, and the particular one brought to bear on the educational sphere.

[v]

The ultimate assumption on which all educational philosophy rests is the postulation that children and young persons deserve special attention, and that they are therefore 'privileged' people. Even though the notion of juvenile privilege has only in the most recent period been formulated into something like a child's bill of rights, the notion itself has always been present and operative, even without any ideological declaration of a formal nature. At the base of this assumption there lies an ethical attitude of decisive import, which provides the key to the understanding of the whole educational process from the point of view of the ethical significance immanent therein.

Let us begin, for the sake of clarifying this aspect of the matter, by posing the following question: 'How far can the notion of the privilege of children, or of persons in receipt of formal education, be reconciled with the notion of the equality of human rights?' One possible answer is that the child is entitled to such privilege by way of compensation for his objectively inferior situation, and as a means of (in some way) raising towards adequacy the inferiority that is contingent upon a weakness that is not merely social but also physical, etc. The special care provided within the sphere of education creates conditions for the *plus* essential for the child's survival in a world that is not his own. For the sake of restoring something like equality, we consequently create for him conditions of life unlike normal ones, set apart from the stresses that automatically flow from the workings of the social Leviathan.

Such an accounting for juvenile privilege throws into relief the generic distinction between education as understood to refer to the young, and adult education. It is true that we nowadays

s   243

emphasise the unending continuity of the educational process, in order to show that it is, or at any rate ought to be a *continuum* running on into adult life; but there still remains a clear and fundamental distinction in regard to the justification proffered for education, that justification corresponding in each case to the age-group concerned. The ideology of adult education stresses the importance of such education's proceeding from the kind of existence in which the adult himself happens to be actually involved; and the fact that it is at pains to stress this, derives indirectly from the differing anthropological (or ethical) approaches to juvenile and adult education respectively.

But the justification for 'entitlement to special treatment', to which our oblique investigation of the theory of equal rights has led us, is merely one side of the coin. Another motive may also be operative in our reaching conclusions with an ethical dimension when we assume that someone is entitled to privileged treatment. This latter viewpoint is reflected, for example, when we extend certain extra rights in the social scheme to ex-servicemen, etc. We do not, in this instance, emphasise the inferior status of the privileged person or claimant of privilege, but, on the contrary, his superior status as being a factor obliging us to accord him due practical recognition. Paradoxical though it may seem, it must be said that in qualifying for treatment as a special case the child does so not only in virtue of his *inferior* status in the world around him, but also on account of the *superiority* that he represents in the context of the world around him, *viz.* an as yet unrevealed potential superiority of human qualities. All education is based on the appreciation – or at any rate the cognisance – of what the child represents potentially from the point of view of human behaviour and achievement. As far as education is concerned, the future is a line running in parallel with the present, even though the parallel is, in terms of actuality, non-existent. It is in the name of the future, i.e. in the name of something that he may now merely represent and which can become palpably visible in the future only, that a young person qualifies for his privilege, since he represents potentially something more than is actually existent. And further, within this same accepted notion of the child's superiority there are two aspects; *viz.* (i) that the child potentially represents something more than he himself is now, and (ii) that he represents something over and above what we, members of the community at large, ourselves have in us under our own contemporary conditions. 'Superiority' therefore, in the present context, carries simultaneously both an individual and a general signification, since it is used with reference both to the young person himself and also to the status of a given society within a determinate historical period. Entitlement to something *plus* is therefore accorded to the young, thanks to an extension of our horizon that prompts us to take into consideration an as yet non-existent dimension – the future – and to assess it as one of the factors that direct, and indeed determine our behaviour in the present.

[VI]

The foregoing assignment of the *potentiality* of the child to its proper place within the series of concepts of ethical significance in pedagogics, brings us to the consideration of a problem that is rather one of principle, *viz.* the status of man in ethics *vis-à-vis* his status in education. Here, once again, we shall find that a clear parallel obtains between the two spheres.

From the ethical point of view, man is a phenomenon possessed of two aspects. On the one hand, he is a fact – a *datum*; as much part of the world of reality that impinges on us as are any other objects which we may happen to come up against, and as the situations of remorseless actuality in the midst of which we live out our lives. Man, being a fact, is (whether I happen to like it or not) one of the determinants of my personal situation. But the ethical situation superimposes a second angle of vision on this factual one – the angle from which the assessment of values is made; this being the only additional point of view that ethical consideration is designed to contribute. From this ethical standpoint the next man, being already a *fact*, becomes also a *value*: we no longer merely rub up against him – we acknowledge him. And the practical expression that this acknowledgment takes is the conception that other people, too, have certain rights which they may expect us to honour.

There is, however, a cardinal ambivalence involved in this double-sided status of man, and it is an ambivalence of some importance for the understanding of both ethics and education. The question may legitimately be asked whether man, *qua* fact, is already a value, or whether he is merely the vehicle of values – so that his own value-quality becomes secondary, and dependent on the extent to which he meets the claims upon him in regard to certain modes of behaviour, the fulfilment of certain duties, and so on. One uses the expression 'the sanctity of life', thereby meaning both that life is sacred in itself and that it is the indispensable basis for the implementation of values or, at the very least, that life has the status of a value because (and only because) of its furnishing that indispensable basis. If we may translate this attitude of mind into the language of the concepts of rights and obligations, we shall have to say both that man possesses certain rights *qua* man, and that he possesses those rights in virtue of his fulfilling certain obligations that are, incidentally, the expression (or implementation) of certain values. If that is correct, the conclusion may follow that man still retains his title to those rights when he fails to fulfil certain obligations, or even when he acts in opposition to them. As is well known, this last ethical consideration can be a very practical one in such serious human situations as, for example, determining the relationship of society towards the offender. In any event, it is now clear that man figures within the ethical sphere as the possessor of a complex of values establishable from two points of view: *either* as himself having inherent status as a value, *or* as having a secondary status as a value, this being conferred upon him by the values that he himself implements.[4]

This ambiguity of meaning, characteristic of the problems involved from the ethical point of view, is likewise to be observed within the educational process. A young person or pupil possesses certain rights *per se* within the educational framework, and not merely because of the values, the potential future implementation of which he carries within him. On the other hand, he has a value-status precisely because we do take his potentialities into account as well, and see in him the vehicle of values yet to be realised in or by him. Without doubt, one of the ideological achievements of modern educational thought is bound up with this notion: modern education (to take a glance at its philosophical aspect) has taken up the notion that man, *qua* man, has some value-status and has injected it into the sphere of education; postulating (or presupposing) that every young person has a value-status, quite apart from the question of any values in terms of specific content such as justice, truthfulness, etc., which he may be in process of realising now, or capable of realising in the future. Here we glimpse the danger to which modern education is exposed — a danger that becomes understandable if we take a look at it from the angle of ethical teaching. Modern education, having made clear the value that it sets on the pupil *per se*, is prone to let the other aspects of the ethical situation slip out of its field of vision, i.e. to pay too little attention to the fact of the young person's possessing a value-status in virtue of *objective* values — or values in terms of specific content — that he is capable of realising in his character as later to be developed, and in his future activities. This mental conviction of the inherent value of the pupil, for all that it gives expression to an attitude that is one of real ethical principle, does nevertheless run the risk of circumscribing the very horizon of all ethical thinking itself; by subtracting therefrom the perspective of futurity that constitutes an interior line round which, as round a centre of interest, the whole vista is coordinated.

Modern educational theory is sometimes constructed on the presupposition that the free development of the personality takes place in step with the subject's striking his roots in the world of objective ethical values. The basis of such a conception rests on considerations of a psychological nature, i.e. the opinion that so long as a person becomes habituated to any given norms on a voluntary basis, his attachment to those norms is one of substance; but that so long as they appear as something imposed on him from without, his *ego* rejects them, this resulting in a split personality, and in norms without any foothold in reality. In this connection it may be remarked that, if what is here said concerns no more than the *method* by which sundry norms of civilised behaviour may best be imparted, and nothing else is asserted than the desirability that self-habituation to those norms should spring out of situations intelligible to young persons themselves rather than that they be submitted to as a matter of formal discipline, then this modern psychological attitude raises no consideration affecting principle; what it has to say remains within the limits of technical advice on the pedagogical plane. If, however, the burden of this whole concept of education is to posit the thesis that such norms grow naturally out of their corresponding situations, and that (at the root of the matter) there is, in such norms, no objective substance with any imperative character about it, then the concept abolishes in one blow the entire basis of human existence itself. All human existence consists of contacts between poles of experience: and it is simply not the case that one pole emanates from the other as if through some process of evolution. If we start from the example afforded by book-learning and the study of an academic subject, we find high-lighted for us the focus of a line that runs through all human existence. An academic syllabus is something that is set before the student; and it would be sheer optical delusion to make out that that syllabus could be deduced from inside the mind of the student himself. To adopt Francis Bacon's simile,[5] man is not like a spider that spins its web from within itself, but resembles rather a bee that gathers nectar from the pollen of the flowers outside it. Even though academic syllabuses are drawn up by men who are scholars, they are not the fruit of the mind of the man who, as a student, is himself under an academic obligation towards those syllabuses; he is simply presented with them. It is, of course, easy for his own address to them to spring out of an enthusiasm engendered by the educational situation, but that does not mean to say that it is that situation which has itself sprouted the syllabuses. Insofar as modern education makes the latter claim its thesis, it is guilty of confounding the difference between the *address to norms* that arises out of empirical situations, and the *status of those norms* themselves when confronted by those same situations.

We see, then, that the educational process takes place against a background of twofold vision, focussed simultaneously on man in general and youth in particular. On the one hand, human existence is in itself elevated to the rank of being treated as a value, and on the other it is conceived to be no more than the necessary condition for any system of values to operate, without being credited with a value status of its own. The internal logic of education is closely linked to the logic that governs ethical evaluation: and, try though one may to replace the dualism of ethical evaluation by some other means of assessment of a monistic kind, one only runs up against difficulties and objections. These difficulties are the outcome of a conscious or subconscious will to be free of the logic that governs the sphere of ethics, and to create for education a realm that shall be independent of it. But this will to self-liberation is impracticable, for one very simple and decisive reason: because these problems, problems of ethical evaluation though they be, are also, through and through, the problems of education itself. The structure of education, and the problematics of principle involved in it, are not other than the structure and problematics of the general sphere of ethics. If the truth be known, when we 'leave' education to its own devices, we leave it saddled with all its old problems, neither lightening the burden nor removing it. For those problems are, from their roots upwards, problems of ethics.

[VII]

This connection between education and the internal problematics of ethical life likewise stands out prominently in something else, *viz.* our relationship towards obligation in general. The late Ezekiel Kaufmann, in his study of soul and spirit in education,[6] has described the two schools of educational theory and practice – one of them with its gaze set towards the objective values of 'culture', the other staking everything on the uninhibited development of the *psyche* or 'soul' of the pupil. In dealing with these two attitudes, Kaufmann adopts a typological method of treatment, cutting them clearly off from one another as if in watertight compartments; and it is but very rarely that he betrays a consciousness of any internal dialectic in their reciprocal relationship. In point of fact, however, we have not here to do with two distinct conceptions of education, but rather with two principles that have been set opposite-wise, in a state of complementary tension. Within the sphere of ethics, we are aware enough of the presence of objective obligation on one side, and the development of the personality on the other; and these two concepts illustrate, in the history of ethical thought, two ethical ideals, one of which derives from a willing (or even an enthusiastic) acceptance of the doctrine of obligation, and the other from a no less enthusiastic acceptance of the doctrine of the progressive sublimation of self. Any physical and biological entity endowed with personality may at times reveal itself as rising, step by step, on the scale of values, by so to speak ingesting some established value-content communicated to it in terms of a categorical imperative; and again, at other times, as moving forward under its own spontaneous steam, as it were taking some given level in life in which it finds itself, and shaping it into an ethical pattern. We are faced here with the tension between a view of the value-system that sees in it a pole of energy to which an individual reacts, and a view that sees it as something identical in essence with the spontaneity of that personality itself. In the usual way where problems with an inconvenient dialectical dimension are involved, the dialectic is disposed of (in such approaches as that of Kaufmann) through formulation in terms of discrete lines of argument, in such a manner that the dialectic falls apart. This leaves each of its determining factors with a spurious appearance of independence, so that each one of them gives the false impression of furnishing a nucleus round which a complete concept of the subject can form.

We meet the same tension within the educational process, which in transferring objective values to the possession of the pupil, seeks also to develop his personality – on the assumption both that that personality is itself a value, and also that by the development of personality is meant the bringing out into actuality – the *educating* – of objective values, through the internal spontaneity of the personality itself. It may be said that, from this point of view, the educational process is richer than the generality of ethically orientated endeavours, in virtue of its being comprised within an essential dualism; a dualism which it is not feasible to dismantle and rebuild upon its component portions in isolation from each other. This is so, for the simple reason that the educational process is brought into contact with the living personality of the pupil and is constrained to recognise the actuality of his personality as a fact, whether or not it chooses also to acknowledge in it an entity with a value-status *ab initio*. Thus the dialectical character of education's existence makes it the richer, precisely as every experimental undertaking is richer and more multi-coloured than some cast-iron systematic formulation. Its dualism, or its inherent tension, hits us in the eye when we pass from the territory of education in its conventional sense (where an educator confronts his pupil) to that of the self-education of the individual, where educator and pupil are doubled up within the physical dimensions of the same personality. In the latter case it is clear enough that the process of education means both the process of development of personality by means of widening its horizons, and also the absorption within it of sundry objective contents, inasmuch as the process is one of the infixation of an ethical content into the background of character in the personality concerned.

Yet for all this, educational thought does occasionally endeavour to surmount the dialectical tension obtaining between the two fundamental constituents in education, *viz.* that of developing the personality and that of shaping it by means of established norms; basing its endeavour on the unitary assumption that, in the final analysis, the objective content of the norms grows hand in hand with the development of the personality, as the latter crystallises out into identifiable traits of character. In making that assumption, educational thought is inclining towards the postulation of a kind of predetermined harmony as between different

251

poles. That supposed harmony is but another name for the fundamental optimism that characterises the educational process, and which takes it for granted that what you begin by having to do despite yourself, you will end up by doing voluntarily and spontaneously. But it is clear that this optimistic assumption – one that is particularly prominent, as is well known, in the thinking of Rousseau – comprises rather a kind of 'technical solution' of the problems in education, or a sort of attempt to prove that when all is said and done, the tribulations involved in the educational moil and toil are but incidental ones, or even phantoms. This is really a kind of attempt at overcoming the tension between the two fundamental constituents, not by any acknowledgment of their discrete existence, but by building a bridge – a bridge, however, that exists in the world of supposition only.

[VIII]

The foregoing remarks on the relationship of education and ethics point to two conclusions as to method and systematic analysis, each of them relevant to both of the elements here related.

(1) From the educational point of view, we may now assert that education is, fundamentally, a humane process that is at one and the same time factual, and possessed of a value-significance. No matter how much it may be based on facts of a biological, emotional or social order, it is impossible to separate it from its additional aspect, i.e. the value-aspect that confers on it its essential significance. All attempts to construct a theory of educational procedure on its procedural (i.e. functional) aspects alone, be those attempts psychologically or sociologically orientated (and many such are nowadays essayed), are doomed: they share the same fate as that which dogs the attempts to derive such concepts as *value*, *propriety*, and *obligation* from (for example) the circumstance that within human society there are certain areas of life that are taboo, or from the fact that society has resort to sanctions against its offenders. Educational thought finds such attempts at simplification attractive, because it assumes that they can lighten its own task of finding a basis for the essence

of education and for educational practice. It is inclined towards them on the supposition that it is easier to concern oneself with matters that are factual and experimental, without getting 'bogged down', as it would seem, in problems of significance which, of their very nature, are open to conflicting interpretations. But even a superficial understanding of what education means will suffice to show that it is saturated with value-significance, and that that significance constitutes an inseparable element of its very essence.

(2) From the angle of ethical teaching, there is a conclusion of a different category to be drawn. If the question be asked, 'Where are there to be found facts within human experience that lend themselves as a starting-point for ethical interpretation?' it is usual to point to custom, the role of law, to the value-judgments implicitly operative in the daily round, and so on. But ethical teaching has an inherent tendency to fasten onto the educational process, as being a fundamental function in any life that may be reckoned humane; and by way of answering the question, one may well find in the process of education itself the field of ethical experimentation. Not, perhaps, its sole field; but certainly one of the more important ones.

NOTES

* Translated by the Editor from the Author's Hebrew.
1 John Dewey, *Democracy and Education*: An Introduction to the Philosophy of Education, New York, 1926.
2 A. D. Lindsay, *The Modern Democratic State*, Oxford, 1943.
3 V. I. Lenin, *State and Revolution*, New York, 1932.
4 See the present author's *Humanism in the Contemporary Era*, The Hague, 1963, pp. 87 f.
5 Francis Bacon, *Novum Organum* xcv, *Philosophical Works*, ed. J. M. Robertson, London, 1905, p. 288, cf. Stobaeus, *Florilegium* §82.
6 *Nephesh wa-ruaḥ ba-ḥinnukh*, included in '*Al ha-ḥinnukh hat-tiykhoni ha-'ibhri be-'ereṣ yisra'el*, ed. Ḥ. Y. [=Leon] Roth, Jerusalem, 1939, pp. 245 f.

12

Herbert Samuel's
Moral Philosophy

HELMUT D. SCHMIDT

[I]

Herbert Samuel (1870–1963) was the last great philosopher of the English liberal tradition. Although he did not develop his philosophy systematically before the 1930s, his mind was decisively moulded in the early 1890s, when he was an under-graduate at Oxford and in close contact with the Fabians. He shared with them the outlook of meliorism, based on social justice and liberal democracy; like the Fabians he believed man to be intelligible, consistent, capable of becoming permanently rational and peaceful and crime to be the outcome of social evils such as poverty, ill health, illiteracy, or bad housing. It was the time when social field-studies undertaken in the East End of London had brought out new, disquieting facts about life 'in darkest England', the time of Booth's Salvation Army, and the beginning of the mass exodus of Jews from Russia. Public debate, too, drew attention to social problems. Parliament debated pro-posals for an old age pension to be paid by the state to the 'industrious poor'.

While still at Oxford, Herbert Samuel decided to devote his

life to the combat of social injustice, to public service in the field
of social legislation. In 1902, after several years of study, he
expounded a social programme in his book on Liberalism, including progressive taxation and old age pensions. He revived
Owenism and foreshadowed Keynes by his demand for public
spending and expansion to provide employment. It is the duty of
the state, Samuel argues, to help its citizens to lead the best life
of which they are capable. Then comes the sentence, 'the trunk of
the tree of Liberalism is rooted in the soil of ethics'. The young
writer felt that politics with its conflicting interests, economics
with its choice of priorities, and jurisdiction were all ultimately
philosophy in action and the practical application of ethics.

Besides social reform there was another topical issue prominent
at Oxford in the 1890s. The meaning of evolution was still in
doubt, and the impact of Charles Darwin was still to be felt in
heated undergraduate discussions. Not many students were as
yet familiar with the new Darwinian philosophy of Nietzsche's
superman, but the subject figured in the secular sermons of
Herbert Spencer and Thomas Huxley. Samuel was present in the
Sheldonian Theatre when the latter delivered his Romanes
Lecture of 1892. The subject was Evolution and Ethics. The gist
of that lecture was the contention that the survival of the fittest
is not the same thing as the survival of the best, and that ethical
progress takes place not in accordance with but in combat
against a hostile cosmos inside and outside ourselves. The cunning
and the destructiveness of the human animal, which at one
stage assisted man to subject the whole animal world, has now
become a defect and an obstacle to ethical progress. Human
awareness must turn ethical man into an active factor that can
increasingly shape and control a conscious evolution. Herbert
Samuel accepted that interpretation of evolution. *Conscious
evolution* became a major principle in his philosophical orientation.

The twenty years of public service in high government positions, in the British Cabinet and as first High Commissioner of
Palestine, left their mark on the method of Samuel's philosophy
and on his approach. Essentially, his philosophy was practical
public service. It was intended to be widely understood and to

reflect issues of private and public life. The following brief presentation of Samuel's moral philosophy sums up his published
work of the period 1931–61.[1] It is inevitable that such a concise
exposition as that here essayed will give Samuel's thoughts a
more dogmatic appearance than they have in their original
context.

Samuel believed that moral philosophy had suffered from two
defects, which he hoped to correct. It was presented to the public
in obscure language, and it had been divorced from experience
by abstract speculations. Whatever a critic might say about
Samuel's philosophy, he cannot possibly argue that it is unintelligible. It was written for the general public and every ordinary
English reader could, and can understand its meaning. As for
abstract speculation, he would never split non-existent hairs.
Samuel remained a staunch Baconian in his empirical approach.
Observation and experiment, collective and personal experience,
were essential to establish facts, to bring out the truth; and where
the truth was found to be in conflict with custom or tradition,
truth must win and tradition must yield. Bronze-age man
believed that gods directed events and could be influenced by
human sacrifice. Children were walled into houses for better
protection of the newly-built homes, daughters were slaughtered
when their parents desired a good harvest or a victorious battle.
Experience, however, proved that neither houses nor soldiers
could be immunised by religious slaughter. A sentimental
century, nearer to our epoch, condemned the killing of flies and
other defenceless insects. Experience proved, however, that those
insects carried deadly germs. Such a discovery altered the views
of generations about what was right or wrong concerning the
killing of insects. 'Civilisation', Samuel wrote, 'emerges from
barbarism precisely through the discovery that right is not
identical with the customary.'

Developing on the basis of observation and experience, moral
thought is a reflection of life. It cannot be stated in abstract
assertions without proof. It can never be stated in absolute and
general terms. It must needs be specific and subject to change
in the light of new facts. Above all, it must serve human welfare.

Ethics cannot be an autonomous discipline supported by *a priori* statements and formal logic alone; it is a practical art, the art of living. The art of living cannot be blind to circumstances, for circumstances are the substance of moral behaviour, because they mould our actions and ideas. With Spinoza, who inspired Samuel's quest for a scientific approach to political ethics, Samuel's own philosophy was in agreement about the desirable ends – first life, then the good life. The avoidance of unnecessary suffering, the wickedness of killing for pleasure, were axiomatic. There was no final vision of a new earth. Ethics reflected the process of human evolution. Its issues revolved around means, not around ends. Each generation could make some contribution towards moral improvement and a better life. The elimination of private feuds and of duelling has been such a contribution, as was also the abolition of slavery.

Samuel was no atheist. He believed that the cosmos reflected a superior mind, that the evolution from cosmic dust and gases to Einstein and Bertrand Russell could not be explained in terms of mere chance. The uniformity of nature, the principle of causality, the law of evolution, above all, the human mind bore witness to a creator. The universe was not self-explanatory. 'We are asked to believe many incredible things', Samuel said in 1931 (and frequently thereafter repeated), 'but that there should be nothing to be believed would be the most incredible thing of all'. On the other hand, there was no evidence in human history to suggest a watchful and benevolent providence. Samuel, therefore, did not link his moral philosophy with any theology. 'The problem of evil is one of human action more than theology.' Man was free to act and to suffer for his own follies. If suffering made any sense at all on a cosmic scale, it could only be interpreted as a guide along the path of self-directed evolution. Countless generations had to suffer famine and epidemics, yet their suffering, collectively speaking, was not in vain. It led mankind to agricultural improvement, to social medicine, and to a world food and health organisation. Devastating world wars have forced mankind to develop a world security authority, imperfect though it still is.

The foregoing interpretation of evil and suffering led Samuel to a social justification of death. Death, like birth, is the mighty engine of evolution. Both are welcomed. Without birth or death new hopes, new ideas, new effort would wither; 'there is pathos in the things that pass, but in things that never passed there would be despair.' Death is no evil; only premature, painful, or violent death is. Samuel, the self-confessed meliorist, believed that the present was better than the past and that the future would be better than the present. Each new generation is a 'fresh invasion of savages' but as it grows into the inheritance of the preceding generations, its young, fresh, critical minds examine the old values and traditions anew and step out further afield, seeking new answers to their own problems. The alternative to that process of evolution by mortality is stagnation through immortality and division – the world of the *amoeba*.

The centre of the moral law is the individual, who is accountable for his actions. Each person is a member of many groups such as the family, the village, the religious congregation, professional and political bodies; but these groups are mere patterns of individuals. The actions of a party or a church are the actions of responsible individuals. They have to bear the blame or receive the praise. But how can the principle of causality leave the individual with any moral responsibility? Samuel found the solution in relativity physics and in Spinozistic determinism.

Statements about reality may often seem contradictory, but the contradiction can be resolved by reference to the different scales or different positions of the observers. A person may be at rest in his bed and yet rotate around the axis of the earth. On the human scale a person has individuality, though he may be regarded by the biologist, on a different scale, as a cell-pattern. *Sub specie aeternitatis*, to use Spinoza's expression, all the actions of a person and his motives are caused by previous events. An omniscient being would know all the causes and could predict all the actions of mankind. Man's will and decisions, Samuel wrote, 'apparently free and spontaneous, are in fact no more than the necessary consequences, either seated within the mind itself or else external and social, which are altogether beyond his power to control.'

Factors controlling man's thoughts and actions are heredity, personal history, physical and social environment, training, habits, and group history. Man shares in the ideas of his time, some of which came into existence long before his birth. Man is not fact, but history; yet not a mere accumulation of factors. As he grows up his self takes an increasing share in his self-direction, control, and choice of actions. A person is an integrated whole partaking of three different worlds, the physical, the organic, and the imaginative. A person's mood and reactions may be determined by temperature, by his age, or by sentiment — that is, by causes pertaining to those different worlds. The result of an infinite chain of causes, yet at the same time no mere puppet, man is responsible for his actions and for their foreseeable consequences.

Looking back, one may discover the causes of one's action; looking into the future, a person feels that he is free to choose. Each act modifies the *ego*. A person is regarded as insane and not responsible for his actions, if it can be observed that he has lost control over them, and that they are entirely determined by the consequences of a disease or by a drug, or by an external force. There is a difference in the amount of personal responsibility of a driver according as to whether he drives into a shop window or whether his car is pushed into a shop window by another car. Somebody may jump on me or he may be pushed on me. In each case my own reaction will be different. If a person feels he is in control of himself and a responsible being, we must treat him as responsible and judge his actions by his motives, by the circumstances, the existing law, and the consequences which he could reasonably foresee. Only on such terms can the practical affairs of life be conducted. Society may impose sanctions, approval, or social pressure, thereby adding factors which cause action or inaction.[2]

The assertion of individual responsibility does not, however, mean a denial of social co-responsibility. Poverty, illiteracy, disease, and bad housing may cause crime. Every crime has a personal and a social aspect. A child is run over by a car on a busy thoroughfare. It is the driver who is indicted, but together with the driver there stand in the dock – invisibly – the local and central authorities that failed to provide better lighting, a necessary underpass, or alternative roads. Man can be understood and judged in the context of society only. Herbert Samuel, as administrator and statesman, gave to his moral philosophy the character and purpose of public service.

Every individual lives inside and by society. His art of social living consists in balancing personal and social claims, self-assertion and self-discipline, egoism and altruism, initiative and obedience, conformity and dissent. Abstract generalisations solve nothing. It is the specific situation, in all its complexity, that alone matters. The man who refrains from saving a drowning child may be a bad swimmer. Had the child been in shallow waters on a calm day, the situation would have been different from one where the child is far out in a rough sea. A general injunction such as *Thou shalt save a drowning child* is of little use.

As slogans, fictitious abstractions can be dangerous, and political or religious myths are bad guides to public ethics. Some systems of ethics have in the past claimed to have God on their side. Atrocities and wars were waged in the name of God. *Gesta Dei per Francos* was a slogan of the crusaders. Samuel, however, was more concerned with modern will-o'-the-wisps, with the deadly doctrine that the end justifies the means. Men are no longer sacrificed to Moloch or Juggernaut: but to party, race, and national states – to fictitious *-isms*. Time and again Samuel emphasised that in human affairs it is the individual that counts. State, party, society are mere associations of persons. The British have been more suspicious than have other peoples of ideological slogans, and have insisted on putting competing ideas to the test of social experiment and practical experience – the only valid test in public ethics. Practice matters more than principles; more important than the neat logic of *either-or* is the practical – and often illogical – art of balance and compromise. Samuel, particularly during the critical days of the second world war, was a staunch believer in the achievements of the English-speaking peoples in the field of political administration and public ethics.

From the seventeenth century onward there has developed in the Low Countries and in England a new civilisation – democratic, scientific, and tolerant. It became the civilisation of North America, the British Commonwealth and Western Europe. Its characteristics were the separation of public morals from theology, freedom of inquiry and expression, toleration of other views, and the abolition of the traditional authority of sacred texts. Bacon, Spinoza, and Locke symbolised that new age. In the name of new knowledge every idea is to be tolerated except intolerance; every person is free to do as he pleases, except to interfere with the freedom of his fellow-citizens. The gangster is not free: against violence there is no protection but force. Firm government is not the opposite of free government. Those who conspire to destroy freedom, Samuel taught, must not have the freedom to conspire. There is no worse calamity than force without justice, or justice without force. Society must be in a position to ward off crimes against itself. In a free society every citizen has the right to have access to truth. A social and scientific democracy requires factual and full information. For Samuel the lesson of North America and the British peoples was plain: individual happiness and public welfare grow best where there is tolerance, justice, liberty, government by consent, and international peace.

It is impossible to determine a quantitative scale of happiness, as the utilitarians believed. It is equally impossible to give precise meaning to the term. Yet a system of public morality does not exist in an abstract void. All public administration has to make moral decisions, and all public morals have certain long-term social aims. Peace, liberty, and toleration are not *objectives* in themselves. They are the *conditions* required to operate and implement a plan of social, ethical, scientific, and democratic humanism. Eventually a universal system of public morals must emerge which would aim, Samuel was convinced, at the achievement of human welfare, material, intellectual, moral, and social, the result of step-by-step improvement. It is forever the *next* step that matters. Once the fight against cholera and tuberculosis is won, the battle against cancer and heart diseases will forthwith have to be fought. Where human welfare is concerned there is no room for ethical relativism. Welfare remains the aim and conscious evolution, the principle of action. Social experience is the criterion, and the consequences of any act are the basis of moral judgment. As for motives, they, too, are consequences of previous actions. And so the cosmic process of struggle for survival and self-assertion is gradually modified into an ethical process of self-restraint, i.e. self-improvement by the control of a reasoning mind. Each group improves its own members, and each state carries out its duty towards its own citizens and its neighbouring states. Thus an emergent world society inherits what is best in each tradition.

[II]

Few critics of Samuel's moral philosophy will disagree with him on questions of method; with his insistence on clarity of expression, on lucid style, on observable facts, and on social experience. Historical evidence is on Samuel's side and supports his view of ethics as constantly evolving with each generation facing new problems. Samuel taught that what had been would not be, and that there are indeed new things under the sun. The ultimate criterion of tradition is its *social usefulness*. Each generation, however, advances into unknown lands, faces perplexing situations and new conflicts. Samuel believed that in such situations of crisis reason would prevail over fear, because he was an eminently reasonable man himself. At this point doubts about the assumptions of his philosophy in the public and in the private sphere begin to be felt. What if fear is stronger, sweeping away reason in times of crisis? History is littered with the ruined plans of reasonable men. Samuel himself had a reasonable solution for an economic federation of the Levant integrating Palestine, Transjordan, the Lebanon, and Syria; yet in the end, the decisions were made on the battlefield.

In 1938 Samuel predicted 'that with more education and prosperity crime will diminish'. This has not been the experience of affluent Britain in the 1960s. One could understand why illiteracy and poverty led to crime. It is harder to understand why comfortable houses, compulsory general education to the age of 15, and social security should lead to crime. Why, then, go on with welfare and progress? Samuel assumed that the progress of knowledge and the increase in human welfare would always benefit humanity. It could be, however, that the curve of knowledge and welfare yields diminishing returns, and that after a point further welfare, more leisure, and greater security might produce disappointing or even harmful results; or a point might be reached in our scientific investigation that revealed a truth which could make too many people incapable of leading a satisfying and happy life, a truth that might undermine a person's morale to face life at all. In that case we should be tempted to return to Plato's suggestion and to look for a Phoenician tale so as to make life bearable for humanity. It might prove to be our social experience, to put it in a more paradoxical way, that human progress is better served, if social welfare and truth made a little less progress. Samuel believed that truth must be known before the right action can be taken. There are occasions, however, when the right course of action is to prevent truth from becoming known.

In an age of revolution in communication, knowledge spreads fast and indiscriminately. The Victorians thought that the faster and wider knowledge spread, the greater would be the gain for humanity. Again, a point has been reached when this assumption has become doubtful. Once a perfected television service makes news instantaneous, global, and universal, the problem of disseminating truth indiscriminately will become more pressing. Once more we might be forced by our social experience to return to the Greek philosophers, who held that man can stand only so much of the truth as his age and intellectual maturity enable him to absorb for the fruitfulness of his own life. The little girl who desires affection and reassurance is not assisted in her development by scenes of rape and murder on the television screen.[3] The truth that life is full of hazards and nature without sentiment in the struggle for survival, shocks no healthy person of eighteen, but it can do positive harm to young children of six.

Sound education demands that the truth should not be known to all. A similar demand can be justified in the name of security by a government, which might fear that the disclosure of certain facts might threaten the safety of the country.

The political objection to a programme of peace and welfare may be based on moral grounds as well. Peace is never neutral. It always serves the *status quo*, which will, therefore, suit the victors. Welfare is not neutral either. People seek welfare for a variety of motives. Some governments interest themselves in the welfare of distant countries because they fear communism or American influence, not because they are motivated by any altruistic desire to promote the welfare of an underdeveloped country. For other groups, assistance offered to underdeveloped areas is good business. In 1947 the Soviet Union supported the establishment of a Jewish State in Palestine, not because Communist leaders were interested in the promotion of social justice – it was in that light that Samuel himself regarded the Jewish national home and Zionism[4] – but because they were interested in ousting Britain from Palestine. Thus human welfare may be undertaken for many motives, not all of them praiseworthy; and the promotion of welfare is not always tantamount to moral progress.

A last objection to Samuel's moral philosophy in the field of public affairs may be raised by those who maintain that every public action is likely to harm certain groups of people and their interests, and that there are many cases in history where social progress has been achieved at the price of bitter conflict and even moral transgression. The American continent – north and south – was not developed by its original inhabitants, but by invaders, who ruthlessly exterminated the original Americans. The meliorist theory of progress is evidently not always supported by historical reality.

'In all human affairs', Samuel said, 'it is the individual that counts – his character and will, his choices, his actions.' The responsible individual is the centre-piece of Samuel's moral philosophy. Yet it may be true that such an individual as envisaged by Samuel does not, in fact, exist.

Samuel's responsible individual, one must assume, is capable of choosing between two or more courses of action, of foreseeing and weighing some of their consequences and judging them in the light of the existing law. It is evident that many individual actions do not arise in that fashion. Some actions are automatic responses, others are governed by emotion, association, and instinct, not by reason. Something, one suspects, is wrong with the concept of human action and the notion of the individual. If it were the case that a person could not simultaneously both act properly and reflect effectively, the responsible individual would become a myth. There is some evidence that man's action is adversely affected by reflection and *vice versa*. The moment of action can never be the moment of reflection. A person who speaks a foreign language, for instance, will find that his fluency in that language is interrupted the moment he is forced to analyse a point of grammar. Should further psychological research come to the conclusion that a person can never act and reflect at the same time, the notion of personal responsibility would have to be modified.

Samuel maintained – without proving – that a person is more than a mere historical accumulation, that he is an entity capable of creative activity, and that his own insight offered evidence of free will. Introspection, however, is no safe guide – besides, it shows that decisions are often made on the basis of associations and circumstances. Experiment has proved that the impression of free will can be an illusion. No evidence of uncaused volition has been forthcoming. Post-hypnotic suggestions have led to actions whose remote causes the persons concerned did not realise. Their belief of having acted freely, and their intriguing rationalising explanations of their actions, have thrown additional doubt on the value of introspection.

There is little evidence that the human mind is more than a historical accumulation contained in a constantly changing organism which is a mere speck in space and time. As far as mind contains language, its character is social rather than individual; for language is a form of social communication. No man can call his language truly his own. From elementary ideas and terms a mind builds up more complex notions in the course of time. Without those elements of thought and language the human mind could not function at all. Research concerning the origin of new ideas is still very far from complete. Nothing in the process suggests that any truly new creation is produced by an autonomous, self-determining mind. All that the mind seems capable of doing is finding new *connexions* among *existing* elements. The experience of a new situation may give rise to a new connexion in a person's mind. Oxford's traffic chaos on a Friday afternoon might give birth to the idea of closing city centres to heavy traffic at certain hours of the day. There is nothing new in those elements of thought and language except their combination. History can furnish many similar instances of how new ideas have arisen.

One of the most impressive collective experiences of seventeenth-century Britain was the spectacle of the rise of Holland after her successful struggle against the might of Spain. English observers drew the lesson that trade, not gold, was the true source of wealth, and that political power was rooted in prosperous trade. Furthermore, it was observed that power and wealth were assisted by tolerance and free inquiry and observation. With persons like William Temple and John Locke political experience came first and theory afterwards. Society furnishes the general pool of ideas, and the individual mind forges the new combination out of the elements that it acquires or selects from the existing social reservoir.

The minds of Adolf Hitler or Joseph Goebbels respectively contained no original element. Their mental work was achieved through the combination, focus, and expression of existing thought. The rise of the House of Rothschild during the Napoleonic wars, and its influence after 1815, created the impression of Jewish financial rule, which already Byron expressed in verse. Mind, therefore, is a group phenomenon having *social* rather than *individual* existence. All moral responsibility must ultimately be that of the group.

The amount of personal prudence and calculated self-interest which a person exhibits is not independent of group culture. It is greater in Western Europe and North America than in India, China, or Russia, but even in Britain or in America the rational, prudent, calculating individual, assumed by Samuel to exist, is nowhere to be found; for calculating prudence is a characteristic of collective action rather than of individual action. Every person may well have *moments* of prudence and sober reasoning, but he also has moments of anger, self-forgetfulness, recklessness, conflicting urges, and loss of self-control. When a person plays an instrument in an orchestra, there are moments when his self becomes fully merged into one melody. In a choir the self is united with many others in song, in the experience of harmony. There are moments in battle when man – the individual soldier – may not and does not exist and act as self. Man in the morning is different from man in the evening, and the person of today is different from the person of yesterday. There are strange changes of role according to whether a person is in social contact with a German, an Arab, a Jew, or an American, if that person happens to have been personally involved with all those communities in his history. Personal identity can have nothing other than a legal reality, for the biological as well as the psychological principle governing the individual is *impermanence*. It was a mistake of Plato to believe that once a person had attained the knowledge of the true and the good, he would for ever remain conscious of it. Samuel believed a person who knew what was true would be in a better position to do what was right. Social experience has furnished no proof for that assumption. Students might earnestly study Plato and Aristotle by day and slaughter innocent women and children by night. Something of the sort was the tragic experience of Leon Roth, as a professor in Jerusalem in the dying years of the Mandate, with his own students of philosophy. The liberal model of man as an autonomous, responsible, self-determining, consistent, and reasonable person has nowhere been vindicated.

[III]

The preceding criticisms can be summed up in one sentence: Samuel's philosophy, like all liberal philosophy, is based on a false conception of the role of reason in human society and the nature of the individual person. Liberal meliorism, therefore, is too utopian to be of any significance today and is not supported by the evidence of history. Herbert Samuel's probable reply to these criticisms would have been the same as he gave in his last book, *A Threefold Cord*; when replying to his partner in the dialogue, Professor Herbert Dingle, he noted 'that one of the main weaknesses of philosophy itself, all through its history, has been the tendency of philosophers of each generation in turn to devote their energies, first and foremost, to destructive criticism of the theories of the preceding generation.'[5] The record of the constructive ideas offered by anti-liberal critics, and the history of anti-liberal practices, have not so far been impressive.

It is not true that history presents a succession of unreasonable solutions to human conflicts. The settlement of the American-Soviet conflict over Cuba in 1962 is not the only instance of a major military conflict's being avoided. In the nineteenth century certain potentially major wars did not break out, such as war between Britain and America in 1861, and between Britain and France in 1898. The greater the threat of suffering, the more urgent the desire to seek peaceful means of settling disputes. The catastrophe of mass human self-destruction is the ultimate biological sanction against man's failure to employ his reasoning faculties. If man cannot profit from his rational nature, he must learn his lesson with tears. The responsible individual – circumspect, far-sighted, reasonable, calculating, prudent – may not exist at all times, but a person in *authority* in public affairs is usually a member of a collective body. He may have lapses and act reasonably intermittently only, but the collective *public authority* can and must be expected to act rationally at *all* times; to give careful consideration to alternative courses and their consequences, to know the law and to respect it, to reflect the principles of their action, and to plan the best means of implementation. A public authority and, indeed, the leadership of any human group cannot plead collective irrationality to justify its action, as an individual may occasionally plead reduced responsibility in a law court. Every authority must be able to show good reason for its public acts, and endeavour to be in possession of the relevant facts; its workings must be open to public inspection so as to prove to the public that the best course of action was taken in the known circumstances. This is possible in a democracy only, because only in a democracy may the public have recourse to legal, constitutional, and public changes or to sanctions against a defaulting authority.

Herbert Samuel insisted on the criterion of social experience and the principle of a flexible public morality that could be adjusted in the light of public experience. Crime has not diminished in prosperous Britain, contrary to the expectations of Liberalism. But certain *types* of crime that were the result of poverty and ignorance have diminished. The new types of crime will have to be studied and analysed as will, no doubt, new types of diseases. It might well be that too much security and leisure have adverse effects on the young. That ought not to be a pretext for a philosophy of despair, or for a flight into irrational and obscurantist doctrines. Perhaps more thought should be given to challenging and creative tasks for the young.

Those who argue that truth is not always beneficial to the young, and that there are circumstances when truth should be withheld from the public, do not invalidate Samuel's contention that truth must be prior to tradition and should form the basis of morality. It is easy to see that the indiscriminate dissemination of facts can do harm to young people and may cause needless distress and anxiety. Yet at the same time truth must be *accessible* to all who seek it. If society is cut off from the facts and wrapped up in half-truth and myth, it loses the means to know reality, to redress its own shortcomings, and will eventually relapse into barbarism.

Samuel always realised the social character of mind; but however social the mind is, it is lodged in an individual body. That body is identifiable in time and space, as well as in law. The public has to be protected against a faulty body or a faulty mind or both, if need be, even as it has to be protected against a defective vehicle or a defective driver. The driver has a name, the vehicle carries a number. From the point of view of physics the car is a

270

mere pattern of metal engineering, but in the eyes of the law the car has individuality as well as the driver. By admitting social co-responsibility for a crime we do not deny individual responsibility. Evolving law must take both aspects into account.

Even those who maintain that the mind is not capable of producing more than was originally put into it, do not deny the ability of the human mind to establish new connections among the elements of thought that it contains. Such an interpretation of mind does not deny man's creativeness or genius. After all, it was precisely from Newton's ability to link the falling apple with the moon's orbit that man's understanding of the universe grew; it was precisely through the linking of swamps and mosquitoes that the malaria germ was traced. Each advance of human genius in turn influences other human minds. In the future, machines will assist man in storing and linking data, and thereby human knowledge may expand even more rapidly. In all this evolution, from primeval dust to Darwin, from the wooden plough to an atomic power station, from tribal feuds to the United Nations, cosmic forces transcend man. In his own human sphere man is engaged in an increasing social effort to modify instinct by reason, and to expand rational control over destructive emotional forces. Creative man is active in many fields; but Samuel believed that *'the creativity of Man culminates in the Moral Law'*.

NOTES

1   The following is a list of books and addresses by Herbert Samuel which bear on moral philosophy:

Liberalism	1902
Philosophy and the Ordinary Man	1932
The Tree of Good and Evil	1933
Practical Ethics	1935
Belief and Action	1937
Is the Criminal to Blame or Society?	1938
Liberty	1939
Style	1941
Democracy	1941
An Unknown Land	1942

Memoirs	1945
Creative Man	1947
Persuasion or Force	1947
Spires of Liberty	1948
Religion in the Modern World	1952
A Century's Changes of Outlook	1953
Sir Francis Younghusband	1953
A Book of Quotations	1954
The Good Citizen	1954
In Search of Reality	1957
A Threefold Cord	1961

2 Herbert Samuel's treatment of the problem of causality and the free will is very close to Leon Roth's interpretation which was presented in his book *The Science of Morals*, London, 1928. Two quotations may serve to illustrate the similarity of their approach.

'Society consists of the dead and the living . . . the part of the living in determining its life is but insignificant compared with the part of the dead' (p. 119).

'I may feel myself as free, but if I wish to know myself, I cannot but know myself as determined. If I knew myself as free, there would be in my mind not knowledge or thought but chaos; and if I felt myself as determined, . . . I should never perform any action at all' (p. 44).

3 An apposite example is brought to my attention by the Editor of this volume. President Kennedy's alleged assassin, Harvey Lee Oswald, was feloniously killed by Jack Ruby in full view of the television cameras that had been ranged to record Oswald's removal from Dallas prison, on Sunday, 24th November, 1963. The resultant picture was not merely shown on American television networks; but, having featured at the normal speed, it was repeated (at least on one programme) in slow motion, in order that every detail of the murder might be observed by the public. The problem of empanelling a suitable jury to try Ruby was consequently rendered yet more complicated.

4 *Zionism*, 1920.

5 1961 edition, p. 214.

13

Thought Categories in
the Hebrew Bible*

EDWARD ULLENDORFF

Linguists, anthropologists, and philosophers have in recent times
all been concerned with the problem of universals. As a linguist
working in the field of oriental and other languages basically
different from those commonly used in our civilisation and cultural environment I am frequently confronted by colleagues who
are philosophers or anthropologists with the question whether
and to what extent different languages reflect different realities,
to what degree translation from one language into another is
possible (and especially so in the case of tongues far removed
from each other); and, above all, to what extent meaning affects
and is affected by varying language structure, so that in the last
resort we may, in fact, never appreciate properly the differing
modes of thought and thinking hidden behind impenetrable
linguistic and logical barriers. In this connection we cannot have
recourse to the real or alleged mental or psychological features
said to be common to all mankind, for those features cannot be
expressed except in terms of language, so that the argument
becomes circular. In order to decide whether there exist certain
mental characteristics that are universal to all human beings,

we would first have to establish whether there exist certain grammatical and linguistic features that are universally present and thus permit at least a minimum of convertibility of thought.

Of course, things were easy in the past. It was only in the nineteenth century that we did away with the idea that Hebrew or Greek or Latin conceptions of grammar had a universal application. But it has proved to be a painful and slow process to rid ourselves of the methods of grammatical and philosophical analysis applied since antiquity which conceived of grammar and language as based on a supposedly universal metaphysical structure of reality. In fact, however, every language structure carries its own metaphysics or basic concepts by which the world of our experience is ordered and systematised. A different language – not based, as ours is, on Euclidean conceptions of space and time – might involve a different metaphysics, might, in fact, give an altogether different account of reality. In speaking to you at this moment I cannot break through our conventionally established bonds of language, I cannot break through the barrier of thought and tongue and convey to you the idea of an entirely different reality, though recent scientific advances in non-Euclidean geometry and atomic physics have successfully broken through the patterns imposed on us by our language, our modes of thinking.

It used to be argued that, since we all inhabit a world with a common metaphysical structure, our languages must exhibit a common structure. That argument is, however, fallacious, and we must now proceed in roughly the reverse direction and say: If it is found (and that is by no means certain yet) that certain basic linguistic forms, such as verb-like and noun-like categories, exist in one form or another over the ever-growing field of languages that become known to us, we may be justified in inferring from that circumstance that the experience, metaphysical and other, of different human societies is similarly constituted. We cannot state that any particular concept – space, time, process, etc. – is linguistically represented universally. But we may state, I think, that the conceptual frames carried by the various types of language structure are usually convertible, at least to some extent. In other words: sentences in one language can usually be translated into sentences in another language. I stress sentences, complete utterances, *not* words. We have not hitherto come across any totally untranslatable languages representing a reality so fundamentally different from our own that it would be impossible to convert their conceptions into modes intelligible to us, or that it would be impossible to approximate our conceptions to theirs to an extent where purposive intercommunication became feasible. But we have, in recent years, found some languages which come pretty near to being untranslatable: that is to say that, for the most part, they do not see what we see, and what they do see they receive and digest in a manner fundamentally different from our own. Lacking or severely limited translatability entails basically other categories. And here is the linguist's dilemma, the anthropologist's dilemma, the philosopher's dilemma – and, I suppose, the theologian's dilemma, though I am not competent to say what the latter's reaction would be.

Now in our present case, the Hebrew Bible, we are concerned with Hebrew, and to a lesser extent Aramaic, and its translation, linguistically and conceptually, into English or any other European language. I do not, of course, claim that the considerations which I have set forth are directly and immediately applicable to Hebrew. As a semitic language, Hebrew belongs to a group of tongues which are not basically and fundamentally different from the Indo-European group. Nevertheless, vast distinctions there are, in language as well as in modes of thought. And I do claim that far too little attention has been given to those distinctions, and that the Hebrew Bible has far too often been rendered into a Western setting which has little or nothing in common with its own world of categories. We usually seek to understand the Hebrew Bible in terms of our own modes of thinking instead of allowing its categories, strange, different, absurd, incomprehensible as they may well on occasion seem, to come to us. In fact, we indulge in *eis*egesis rather than *ex*egesis.

Before giving chapter and verse for these allegations, I should like to make two general observations: In what I have to say I am not concerned with value-judgments: I wish to state differences, but I am quite incompetent to judge as between good and bad and have no intention of doing so. And secondly: it is my intention to show that the modes of thought in the Hebrew Bible are often very different from what they are commonly assumed to be, that many passages have therefore been misunderstood, or at least been imperfectly understood. Beyond that, I seek to prove nothing; this is an analysis and exposition *sine ira et studio*.

In *Lev.* 19: 18 we find the famous verse: ואהבת לרעך כמוך 'thou shalt love thy neighbour as thyself'. But we have to find out whether the rendering of the Authorised Version (or any other translation) does, in fact, translate the language and the thought of this verse accurately.

The Septuagint with its καὶ 'ἀγαπήσεις τὸν πλησίον σου ὡς σεαυτόν agrees with the Authorised Version. And the Septuagint translation of this verse will also be found, without any change whatever, in *Matt.* 22: 39; *Luke* 10: 27, etc. The semitic translations (Syriac, Ethiopic, Arabic) do not render the Hebrew כמוך, but use expressions which clearly reflect the Greek σεαυτόν (i.e. *nfs*, *r's*). A notable exception is the Targum, which offers a faithful rendering of the Hebrew original: תרחם לחברך כותך and *not*: כנפשך as the Syriac version has.

Now the point at issue is that the Hebrew כמוך simply does not mean 'as thyself', does not mean σεαυτόν, but can only be translated as 'as you', i.e. 'as thou', *not* 'as thee', and certainly not as 'thyself'. In other words: the Hebrew text has neither a reflexive pronoun nor an accusative. If I were to translate σεαυτόν, 'as thyself', back into Hebrew, I would have to say, כאת עצמך or כאת נפשך, but *not* כמוך.

The reason why the translators have failed to appreciate the real meaning of this verse probably lies in the typically semitic brachylogy which omits the conjunction כי; for the translation of *Lev.* 19: 18 can only be: '*thou shalt love thy neighbour, for he is as thou*'; he is like you, a human being created in God's image – just like you. This can, of course, easily be proved not only by recourse to one's linguistic feeling, but by reference to other occurrences of כמוך in the Old Testament. Take, for instance, *Ex.* 15: 11, מי כמוך באלים, 'Who is like you among the gods?'

I find conclusive proof of this view in the same chapter 19 of *Lev.*, verse 34, where the same phrase occurs again: here the treatment of the stranger is discussed: כאזרח מכם יהיה לכם הגר הגר אתכם ואהבת לו כמוך

'The stranger that dwelleth with you shall be unto you as one born among you, and thou shalt love him for he is as thou; for ye were strangers in the land of Egypt.'

This verse shows that the stranger is to be treated as one of you, for he is a human being as yourself. You should love him, for he is just like you, but you are *not* commanded to love him as you love yourself.

But this verse offers additional difficulties. It is only in this chapter 19 of *Lev.*, verses 18 and 34, that the Hebrew verb אהב 'to love' is construed not with the usual accusative sign את, introducing a direct object (and thus it occurs dozens of times in the Hebrew Bible), but with ל introducing the indirect object. And there clearly is a significant difference between אהב את and אהב ל. The former is used of loving a woman, of loving God; e.g. *Deut.* 6: 5, ואהבת את יהוה אלהיך 'And thou shalt love the Lord thy God.' But אהב ל means something slightly different, slightly less, if you like: it means to have love, liking *for* somebody, to treat kindly.[1]

Thus I suggest that the great verse 18 in *Lev.* 19 cannot be translated 'thou shalt love thy neighbour as thyself', but its meaning is 'you shall treat kindly, lovingly, your neighbour, for he is a human being like yourself'. I do not know if the Septuagint misunderstood the Hebrew original and thus gave rise to this long chain of inaccurate translations or – as is quite possible – based its version on a midrashic interpretation of the verse current at that time.

It may, perhaps, be claimed that the ethical and theological implications of this linguistic reappraisal are slight. I do not know. But I do myself seem to see a pregnant distinction between loving one's neighbour quite as much as one loves oneself and showing liking, kindness, to my neighbour, for he is human just like me. And this latter interpretation is not only demanded by the language of the Old Testament, but also by the thought of the Hebrew Bible. The Old Testament shows above all a very practical, human, approach; it sometimes makes ideal, but never superhuman demands. As far as I can see, the injunction to love one's neighbour as much as one loves oneself would be quite alien to the eastern mind and alien to the world of the Hebrew Bible or the world of Islam.

Let us turn to a different matter altogether: to prayer. When we use the word 'prayer' with reference to the Hebrew Bible, we must be clear that we are introducing a concept with a meaning-range very different from that which naturally arises from the Hebrew Bible, ancient oriental religion, or Islam. The word 'prayer' in the western, the Christian, sense has a sublimated significance which has little or nothing to do with prayer as practised in the Old Testament.

The *Encyclopaedia Biblica* defines Christian prayer in this way:

Prayer to Jesus was not an occasional thing to be used under the pressure of urgent need, or whenever the religious authorities might decree, but a constant aspiration towards God. There was no magic spell in it. There is importunity in the prayers – if so they can be called – of the psalmists; there is argument, there is persuasion. But in Christianity there is no longer an attempt to turn the director of the world from his purpose by persuasion.

In the Hebrew Bible – with some partial exceptions which I shall mention presently – there exists no prayer accompanied by disinterested homage without the character of entreaty and petition – passing into mystic communion with God. Prayer in the western, Christian, tradition is a religious, devotional discipline – intercourse with God – and quite distinct from petition for fulfilment of some specific want.

I think I know two words in biblical Hebrew which are

commonly translated as 'to pray': עתר (העתיר) and התפלל.
עתר originally means – as the Arabic cognate '*atara* still does
today – 'to offer a sacrifice', 'to slaughter', i.e. to offer something
to the god, so that he in turn may grant our requirements.
That is the gift-theory of sacrifice: *do ut des*, on a *quid pro quo*
basis. So if we render this as 'prayer', we must be very clearly
aware that in the Bible the Hebrew word carries none of the theological load, none of the associations, which the English word
'prayer' naturally evokes. I am putting these considerations
before you without – if I may stress it again – in any way trying
to indicate that one is good and the other bad. I am stressing
differences of approach without labelling them with value-
judgments.

The other Hebrew word for prayer התפלל means – again like
the Arabic *falla* – 'to cut oneself', 'to make incisions', i.e. to
inflict pain upon oneself with the object of swaying the divine
power to grant one's request, one's prayer. The טוטפות of the
Bible (*Deut.* 6: 8, etc.) or the תפלין of post-biblical Hebrew, the
phylacteries, are worn by the orthodox Jew during morning
prayer to this day; they appear to serve as substitutes for the
sacred marks cut in the flesh of the arm. And it is interesting to
note that the biblical Aramaic word for 'to pray', צלא, originally
means 'to roast', and this is also true of the same word in Arabic
ṣly, and Ethiopic *ṣalaya*, though lexicographers have frequently refused to acknowledge this obvious connection and have
artificially separated two identical roots, probably because a
semantic development from *roasting meat* to *praying* seemed
obnoxious to them.

We have to recognise the bargaining spirit of early oriental
prayers. The Egyptians bullied their gods – and Zulus 'pray':
'Help me, or you will feed on nettles.' And there is the magical
spell which is present in oriental religion (also in oriental
Christianity) among Nestorians, monophysite Christians (Ethiopians, Copts).

Or take a typical prayer of Assyro-Babylonian times so closely
akin to the biblical atmosphere:

279

O Namrasit (the moon god) unequalled in power, whose
designs no-one can conceive,
I have spread out for thee a pure incense-offering. . . . I have
poured out for thee the best sweet drink.
I am kneeling. . . . I seek after thee.
Bring upon me wishes for well-being and justice. . . .

(Pritchard, *Ancient Near Eastern Texts*, p. 386)

And closest to the world of the Hebrew Bible are the Ugaritic hymns where one may read:

Hearken, I pray thee,
Ask for silver and I'll give thee,
For gold and I'll bestow on thee,
But give Thou victory to my bow.

(*Aqht cycle*)

With the Babylonian prayer of incense and sweet drink one may well compare *Gen.* 8: 20–1, when after the flood Noah 'built an altar unto the Lord . . . and offered burnt offerings on the altar. And the Lord smelled a sweet savour; and the Lord said in his heart: I will not again curse the ground any more for man's sake.'

Or Hannah's prayer in *I Sam.* 1: 10:

Hannah prayed unto the Lord . . . if thou wilt give unto thine handmaid a man child, then I will give him unto the Lord all the days of his life.

There is, of course, Solomon's long and noble prayer in *I Kings* 8: 23–53; but Pfeiffer in his *Introduction to the Old Testament* is on the whole right in stressing (p. 33) that prayer in the true sense is not well developed in the Hebrew Bible. Nor must we confuse prayer with hymn. The book of Psalms is not a collection of prayers, but of hymns which – as everything else in the East – were chanted or sung.

The Church – as indeed its etymology τὸ κυριακὸν δῶμα testifies – is a 'place of worship, a place of prayer', but the Synagogue –

συναγωγή – בית הכנסת – is 'a place of assembly'. People go there to meet and to talk – not necessarily to pray. There is no solitary prayer, but an assembly of at least ten men is required. There are only set prayers, and you cannot normally formulate a prayer yourself. In Islam, too, prayer is almost a mechanical act, repeated five times a day, throughout life without variation of text. The Hebrew and the Muslim can pray in Hebrew and Arabic only; the Christian may pray in any language. For some prayers, the Talmud asserts, כוונה, i.e. 'devotion', 'intention', 'attention' (a difficult word to translate) is not necessarily required: they are simply a matter of 'routine' (though this term must not be taken to possess a pejorative connotation).[2]

I have dwelt on the subject of prayer at some length (and, of course, a good deal more can and should be said), because it seems to me important to realise that 'prayer' in the Hebrew Bible has a very different connotation from the conventional one; and if we wish to use the term with reference to the Hebrew Bible, we must at least relieve it of the heavy burden of western and Christian associations which it has accumulated.

The word and conception of *Satan* seem to me another instance of a wide divergence between the biblical notion and the use of the term in our civilisation. The *Encyclopaedia Britannica* explains Satan (or Devil) as 'the generic name for a spirit of evil, especially the supreme spirit of evil, the foe of God and man'. That is not, however, the conception of the Hebrew Bible. In post-biblical Jewish and Christian legends Satan is pictured as an evil creature with horns and hooves who is intent on causing pain to man. In the *Book of Enoch* Satan is represented as the ruler of a rival kingdom of evil.

The Hebrew Bible's Satan, on the other hand, is variously described as an adversary (*I Kings* 11; *I Sam.* 29: 4; etc.), an opponent (*Num.* 22: 22–32, where an angel of the Lord acts as an opponent), and as an accuser (*Zech.* 3: 1–2). The Septuagint renders Hebrew שטן as διάβολος, i.e. the informer, the calumniator; and it is from this Greek word διάβολος that the words 'devil' in English, *diabolo* in Italian, *diable* in French, *Teufel* in German, etc., are derived.

The most compact and complete references to Satan in the Hebrew Bible will be found in the two introductory chapters of the book of *Job* – which, incidentally, form the basis of the 'Prologue in Heaven' in Goethe's *Faust* (which reveals an astonishing insight into the biblical narrative). In *Job*, chapter 1, Satan appears before God as one of בני האלהים, 'the sons of God'. The sons of God no doubt are the servants of God – and one of these is Satan who, in the conception of the Hebrew Bible, belongs to the divine Court. The only question is, what exactly is his function as a courtier of Yahweh? In a similar context in *Zechariah* 4 we are told (in verse 10) of the 'seven eyes of the Lord' המשוטטים בכל הארץ 'which run to and fro through the whole earth'. That these seven eyes are, in fact, seven persons (or divine servants) can be clearly recognised from the masculine המשוטטים, for otherwise 'eyes' in Hebrew is construed as a feminine. They are the divine messengers who run to and fro on earth to report to the Lord on the deeds of man. And one of these משוטטים 'runners to and fro' is Satan – as is clearly explained in this passage in *Job*: When Satan, in company with the other 'sons of God', came to present himself before the Lord, God asked him: 'Whence comest thou?' and Satan replied: 'From going to and fro in the earth, and from walking up and down in it.' The Hebrew text of this reply is: משוט בארץ ומהתהלך בה. And here again we have the verb שוט 'going to and fro' which we have already encountered in the passage from *Zechariah* 4. Satan's task, therefore, is to 'go to and fro' and to report to the Lord, in Hebrew, משוטט, שוט; and it seems thus very probable that the form of his name is *Shatan* rather than *Satan*. sin and šin in Hebrew have the same graphic symbol distinguished merely by a diacritical dot placed either over the left or right side of the letter. The difference, if it existed at all, was a purely dialectal one – as we know from the famous *Shibboleth-Sibboleth* story in *Judges* 12: 6. This recognition of Satan-Shatan as the 'goer to and fro' was first advanced by S. D. Luzzatto in 1876, but has never penetrated the scholarly world – perhaps because Luzzatto's work was written in Hebrew.[3] He speaks of Satan's function to go to and fro to investigate the deeds of man and to report on them to his divine master. He was thus a sort of spy and informer, and this is, in Luzzatto's view, probably the reason why Shatan was changed to Satan, for the root *stn* means 'to oppose'. However, that the original derivation of Satan is from שׁוט 'to go to and fro' can still be seen from the Ethiopic and Arabic form *šayṭan*.

Satan, as the roving ambassador of the Lord, more often than not had unfavourable things to report about man, and so there developed the idea of Satan as the opponent, the calumniator – and finally even the incarnation of evil. Often, indeed, he had to act as an *agent provocateur* in his task of policeman and informer. But the original conception of Satan in the Hebrew Bible was innocent enough: one of the 'sons of God', even if one whose task was not particularly congenial to man.

It is interesting to observe, incidentally, that the other word for Satan's function in this *Job* narrative – parallel to שׁוט – is מתהלך 'walking up and down'; and the etymological equivalent of מתהלך in the cognate Akkadian is *muttalliku* 'walking up and down' – and this term, too, has from a fairly innocuous beginning acquired the additional meaning of 'demon'.

What I wish to establish, then, is briefly that the thought-complex 'Satan' in our thinking is something radically different from the Satan of the Hebrew Bible, though not necessarily from the associations attached to the idea in later Jewish writings. But this *Job* passage – as an early layer of the Hebrew Bible – has preserved Satan in his original function as a roving messenger, an ambassador at large, perhaps a secret policeman.

After these three detailed instances I should like to give a few brief and isolated examples of the thought categories of the Hebrew Bible with which I am at present concerned.

The Hebrew verb ברך (which occurs some 250 times in the Bible) is rendered into English as 'to bless'. And that is, indeed, an adequate translation. But the word 'blessing' carries a very large load of associations which have nothing whatever to do with the conception of the Hebrew Bible. It is not my intention to query the translation as such but to invite attention to the fundamentally differing associative and emotional value which Hebrew ברך and English 'bless', or French *bénir*, or German *segnen*, evoke. Every word in a living language has a precise 'feel' about it on which most of its native speakers are agreed; it has a tune, a colour, a key of its own which its use in literature and in life has brought about. The Oxford dictionary defines 'to bless' as 'to consecrate', 'to call holy', 'to adore', 'to pronounce words that bring supernatural favour'; and in general there is an element of abstractness in the concept of blessing. To the Hebrew speaker, however, to the man of the Old Testament, ברך is a very concrete thing: ברך means 'knee' and the verb is 'to kneel'; more often it is used in the causative form ברך 'to make kneel', for usually, though not invariably, God is the one who blesses and man kneels. In the Hebrew Bible, therefore, ברך simply expresses the concrete action of kneeling down, of making obeisance, of rendering homage, respect, physical submission. And even though the biblical Hebrew term came later to be associated with a more abstract, transferred meaning, to the Hebrew speaker the original significance is never lost; and ברך thus expresses associative elements which are very different from those of 'to bless'.

Very similar considerations apply to the even more frequent word קדוש, 'holy'. Now, if I understand the English word correctly, it connotes something sacred, spiritually perfect, etc. But the Hebrew קדוש does not. The original meaning of the verb קדש is 'to separate', 'to put apart'. קדוש would in many ways be better translated by 'particular', in its real and literal sense, than by 'holy', which has so very different an emotional value. The קדש הקדשים of the Temple is not really the 'Holy of Holiest', but the 'most separate', 'most distinguished' – and it is only because it was the most separate, the most difficult of access, that it also became the holiest. And when, in *Ex.* 19: 5–6, we hear that Yahweh chooses Israel, he makes them 'peculiar (סגולה) unto me above all people' – and גוי קדוש, not a 'holy people', but a separate, different people, a community apart. Of the same Hebrew root *qdš* we have a noun like קדשה, 'a prostitute', usually a temple prostitute. The קדשה is, of course, not a 'holy woman', but – as a prostitute – a woman set apart, different, separate from the remainder of women. All this is, of course, not an etymological problem concerning the philological derivation of the word, but a question of the currency value, the use, the semantic status of this concept. Again, I do not mean to question the adequacy of 'holy' as a rendering of קדוש; but I rather come to doubt the possibility of translation in the most general sense. The word קדוש conveys something very specific to me, and so does, I suppose, the English 'holy', but their antecedents, their history, and semantic development are completely different. Modern linguists and semantic scholars have come to operate more and more with the concept of the 'linguistic field', and in that sense קדוש and 'holy' simply do not belong to the same 'field', to the same category of semantic classification. If I may overstate the point a little in order to make my intentions somewhat clearer, קדוש is a geographical term connoting physical apartness, separateness; 'holy' is a theological term, permeated by a deep spiritual significance.

There are countless other examples with which I have not space here to deal; נביא is simply an announcer (as Arabic *naba'a* testifies) and may originally have been well rendered by Greek προφήτης, but it carries none of the meaning of 'prophet' as one who is inspired, who reveals – let alone predicts future events. All that is, of course, well known, but if we still insist on translating נביא as 'prophet' we should each time tell the unwary student of the Hebrew Bible that נביא is 'prophet' *minus* nearly everything that 'prophet' means and connotes.

Or take a term as heavily charged with theological meaning as 'forgiveness'. Many a paper has been written, and many a lecture has been delivered on 'sin and forgiveness' in the Hebrew Bible, yet few have been troubled by the deep-seated incongruence of meaning and association between 'forgiveness' and the Hebrew סליחה. But סליחה in the Bible is only used of God, and never of forgiveness between man and man. And the reason is simple: סלח has a very concrete meaning – 'to spray', 'to rain upon'. Nothing in the Near East is more important than to receive the sign of grace, dew or rain; and the beginning of the rain was the annual confirmation of Yahweh's forgiveness, his willingness to maintain mankind. Of course, this concrete meaning is not present in every layer of the Hebrew Bible; there is semasiological development also in the Old Testament, but the original meaning is not entirely lost from linguistic consciousness and plays a part in the value and use of the term.

Naturally, as far as the Hebrew Bible is concerned (though this does not apply to the Hebrew language), the development of meaning and thought has been arrested, but in the languages into which it has been translated semantic evolution proceeds further every day. A translation which may have been perfectly adequate in, say, the seventeenth century, may now have become quite unsuitable, because words are not static but acquire fresh meaning-variants with use and development. For that reason a rendering into Latin – a language which has now lost living evolution – might be preferable; at least you avoid the growth and increase of incongruence and imbalance.

I had wanted to give a few more concrete examples, and to show that אריה in the Hebrew Bible is not a 'lion', but simply a big animal; it is only to us that the lion figures as the king of animals, but there were apparently no lions in Palestine. לחם is not necessarily 'bread' but whatever the staple diet may have been at a given period. ידע is not 'to know', but 'to be intimate with'; in *Gen.* 4: 1 it is not that Adam *knew* his wife Eve but something rather more meaningful; and when I am intimate with a piece of information, then I *know* it. Hebrew ידע and English 'know' (which in etymology as well as association carries Greek γνῶσις within it) are poles apart – but I must conclude.

The categories of the Hebrew Bible are not closed to us; they are not untranslatable, but they are very different, and *our* associations must not be introduced, however unwittingly, into biblical Hebrew thought, at least if we wish to understand the Hebrew Bible in its true and original setting and sense rather than in the interpretation which we might wish to give to it.

The Bible was written in Hebrew; and this is a fact of paramount importance, for – as the philosopher Cassirer has well said – 'the difference between language derives less from differences in sounds and signs than from differences in worldview.' Language is not a simple reflection of the world of objects, but rather embodies the results of an intellectual remoulding of this world. The Hebrew of the Bible – as indeed every other language – has a semantic structure of its own; and we must recognise that a particular manner of viewing the universe is implicit in the organisation of the individual meaning-elements of a language.

If this view is correct – as I believe it is – then the particular thought categories of the Hebrew Bible are to some extent the result of Hebrew and Hebraic thinking, and any conversion, translation, of these thought-processes into those of another language will be several steps removed from the original meaning.

Human beings do not live in the objective world alone, but are very much at the mercy of the particular language which has become the medium of expression for their society. It is an illusion to imagine that language is merely an incidental means of solving specific problems of communication or reflection. The fact of the matter is that the 'real world' is to a large extent unconsciously built upon the language habits of the group. No two languages are apparently ever sufficiently similar to be considered as representing the same reality. The worlds in which different societies live are distinct worlds, not merely the same world with different labels attached.

The understanding of a simple poem or piece of prose – let alone the whole body of the Hebrew Bible – involves not merely an understanding of the single words in their average meaning, but a full comprehension of the whole life of the community as it is mirrored in the words or as it is suggested by their overtones.[4]

Wittgenstein said (and in this he has been echoed by Gilbert Ryle) that 'all philosophy is critique of language'. In a similar sense, I would suggest, Old Testament theology is all in the last resort critique of language – critique of the language of the Hebrew Bible.

NOTES

*A paper read to the St. Andrews Summer School of Theology and the St. Andrews University Linguistic Circle. I dedicate these lines to the memory of Leon Roth, an inspiring teacher, a true friend, and a man in whom greatness of mind and character met in rare unison.

1 Cf. Ibn Ezra and Naḥmanides to *Lev.* 19: 18.
2 Cf. Babylonian Talmud, *Berakhoth*, 13a–b.
3 See now also N. H. Tur-Sinai, *The Book of Job*, Jerusalem, 1957, pp. 38 ff.
4 Cf. E. Sapir, *Language*, 1921; *Culture, Language and Personality*, 1956; H. Hoijer, *Language in Culture*, 1954; B. L. Whorf, *Language, Thought and Reality*, 1956; R. H. Robins, *Ancient and Mediaeval Grammatical Theory in Europe*, 1951.

14

The Idea of
Humanity in Judaism*

KURT WILHELM

[I]

The unity of the human race is a doctrine of Judaism. The Bible
opens with a sole God, creator of Adam, Man, the father of all
men; and the God of Israel is not only God of humanity, but
God for humanity, what may be termed 'monanthropy' being
the logical consequence of monotheism.[1] For even though the
notion of Adam's having been created as a single individual is
cardinal to all Jewish thinking about humanity, yet more
decisive still is the circumstance of his having been created by a
uniquely sole God. The Babylonian epic of creation likewise
knows of a solitary man as the source of all his kind: but its gods
are a plurality. It is the unity of God which points inexorably
towards the unity of man, and *vice versa*. In his posthumous
work *Religion der Vernunft aus den Quellen des Judentums*,[2]
Hermann Cohen represents this conditioned reciprocity by the
term *Korrelation* or correspondence (*Entsprechung*); the concept
by means of which the co-relativity of God and man realises
itself being the concept of moral discernment – a quality common
to both parties. The correlation is, moreover, absolutely reci-

procal, so that man, in virtue of his God-given perceptivity, is not merely the creature but the discoverer of God. It necessarily follows that God is one if, and only if mankind is one; or in other words, that the completion of that correlation falls within the Utopia of Judaism's messianic future. 'And the Lord shall be king over all the earth; in that day shall God be one, and His name one.'[3] In Cohen's own words, the divine Name is equivalent in meaning to the divine kingdom.[4]

The doctrine that the unity of mankind will find its completion in a messianic age yet to come has produced, within Jewish speculative theology of the last hundred years, a belief in progress – a belief to which other movements of social and political philosophy as well as the religious liberalism of western Europe and America have also come to subscribe. The final significance of Judaism would then lie in its sense of development from Peculiar People to Mankind, from the sum total of all individuals to the revelation of true Humanity within the messianic union of all men. The Bible purports to describe – or rather to anticipate – this historical process, in which a personal God at the final stage of a long development chooses for Himself humanity as a whole: and it hints that this development corresponds to the spiritual and moral nature of man himself. But within the doctrine of the moral progress of humanity there is to be found a wide range of tones.

In his *Wesen des Judentums* – not, strictly speaking, a theologically orientated book – Leo Baeck did not fall for this kind of formal ethical monotheism. More than any of the theologians who were his contemporaries, Baeck traced out the paradoxes in the religious ideas and institutions of Judaism, and remained on his guard against the making of messianism into an abstract ideal in which the unity of humanity should be achieved. In any theological formulation of a Jewish belief in progress the concept of the Messiah becomes distorted: for Jewish messianism is something more than a mere symbol for a belief in the moral progress of humanity. To quote Max Wiener, who is one of the few modern liberal theologians to pose the whole problem correctly, the hall-mark of traditional Jewish messianism is 'miracle in its most stupendous proportions – the transcendental intervention of a living, personal God in the fate of man.'[5] Like creation, messianism is unique in its wondrous quality; whereas the extensive speculations of the rabbis concerning the coming of the Messiah have little to say on the subject of the moral development of mankind. On the contrary: the so-called 'footsteps of the Messiah' – the days that will precede his arrival – are to be distinguished by a godlessness and a negation of morality that will form, so to speak, the shadows heralding the appearance of the Redeemer. A whole series of speculations regarding these fateful forerunners is to be found in the Talmud, for example the following[6]: 'With the footprints of the Messiah presumption shall increase and dearth shall reach its height . . . the empire shall fall into heresy and there shall be none to utter reproof. The council-chamber shall be given to fornication. . . . The face of this generation is as the face of a dog, and the son will not be put to shame by his father. On whom can we stay ourselves? On our Father in heaven.' In talmudic Judaism the messianic epoch stands in connection with the so-called 'weeks', i.e. *aeons* into which world history is divided, itself constituting the climax of them. Even though the 'weeks' originally ordained to precede the messianic period have now all elapsed, the Messiah has nevertheless not yet appeared: his coming will materialise when Israel merits the messianic age, or else in God's own good time. The actual date of his coming is one of the seven things that remains concealed from all.[7] Eschatological speculation is unanimous to the effect that at the onset of the messianic kingdom God will bring about a visible miracle analogous to the miracles associated with creation and revelation. Jewish excitement concerning the miraculous aspect of messianic redemption may be descried in the fever of anticipation that has invariably gripped Jewry on the occasion of each successive pseudo-messianic phenomenon. The days of the Messiah signify the rendering visible, in an experience of overwhelming emotional intensity, of God's own very Act – or, in the words of a familiar messianic prayer, 'in His loving-kindness He will yet again cause us to hear, before the eyes of all that live, [His promise] "to be to you for a God".'[8]

Nevertheless, traditional Jewish expectation of the Messiah's coming has the following in common with modern Jewish messianic notions, *viz.* that it is here, on earth, that the divinely intended messianic kingdom of the future will find its implementation. The time of the messianic *eschata* is historical time, and the kingdom *is* of this world. Furthermore – and this appears to be of fundamental importance for the presentation of the concept of humanity in Judaism – it is God's purpose to unify the whole of mankind in the messianic period into a single community that is morally one. The messianic kingdom is the kingdom of justice and of moral order. And yet, together with this aspect of messianic expectation, belief in the special position of the people of Israel never disappears. Israel's redemption coincides with the redemption of mankind – or rather, it introduces it alongside itself. On the other hand modern Jewish theology, in representing Judaism as the simplest and most direct method of implementing moral good with the messianic concept as its guarantor, makes use of traditional Jewish messianism as a foundation for a universal ethical creed of mankind – a Judaism set free from religious law.

The contradiction has often been sensed, and the attempt made to overcome it by representing Judaism as a world-religion in tension, between universalism and particularism or universalism and nationalism; it being claimed that in times of persecution or oppression it is particularism that has been the centre of interest, and universalism in times of external freedom. Precisely so, the Jewish concept of election is alleged to have both its particularistic and its universalistic traits, Israel's own domestic election falling in the here and now and the election of humanity at the end of days. Universalism and particularism are, however, inextricably interwoven in Judaism, and it is in the perpetual interpenetration of national and universal religious elements that Judaism itself both consists, and asserts its own specific God-idea, *viz.* that the God of Israel is the God of all humanity.

These preliminary remarks are necessary, in order that the concept of humanity in Judaism may be represented without resort to apologetics. Meagre are the attempts that have been made to prepare the way for a statement of the concept of humanity in Judaism, if we are to disregard (as, for reasons already stated, we have to) Jewish theological writing of the last hundred years. We may limit ourselves to reference to the outline by Max Wiener, who was a rabbi and lecturer at the Berlin Hochschule für die Wissenschaft des Judentums, entitled *Aufriss einer jüdischen Theologie*.[9] As his starting-point for an appreciation of the Jewish concept of humanity Wiener no longer postulated a polarity between universalism and particularism; for him it is '*people* and *history* [that] are the two poles between which the particular life of our religion moves.' God is, from the outset, the God of history, who creates the world as the stage on which the human drama is to be played out. Human events can be individual or ethnic ones. In Christianity, as already in Stoicism and the thought of late antiquity in general, history is a process that moves from individual to humanity, whilst in Judaism history predominantly means happenings as between one people and another and as between God's people and the community of peoples. The peoplehood of Israel is consequently an indispensable component of the religion of Israel; and this is the reason for the election of Israel *qua* people. The chosen people is Israel because of considerations that are neither racial nor statistical, but because it occupies a special position *vis-à-vis* the God of history. It has chosen the God who chose it for Himself.

[II]

To assert that the early chapters of *Genesis* had, right from their earliest beginnings, the unity of mankind in view might be regarded as a debatable claim. The narratives of the creation of the world and of the first human pair, if taken in themselves, evince rather a cosmological and anthropological interest, into the fabric of which a religious concern has been woven.[10] Be that as it may, these chapters have been not merely inserted into the Bible, but rather stand as a preface to *Genesis* as being documents of Israel's pre-history, and form with it a self-contained unity: and this circumstance lifts the biblical history of man's creation on to the ethical plane, providing Judaism with a *locus classicus* for the idea of the unity of the human race. Deutero-Isaiah, too, recognises that the chronological process of the time-span of human history begins in the very moment of the transcendent act of creation effected by the God of the cosmos, 'calling the generations from the beginning it is I, the Lord, who am first, and with the last I am the same as I ever was.'[11] The idea of humanity orientated on the future is here indicated as being implicit in the story of the creation of one single man in the beginning.

The doctrine of the unity of mankind runs through the whole of *Genesis*. After the flood, it is Noah who stands for the whole human race as Adam had done in the creation narrative. Jewish tradition finds in the covenant contracted with Noah by God the basis of its conviction of man's perpetual continuance, which no flood will ever again come to annihilate. Noah thus becomes the guarantor of mankind; in place of the biblical description of which as 'children of Adam', rabbinic Hebrew prefers to speak of 'children of Noah' when it is referring to humanity as a moral entity. The so-called Seven Commandments of the sons of Noah[12] constitute a formula whereby recognition becomes possible of a wider humanity, into relations with which of a moral and lawful kind Jewry can enter without requiring of its environment any avowal of Judaism. The 'seven commandments' are, of course, but an artificial postulate which, as affording a minimum programme of human morality, are subsumed in what is binding upon the Jew himself, just as if the seven had once been 'revealed' to the whole non-Jewish (or rather, pre-Jewish) world. But it is specifically as precepts incumbent upon mankind in general that they could provide the basis of a moral order affecting all: and that is why the first of the seven is deemed to be the obligation to administer justice.[13] The Noachides' dispensation belongs to the pre-history of revelation in Judaism, but those still subject to it are reckoned nonetheless amongst 'the righteous of the Gentiles'. Maimonides (1135–1204) writes as follows in his great codification of the religious law of Judaism: 'Whosoever [of the Gentiles] acknowledges the Seven Commandments and is circumspect in fulfilling them is one of the pious ones of the Gentiles and has a

portion in the world to come, provided always that such acknowledgement is on grounds of their divine origin and revelational
transmission.'[14] In Dante's *Divine Comedy* the unbaptised,
together with many of the philosophers and poets of classical
antiquity, find themselves in the uppermost region of Inferno,
albeit immune from the torments of Hell. In the Hebrew imitation of Dante by Immanuel of Rome, poet and exegete (1265–
1330), entitled *Hell and Paradise* (*Hat-topheth we-ha-'edhen*), in
Paradise the Jew meets the righteous of the Gentiles: 'and it
came to pass, as we were strolling along Eden's ways, observing
the eminence of men distinguished by reason of their wisdom. . . .
And forasmuch as I knew not one of them, I asked my guide
about them: he said unto me, "these be the righteous of the
peoples of the earth, every one of them a hero by reason of his
wisdom and understanding".'[15]

W. Eichrodt[16] observes that the genealogical table of *Gen.* 10
is without parallel in the literature of the ancient Orient; and in
this chapter Israel's concept of humanity again finds expression.
By its inclusion of this genealogical tree the Bible renders
racialism as a basis of political theory untenable, since the table
knows of no people that was not worthy of being embraced
within a definition of mankind. Greek concepts of humanity did
not acknowledge the notion of mankind implicit in this table of
Genesis – for Aristotle there are Hellenes and barbarians, those
born to be masters and those born to be slaves. It is from the
genealogy of *Genesis* that there derives the rabbinic idea of the
'Seventy Nations of the world' as comprising between them all
mankind, and the parallel concept of the 'Seventy Tongues' –
notwithstanding sundry difficulties of arithmetical equation with
the text of *Gen.* 10 as it has come down to us. The number 70 –
itself the symbol of completeness – has been laid under contribution by religious thinking on the subject of the inherent unity of
mankind as running through the multiplicity of nations. And
indeed the Pentateuch does not regard their sum of seventy as
being a mere coincidence. In Moses' valedictory song – at any
rate in the Hebrew text authenticated by the Massoretes[17] – we
read 'When the Most High divided to the nations their inheri-

tance, when he separated the sons of Adam, he set the bounds of the peoples *according to the number of the children of Israel.*' The traditional number of the issue of Jacob-Israel was 70, and the allusion in the song to the genealogy of the peoples is obvious enough: the sum of the peoples, themselves each the issue of its own founding father, corresponds to the number of the issue of Israel's own eponymous ancestor. Moreover, *Genesis* places the peoples of the world into a position of responsibility for themselves *vis-à-vis* God like that occupied by Israel, the key word being in each case the *covenant – berith*: a term more decisive than any other with regard to Israel's relationship with God.[18] The first of the post-diluvians (apart from Noah himself and his immediate progeny)[19] with whom God contracted a covenant – a covenant that had in mind an as yet non-existent people of Israel – was Abraham. His own story, and consequently the history of Israel itself, begins with the divine summons to leave his own country and his father's house, to launch out into the unknown where God will contract an everlasting covenant with him. The call to face something new, the full implications of which he could not know, concludes with the words[20] 'and in thee shall all the families of the earth be blessed'. It is in virtue of his being the ancestor of Israel that Abraham's connection with the entire human race is effected.

The biblical notion of humanity avoided the danger to which the universalism of post-classical civilisation succumbed: it did not lose itself in a facile cosmopolitanism. Stoic notions of mankind recognise nought but individual and world-polity, with no middle term between individuality and totality.[21] *Per contra*, Judaism's Utopia of a mankind united at the end of days by an acknowledgement of the one sole God consists of a world-wide fellowship of peoples:

And it shall come to pass in the last days that the mountain of the Lord's house shall be established so as to be at the top of the mountains, and shall be exalted above the hills; and all nations shall flow to it. And the peoples in great numbers shall go and say, Come ye, and let us go up to the mountain of the

Lord, to the house of the God of Jacob, that he may teach us of His ways, and that we may walk in His paths: for it is from Zion that shall go forth Torah, and the word of the Lord from Jerusalem. And he shall judge between the nations, and shall adjust all differences between the peoples in their crowds: and they shall beat their swords into ploughshares, and their spears into pruning-hooks: nation shall not lift up sword against nation, neither shall they learn war any more.[22]

Thus can Isaiah, the contemporary of kings whose faithlessness evoked disillusionment after disillusionment, portray the future of mankind. The prophecy is again taken up, but with slight alterations, in the collection of Micah's prophetic utterances.[23] The temple mount at Jerusalem is the stage towards which the peoples stream in order to find, at God's mountain, their own unification. At present, the temple hill stands lower than the Mount of Olives and the other hills that surround it. The end of days will bring with it the miraculous transfiguration of the physical landscape of the spot where the peoples are destined to meet. Since they will then recognise the one God alone, all barriers that now separate the peoples will fall. As ethnic entities they continue, indeed, to exist; but their contests bring them all alike before the one Lord and Judge for settlement. They will therefore have no need any longer to resolve their disputes by force of arms, and will consequently not learn war any more. In the Holy City there will hold sway a judge of right on whom there will 'rest the breath of God's spirit, the spirit of wisdom and discernment, the spirit of counsel and heroic courage, the spirit of knowledge and fear of the Lord; and it shall be the fear of the Lord that shall inspire him.'[24]

It is the circumstance that through him there breathes the spirit of God that serves to characterise the ideal lord and judge of all. Quite typically, the Messiah is not priest, but judge or king; and as such, he is no less and no more like to God than is any other man. Precisely because Jewish eschatological notions of a united humanity do not reveal a vista of some crowning achievement to consummate the higher development of religious thinking, but signify rather the concrete realisation of the rule of God on earth and in every single department of life, the Messiah's governance of Israel and the nations which comprise the world is a political governance in the fullest sense.[25] The messianic age is one in which the peace of God embraces creation as a whole, the very wild beasts being transformed and changing their relationships towards each other and towards man.[26] A whole series of prophets proclaimed that the ideals implicit in the concept of humanity would find their practical implementation in an international peace founded upon justice; and in the Babylonian exile the second Isaiah was to draw the logical conclusion to the thinking of his great predecessors. It is that the historic charge of leading a unified mankind on to the stage devolves upon Israel. Israel's own redemption is bound up with that of the nations, and *vice versa*. Israel is summoned, from a state of being God's people, to become a 'covenant of the peoples' (*berith 'am*) – a people standing as intermediary between God and the human kind. 'I, the Lord, call thee by way of confirming something as right and do grasp thee by the hand, and will keep thee and assign thee as a people's covenant, as a light for the national families of the world: to lighten the eyes that are blind, to bring out the prisoners from the dungeon, from the prison-house them that sit in darkness.'[27] Such is the role for which Deutero-Isaiah casts his own people while it is itself confined in the prison-house of exile. The comforting of Israel is tied to the comforting of mankind, or rather, as Martin Buber has put it, the redemption of Israel and that of the gentile peoples are but different stages of one single redemptive act that concerns the whole world of man.[28]

Rabbinic Judaism sees in the messianic age the great contrast to the epoch in which, following the Tower of Babel, mankind has fallen apart into the seventy nations. It is the Evil Inclination which, in this world, has divided the peoples into seventy: but in the world to come they will find themselves unanimous in the service of God alone. It is in this connection that *Zeph.* 3: 9 is quoted[29] – 'For then will I change the peoples to a pure language, so that they will all call upon the name of the Lord, to serve Him with a united shoulder.' The 'clear lip' or pure language is the image, in prophetical and midrashic literature alike, for purity of heart and thought; and pure speech here means the mutual understanding of the peoples. But implicit in the thinking here there is also the idea of a linguistic idiom that bonds the peoples into one; and it is no coincidence that the rabbis connect the verse with the story in *Gen.* 11 of the confusion of tongues. The original language of humanity – according to rabbinic notions Hebrew, the speech of Eber (*Gen.* 10: 21) – will in messianic times take the place, as a universal language, of the present seventy. In rabbinic literature there is to be found a rich store of imagery regarding the messianic age, from the overcoming of war to the overcoming of death; and in it thinking about the unification of humanity revolves normally round the role therein that will fall to Israel. This may conceivably be but a passive role, and as such it was formulated by Mar Samuel (*c.* 180–253 C.E.), the most important talmudic scholar of his time, when he declared that 'the only difference between this world and the days of the Messiah is enslavement to the world powers'[30]; i.e., in the messianic age Israel will no longer be subjected by the world-kingdoms to slavery. Maimonides took up this dictum into his code of halakhic Judaism,[31] and states expressly that no alteration in the laws of nature will mark the messianic age, nor any renovation of the act by which the world was created; the world will pursue its normal course. Nevertheless, 'at that time there will be neither hunger, jealousy, nor competitiveness, since good things will be available in prodigious amplitude, luxuries being as common as dust, and the whole world will be engaged in no other pursuit than that of knowing the Lord alone.'[32] Thus the great canonist of Jewish law: But the *'Aggadha* can find scope for the elaboration of a fantastic imagery of the end of days and of a mankind united in them. It may suffice to refer to the vision conjured up for it by *Isa.* 60, *Arise, shine, for thy light is come.*[33] A great light will burst over Jerusalem to attract the Gentiles by its powerful brilliance. On the basis of a decision all their own, they move towards it in streams – mankind coming to the light, and not the light to mankind. Jerusalem will be the metropolis of all humanity; but the idea that the Gentiles will then find it possible to profess Judaism plays no crucial part in this picture.

It is towards a redeemed tomorrow that all our unredeemed todays must orientate themselves. The ideas of redemption and yearning for Utopia consequently form an important theme of the Jewish liturgy, particularly on the days of exalted solemnity, *viz.* the New Year festival and the Day of Atonement. The special prayers for these occasions are distinguished by petitions regarding the Kingdom – that is, the kingdom of the Messiah, scion of David, which is at once the Kingdom of God ruling over a united humanity:

Now therefore, O Lord our God, impose Thine awe upon all Thy works, and Thy dread upon all that Thou hast created, that all works may fear Thee and all creatures prostrate themselves before Thee, that they may all form a single band to do Thy will with a perfect heart, even as we know, O Lord our God, that dominion is Thine, strength is in Thy hand, and might in Thy right hand, and that Thy name is to be feared above all that Thou hast created.

Give then glory, O Lord, unto Thy people, praise to them that fear Thee, hope to them that seek Thee, and free speech to them that wait for Thee, joy to Thy land, gladness to Thy city, a flourishing horn unto David Thy servant, and a clear shining light unto the son of Jesse, Thine anointed, speedily in our days.

Then shall the just also see and be glad, and the upright shall exult, and the pious triumphantly rejoice, while iniquity shall close her mouth, and all wickedness shall be wholly consumed like smoke, when Thou makest the dominion of arrogance to pass away from the earth.

And Thou, O Lord, shalt reign, Thou alone over all Thy works on Mount Zion, the dwelling place of Thy glory, and in Jerusalem, Thy holy city, as it is written in Thy holy words, 'The Lord shall reign for ever, Thy God, O Zion, unto all generations. Praise ye the Lord.'[34]

The foregoing prayer originates from the early talmudic period. Like other prayers that have the Kingdom of God as their main concern, it is characterised by the universal hope that the peoples of the world may bind themselves into a community of mankind in order to acknowledge none but God. No man, no people is excluded from God's Kingdom, which knows neither national nor geographical boundaries: the one condition is that the peoples should renounce their false gods and ascribe honour to God alone.[35] A somewhat later variation on this same theme of prayer forms the latter part of the introduction to the so-called *Malkiyyoth*, or prayers for the inauguration of the divine Kingdom ('Our God and the God of our fathers, do Thou reign in Thy glory over the whole universe . . .'),[36] in the Additional Service for the New Year Festival, whence it has been taken over in the majority of liturgical rights for daily use as a closing prayer:

> We therefore hope in Thee, O Lord our God, that we may speedily behold the glory of Thy might, when Thou wilt remove the abominations from the earth, and the idols will be utterly cut off, when the world will be perfected under the Kingdom of the Almighty, and all the children of flesh will call upon Thy name, when Thou wilt turn unto Thyself all the wicked of the earth. Let all the inhabitants of the world perceive and know that unto Thee every knee must bow, every tongue must swear. Before Thee, O Lord our God, let them bow and fall; and unto Thy glorious name let them give honour; let them all accept the yoke of Thy Kingdom, and do Thou reign over them speedily, and for ever and ever. For the Kingdom is Thine, and to all eternity Thou wilt reign in glory; as it is written in Thy Law, 'The Lord shall reign for ever and ever'. And it is said, 'in that day shall the Lord be One, and His name One'.[37]

It is with this citation from *Zechariah* which, as stated above (pp. 289 f.), is of major importance for Hermann Cohen's theory of Correspondence (*Korrelation*) and its complete implementation in the utopian thinking of Judaism, that the Jewish divine office draws to a close.

Mankind united at the end of days is a Utopia; but Judaism has been able to develop the Utopia of a *Humanitas* precisely because it has also made its own certain definite notions, not conceived of utopianism, regarding the *Societas* from which the true oneness of mankind inevitably follows. It is only the essential principles of a Jewish social theory that will be touched upon here.

The Hebrew language can boast of a marked richness in its vocabulary for expressing the idea of entirety. Conversely, the language does not distinguish between the notions of *entirety* and *totality*, and the same word, *kol*, is applied to mean *the whole* when reference is to a *unit* and to mean *each* or *all* where what is in view is a *plurality*. Characteristic of this double application is the 145th psalm, in which it is this little word that as *leitmotif* binds the various themes of the psalm together and renders it a sublime hymn of universalism. All works of the divine love, all works of the divine justice are manifest to mankind as a whole, and all flesh sings God's praise in melodious unison.[38] Where Hebrew wishes to express individual entirety, it usually employs the root of *tam*, the other meanings of which are *ingenuous* (Latin *integer*), (morally) *perfect, complete* – and so, *whole*. The word for collective entirety, on the other hand, is *shalem*, and is thus intimately related to *shalom*, the word for 'peace'. *Peace* in Hebrew is thus not – or not merely – the opposite of war, and that which overcomes it, but rather a symbol for everything, divine and human alike, that is complete. The last note of the priestly benediction (*Num.* 6: 26) is 'peace' in this deeper sense: the Jew prays for the protection of God's tabernacle of 'peace'[39]; and so *shalom* is the natural word wherewith he extends his greeting. It is by 'peace' that the human race effects its own completeness, and 'peace' is the true token of the messianic age – the Messiah himself being once styled[40] *prince of peace*.

This chain of moral ideals – entirety, totality, completeness and 'peace' – points further (in virtue of their being both social ideals and presuppositions of thinking about mankind) towards notions of human unity. In the tractate *Sanhedrin* – in which the Mishnah

302

deals with judicial processes – there is discussed at length the testimony of witnesses and their interrogation before criminal courts. The following caution is prescribed against carelessness in the witness-box that may involve the deposition of false evidence. After impressing on witnesses (in a capital case) the tremendous responsibility which they bear, the clerk of the court is to continue thus[41]:

> Therefore but a single man was created in the world, to teach that if any man has caused a single soul to perish[42] Scripture imputes it to him as though he had caused a whole world to perish; and if any man saves alive a single soul[42] Scripture imputes it to him as though he had saved alive a whole world. Again [but a single man was created] for the sake of peace among mankind, that none should say to his fellow, 'My father was greater than thy father'; also that the heretics should not say, 'There are many ruling powers in heaven.' Again [but a single man was created] to proclaim the greatness of the Holy One, blessed is He; for man stamps many coins with the one seal and they are all like one another; but the King of Kings, the Holy One, blessed is He, has stamped every man with the seal of the first man, yet not one of them is like his fellow. Therefore everyone must say, for my sake was the world created.

In this passage of the Mishnah the oneness of mankind is elevated into a matter of principle in connection with the creation story that records the forming of one solitary man. The idea of it being monotheism which is the principle whereon the unity of humanity rests has now had injected into it the further assertion that the unity of man is, for that reason, also the refutation of all gnostic systems – 'in order that the heretics (*minim*, i.e. sectarians) should not say . . .'. The final proposition is divided by the Mishnah into two parts. In the first, it is the fact of the derivation of all men from the single Adam that is raised into the principle of the *equality* of all men: each individual represents mankind as a whole, and no one can say to his fellow man, my ancestor was greater than yours. In the second part, the same circumstance is elevated into the principle of the *diversity* of men. True though it be that God fashions every man in the form of Adam, no two men are ever alike in the way that one penny piece is like another. Men are differentiated, physically as well as in matters of the mind, and the peoples, too, are differentiated. This latter doctrine Judaism had, indeed, to maintain in its own interests: for Israel is, in point of fact, something other than the nations of the world. The two clauses of the Mishnah constitute no contradiction; the equality of men and peoples rests on the right of each to be different and on the divine charge to eliminate all social inequalities and asocial differentiations. Those passages of the Bible that speak of *thy brother* or *thy neighbour* or the *brother thou knowest not*[43] are not merely elegant declamatory flourishes, but commandments. And where the commandment requires that there be 'one manner of law, as well for the stranger as for the native',[44] it is followed immediately by the foundation for that one law for all – 'for I am the Lord your God'. And examples could be adduced from elsewhere in the Pentateuch for what *Deut.* (1: 17) means when it declares 'for judgment is God's'.

Judaism has no place for any ideology founded on race, and it knows of no sagas regarding aristocracy of blood wherewith to support the concept of Israel's election. Quite the contrary: the prophet Amos, in a bold picture, can place on the same level with Israel both her neighbouring peoples and peoples from afar. 'Are ye not as the children of the Ethiopians unto me, O children of Israel ('tis the Lord's own word)? Have I not brought up Israel out of the land of Egypt? And the Philistines from Capthor, and the Syrians from Kir?'[45] It is a calculated gesture in which Amos sees to it that the feature shared by the Chosen People with the children of the dark-skinned Kush, Ethiopia, a people held by his contemporaries in universal contempt, is that both are styled *children* (or rather, *sons*); of set purpose it is the uncircumcised Philistine to whom there is compared the people with which God has contracted a covenant itself symbolised by circumcision: and it has to be the Aramaic-speaking people of Syria, traditionally the enemy of Israel, that must put up with being mentioned by God in the same breath as Israel itself. In God's sight they are all equal, inasmuch as it is God who directs the destiny of each. Amos' message had his own contemporary world in view. Looking into the future, Isaiah saw the salvation of the nations in the circumstance that Assyria would one day be linked with Egypt by a road running through Israel. The three peoples would constitute themselves a triad specifically bonded together by covenant, and vouchsafed God's blessing: 'Blessed be Egypt My people, and Assyria the work of My hands, and Israel Mine inheritance.'[46] Egypt, for Israel, meant the house of bondage and the epitome of every aspect of enslavement; and yet, salvation for Israel is to consist in there being a covenantal state between itself and this one arch-enemy and the other that had led Israel's northern kingdom into exile. The terms of affection that have hitherto been applied to Israel alone are the very ones in which God now sees fit to address Egypt, 'My people', and Assyria, 'the work of My hands'. The peoples are to knot themselves together – not to merge themselves in each other beyond all identification. In the Midrash, it is the diversity of the peoples to which reference is made as corresponding with the divine plan: 'God explained the details regarding the frontiers of each several nation, in order that they should not become mixed up in each other.'[47]

That which puts the seal on the recognition of the same rights for diverse groups is love; for the commandment to love one's neighbour is the logical consequence of this attitude towards one's brother and fellow. 'Thou shalt love thy neighbour as thyself' – or rather, to translate it in true accord with both the canons of Hebrew syntax and the essence of Judaism, 'Thou shalt love thy neighbour, he being like thee'[48]; and once again the basis of the commandment follows immediately – 'I am the Lord'. Quite characteristically, rabbinic Judaism has set this commandment regarding loving one's neighbour alongside a verse of *Genesis* (5: 1), 'This is the book of the generations of Adam.'[49] According to Ben 'Azzai, one of the mishnaic scholars of the second generation (*c*. 90–130 C.E.), this latter verse affords a basic principle of Judaism of even wider purview than that covered by the commandment to love one's neighbour, which his contemporary, Rabbi 'Aqiba (c. 50–135), defended as being an all-embracing statement of what Judaism means. All that Ben 'Azzai is doing, fundamentally, is merely to use the *Genesis* text to underscore the commandment to love one's neighbour. The obligation to love one's fellow man is founded upon the brotherhood of all men, each of whom – as the continuation of the verse in *Genesis* explicitly states – was created by God in His own likeness.[50] Ben 'Azzai's exegetical emphasis accords with the circumstance that post-biblical Judaism has introduced a new term for 'fellow man' – or rather, has reminted an old word in this sense (*beriyyoth*, creatures)[51] – and indeed makes use of it in a rabbinic restatement of the commandment to love one's neighbour. In the *Ethics of the Fathers*[52] Hillel (c. 30 B.C.E. – 10 C.E.) is recorded to have said 'be among [those who] . . . love [their fellow-] creatures'. The word *beri'ah* occurs once in the Hebrew Bible[53] in the sense of creation, or rather of a phenomenon newly created; it occurs once, in the sense of *creature*, in the Aphorisms of Ben Sira,[54] and it is in this sense – but restricted contextually to human beings – that it is common in midrashic literature in the form *biryah*, the less frequent singular form *beriyyah* referring still to the divine act of creation.

The final – as well as the primary – requirement of Jewish morality for any common life of humanity is justice. Law is the principle upon which all social existence must rest, but (as the Bible never tires of reminding us) law has to be applied with justice (*ṣedaqah*). This Jewish 'justice' (the inverted commas may serve to emphasise the inadequacy of the translation) is something more than a general principle formally stated in the sense of *suum cuique*, no matter whether the latter be taken to mean 'to each his own task in society' or 'let each enjoy what is his own'. To be sure, the equality of all before the law goes without saying in Judaism: and the commandment not to countenance a poor man in his cause,[55] or 'Ye shall do no unrighteousness in judgment, thou shalt not respect the person of the poor'[56] is an injunction regarding which Geiger could

306

remark[57] that as a warning against the perversion of justice expressed within the context of a legal code, it is probably not to be paralleled. But this in itself does not suffice to characterise what is essential in the Jewish notion of 'justice', which is a dynamic and active principle even as is love. For both Philo and the Midrash the twin cherubim above the ark of the covenant represent 'love' and 'justice'.[58] This 'justice' – *sedaqah* – constitutes in Judaism the *imitatio Dei*, it being said of God[59] that 'all His ways are judgment' (*mishpat*); and it was to Abraham that there was addressed the demand, for himself and those who should come after him, that 'they will keep the way of the Lord, to do "justice" (*sedaqah*) and judgment' (*mishpat*).[60] God is 'the Just' – *saddiq* – and it is as *'El saddiq* that He effects a just settlement between nations.[61] And where man is described as *saddiq* he is, quite simply, piously God-fearing and his doings are doings of beneficence (*sedaqah*).

A presupposition of the existence of human society is the acknowledgment of a humanity the members of which are actively concerned in manifesting 'acts of piety' (*gemiluth hasadhim*) each towards the other. According to the Talmud[62] it is this spirit of humanity that constitutes the beginning and the end of the Torah. At the beginning of the Pentateuch[63] God clothes man's nakedness as he goes forth from Eden, and at the end of it, it is God again who, according to a bold midrashic interpretation,[64] Himself buries Moses in the fields of Moab. Thus the Torah begins and concludes with examples of God's own evincing of 'acts of piety', in order to teach that man may learn from them to imitate God.

It is through maintaining this attitude towards human society that Judaism has been able to pave the way for its own Utopia of a united mankind at the end of days. For the concept of humanity has never been, for Judaism, a matter for the intellect alone; and Hermann Cohen rightly observes[65] that it is no accident that Herder, the author of *Ideen zur Philosophie der Geschichte der Menschheit*, also wrote a book entitled *Vom Geist der ebräischen Poesie*.

NOTES

* An article entitled *Der Menschheitsgedanke im Judentum* appeared in *Studium Generale* 15, 9, 1962, pp. 571 f., over the name of (the late) Dr Kurt Wilhelm, who suggested to the Editor of the present volume that an English version of it might be a fitting contribution to a volume in memory of Leon Roth. In accordance with a freedom of treatment which he gave the Editor, it has here been slightly abridged in a few places; unfortunately Dr Wilhelm died before the English draft could be submitted to him.

For the biblical passages cited in the German original Dr Wilhelm had quoted the translation of M. Buber and F. Rosenzweig. Where this version differs from King James' either in emphasis or in exegesis, the Editor has, in translating the article into English, endeavoured to follow it closely.

1 M. Guttmann, *Das Judentum und seine Umwelt*, Berlin, 1927, p. 2 f.
2 2nd edition (reprinted Cologne, 1959), pp. 95, 154.
3 *Zechariah* 14: 9.
4 *Op. cit.* (note 2), p. 403.
5 'Der Messiasgedanke und seine Umbiegung im modernen Liberalismus', in *Festgabe für Claude G. Montefiore*, Berlin, 1928, pp. 151 f.
6 Mishnah, *Soṭah* 9, 15, H. Danby's translation, p. 306.
7 *Baraita* in T.B. *Pesaḥim* 54b, *supra.*
8 S. Singer, *Authorised Daily Prayer Book* (1929 ed.), p. 161.
9 *Hebrew Union College Annual* 18, 1943–4, Cincinnati, pp. 353 f.
10 G. von Rad, *Theologie des Alten Testaments*, i, p. 144.
11 *Isaiah* 41: 4.
12 On the Noachide Commandments see more fully R. Loewe, *supra*, pp. 125 f., and S. H. Bergman, *supra*, pp. 52 f.
13 Guttmann, *op. cit.* (note 1), pp. 98 f; S. H. Bergman, *supra*, p. 56 f.
14 *Hilekhoth Melakhim*, 8, 11. For the significance of the concluding proviso, see R. Loewe, *supra*, pp. 143 f.
15 *Maḥbereth* 28, part ii (*ha-'edhen*), ed. Dov Yarden, Jerusalem, 1957, vol. 2, p. 542, l. 715 f; L. Goldschmidt's edition, p. 45.
16 *Das Menschenverständnis des Alten Testaments*, p. 35.
17 *Deut.* 32: 8; but the Septuagint, in which the verse ends *according to the number of angels of God* (i.e. *beney 'elohim* instead of *beney yisra'el*) quite possibly preserves an earlier text, according to which the number of the peoples tallies with that of their respective champion or guardian angels. For the traditional figure of 70 for the sons of Jacob, reflected in the massoretic text here, cf. *Ex.* 1: 5, *Deut.* 10: 22, and the arithmetical and syntactical gymnastics of *Gen.* 46: 26–7 that are resorted to in order to achieve this total.

THE IDEA OF HUMANITY IN JUDAISM

18 Eichrodt, *op. cit.* (note 16), p. 36.
19 *Gen.* 9: 8 f.
20 *Gen.* 12: 3.
21 I. Heinemann, 'Die geschichtlichen Wurzeln des neuzeitlichen Humanitätsgedankens', *Der Morgen*, 6, 1930, pp. 112 f.
22 *Isaiah* 2: 2–4.
23 *Micah* 4: 1–3.
24 *Isaiah* 11: 2–3.
25 M. Buber, *Der Glaube der Propheten*, pp. 218 f.
26 *Isaiah* 11: 9.
27 *Isaiah* 42: 6–7.
28 *Op. cit.* (note 25), p. 309.
29 T.B. *'Abhodhah Zarah* 24a. For the linking of the verse with the story of Babel in *Genesis* cf. *Yalquṭ Shim'oni* to *Zephaniah* (ii, 567; R. Yosē).
30 T.B. *Berakhoth* 34a.
31 *Hilekhoth Melakhim* 12, 1–2.
32 *Ibid.* 12, 5.
33 T.B. *Babha Bathra* 75a, *Exodus Rabbah*, 23, 10, ed. Wilna, f. 43b, col. ii. Cf. also *Pesiqta Rabbathi*, 36, *end*, ed. M. Friedmann, f. 162b. The basic text is of course *Isaiah* 60: 1–3.
34 S. Singer, *op. cit.* (note 8), p. 239a.
35 I. Elbogen, 'Die messianische Idee in den alten jüdischen Gebeten', *Judaica* (*Hermann Cohen Festschrift*, 1922), p. 669.
36 S. Singer, *op. cit.* (note 8), p. 249.
37 *Ibid.*, p. 37 f.
38 Leon J. Liebreich, 'Psalms 34 and 145 in the light of their key words', *Hebrew Union College Annual*, 27, 1956, p. 190. Cf. also C. G. Montefiore and H. Loewe, *A Rabbinic Anthology*, 1938, p. lxxxvii.
39 S. Singer, *op. cit.* (note 8), p. 99 f., *infra*.
40 *Isaiah* 9: 5.
41 *Sanhedrin* 4, 5, H. Danby's translation, p. 388.
42 Some texts add, at both these points, 'from Israel'. In regard to the comparative lack of modern Jewish attention to the ethical question raised by the insertion or omission of these words, see Leon Roth's remarks in his 'Moralization and Demoralization in Jewish Ethics', *Judaism*, 11, no. 4, Fall, 1962, p. 292.
43 *Deut.* 22: 2.
44 *Lev.* 24: 22.
45 *Amos* 9: 7.
46 *Isaiah* 19: 25.
47 *Siphrē, Deut.* 311 (to 32: 8), ed. L. Finkelstein, p. 352, l. 1.
48 *Lev.* 19: 18. Cf. E. Ullendorff's article, *supra*, pp. 276 f.

49 *Siphra, Qedoshim* 4 (on. *Lev.* 19: 18), ed. I. H. Weiss f. 89a, col. ii, (12).

50 See Leon Roth's illuminating analysis of the passage, *op. cit.* (note 42), pp. 295 f.

51 See further on this term R. Loewe, *supra*, pp. 127 f.

52 1, 12, Danby's translation, p. 447.

53 *Numbers* 16: 30.

54 *Ecclesiasticus* 16: 16 (*biryothaw* parallel to *beney 'adham*); but the verse – which is omitted by nearly all MSS of the Greek version – is regarded by many as a later insertion. Cf. W. O. E. Oesterley's commentary, Cambridge, 1912, p. 111.

55 *Exodus* 23: 3.

56 *Lev.* 19: 15.

57 A. Geiger, *Das Judentum und seine Geschichte*, 1864, p. 25. Cf. Z. Diesendruck's Hebrew article on 'The perfection of society according to the teaching of Judaism', *H. N. Bialik Festschrift*, Tel Aviv, 1934, 3, p. 51, a study to which I am indebted for a number of references.

58 Philo, *Cherubim*, 9, 27, 144, ed. Cohn-Wendland, i, p. 176, Loeb translation by F. H. Colson and G. H. Whitaker, ii, p. 24. Cf. *Midrash Tadeshē*, A. Jellinek, *Beth Ham-midrash*, 3, p. 164, *infra*.

59 *Deut.* 32: 4.

60 *Gen.* 18: 19.

61 *Isaiah* 45: 21.

62 T.B. *Soṭah* 14a (R. Simla'i); cf. *Tanḥuma*, ed. Buber, *Genesis, Way-yera'*, 4, f. 43b, note 30.

63 *Gen.* 3: 21.

64 *Deut.* 34: 6.

65 *Op cit.* (note 2), p. 282.

15

Maimonides on
Modes and Universals

HARRY A. WOLFSON

In a passage dealing with the problem of divine attributes, Maimonides says: 'You must know that God has no essential attributes in any manner (*wajh: panim*) and in any mode (*ḥāl*: *'inyan*) whatsoever.'[1]

At the time of Maimonides, the problem of attributes did not present itself simply as a contrast between the affirmation of attributes and the negation of attributes. Between these two contrasting theories there was a third theory, known as the theory of *modes*. The Arabic term for mode in this technical sense is *ḥāl*, which the Modalists say is used by them as the equivalent of the term *wajh*.[2] A few salient points in the history of the theory of modes, as I have reconstructed it in my forthcoming work *The Philosophy of the Kalam*, are necessary as prefatory to the discussion as to the use of these terms in the passage quoted.

The theory of modes originally appeared as a theory of universals, and it was the culmination of a discussion of the problem of universals which had arisen about a century earlier, in an attempt to answer the question posed by Porphyry as to the nature of *genera* and species. From a theory of universals, which is also a theory of predication, the theory of modes was applied to

311

divine attributes; and it resulted in a view which was at once opposed to both the orthodox affirmation of attributes and to the Mu'tazilite denial of them. In the course of time, however, certain orthodox Attributists harmonised modes in the sense of divine predicates with their own affirmation of attributes, and certain Mu'tazilites harmonised them with their own denial of attributes.

Although, on the whole, various distinctive formulae were used by exponents of these three theories in the description of their respective views, sometimes the same formula was used by them in different senses. The most common formula used for modes in the sense of both universals and divine predicates was that modes are neither existent nor non-existent. The most common formula for modes in the sense of only divine predicates was that modes are neither the same as God nor other than God. A stock objection to the theory of modes was that it infringed upon the Law of Excluded Middle. The answer to this stock objection was that modes have a conceptual existence and that a conceptual existence is a special kind of existence, which is intermediate between the existence of things which correspond to words and the non-existence of mere words for which there is no correspondence in things; and, since the existence of modes is an intermediate between two extremes, the negation of both the extremes is no infringement upon the Law of Excluded Middle.

In view of the fact then, that by the time of Maimonides modes had already been harmonised with either the affirmation of attributes or the denial of attributes, when Maimonides says here that 'God has no essential attributes in any *wajh* and in any *ḥāl* whatsoever', the following question arises: Does his rejection of attributes here include also a rejection of modes or does it not include a rejection of modes? In the former case, the phrase 'in any *wajh* and in any *ḥāl*' will have been used by him significantly, in order to emphasise the inclusion of modes among the attributes rejected by him; in the latter case, the phrase will have been used by him to emphasise merely that attributes are to be rejected, no matter how their real meaning may be disguised by the use of some evasive formula.

The same question with regard to Maimonides' attitude toward modes arises also in connection with another passage, which reads as follows: 'Some people of speculation got to the point where they said that the attributes of God are neither His essence nor anything extraneous to His essence.'[3]

This type of formula, though usually associated with the name of Abū Hāshim[4] and the theory of modes of which he is the founder, was used long before him in the sense of the affirmation of attributes, first by Sulaymān b. Jarīr and his followers[5] and then by Ibn Kullāb and his followers.[6] Subsequently among the Ash'arites it was used by some in the sense of the affirmation of attributes[7] and by others in the sense of the affirmation of modes.[8] Accordingly, in Maimonides' ascription here of this type of formula to 'some people of speculation', the following question arises: Does he use this type of formula in the sense of an expression of a belief in attributes only, or does he use it in the sense of an expression of a belief in modes?

In his refutation of this formula, Maimonides goes on to say as follows:

But this is similar to the saying of some others that the modes (al-aḥwāl: ha-'inyanim), that is, the universal concepts (al-ma'ānī al-kulliyyah: ha-'inyanim hak-kelaliyyim), are neither existent nor non-existent and similar to the saying of still others that the atom is not in a place (makān: maqom) but it occupies space (yushghal al-ḥayyiz: yaṭridh hag-gebhul) and that man has no action at all but he has acquisition (al-iktisāb: haq-qeniyyah). All these are sentences (aqāwil: debharim) which are only said, so that they exist in words (alfāẓ: milloth) and not in rational judgments (adhhān: de'oth), and all the more, they have no existence outside the mind (dhihn: sekhel).[9]

At first sight, his statement that the formula which he has previously ascribed to 'some people of speculation' is similar 'to the saying of some others' about 'modes', would seem to indicate that the 'some people of speculation' to whom he ascribed the aforementioned formula were not those who believed in modes.

But when, right after mentioning the term 'modes', he explains that he means by it 'the universal concepts', he clearly indicates that he is aware of the distinction between modes as universal concepts and modes as divine predicates. The same question with regard to Maimonides' attitude towards modes thus arises again: Do the 'men of speculation', to whom Maimonides ascribes the formula which he compares to the formula used for modes in the sense of universals, include those who used the same formula for modes in the sense of divine predicates, or do they not include them? In the former case, it would indicate that Maimonides agreed with those who harmonised modes in the sense of divine predicates with the affirmation of attributes; in the latter case, it would indicate that he agreed with those who harmonised modes in the sense of divine predicates with the denial of attributes.

But then there is another question in connection with this refutation. Why should Maimonides object to the formula that modes in the sense of universals are neither existent nor non-existent? Those who considered universals as modes held, as said above in the prefatory remarks, that universals have a conceptual existence, and that a conceptual existence is a kind of existence which is intermediate between the existence of things and the non-existence of words; and that, because universals are intermediate between existence and non-existence, to say of them that they are neither existent nor non-existent is not a violation of the Law of Excluded Middle. Now Maimonides himself admits that universals, while they are not extra-mental things, are mental things (*ma'ānī dhihniyyah: debharim sikhliyyim*).[10] Moreover, from his contention that a definition implies that the *definiendum* is composed of genus and specific difference which are causes of the *definiendum*,[11] it is to be inferred that universals, described by him as 'mental things', do have some kind of existence. The kind of existence which, according to him, universals could have would be, we may assume, like that ascribed to them by Avicenna in his triple stage theory in the existence of universals, namely, before multiplicity (*qabl al-kathrah*), in multiplicity (*fī al-kathrah*), and after multiplicity (*ba'd al-kathrah*), which, as I have shown, is traceable to Ammonius Hermiae.[12] Now, according to this theory, universals in their after-multiplicity stage, that is, the stage during which they exist in the human mind, may be said to have a conceptual existence[13] analogous to that ascribed to them by the Muslim Modalists, and may thus be described as being neither existent like extramental things nor non-existent like mere words. In view of this, why should Maimonides object to the formula that universals are neither existent nor non-existent, when that formula can be interpreted as not being an infringement upon the Law of Excluded Middle?

Let us see how Maimonides would answer this question as to why he objects to the modalistic formula about universals, and from his answer to this question we shall try to find out what his answer would be to the questions we have raised with regard to his view on modes in the sense of divine predicates.

In his answer to this question, Maimonides, I imagine, would say that although he was willing to admit that the formula could be interpreted so as not to infringe upon the Law of Excluded Middle, he still objected to it on the ground that in its form, in its phrasing, it does infringe upon that Law. To him, he would argue, for a formula to be right is must be one which, both in form and in substance, is logically sound. By such a logically sound formula, he would go on to explain, he meant a formula which conforms to what Aristotle calls an 'enunciative sentence' (λόγος ἀποφαντικός: al-qaul al-jāzim), by which Aristotle means a logical proposition which is subject to the description of being either true or false[14]: and the test as to whether it is true or false is, according to him, its correspondence or non-correspondence to something outside the mind.[15]

It is in accordance with this conception of his as to what constitutes the right kind of formula that Maimonides goes on to reject as unsound the four formulae under consideration. The formula that 'the atom is not in a place (makān) but occupies space (yushghal al-ḥayyiz)' may, indeed, in its external form be a well constructed logical proposition; for externally it appears that the predicate that is negated in the first part of the proposition is not the same as the predicate that is affirmed in its second part. Still, in meaning the proposition infringes upon the Law of Contradiction; for, inasmuch as by definition 'place' (*makān*) is that which is occupied by an extended body only,[16] the statement in the first part of the proposition, namely, that 'the atom is not in place', implies that the atom is not an extended body; but, inasmuch as only those who believe that the atom is an extended body say that the atom occupies space,[17] the statement in the second part of the proposition, namely, that the atom 'occupies space', implies that the atom *is* an extended body. Similarly the formula that 'man has no action at all but he has acquisition' may, again, be a well-constructed logical proposition in its external form. Still, in meaning it is an infringement upon the Law of Contradiction, for the 'acquisition' affirmed in its second part is itself an 'action', and thus it is contradictory to the denial of 'action' in the first part. As for the formula quoted by Maimonides from certain Attributists, we may assume that he knew that Ibn Kullāb and the others after him had used it, as can be shown, in such a way that, by their denying that attributes are 'His essence', they meant to deny the Muʿtazilite view that the attributes of God are 'His essence'; and that by their denying that attributes are 'extraneous to His essence', they meant to deny the view of the Zurariyyah and Karrāmiyyah that the attributes are created, and hence are 'extraneous to His essence': so that in meaning the formula does not infringe upon the Law of Excluded Middle. Still, in its external form it is an infringement upon that Law, since it denies both that the attributes are 'His essence' and that they are 'extraneous to His essence', that is to say, they are neither the *same* as His essence nor *other* than His essence. Similarly, we may assume that he knew that the Modalists by their denying that universals are 'existent' meant to deny that they are existent like extra-mental real things, and that by their denying that universals are 'non-existent' meant to deny that they are non-existent like mere words; so that the formula is no infringement upon the Law of Excluded Middle. Still, in its external form it is an infringement upon that Law. What, according to Maimonides, would be the right formula for conceptual universals is suggested by him in his statement that 'no species exist outside the mind, but species and other universals are mental things'.[18] The right formula would thus be that 'universals are non-existent outside the mind, but they are existent in the mind'.

That Maimonides' criticism here is aimed exclusively at the formulae used in the four theories he mentions, and not at the theories themselves, is evidenced by his use of the term *aqāwil* in his opening statement, namely, 'these are all *aqāwil* (Hebrew: *debharim*)'.[19] The term *aqāwil* is the plural of *qaul*, which in the Arabic translation of *De Interpretatione*[20] translates the Greek term λόγος in the passage quoted above. In that passage Aristotle, starting with an explanation of the general meaning of the term λόγος, 'sentence' (of which he subsequently says that it may be either enunciative, which conveys judgment as to truth and falsehood, or verbal, which does not convey judgment as to truth and falsehood), goes on to say that 'a word' (φάσις, *lafẓah*), such as the word 'man', which is part of a sentence, never does convey 'affirmation or negation',[21] that is, it never conveys judgment as to truth and falsehood. Thus Maimonides' opening statement means to say that all these formulae are only what Aristotle would consider as mere verbal sentences, for, as he goes on to explain, 'they are only said and consequently they exist only in words (*alfāẓ*: *milloth*) and not in rational judgments (*adhhān*: *de'oth*)'.[22] By this he means to say that they are combinations of words which form only verbal sentences that convey no judgments as to truth and falsehood. He then adds: 'and all the more, they have no existence outside the mind (*dhihn*: *sekhel*)'.[23] By this he means to say that, more than merely being sentences which *do not* convey judgments as to truth and falsehoods, these formulae are like words which, according to Aristotle, *never* convey judgments as to truth and falsehood,[24] seeing that there can never exist outside the mind anything to correspond to any of those formulae.

Finally, in trying to explain in concrete terms what his objections really are against the four formulae he has mentioned, he makes two statements. First: anyone who uses these formulae, he says, 'endeavours to make exist something that does not exist'.[25] By this he refers to two of the four formulae quoted by him, namely, those used by some Atomists and the Acquisitionists, both of which, as I have tried to explain, are in meaning infringements upon the Law of Contradiction which, as quoted by Aristotle in the name of Heraclitus, reads: 'It is impossible for anyone to suppose that the same thing exists and does not exist.'[26] Second: anyone who uses these formulae, he says again, 'endeavours . . . to create an intermediate between two contraries (*ḍiddāni*: *shenē hephekhim*) between which there is no intermediate'[27] – that is, they infringe upon the Law of Excluded Middle. Here Maimonides himself indicates that this criticism is aimed at the other two of the four formulae quoted by him, namely those used by some of the Attributists and by Modalists in their conception of universals; for immediately after this criticism he goes on to say that there is no intermediate between the contraries 'existent' and 'non-existent' and between the contraries 'same' and 'other'[28] : that is, the two pairs of contraries denied respectively in the formula of the Modalists in their conception of universals, and in the formula of some of the Attributists. Maimonides' carefully phrased statement that the contraries between which the users of these formulae endeavour to create intermediates are those 'between which there is no intermediate', reflects Aristotle's statement that, with respect to opposites which are 'by way of contraries (ὡς τὰ ἐναντία: *'alā ṭarīq al-muḍāddah*)', some have intermediates and some have no intermediates; and that those which have no intermediates are 'such that the subject in which they naturally exist, or of which they are predicated, must necessarily contain either the one or the other of them',[29] the implication being that the subject cannot be said to contain neither the one nor the other.

The upshot of our discussion is that, with respect to modes in the sense of universals, Maimonides agrees with the Modalists that they have a conceptual existence which is neither existent like things nor non-existent like words, but he disagrees with them as to the logical propriety of the use of their formula. With regard to the use of modes as an interpretation of divine predicates, inasmuch as in his discussion of divine attributes Maimonides has made it clear that no term predicated of God can be a universal,[30] it follows that no term predicated of God can be a mode. Consequently, with regard to divine predicates, he not only disagrees with the Modalists in the use of their formula: he disagrees with them also in their interpretation of divine predicates as modes.

By this we are now able to answer the other questions we have raised. The terms *ḥāl* and *wajh* in the first passage are quite definitely used by him in the technical sense of 'mode', and similarly 'some men of speculation', to whom he ascribes the formula that 'the attributes of God are neither His essence nor anything extraneous to His essence', include both those who use this formula in the sense of attributes and those who use it in the sense of modes, for to him modes as an interpretation of divine predicates are not to be distinguished from attributes; the former, no less than the latter, being to him incompatible with the conception of the absolute simplicity of God.

The conclusion we have arrived at in our interpretation of these vague passages also throws light on a third vague passage in the *Moreh Nebukhim*. In that passage, dealing with those who believe in attributes, Maimonides says: 'Some of them express themselves clearly on the existence of attributes, enumerating them as things superadded to the essence.'[31] This quite evidently refers to those Ash'arites whose formulation of the doctrine of attributes contains the expression 'superadded to the essence'.[32]

Maimonides then goes on to say: 'Others among them do not state this clearly, but that this is their belief is quite clear, even though they do not express themselves in clear-cut language, as is the case of some of them who say that God is powerful in virtue of His essence, He is knowing in virtue of His essence, He is living in virtue of His essence, He is willing in virtue of His essence.'[33] Now the expression 'in virtue of His essence' as a description of terms predicated of God has been used in various senses. According to Ash'arī, the formula that 'the names and attributes of God are in virtue of His essence' was used by Ibn Kullāb, together with his formula that 'they are not God and they are not other than God', as an expression of his belief that 'they subsist in God',[34] by which he means, as he makes even more clear elsewhere,[35] that God possesses real attributes. According to Shahrastānī, the expression 'in virtue of essence' was used by Jubbā'ī in the sense of the denial of attributes and by Abu Hāshim in the sense of the affirmation of modes.[36] From the context of the passage, which deals directly with Attributists, it is not clear whether 'the others among them' who use the expression 'in virtue of His essence' include Attributists only or also Modalists. In the light, however, of our conclusion that Maimonides was opposed to modes no less than to attributes, it is quite certain that 'the others among them' include also Modalists. But although in this passage the use of the expression 'in virtue of His essence' is rejected by Maimonides with reference only to its use as an affirmation of either attributes or modes, it may be inferred from other passages, as I have shown elsewhere,[37] that Maimonides would not use it even in the sense of the absolute denial of attributes; and one of the reasons for his not using it is the fact of its being used by others in the sense of the affirmation of either attributes or modes. To him, any formula describing the meaning of terms predicated of God must be free of any vagueness and ambiguity.

NOTES

1 *Moreh Nebhukhim* I, 50, Arabic, ed. Joel, p. 75, ll. 5–6.
2 Shahrastānī, *Nihāyat*, ed. Guillaume, p. 137, l. 18.
3 *Moreh* I, 51, p. 76, ll. 24–6.
4 Baghdādī, *Farq*, ed. Badr, p. 182, l. 14.
5 Ash'arī, *Maqālāt*, ed. Ritter, p. 70, ll. 8–10; p. 514, ll. 15–16; p. 547, l. 13.
6 *Ibid.*, p. 169, ll. 10–13; p. 514, ll. 15–16; p. 546, l. 11.
7 Ibn Ḥaldun, *Muqaddimah*, ed. Quatremère, III, p. 38, ll. 16–17; cf. discussion in my *Religious Philosophy*, pp. 182–3.
8 Ibn Ḥazm, *Fiṣal*, ed. Cairo, 1317–27, V, p. 49, ll. 2–4.
9 *Moreh* I, 51, p. 76, l. 26 – p. 77, l. 2.
10 *Ibid.*, III, 18, p. 343, ll. 9–10.
11 *Ibid.*, I, 52, p. 77, ll. 19–25.
12 Cf. my paper 'Avicenna, Algazali, and Averroes on Divine Attributes', *Homenaje a Millás-Vallicrosa*, II (1965), pp. 547–50.

13 Cf. my interpretation of Maimonides' theory of universals in terms of Avicenna's triple stage theory of universals in my paper 'Crescas on the Problem of Divine Attributes', *Jewish Quarterly Review* N.S., 7 (1916), pp. 11–13. At that time I thought of Maimonides' triple stage theory of universals as a sort of moderate realism, and hence I described his criticism of the modalistic formula for universals in *Moreh* I, 51, as a criticism of conceptualism. According to my present way of thinking, however, all theories of universals between extreme realism and extreme nominalism are to be considered as various shades of conceptualism. Maimonides' theory of universals is, therefore, one of the various shades of conceptualism. His criticism, as I now try to show, is only of the phrasing of the formula.

14 *De Interpr.* 4, 17a, 1–3.

15 *Metaph.* IV, 7, 1011b, 27.

16 Jurjānī, *Kitāb al-Taʻrifāt*, ed. Flügel, p. 244, l. 20 – p. 245, l. 1; cf. Munk, *Guide*, I, 51, p. 186, n.

17 Abū Rashīd, *Masāʼil*, ed. Biram, p. 38, l. 15, and p. 41, l. 18 – p. 42, l. 2 (German, pp. 46 and 49).

18 *Moreh* III, 18, p. 343, ll. 9–10.

19 *Ibid.*, I, 51, p. 76, l. 29.

20 Cf. I. Pollak's edition of the Arabic translation of the *De Interpretatione* and Badawi's edition of the *Organon*.

21 *De Interpr.* 4, 16b, 27–8.

22 *Moreh* I, 51, p. 77, l. 1. For my translation of *adhhān* by 'rational judgments', see Avicenna's descriptions of *dhihn* quoted by Goichon in *Lexique*, § 263, pp. 132–4. This explains also why Ibn Ṭibbon translated it by *deʻoth*.

23 *Moreh* I, 51, p. 77, ll. 1–2.

24 *De Interpr.*, 4, 16b, 26–30.

25 *Moreh* I, 51, p. 77, l. 6.

26 *Metaphys.* IV, 3, 1005b, 23–4.

27 *Moreh* I, 51, p. 77, l. 6.

28 *Ibid.*, ll. 7–8.

29 *Categ.*, 10, 11b, 33 – 12a, 3.

30 *Moreh* I, 52, p. 77, l. 19 – p. 78, l. 1.

31 *Ibid.*, I, 53, p. 82, ll. 1–2.

32 *Nihāyat*, p. 181, ll. 1–4; Averroes, *Kashf*, ed. Müller, p. 56, ll. 3 and 7.

33 *Moreh* I, 53, p. 82, ll. 2–4.

34 *Maqālāt*, p. 169, ll. 12–13.

35 *Ibid.*, ll. 10–12.

36 *Milal*, p. 55, l. 19 – p. 56, l. 3.

37 Cf. my paper 'Maimonides on Negative Attributes', *Louis Ginzberg Jubilee Volume* (1945), pp. 415–18.

BIBLIOGRAPHY OF THE WRITINGS OF LEON (*Hebraice* ḤAYYIM YEHUDAH) ROTH

A Bibliography of Roth's writings was included in the Jerusalem memorial brochure (see *supra*, p. 11, note 1), pp. 19 f.; it was compiled anonymously by several of his pupils, who acknowledged that it was almost certainly incomplete. It has been possible to add quite a substantial number of items here, and my thanks are due to Professor T. E. Jessop, Mr J. M. Shaftesley, O.B.E., and particularly to members of Leon Roth's family for their help in recovering these titles. The arrangement of the material here differs from the Jerusalem scheme somewhat; and since the present list exceeds the other considerably, it has not been felt necessary to indicate the concordance of its serial numbers where the items also figured on the Jerusalem list. Unfortunately, personal inspection of most of the Hebrew items, and some of the English ones, was not possible for me, and the completeness of detail is therefore not consistent throughout.

It is hoped that it may be possible to arrange for a few of the major libraries in England, Europe, Israel and the U.S.A. to have a microfilm copy of all the items other than books enumerated below. Any such filming will follow the serial numbers of this bibliography.

R.L.

(A) ENGLISH

I. BOOKS

i. *Spinoza, Descartes and Maimonides*. Oxford, Clarendon Press, 1924 (re-issued by Russell & Russell, Inc., New York, 1963).

ii. *Correspondence of Descartes and Constantyn Huygens, 1635–1647*. Edited from manuscripts now in the Bibliothèque Nationale. Oxford, Clarendon Press, 1926.

iii. *The Science of Morals: an Essay in Method.* London, Benn, 1928.

iv. *Spinoza.* London, Benn, 1929.

v. *Descartes' Discourse on Method.* Oxford, Clarendon Press, 1937.

vi. *The Theory and Practice of Government.* Excerpts from *Representative Government* by John Stuart Mill and *The English Constitution* by Walter Bagehot. Jerusalem, D. B. Aaronson, 1945.

vii. *The Guide for the Perplexed: Moses Maimonides.* London, Hutchinson, 1948.

viii. *God and Man in the Old Testament.* London, George Allen and Unwin, 1955 (translation of Hebrew item no. 27, *infra*, p. 331).

ix. *Judaism. A Portrait.* London, Faber & Faber, 1960 (paperback edition, Viking Press, New York, 1962).

II. PAMPHLETS, ARTICLES, LECTURES, REVIEWS, ETC

x. 'David Nieto and the Orthodoxy of Spinozism', *Chronicon Spinozanum* i (The Hague, 1921), pp. 278–82.

xi. 'The *Abscondita Sapientiae* of Joseph del Medigo', *Chronicon Spinozanum* ii (1922), pp. 54–66.

xii. 'Spinoza and Cartesianism', *Mind* 32 (1923), pp. 12 f., 160 f. (later embodied in no. i).

xiii. 'Miscellanies', *Chronicon Spinozanum* iii (1923), pp. 347–8.

xiv. Review of A. Kaminka's *The Thoughts of Marcus Aurelius* (Hebrew), *The Jewish Guardian*, 16th March, 1923.

xv. 'The Goodness of God', *Journal of Philosophical Studies* 2, 8 (1926), pp. 503–15.

xvi. 'Jewish Thought in the Modern World', *The Legacy of Israel*, ed. Edwyn R. Bevan and Charles Singer. Oxford, Clarendon Press, 1927, pp. 433–72.

xvii. 'Spinoza in Recent English Thought', *Mind* 36 (1927), pp. 205 f.

xviii. Review of H. Bergmann's *The Philosophy of Immanuel Kant* (Hebrew), *ibid.*, p. 384.

xix. 'The Jerusalem University. Some Personal Notes', *The Universities Review* 2, 2 (1930), pp. 111–5. (Describes methods employed to produce Hebrew versions of philosophical texts, and the fashioning of Hebrew for university teaching purposes. Cf. no. xxvi.)

xx. 'Jerusalem Letter', *ibid.*, 4 (1932), pp. 126–31. (Describes the introduction of teaching in biological sciences, financial difficulties and administrative experiment in the Hebrew University.)

xxi. 'Note on the Relationship between Locke and Descartes', *Mind* 44 (1935), pp. 414–16.

xxii. 'The Discourse on Method, 1637–1937', *Mind* 46 (1937), pp. 32–43.

xxiii. 'The Descartes-Huygens Correspondence', *Travaux du IXe Congrès international de Philosophie* ('Congrès Descartes'), Paris, 1937, pp. 101–8.

xxiv. 'The First 25 Years of the Hebrew University', *Bulletin* of the English Friends of the Hebrew University, October, 1943.

xxv. *The Hebrew University and its Place in the Modern World*, Lucien Wolf Memorial Lecture, 1945, The Jewish Historical Society of England. (Reported also in *The Jewish Chronicle*, 6th April, 1945, p. 5.)

xxvi. Review-article entitled 'Philosophical Classics' [in Hebrew, vols. 1–22], *Commentary* 2 (1946), pp. 298–300. (Outlines the origin of this series of Hebrew translations and the methods employed to produce it. Cf. no. xix.)

xxvii. 'A Plea for Universality in Education', *Scopus* ii, 1 (March 1948). (Cf. no. 54.)

xxviii. 'Judah L. Magnes and the Hebrew University', *Jewish Education* 20 (1949).

xxix. 'I[srael] A[brahams] and the Hebrew University', *The Zionist Independent* i, 2 (1949), pp. 20f.

xxx. 'General Humanities', in *The Hebrew University of Jerusalem 1925–50* [ed. Manka Spiegel], Jerusalem, 1950, pp. 98–102. (Outlines the history of the establishment of the various schools of humane studies. A Hebrew edition of this book also appeared.)

xxxi. 'Twenty Five Years' [of the Hebrew University], *Scopus* iv, 1 (February, 1950).

xxxii. 'Judaism', *Year Book of Education*, 1951, chap. 6, pp. 192–212.

xxxiii. 'Ambassador' [review editorial of James G. McDonald's *My Mission in Israel*], *Desiderata* iv, 49, 7th December, 1951, pp. 1–3. (Signed A.N.O.R. *Desiderata* was edited by Leon Roth's brother David, the bibliophile.)

xxxiv. 'Boloney' [review editorial of Charles G. Finney's *The Circus of Dr. Lao*], *Desiderata* iv, 50, 14th December, 1951, pp. 1–4. (Signed A.B.F.)

xxxiv a. 'Judah Leon Magnes [:] An Appreciation', *Ner*. Jerusalem, 3rd year, 5–6 (December, 1951–January, 1952), p. 20 (English portion of a Hebrew–English periodical). Cf. *infra*, no. 71.

xxxv. 'Philosophy at the University [of Jerusalem] and the Jewish Mind', *Hebrew University Garland*, ed. Norman Bentwich, 1952, pp. 65–72. Also reprinted as pamphlet, Welwyn Garden City, 1952. (On the indispensability of scepticism, self-criticism, and intellectual cosmopolitanism.)

xxxvi. Letter to *The Jewish Chronicle*, 4th December, 1953, p. 21 (on the morality of Jewish apologia for the Qibya raid).

xxxvii. *Jewish Thought as a Factor in Civilization*, Unesco Series (The Race Question and Modern Thought), Paris, 1954. (Yiddish translation by M. Shenderey, Buenos Aires, 1956.)

xxxviii. 'St. George for England' [review editorial of George Orwell's *England, Your England and Other Essays*], *Desiderata* vii, 2, 15th January, 1954, pp. 1–3. (Signed A.B.F.)

xxxix. Letters to *The Jewish Chronicle*, 16th April, 1954, p. 23, and 30th April, 1954, p. 15. (On Ahad Ha'am: cf. also issue for 9th April, p. 38.)

xl. 'Cartesian Studies' [review of Norman Kemp Smith's *New Studies in the Philosophy of Descartes*], *The Cambridge Journal* 7 (1954), pp. 466–75.

xli. *The Significance of Biblical Prophecy for our Time*, Rabbi Mattuck Memorial Pamphlet no. 1, The London Society of Jews and Christians, 1955 (jointly with W. A. L. Elmslie).

xli a. 'Prophets of All Time' [an abbreviation of the foregoing], *Common Ground* (Council of Christians and Jews) ix, 3 (1955), pp. 3–8.

xlii. Review of J. C. Wordsworth's *Pain and Other Problems*, *The Philosophical Quarterly* 5 (1955), pp. 382–3.

xliii. Letter to *The Jewish Chronicle*, 4th February, 1955, p. 14. (On J. L. Magnes.)

xliv. *Great Jewish Books, Old and New*, Jewish Book Council, London, 1955.

xlv. 'A Contemporary Moralist: Albert Camus', R. R. Marett Memorial Lecture, *Philosophy* 30 (1955), pp. 291–303.

xlvi. *Some Reflections on the Interpretation of Scripture*, Claude Montefiore Lecture, 1955, Liberal Jewish Synagogue, London, 1956.

xlvii. 'The "Cherem" on Spinoza', *The Jewish Chronicle*, 27th July, 1956, p. 15.

xlviii. Address given at the West London Synagogue on the occasion
of the Inauguration of the Jewish Theological College
[subsequently renamed The Leo Baeck College], *The
Synagogue Review* xxxi, 3 (1956), pp. 65 f. (In part incor-
porated in *Judaism* (*supra*, no. ix), pp. 74 f.)

xlix. 'Rabbi and Audience', *The Jewish Chronicle*, 14th December,
1956, p. 17, and 21st December, p. 15.

l. *Baruch Spinoza. His Religious Importance for the Jew of
Today*. International Conference of the World Union for
Progressive Judaism, Amsterdam, 1957.

l a. 'Spinoza and the Religious Jew of Today' [an abbreviation of
the foregoing], *The Jewish Chronicle*, 13th September,
1955, p. 21, and 20th September, p. 21.

li. 'Encounter and Tensions in World Religions', *Forum* (World
Congress of Faiths, London), 32 (1957), pp. 7–15.

lii. Review of W. R. Valentiner's *Rembrandt and Spinoza*, *The
Jewish Chronicle*, 21st June, 1957, p. 23.

liii. Review of Arnold Toynbee's *An Historian's Approach to
Religion*, *A*[*nglo-*] *J*[*ewish*] *A*[*ssociation*] *Quarterly* 3
(1957), p. 34.

liv. 'Judaism, the Elements', *Judaism* (New York), 7 (1958),
pp. 3–13 (an earlier draft of chap. 1 of *Judaism, supra.*
no. ix).

lv. 'Maimonides', *Common Ground* (see no. xli a), xii, 1 (1958),
pp. 23–6.

lvi. Review of M. Waxman's *Tradition and Change*, *The Jewish
Chronicle*, 15th May, 1959, p. 19.

lvii. 'The Resurgence of Hebrew', *The Jewish Journal of Sociology* i, 2 (1959), pp. 177 f.

lviii. 'Authority, Religion, and Law', *The Hibbert Journal* 58
(1960), pp. 115–20.

lix. 'Back to, Forward from, Ahad Ha'am?' *Addresses* given at
the 13th Conference of Anglo-Jewish Preachers, 1960,
pp. 35–47.

lix a. (The same title as the foregoing), *Conservative Judaism* (New
York), xvii, 1–2 (1962–3).

lx. Review of Louis Jacobs' *Jewish Values*, *The Jewish Chronicle*,
1960, p. 20.

lxi. 'Religion and Piety in Spinoza', in *A Seminar of Saints*
(Papers presented at the 2nd Seminar of the Union for the
Study of Great Religions), Madras (Ganesh & Co.), 1960.

lxii. 'Hebraists and Non-Hebraists of the Seventeenth Century',
Journal of Semitic Studies 6 (1961), pp. 204–21.

lxiii. Review of Malcolm L. Diamond's *Martin Buber: Jewish Existentialist, ibid.*, p. 114.

lxiv. Review of Cyrus H. Gordon's *New Horizons in Old Testament Literature, ibid.*, pp. 293–4.

lxv. Review of Samuel Belkin's *In His Image: The Jewish Philosophy of Man as Expressed in Rabbinic Tradition, The Jewish Chronicle*, 17th March, 1961, p. 29.

lxvi. Review of Yehezkel Kaufmann's *The Religion of Israel* (English translation), *The Jewish Chronicle*, 2nd June, 1961, p. 24.

lxvii. 'A Secularist Faith', *World Faiths* (formerly *Forum*, see no. li), 51 (1961).

lxviii. 'Religion and Literature', *The Hibbert Journal* 60 (1961–2), pp. 24–34.

lxviii a. (The same title, reprinted in) *Religion in the Modern World*, World Congress of Faiths, London (no date), pp. 24–34.

lxix. *Foundations*, St Paul's Lecture, 1961, London Diocesan Council for Christian Jewish Understanding, 1962.

lxx. 'Is there a Jewish Philosophy?' Chap. 1 of *Jewish Philosophy and Philosophers*, ed. Raymond Goldwater, The Hillel Foundation, London, 1962, pp. 1–19.

lxxi. 'Moralization and Demoralization in Jewish Ethics', *Judaism* (cf. no. liv), xi, 4 (1962), pp. 291–302.

lxxii. 'Mysticism: Thick and Thin', *World Faiths* (cf. no. lxvii), 55 (1962).

lxxiii. Review of A. C. Bouquet's *Sacred Books of the World, The Jewish Chronicle*, 7th December, 1962, p. 26.

lxxiv. Review of Jacob Katz's *Exclusiveness and Tolerance: Studies in Jewish–Gentile Relations in Medieval and Modern Times, Journal of Semitic Studies* 8 (1963), pp. 137 f.

lxxv. Review of S. G. F. Brandon's *Man and His Destiny in the Great Religions, ibid.*, pp. 217 f.

* * *

lxxvi. The following additional item, not technically published but reproduced in cyclostyled form for private circulation only, may appropriately be recorded here:

Some Observations on Recent Reported Undergraduate Conversions to Christianity, a paper read to the Inter-University Jewish Federation [of England] Summer School, August 1954, pp. 22 f.

(B) HEBREW

I. (A) BOOKS*

Titles are given in English below

1. לזכרו של אחד־העם. מחקרים בפילוסופיה של היהדות, תרצ"ז. (נאספו כאן בכרך אחד ההרצאות לזכרו של אחד־העם שניתנו באוניברסיטה העברית בשנים תרפ"ט־תרצ"ז, ושיצאו כל אחת לחוד בשנים תרצ"א־ תרצ"ז: ואלו הן שמותן.

   (א) הפילוסופיה ואחד־העם, הרצאת פתיחה, תרפ"ט.
   (ב) ההדמות לאל ורעיון הקדושה, תרצ"א.
   (ג) השכל והרצון כגורמים דתיים, תרצ"ב.
   (ד) "על הטעויות. . .", תרצ"ג.
   (ה) האלילות, תרצ"ד.
   (ו) מושכלות אמצעיים במוסר היהדות, תרצ"ה.
   (ז) טעמי המצוות, תרצ"ו.
   (ח) ההתפתחות, ההגדרה והיהדות, תרצ"ז).

2. מורה דרך בפילוסופיה היונית. ירושלים, ר. מס, 1939. מהדורה שניה, תש"ו; מהד' שלישית, תשי"ב; מהד' רביעית, תשי"ד.

3. מורה דרך בפילוסופיה החדשה. ירושלים, ר. מס, 1941. מהדורה שניה, תש"י.

4. למוד גבוה וחנוך הדור. האוניברסיטה העברית ע"י הוצאת "יבנה", תל אביב, תש"ד.

5. שבעה פרקים על אנגליה ודרכי הדימוקרטיה האנגלית. "יבנה", תל אביב, 1945 (השוה למטה, מספר 37).

6. מורה דרך בתורת המדינה. ירושלים, ר. מס, תש"ז. מהדורה שניה, תשי"ב; מהד' שלישית, תשי"ח.

(An asterisk (*) indicates books published by the Magnes Press, The Hebrew University, Jerusalem)

1. *In Memoriam Ahad Haam.* Annual Ahad Haam Memorial Lectures, 1929–1937 (also published annually from 1931). Individual titles are:
   (a) 'Philosophy and Ahad Haam' (inaugural lecture, 1929).
   (b) '*Imitatio Dei* and the Idea of Holiness' (1931).
   (c) 'Intellect and Will as Religious Factors' (1932).
   (d) '*De Erroribus Philosophorum*' (1933).
   (e) 'Paganism' (1934).
   (f) 'Middle Axioms in Jewish Ethics' (1935).
   (g) 'The Reasons for the Precepts' (1936).
   (h) 'Development, Definition, and Judaism' (1937).
2. *Guide to Greek Philosophy.*
3. *Guide to Modern Philosophy.*
4. *Advanced Studies and Contemporary Education.*
5. *Seven Chapters on England and English Democracy.*
6. *Guide to Political Thought.*

7. החינוך וערכי האדם. פרקים בהשתלשלות הרעיון ההומניסטי בחנוך.
"דביר", תל אביב, תש"ט. מהדורה שניה מאמהות, תשכ"א.

8. שלטון העם על־ידי העם. רעיונות יסוד בדימוקרטיה. "יבנה", תל
אביב, תש"ט.

(B) TRANSLATIONS FROM THE GREEK

(*The original works are here indicated in English, the Hebrew title and details being given in the footnotes*)

9. *Aristotle, Metaphysics Book I.*
10. *Aristotle, Metaphysics Book XI.*
11. *Aristotle, Politics Books I–II.*
12. *Aristotle, Ethics Books I–II.*

(C) WITH THE FOLLOWING PRODUCTIONS ROTH WAS CONNECTED EITHER AS GENERAL EDITOR, OR AS BEING RESPONSIBLE FOR ANNOTATING OR SELECTING THEIR CONTENTS. THE TITLES, AND THE NAMES OF THE TRANSLATORS, ARE GIVEN IN ENGLISH BELOW

13. לייבניץ, ג"ו. השיטה החדשה וכתבים אחרים על תורת המונדות*.
תרגם י. אור. תרצ"א. מהדורה מתוקנת, תשי"א.

14. דיקרט, ר. הגיונות על הפילוסופיה הראשונית*. תרגם י. אור. תרצ"ב.
מהדורה מתוקנת, תש"י.

15. רוסו, ז"ז. על האמנה החברתית או יסודות המשפט המדיני*. תרגם
י. אור. תרצ"ב. מהדורה שניה, תש"ז; מהד' שלישית, מתוקנת ומוגהת,
תשט"ז.

16. מיל, ג"ס. התועלתיות*. תרגם אריה סימון. תרצ"ד. מהדורה מתוקנת,
תשי"א.

7. *Education and Human Values.* Chapters on the Involvement of Humanism in Education.
8. *Government of the People by the People.* Fundamentals of Democracy.

9. אריסטו. המטפיסיקה*. ספר א' (על הפילוסופים שקדמו לאריסטו)• תרגם מיוונית• תרצ"ד•
מהדורה שניה, תש"ס•

10. אריסטו. המטפיסיקה*. ספר י"א (על העצם ובייחוד על העצם העליון הוא האלוהים)• תרגם
מיוונית• תרצ"ד•

11. אריסטו. הפוליטיקה*. ספרים א'־ב'• תרגם מיוונית• תרצ"ו• מהדורה מתוקנת, תש"י•

12. אריסטו. המידות*. ספרים א'־ב'• (על התכלית המוסרית ועל דרכי החינוך המוסרי)• תש"ג•
מהדורה מצולמת, תשכ"ב•

13. *Leibniz, The Nova Methodus and other writings on Monadology.* Translated by Y. Or.
14. *Descartes, Meditationes de Prima Philosophia.* Translated by Y. Or.
15. *Rousseau, Contrat Social.* Translated by Y. Or.
16. *J. S. Mill, Utilitarianism.* Translated by Y. Or.

17. אפלטון. תיאיטיטוס* . תרגם אריה סימון. תרצ"ד. מהדורה מתוקנת,
תשי"א.

18. יום, ד. מחקר בדבר עקרוני המוסר* . תרגם י. אור. תרצ"ד.

19. לוק, ז'. מסה על שכל האדם* . עפ"י קיצור של א"ס פרינגל־פטיסון.
תרגם י. אור. שלושה כרכים, תרצ"ה.

20. משה בן מימון. ספר מלות ההגיון לר' משה בן־מימון, בהעתקת
ר' משה ן' תבון* . ערוך על־פי דפוסים ראשונים ומפורש על־ידי ח"י
רות. תרצ"ה.

21. דיקרט, ר. מאמר על מיתודה, ביחד עם מכתב המחבר המשמש מבוא
לעקרוני הפילוסופיה* . תרגם י. אור. תרצ"ו. מהדורה שניה מתוקנת
ומוגהת, תש"ב.

22. מיורהד, י"ה .ראשי פרקים בתורת המידות* . תרגם י. אור. תרצ"ז.

23. רסל, ב. בעיות הפילוסופיה. תרגם מ. שטרנברג. תרצ"ח.

24. ילקוט הדעות והמידות. פרקים מתוך ספרות המחשבה ומוסר של
עם ישראל מתקופת בית שני עד המאה העשרים. לקט, סדר וערך ח"י
רות. ירושלים, הוצאת ר. מס, 1938. מהדורה שניה, תש"ו.

25. ברקלי, ג. עקרוני הדעת של האדם* . פרקים נבחרים. תרגם י. אור.
תרצ"ט.

26. על החינוך התיכוני העברי בארץ ישראל (לכבוד א. בירם). 1939.
מאמריו של ח"י רות: על בעיות החינוך התיכוני העברי בארץ ישראל;
על למוד הלשונות; על הספורט.

27. תנ"ך (ליקוטים). מפי עליון. פרקים מתוך ספר הספרים. תש"ד.

28. אפלטון. ספר המדינה. על־פי תרגומו של צבי דיזנדרוק, מקוצר וערוך
על־ידי ח"י רות, עם הקדמה מאת העורך. הוצאת שוקן, תל אביב. תש"ה
(ועוד מהדורות).

17. *Plato, Theaetetus.* Translated by Aryeh Simon.
18. *Hume, Inquiry concerning the Principles of Morals.* Translated by Y. Or.
19. *Locke, Essay concerning Human Understanding.* Abridged translation by
    Y. Or.
20. *Maimonides, Treatise on the Terminology of Logic.* Moses ibn Tibbon's
    Hebrew translation from the Arabic, edited with commentary by
    L. Roth.
21. *Descartes, Discours de la Méthode.* Translated by Y. Or.
22. *J. H. Muirhead, Elements of Ethics.* Translated by Y. Or.
23. *Bertrand Russell, The Problems of Philosophy.* Translated by M. Stern-
    berg.
24. *Illustrations of Post-Biblical Jewish Ethical and Religious Thought,*
    selected and edited by L. Roth.
25. *Berkeley, Principles of Human Knowledge.* Translated by Y. Or.
26. *The A. Biram Presentation Volume (Topics of Hebrew Secondary
    Education in Eretz Israel)* includes articles by Roth on *Problems* rela-
    tive to the main title of the book, on *The Teaching of Languages,* and
    on *Sport.*
27. *'Out of the Mouth of the Most High.'* An anthology chosen from the
    Hebrew Bible, by L. Roth (published also in English translation, see
    supra, p. 324, no. viii).
28. *Plato, The Republic.* Abridged and edited by L. Roth from Z. Diesen-
    druck's translation.

29. על חינוך האזרח*. קובץ הרצאות מאת א. סימון, ח"י רות, א.
בונה, ע"א סימון, ק. פרנקנשטיין, א"א אורבך, מיכאל וייזינגר, ח.
אורמיאן, י. בנטואיץ, א. בירם. תש"י. מאמרו של ח"י רות: שלטון־עם
הלכה למעשה.

30. בוזנקט, ב. עיקרי תורת ההגיון*. תרגם ישורון קשת (יעקב קופלביץ).
תשי"ב.

II. ARTICLES, LECTURES, INTRODUCTIONS

(*Note.* Several of the articles listed below (e.g. no. 59), although they
are printed, include no indication of the publisher: they will presumably have been issued by the Hebrew University of Jerusalem. The
same doubtless applies to some of the cyclostyled items (e.g. no. 60)
which, in the light of the conditions prevailing in Palestine at the
time, are to be regarded as having been virtually published in the
same way as is no. 66, a periodical publication issued in cyclostyled
form. There may, in some cases, be room for doubt as to whether such
items were technically published: but since Leon Roth preserved them
together with the file copies of his articles published in conventional
form, I have felt it right to include them here.)

The titles are given in English below.

31. יובל שפינוזה. הארץ. 1932 .11 .25

32. משנתו של שפינוזה ביהדות. מאזנים, ד', גל' כ"ו, ט"ז בכסלו, תרצ"ג.

33. "שלטון השכל?" (על הרמב"ם). מאזנים, כרך ג', תרצ"ה, עמ' 380־370.

34. אפלטון בעברית. בתוך "ספר קלוזנר", תל־אביב, תרצ"ז, עמ' 329־324.

35. שמואל אלכסנדר. מאזנים, כרך ח', תרצ"ט, 391־383.

36. "מה נוכל ללמוד מבית־הספר הקלאסי?" חנוך, י"ג חוברת ב',
ירושלים, ת"ש.

37. אנגליה והאנגלים. מאזנים, כרך י"א, ת"ש־תש"א, עמ' 66־57 (הרצאת
ההקדמה לשורת ההרצאות על אנגליה והאנגלים שניתנו באוניברסיטה
העברית בחורף ת"ש (השוה למעלה, מספר 5).

29. A collected volume of essays on *Educating the Citizen* includes one by
    Roth entitled *The practical import of the sovereignty of the people*.
30. B. Bosanquet, *Logic: or the Morphology of Knowledge*. Translated by
    Y. Qeshet (Jacob Kopelowitz).
31. The tercentenary of Spinoza.
32. Judaism and the thought of Spinoza.
33. The authority of the intelligence? (on Maimonides).
34. Plato in Hebrew.
35. Samuel Alexander.
36. What have Greek education and the Classics to teach us?
37. England and the English (introductory lecture to a course with the same
    title given in the Hebrew University, 1939–40).

38. לביסוס הדמוקרטיה. מאזנים, כרך י', ת"ש, עמ' 458–449 (הרצאה שנקראה לפני אגודת שוחרי האוניברסיטה, טבת, ת"ש). (השוה למטה מספר 78)

39. לזכרו של הנרי ברגסון. מאזנים, כרך י"ב, תש"א, עמ' 8–206 (לפי שיחה בעתון העתונאים בירושלים, טבת, תש"א).

40. הרצאת פרופ' ח' י' רות רקטור האוניברסיטה העברית, פתיחת שנת הלימודים תש"ב, ביום ט"ו מרחשון. 8 עמודים. דפוס אחוה, ירושלים.

41. מה עשתה האוניברסיטה למען הלשון העברית? הרצאת רקטור האוניברסיטה פרופ' ח' י' רות באסיפה הכללית של אגודת שוחרי האוניברסיטה בירושלים, כ"ד טבת, תש"א. העולם. תש"א, גל' כ"ז־כ"ח, עמ' 422–420.

42. מקום הדת בבנין הארץ. גליונות, כרך י"ג, תש"ב, עמ' 79–74 (הרצאה בבי"הכ "אמת ואמונה" בירושלים, לרגל חגיגת השנה החמישית להוסדו, שבט תש"ב).

43. דרכה של האוניברסיטה שלנו. העולם, תש"ב, גל' ז', עמ' 3–52.

44. אחד־העם ואחדות־העם. מאזנים, כרך י"ד, תש"ב, עמ' 78–73 (ט"ו למותו; מתוך הרצאה).

45. מכתבים על הצופיות העברית. חליפת מכתבים בין אריה כרוך... לבין ח' י' רות . . . ירושלים, תש"ב.

46. לימוד הספרות בבתי הספר התיכונים (הרצאת פתיחה בסימפוסיון בירושלים, כ"ה־כ"ו תמוז, תש"א). בתוך "מבעיות חינוכנו", קובץ תש"ב, עמ' 35–30.

47. לעניין "אפלטון ומנדלי". בתוך "מבעיות חינוכנו", תש"ב, עמ' 63.

48. לשון ותרבות. בתוך "עם וספר", הוצאה חד־פעמית של הברית העברית העולמית, תל אביב, תש"ב, עמ' 6–15.

49. הרצאת רקטור האוניברסיטה העברית, 42. 11. 24, 4 עמודים.

50. היהדות בתקופה זו. הרצאה לחוג הדתי, 43 .2 .6. משוכפלת, 3 עמודים.

51. האוניברסיטה וחינוך הדור. הארץ, 43 .4 .12.

38. Towards the basis of democracy (cf. *infra.* no. 78).
39. Henri Bergson, *in memoriam.*
40. Rector's opening address, for the academic year 1941–2, the Hebrew University.
41. What has the [Hebrew] University achieved for Hebrew?
42. The place of religion in the upbuilding of the Land of Israel (synagogue address).
43. How our University goes about it.
44. Ahad Haam and the unification of the [Jewish] people.
45. The Hebrew Scout movement. Correspondence with Aryeh Kroch.
46. The study of literature in secondary schools (opening address at a symposium).
47. Plato and Mendele Mokher Sforim.
48. Language and culture.
49. Rector's address, The Hebrew University, 24th November, 1942.
50. Judaism in the present age.
51. The University and contemporary education.

52. על הכיוון הרצוי של לימודי אנגלית. מאזנים, כרך ט"ז, תש"ג, עמ'
49–144 (הרצאה בשעורי ההשתלמות למורי האנגלית מטעם מחלקת
החינוך של כנסת ישראל והמכון הבריטי, כ"ז ניסן תש"ג).

53. לשרות הלאום. שיחה ברדיו לבוגרי השמינית, רדיו ירושלים, 7. 2. 4.
עמודים.

54. הרחבת הגבולין באוניברסיטה. רדיו ירושלים, 7. 2. 45, עמ'
1–2 (השוה למעלה, מספר xxvii).

55. על הפצת התרבות. הגלגל, 1, גל' א', 7. 22.

56. נאום בועידה הארצית של אגודת שוחרי האוניברסיטה, 7. 25. 43. כתוב
במכונה, 4 עמודים.

57. חינוך למבוגרים. הגלגל, 1, גל' ז', עמ' 14. 43. 10. 13.

58. אמונה לשם החיים. הגלגל, 1, גל' ח'. 43. 10. 28. בקורת ספר אנגלי
"המלחמה לתנאי השלום". (וביתר אריכות בתוך הד"ח הנרשם במס' 62).

59. דברי הרקטור היוצא בפתיחת שנת הלימודים תש"ד, 43. 11. 14. 6
עמודים. דפוס אחוה, ירושלים.

60. דברי הרקטור בטכס חלוקת התעודות. משוכפל, 2 עמודים (בלי
תאריך; מתוך שנות ת"ש לתש"ג).

61. דברי פתיחה בסימפוסיון על השכלת העם בארץ והחינוך העברי
בתפוצות, שנתקיים בירושלים בח"ט' אלול, תש"ג. בתוך "השכלת העם
בארץ והחינוך העברי בתפוצות", ירושלים, תש"ד, עמ' 1–11.

62. החינוך והדת. מאזנים, כרך י"ז, תש"ד, עמ' 48–344. (השוה "דת
וחינוך", בתוך ד"וח על הסמינריון לחנוך דתי שנערך בירושלים
בשנת תש"ג, האגודה הדתית, ירושלים).

63. אחרי חמש־עשרה שנה [לפטירת אחד־העם.] העולם, תש"ד, גל' מ"ה, עמ'
308–9.

64. משמעת לאומית וחופש הפרט. מאזנים, כרך י"ח, תש"ד, עמ' 7–84.

65. על הדת והמדינה והמסכת התיאולוגית־פוליטית של שפינוזה. מאזנים,
כרך י"ט, תש"ה, עמ' 32–227, 4–170.

52. The appropriate orientation for English studies (an address to teachers).
53. National service: a broadcast talk to school-leavers.
54. Widening the University's horizons; a broadcast (cf. *supra*, no. xxvii).
55. The diffusion of culture.
56. Address to the Palestine section of the Friends of the Hebrew University, July 1943.
57. Adult education.
58. Faith for living (review of E. H. Carr's *Conditions of Peace*.)
59. Rector's valedictory address, commencement of the academic year 1943–4, The Hebrew University.
60. Rector's address at degree-giving ceremony (undated: between Autumn 1940 and Summer 1943).
61. Opening address at a symposium on Popular enlightenment in Eretz Israel and Hebrew education in the Diaspora.
62. Education and religion.
63. Ahad Haam in retrospect—15 years.
64. National discipline and individual freedom.
65. Religion, State, and Spinoza's *Tractatus Theologico-politicus*.

‎66. דת בלי סוציאליזם. הרצאה לחוג הדתי. עלון של האגודה הדתית,‏
‎שנה ב׳ מס׳ 2–1, טבת, תש"ו, 45 .12 .22, עמ׳ 25–14. משוכפלת.‏
‎67. יוסף צבי הרץ ז"ל. דברי אזכרה ביום השלשים לפטירתו (י"ב‏
‎שבט תש"ו).‏
‎68. הדין וחשבון של ועדת החינוך הממשלתית. עמודים, גל׳ ל"ה, עמ׳ 8–7.‏
‎יולי תש"ו(?).‏
‎69. כיצד צמחה הפילוסופיה ? הוצאת עלה, תל אביב, תש"ז.‏
‎70. נאום בטכס פתיחת הקורסים להכשרת מורים, 47 .9 18. ידיעות‏
‎למורים של בית־הספר הריאלי, שנה 12 גל׳ 2, 47 10. 5, עמ׳ 6–5.‏
‎משוכפל.‏
‎71. על איש הפוליטיקה. דברים שנאמרו באזכרה לד"ר י׳ ל׳ מגנס. בעיות‏
‎הזמן, 48 .12 .7, עמ׳ 8–7. (השוה למעלה, מספרים xxviii, xxxiva)‏
‎72. דינא דמלכותא. (לחינוך האזרח במדינת ישראל). ירושלים, הסתדרות‏
‎המורים העברים. תש"ח.‏
‎73. המשורר וורדסוורת וערכי הספרות והחינוך. מחברות לספרות, כרך‏
‎ד׳, מחברת ג׳–ד׳, תשרי תש"י (אוקטובר 1949) עמ׳ 55–47.‏
‎74. זכויות האדם. הרצאת הפתיחה בסימפוסיון לארגון האגודה הישראלית‏
‎למדע המדינה, 50 .11 .5, 3 עמודים. משוכפלת.‏
‎75. דת ומוסר. ידיעות למורים, שנה 15, גל׳ ג׳, 50 .12 .1, עמ׳ 22–15.‏
‎76. אגוד לזכויות האזרח למה ? הוצאת האגוד לזכויות האזרח, 1950 (או‏
‎1949). 11 עמודים, דפוס ישראל, גבעת הרצל.‏
‎77. לזכרו של יצחק גוטמן. עיון, כרך ב׳, חוברת א׳, ינואר 1951, עמ׳‏
‎10–3.‏
‎78. לביסוס הדימוקרטיה. חיפה, בית־הספר הריאלי העברי, תשי"ד. (=מספר‏
‎38; נדכס מחדש)‏
‎79. צדק וצדקה בישראל (רשימת ספר "הצדקה בישראל" של ש׳ ברגמן).‏
‎מאזנים, כרך י"ח, תשי"ד, עמ׳ 322–3.‏

66. Religion without socialism.
67. Joseph Hermann Hertz, Chief Rabbi; *in memoriam*.
68. The *Report* of the British Government's Royal Commission on Education in Palestine.
69. The beginnings of philosophy.
70. Address to a teacher's course.
71. *Homo Politicus* (politics as a branch of ethics): *in memoriam* J. L. Magnes (cf. *supra* nos. xxviii, xxxiva).
72. The law of the land (education for citizenship in the State of Israel).
73. Wordsworth, literary values, and education.
74. The rights of man (opening address to the Israel Society for Political Science).
75. Religion and ethics.
76. Why is an Association for Civil Rights necessary?
77. Julius Guttmann, *in memoriam*.
78. Towards the basis of democracy (reprint; =no. 38).
79. Review of S. H. Bergman's *Righteousness in Israel*.

80. מדיניות ופוליטיקה בתורת אפלטון. בתוך אשכולות*, קובץ מוקדש
לחקר התרבות הקלאסית והסברתה. קובץ א', תשי"ד.
מבואות

81. הקדמה ל"חירות ומשטר", בעריכת ח' מרחביה, הוצאת גורן, ירושלים
1945, עמ' ה'-ר'.

82. מבוא ל"כל כתבי אחד-העם", הוצאת דביר, תל אביב, והוצאה עברית,
ירושלים, תש"ז (ועוד מהדורות) עמ' xii–v.

83. מבוא ל"מלון למונחי הפוליטיקה" מאת ח"ה בן-ששון, הוצאת מ'
ניומן, תל אביב, תש"י, עמ' 6–5.

80. Statecraft and politics in the thought of Plato.
81. Introduction to H. Merhavya's *Freedom and Government*.
82. Introduction to the *Collected Works* of Ahad Haam.
83. Introduction to H. H. Ben-Sason's *Dictionary of Political Concepts*.

INDEX

Aaron b. Jacob Cohen of Narbonne, 195 n.34
'Abba b. Zabda, R., 183
'Abbahu, R., 137, 195 n.24
'Abhodhah (work, service, worship), 156, 157, 166, 178
Abraham, and belief in God, 133, 153, 183f.; and gentile environment, 48, 176f., 182f., 185; and humanity, 51; and Israel, 118–20, 153, 175, 178, 296, 307
Abraham ibn Da'ud, and active intellect, 93; on faith and philosophy, 215f., 217–22, 226, 229 n.4
Abraham ibn Ezra, 288 n.1
Abrahams, Israel, 1f., 325
Abudarham, David, 112, n.55
Abū Hāshim, 313, 320, 321 n.36
Abu Rashīd, 316, 321 n.17
Accountability, individual moral, 259; *see also* Individual
Acquisition (*iktisāb, qeniyyah*), 313, 316; Acquisitionists, 318
Active intellect, 93
Acts of piety (*gemiluth hasadhim*), 307
Adam, and human equality and diversity, 289, 294, 303–4; and Job, 78f., 82f.; and love of neighbour, 305; and sin, 106, 119–20, 179; and soul, 91–2, 96–7, 106; recipient of divine commandments, 125f., 137; *see also;'Adham Qadhmon, Beney 'Adham*
Adequate and inadequate ideas, in Spinoza, 28
'Adham qadmon (primordial Adam), 94
Adhhan, see Dhihn
Adiabene, 134
Adjustment, as object of education, 233f., 235, 236

Adler, N., 195 n.28
Aequilibrium indifferentiae, 16
'Aggadha, area of, 117; and ethics, 171, 175; impingement on *Halakhah*, 117, 195 n.32
Ahad Ha'am, 4, 109f., n.25
Ahwal, see Hal
'Alack for those who are perished, etc.', 194 n.9
Albo, Joseph, and Aristotle, 230 n.14; on human and divine law, 223, 226–7; on Job, 81, 85 n.21; on Torah and prophecy, 225; on Torah and happiness, 228; *'Iqqarim I, 79–80*, 228, 230 nn.16–17; *I, 93*, 227; *I, 173*, 226, 230 n.13; *III, 46*, 230 n.17
'Alenu leshabbeah ('it is our duty to praise, etc.'), 50, 191
Alexander, Samuel, 3, 332
'Al ken neqawweh lakh ('we therefore hope in Thee, etc.'), 50, 191, 301
'Alter Rebbe' (Schneur Zalman of Liady), 90
Altmann, A., 110 n.35
'Am ha-'ares (non-pharisaic proletariat), morals of, 132
'Ammi, R., 141f., 150 n.60
Ammonius Hermiae, 315, 320 n.12
Amos, 304
Ancelet-Hustache, J. 108 n.4
Andala, R., 22, 42 n.33
Angelus Silesius, 154–5, 158–9, 167, 168 n.1
'Anokhi ('I'), *see* 'I'
Antoninus, Judah the Patriarch and, 132
ἀποφαντικός (enunciative), 315
Apologetics, 115, 138, 147 n.13, 292; cf. 49
Apostasy, constructive, 142
Apt, N., 86, n.29, n.31

337

z+

z*

Simeon and Levi, execrated by
Jacob, 185
Simeon b. Yoḥai, R., 68, 71 n.12,
101, 128, 148 n.23
Simḥah shel miṣwah (joy experienced through fulfilment of
commandment), 228
Simla'i, R., 307, 310 n.62
Simon, E., 61, 65 n.16
Simonsohn, S., 111 n.52
Sinai, 220–1, 227
Singer, S., 148 n.18
Siphrā, Qedoshim 4, 305, 310 n.49
Siphrē, 128, 148 n.20; *Numbers
111*, 137, 149 n.42; *Deutero-
nomy 40*, 70 n.12; *49*, 222,
229 n.7; *306*, 92, 109 n.20;
311, 305, 309 n.47
Slaves, for Aristotle, born to
servitude, 295; 'natural' obligation to master, 209–10;
slavery, abolition of, 258; a
temporary status in Judaism,
122
Spain, Holland's recovery from,
267; Jewish expulsion from,
180
Spark, divine, as the soul, 87f.,
103f.; from the soul, 106
Species and genera, 311, 314, 317
Spencer, Herbert, 256
Spies, incident of the 179–81,
189f.
Spinoza, B., and Leibniz and
Mendelssohn, 13f.; and Maimonides, 221; rationalism of,
197, 199; L. Roth's interest
in, 3, 4, 198, 215, 323f.; and
Herbert Samuel, 258–9; typifies
new 17th cent. era, 262; *Ethics,
I, 7*, 19; *10, schol.*, 19; *17*, 20;
25, cor., 18; *32*, 20; *33,
schol. 2*, 20; *II, Def. 1*, 33;
axiom. 3, 44 n.56; *prop. 7*, 37;
schol. 5, prop. 12, 37; *6*, 31,
7, 21, 29; *7 schol.*, 30; *9*, 19,
41 n.18; *12–13*, 33, 41 n.19;
21, 30, 33; *21 schol.*, 37; *23*,

33; *III, 2*, 27f., 34; *schol.,
prop. 2*, 37; *V, 1*, 30; *Oeuvres
posthumes*, 36f.
Social character of language, 275;
contract, 204, 209–10; co-
responsibility, 260f., 271;
existence of mind, 267; experience, as criterion, 270; justification of death, 259; philosophy, 211, 213; science, 211,
213; theory, 219, Jewish, 126,
302f.; usefulness, as criterion
of tradition, 263; society,
determined mainly by its past,
272 n.2; and individual, 234,
235, 260f.; language and,
266f.; A. D. Lindsay's conception of, and Lenin's, 240;
self-protection of, 262; *see also*
Education and society
Sodom, Abraham and, 177
Solomon, prayer of, 280
Soul, animal (natural) and
divine, 103, 107; cogitative,
220; as divine spark, 87f., 94f.;
doctrines of, 109 n.25; Jewish,
57; Leibniz and Spinoza on,
16f., 25, 28, 37; Philo on, 91f.,
93, 109 n.15; *see also
Nephesh, Ner, Neshamah, Ruaḥ*
σωφροσύνη, defined as contentment, 219
State, the: *Abraham ibn Da'ud*
on relevance of Decalogue,
219; *Hobbes on*, 202f.; its
administration unlike that of
prison, 210, as artificial, 204,
as protective, 202, obedience
due to, 203, 209, 212; *A. D.
Lindsay and V. I. Lenin* on,
240; *Herbert Samuel* on, as
association of individuals, 261,
as owing duty towards neighbouring states, 263, and citizens, *ibid.*, to promote their
happiness, 256; *see also*
Obedience, Society, Unethical
orders